REAPPRAISING POLITICAL THEORY

REAPPRAISING POLITICAL THEORY

Revisionist Studies in the History of Political Thought

TERENCE BALL

CLARENDON PRESS · OXFORD

1995

Oxford University Press, Walton Street, Oxford OX2 6DP

Oxford New York
Athens Auckland Bangkok Bombay
Calcutta Cape Town Dar es Salaam Delhi
Florence Hong Kong Istanbul Karachi
Kuala Lumpur Madras Madrid Melbourne
Mexico City Nairobi Paris Singapore
Taipei Tokyo Toronto
and associated companies in
Berlin Ibadan

Oxford is a trade mark of Oxford University Press

Published in the United States
by Oxford University Press Inc., New York

British Library Cataloguing in Publication Data
Data available

Library of Congress Cataloging in Publication Data
Ball, Terence.
Reappraising political theory: revisionist studies in the history
of political thought / Terence Ball.
Includes bibliographical references.
1. Political science—History. 2. Political science—Philosophy.
1995 I. Title.
JA81.B253 1994 320'.01—dc20 94-21129
ISBN 0-19-827953-1
ISBN 0-19-827995-7 (Pbk)

Set by Hope Services (Abingdon) Ltd.
Printed in Great Britain
on acid-free paper by
Biddles Ltd.
Guildford & King's Lynn

For
Jean and Glenn Willson

Although I do not believe the classics beyond criticism, I hold that they have merits especially well-calculated to counterbalance our defects. They provide support just where we are most likely to fall.

De Tocqueville, *Democracy in America*

PREFACE

THIS is the second in a series of three companion volumes travelling under the general title 'Political Theory and the Human Sciences'. The first, *Transforming Political Discourse* (Blackwell, 1988), dealt with the ways in which political theorizing, argumentation, and criticism change the meanings of the concepts with and through which political discourse is conducted. The third volume—*Positivism, Politics, and the Social Sciences*—will examine aspects of the history and philosophy of the social sciences, as seen from within, and criticized from outside, the positivist tradition of political and social enquiry. Taken together, this trilogy—if that is not too kind a term for a rough-hewn three-legged stool—is intended as a commentary on, and criticism of, several key features of modern social and political theory.

The present work proceeds from the premiss that political theory is in part, and inescapably, a backward-looking historical enterprise. This second volume accordingly consists, in the main, of a series of studies in the history of political thought. I tend to favour the essay as a form and a forum for these reappraisals. For an essay, in its original meaning, is not only a literary form or genre but a 'test' or 'trial' in which an author's views are tried out, tested, and considered from several sides. An essay is also an 'assay' or 'appraisal' of the adequacy or worth of an idea or argument. This is not merely a way of writing but one of thinking and even, one might say, of living one's life. As Robert Musil says of his protagonist Ulrich in *The Man Without Qualities*: 'It was approximately in the way that an essay, in the sequence of its paragraphs, takes a thing from many sides without comprehending it wholly . . . that he believed he could best survey and handle the world and his life.' For a student of political thought, the world and one's life are inextricably bound up with one's studies. That, it seems to me, is why the essay is especially well suited to the study of political theory and the reappraisal of the thinkers and texts that comprise it.

Different though these essays are, all are connected by a common thread. That thread is the idea that the study of political thought requires the reinterpretation and reappraisal of—to use a now-contentious term—the 'classics' of political theory. That indeed is how they retain their status as classic works. But it is important to note that this 'canon' (if indeed that is what it is) does not consist of timeless truths preserved unchanged for those fortunate few who can decipher the coded messages contained in The Great Books. The ideas that inform and constitute political discourse are not, *pace* Plato, eternal entities, ideal forms floating freely above the political fray. Political ideas and concepts are conceived and articulated—and amended or transformed—within particular political contexts, at specific sites, and within a determinate range of rhetorical possibilities. Although bound by context, political ideas are historical artefacts which can, and characteristically do, exist in several contexts at once. They can, for one, be traced to, and placed back in, the context of their origins, as the tool or brain-child of this or that writer or party with a particular political agenda. Or they can be placed in the context of their subsequent reception by this or that audience, each having its own political problems and agendas, and its own reasons for reworking old ideas for new purposes—purposes unforeseen and perhaps even unforeseeable by an earlier author. One of my purposes in the present volume is to show, by way of a fairly wide-ranging series of studies, how tensions and confusions arise when contexts of origin and reception are confused or are not taken into account by those attempting to write the history of political thought—or, more often, particular episodes therein—for various purposes, be they political or scholarly. To expose, criticize, and solve such interpretive problems is, at the same time, to reappraise the theorist and theory under discussion. Such reappraisals, I contend, are a necessary feature of the political theorist's craft, inasmuch as they inform and enrich our understanding of our predecessors' contribution to the political traditions to which we are heir and to which we contribute even as, and because, we think and write about them.

But how, exactly, ought we to think about these works? How, that is, should they be read and understood, i.e. interpreted? My approach in the present study can be characterized in two words: *pluralist* and *problem-driven.* That is, no one method of interpretation will suffice in all cases; which of many methods one chooses depends on the particular problem being addressed, and not the other way around. Mine might be termed the Gertrude Stein approach. Legend has it that, as Stein lay dying, her friend Alice B. Toklas, apparently believing the near-dead to have clairvoyant powers, asked, 'Gertrude, what is the answer?', whereupon Stein rather sensibly replied, 'That depends, Alice, on what the question is.' So it is with textual interpretation. An interpretation is an attempted answer to a question or a tentative solution to a problem. Interpretations therefore follow from some problems and, of course, give rise to others. Students of political theory need never fear the spectre of intellectual unemployment.

This account of my aims is, of course, unduly abstract. It will be vindicated—or not, as the case may be—in the following studies. My studies have been supported by several institutions: the University of Minnesota, which has been generous in granting financial support and leaves; the University of California at San Diego, where I was a visiting professor in 1984; Nuffield College, Oxford, where I was a visiting fellow in 1978–9; Christ Church, Oxford, which elected me to the Fowler Hamilton Fellowship in 1993; the National Endowment for the Humanities, which awarded me a Fellowship for Independent Study and Research in 1978–9; the Woodrow Wilson International Center for Scholars in Washington, DC, where I was a fellow in 1987. And, not least, six magnificent libraries—the Bodleian, the British Library, the London Library, the Cambridge University Library, the National Library of Scotland, and the Library of Congress—supplied the serenity and the resources without which my work would never have been undertaken, much less completed.

I owe a special debt to Tim Barton, my editor at OUP, for his initial interest in and continued support of my work. I should also like to thank two anonymous readers for the OUP for the care and thoroughness with which they reviewed my manuscript. I am also much indebted to Mary Ellen Otis for transforming my rough typescript into a readable manuscript.

I owe a much more unusual debt to my brother, David Ball, for painting 'The Hermeneutic Circuit', a picture with a punning title that captures in one succinct image what I have tried to convey in many thousands of words. Since he has kindly allowed me to use that picture on the dust-jacket, I would like to think that this is one book that can be judged by its cover.

The studies comprising the present volume have benefited

greatly—though not, I fear, nearly enough—from the suggestions given (and warnings issued) by many friendly critics, none of whom should be held responsible for what I have done, or failed to do, with their criticisms. For friendly criticism, companionship, and conversations from which I always learn a good deal—and, not least, for reading all or part of the present work—I thank Elias Berg, Isaiah Berlin, Terrell Carver, Janet Coleman, Richard Dagger, Fred Dallmayr, Mary Dietz, John Dunn, Peter Euben, James Farr, Bruce Haddock, Iain Hampsher-Monk, Jeremy Jennings, Gregory Leyh, Douglas Long (for musical companionship and scholarly criticism), James Miller, Donald Moon, the late Christopher Morris, John Pocock, the late John Rees, Quentin Skinner, Giorgio Tagliacozzo, William Thomas, James Boyd White, and Donald Winch. It is customary—and in this instance true—to say that all errors are my own.

T.B.

Madeline Island in Lake Superior
May 1994

ACKNOWLEDGEMENTS

WITH the exception of the first chapter, these studies originated as papers presented to audiences in North America and Europe. Several studies in the present volume—Chapters 2, 3, 4, 8, 9, 10, and 11—have, in shorter and sometimes quite different versions, already appeared in print. Chapters 1, 5, 6, 7, and 12 appear here for the first time. Chapter 2 was first presented as an invited 'theme' paper at the 1989 Midwest Political Science Association and appeared in *Political Science: Looking to the Future*, edited by William Crotty and published by Northwestern University Press in 1991. Chapter 3 was in its first incarnation a paper presented at the University of California at San Diego in 1984 and, under the title 'The Picaresque Prince: Reflections on Machiavelli and Moral Change', appeared in *Political Theory*, 12/4 (November 1984), 521–36. Chapter 4 began as a paper presented at the 1983 meeting of the American Political Science Association and was, in substantially revised form, subsequently published in *Polity*, 17 (1985), 739–60. Chapter 5 was the first Elias Berg Lecture in Political Theory, given at the University of Stockholm in 1988. Chapter 6 began as a paper presented to the conference on 'The Scottish Enlightenment in its European Context' at the University of Edinburgh in 1986 and, in a revised version, to John Dunn's and Quentin Skinner's political theory seminar at Christ's College, Cambridge, in the Easter Term 1993. Chapter 7 was my contribution to the International Utilitarian Studies Conference at the University of Western Ontario in 1992 and, in a much revised version, was my 1993 Fowler Hamilton Lecture at Christ Church, Oxford. Chapter 8 began as a paper presented to the Politics Seminar at Nuffield College, Oxford, in 1979 and, under the title 'Utilitarianism, Feminism and the Franchise: James Mill and his Critics', appeared in *History of Political Thought*, 1 (1980), 91–115. Chapter 9 was published as 'On "Making" History in Vico and Marx', in *Vico and Marx: Affinities and Contrasts*, edited by Giorgio Tagliacozzo (Humanities Press, 1983), 78–93. Chapter 10 was originally a paper presented at the universities of Stockholm and Swansea in 1978, and subsequently appeared as 'Marx and Darwin: A Reconsideration', in *Political Theory*, 7 (November 1979), 469–83. Chapter 11 was in an earlier and much shorter version a paper presented at the 1987 meeting of the American Political Science Association and, under the title 'Constitutional Interpretation and Conceptual Change', was my contribution to *Legal Hermeneutics*, edited by Gregory Leyh and published by the University of California Press in 1992. Finally, Chapter 12 was a paper presented at the 1993 annual meeting of the American Political Science Association in Washington, DC.

CONTENTS

ABBREVIATIONS

AJPS	*American Journal of Political Science*
APSA	American Political Science Association
APSR	*American Political Science Review*
ASJJR	*Annales de la Société de Jean-Jacques Rousseau*
Bentham, *CW*	*The Collected Works of Jeremy Bentham*, ed. J. H. Burns, J. R. Dinwiddy, and F. Rosen (London, 1968–)
Bentham MSS, UCL	Bentham manuscripts, University College, London
Bentham, *Works*	*The Works of Jeremy Bentham*, ed. J. Bowring, 11 vols. (Edinburgh, 1838–43)
BL Add. MSS	British Library Additional Manuscripts
EW	*The English Works of Thomas Hobbes*, ed. W. Molesworth, 11 vols. (London, 1839)
HPT	*History of Political Thought*
JHI	*Journal of the History of Ideas*
Lev.	Thomas Hobbes, *Leviathan*, ed. C. B. Macpherson (1651; Harmondsworth, 1968)
LW	*The Latin Works of Thomas Hobbes*, ed. W. Molesworth (London, 1839)
MC	Thomas Hobbes, *Man and Citizen*, ed. B. Gert (Eng. trans. of *De homine*) (Garden City, NY, 1972)
MESC	K. Marx and F. Engels, *Selected Correspondence* (Moscow, 1975)
MESW	K. Marx and F. Engels, *Selected Works*, 1 vol. edn. (New York, 1968)
MEW	K. Marx and F. Engels, *Werke*, 39 vols. (Berlin, 1968–)
Mill, *CW*	*Collected Works of John Stuart Mill*, ed. J. M. Robson, 29 vols. (Toronto, 1963–89)
NS	G. Vico, *The New Science* (Eng. trans. from *Scienza nuova*), trans. T. G. Bergin and M. H. Fisch (1744; Ithaca, NY, 1984)

OC	*Œuvres complètes de Jean-Jacques Rousseau*, ed. B. Gagnebin and M. Raymond (Paris, 1959–)
PW	James Mill, *Political Writings*, ed. T. Ball (Cambridge, 1992)
SC	Jean-Jacques Rousseau, *Social Contract* (my trans. from Rousseau, *Contrat social*, *OC* iv)
SPD	Sozialdemokratische Partei Deutschlands (German Social Democratic Party)
WPQ	*Western Political Quarterly*

I
BEARINGS

I

REAPPRAISING POLITICAL THEORY

1.1 INTRODUCTION

Several years ago a colleague asked me why it was that scholars specializing in political theory continued to write about the 'great thinkers' of the past. Had not everything that could be said already been said? Why had no one had the last word on, or written the definitive work about, Rousseau or Mill or Marx? Were we too dim to understand what our elders and betters were up to? Or were we merely multiplying the number of articles and books about the great political thinkers in order to secure tenure and promotion? And why all the fuss about 'interpretation'? Why do we bother to devise (or to read) this or that interpretation instead of going straight to the source and seeing what the author has to say?

It was an astonishing and unsettling series of questions for which I had no fully satisfactory answers. Some of us, I readily admitted, probably are rather too dim to understand what Plato or Machiavelli or Marx were about. And some scholars do, to be sure, write with the instrumental intention of getting tenure or being promoted (although this phenomenon is hardly unique to political theorists). But for the other questions I had no good answer, save to mutter something about the perennial fascination of classic works for succeeding generations of readers, each of which reads them anew and from their own vantage-point. And besides, I added, these authors and their works comprise an important aspect of our Western political tradition, which we renew and enrich by reading, reflecting upon, and criticizing these 'classics'.

These answers satisfied neither my colleague nor me. I have often thought about this exchange, especially when hearing complaints about a 'canon' of works by 'dead white men' whose ideas are pickled and preserved (in much the same way, one imagines, as Lenin's and Bentham's corpses continue to be). Such complaints have, if anything, become even more numerous (and nasty) of late. And, perhaps surprisingly, they have a long ancestry and a familiar ring.

Earlier but similar criticisms were once heard from 'scientifically' minded political scientists, who complained that the worship of long-dead thinkers was impeding the development of genuinely scientific theories of political behaviour. Nowadays, however, such criticisms come more often from quarters that one would expect to be sympathetic if not friendly to the historical study of political thought. The first include advocates and practitioners of analytical political philosophy, some of whom see a sustained and systematic interest in the history of political thought as an antiquarian distraction and an obstacle to our thinking for ourselves in more modern, and presumably more fruitful ways, about the pressing political concerns of our own time. They tend to favour, not the historical study and interpretation of old texts, but the application of economic, rational choice and game-theoretic models and theories to questions of freedom, justice, political participation, and other concerns. Or, if they do study classic works, it is to mine them for insights or to look for forerunners and ancestors who share their views. Thus (to mention merely one of many examples) Hobbes becomes a proto-rational choice theorist and the Hobbesian state of nature a model of decision-making under conditions of perfect rationality and imperfect information.

A second set of objections comes from proponents of 'multiculturalism' in the modern curriculum. We should not, they say, be in the thrall of old books by 'dead white men', since these 'canonical' texts tend to preserve and legitimate the power of living white males, and to 'marginalize' the views of women, blacks, gays, and other minorities. We need first to deconstruct this 'canon' in order to show how it functions to empower some while disempowering or oppressing others; and we need next to discard, or at least delegitimize and move to the margins, the very idea that there are 'classic' works in political theory that repay careful study by both sexes, regardless of race or nationality or sexual preference.

Such sweeping criticism has, perhaps predictably, provoked

howls of protest from defenders of 'the great books' and the 'timeless truths' that they teach to the fortunate few. The disciples of the late Leo Strauss have been particularly vocal on this score and have, in the main, succeeded in conforming closely to the stereotype or caricature created by postmodern critics of the texts comprising the canon. Since this is a book about the problems and pleasures of interpreting such texts, I suppose I should begin by saying something in defence of my enterprise, if only to distance myself from certain of its latter-day defenders.

Consider first the matter of method. There is in modern academic discourse much ado about one's method or approach to the interpretation of texts. Now of course being aware of, and attentive to, matters of method is no doubt necessary, and to proceed methodically is an altogether admirable trait for a scholar (as indeed it is for a motor mechanic or a carpenter or anyone who practises a skilled craft). The danger is that these means have a way of becoming, at least in academic settings, ends in themselves: method becomes 'methodology', and a driving force in its own right. I wish it could be otherwise. The proof of the pudding being in the eating rather than in the recipe, my reappraisals would, if I had my way, be judged according to their merit, or lack thereof. But ours is for better or worse an age in which method precedes matter and sometimes pre-empts substance. If one's enquiries are to be both intelligible and legitimate, one must conform to the norms of one's own age and culture, and ours requires that one begin by describing and defending one's method or approach.

My defence of the approach taken here proceeds in the following way. I begin with a brief defence of the claim that interpretation is both inescapable and necessary. Next, I consider several strategies of interpretation now competing for attention and even, one might say, allegiance. I then go on to claim that several of these strategies are mutually compatible, inasmuch as each answers to quite different but entirely legitimate interests. I then offer a defence of a problem-centred and multi-method approach to interpretation. And, finally, I provide a brief overview of the revisionist reappraisals comprising this book.

1.2 THE INESCAPABILITY OF INTERPRETATION

Disputes over interpretation are almost certainly as old as the human species itself. Although unwritten, the first 'texts'—omens and portents, animal bones and entrails—had to be 'read' and their meaning made clear. Later still, the singers of tales told and retold stories whose meaning was interpreted and reinterpreted from one generation to another.[1] With the advent of the written word came new and even more intractable problems of interpretation, and along with it a written record of the sorts of difficulties faced by interpreters, commentators, and critics.[2] Aristotle's *Poetics* is perhaps the most famous, if not the earliest, example of the genre. Nor were questions of interpretation merely pleasant pastimes enjoyed by the idle and affluent. Then, as now, lives were often at stake in the interpretation of legal and religious texts. What counts as a capital crime, or as heresy or blasphemy, is a matter of interpretation not only of legal or religious texts, but of the intent of the accused. Thus questions of interpretation constitute what I call 'deadly hermeneutics'—deadly inasmuch as people's lives, liberties, and happiness hang in the balance.[3]

Another feature of this long history is the periodic and recurring call to 'get back to basics'—to the text, the author, the author's intention, or whatever—and eschew interpretation altogether. This is the move made with almost predictable regularity by fundamentalists in law and literature as well as in religion. The law or the scripture, they say, has become encrusted with interpretation, each successive layer of which skews or distorts the original or 'true' meaning of the text and/or its author (or, in the case of holy scripture, Author). The first task must accordingly be to undo the damage done by earlier commentators. Hence Luther's claim that interpretation is 'the scum of holy scripture' and his call for a return to the 'straight road' of scripture, unadorned and undistorted

---

[1] See A. B. Lord, *The Singer of Tales* (Cambridge, Mass., 1960).

[2] R. Thomas, *Literacy and Orality in Ancient Greece* (Cambridge, 1993).

[3] See my 'Deadly Hermeneutics', in Ball (ed.), *Idioms of Inquiry* (Albany, NY, 1987).

by commentary or interpretation. As he remarks in the preface to his translation of the New Testament, his own preface is necessary only because earlier interpreters 'have perverted the understanding of Christian people till they have no inkling of the meaning of the gospel. ... This distressing state of affairs calls for some sort of guidance by way of preface, to free the ordinary man from his false though familiar notions [and] to lead him into the straight road ...'[4] The irony is, of course, that Luther's fulmination against interpretation is itself inescapably interpretive, inasmuch as it amounts to a defence of one kind of interpretive strategy against other alternatives.

Even now, in one version or another, variations on Luther's complaint can be heard not only from religious fundamentalists, but from judges, lawyers, and literary critics. In the United States some conservative jurists call for a return to the 'original intent' of the Founders.[5] And among literary critics some, such as Susan Sontag, take their stand 'against interpretation'.[6]

But surely it is as absurd to be 'against' as it is to be 'for' interpretation, much less to 'love' it, as Professor Fish professes to do.[7] Whether one likes or dislikes interpretation is quite beside the point, for one really has no choice in the matter. The decision to interpret or not to interpret is not an option open to human beings, but a requirement that comes, so to speak, with the territory of being human. For our language-using and meaning-seeking species, interpretation is inescapable. Heidegger put the point with uncharacteristic clarity when he said that for human beings interpretation is an ontological category. And Gadamer has underscored the point by saying that hermeneutics—the art and practice of interpretation—is a matter not of method but of ontological necessity.[8]

The world we inhabit and the texts we read, says Gadamer, are never raw sense-data or some ideal *objet trouvé* but are

[4] Luther, *Selections*, ed. J. Dillenberger (Garden City, NY, 1961), 14.
[5] See Ch. 11 below.
[6] S. Sontag, *Against Interpretation* (New York, 1966).
[7] S. Fish, *Is there a Text in this Class? The Authority of Interpretive Communities* (Cambridge, Mass., 1980).
[8] H.-G. Gadamer, *Truth and Method* (New York, 1984).

'always already' interpreted and invested with meaning. We are born and grow into a world made meaningful by the language we speak and the traditions we inherit. And these in turn supply us with our own culturally and historically specific standpoint or set of 'prejudices' (*Vorurteile*) from which vantage-point we make sense of our world and the creatures, texts, signs, and artefacts that comprise it. But Gadamer also insists that this standpoint, far from being static and unchanging, is historically situated and subject to criticism and alteration. Indeed, the central thrust of Gadamer's hermeneutics is that, while we necessarily *begin* with our own present-day prejudices, we need not *end* with them unchanged and forever intact. We extend or expand our present horizon of understanding by encountering and attempting to understand prejudices and practices that at first sight seem strange or alien. By encountering and trying to come to some understanding of the alien and unfamiliar, we gain a better sense of the historically specific limitations of our own parochial horizon. We attempt to make a distant horizon compatible with our own. In thus effecting, or at least attempting, a 'fusion of horizons' (*Horizont verschmelzung*), we at once appreciate our distance from and kinship with those whose perspectives differ markedly from our own. And in so doing, we also come to appreciate our common, if differently expressed, humanity. The art of interpretation, on this telling, is an essential part of the art of living the life of a human being.

This art, however, is not a luxury but a necessity. We cannot dispense with interpretation or get by without it. As communicating and interacting social agents, each of us must in our daily lives interpret the meaning of the actions, practices, and utterances of other people. Suppose, for instance, that I see coming towards me a large man, knife in hand and wearing a blood-smeared smock. How I respond depends on how I interpret the meaning of what I see. Placing that sight in a larger interpretive context constituted by certain customs, conventions, and social roles—this is a meat market, that man is the butcher, and I am a customer—permits me to arrive at a correct interpretation and to act accordingly. Instead of fleeing in terror, I engage in a series of socially appropriate and recognizable acts—placing an order, making a purchase, paying for it, and the like. Of course, this and other aspects of the everyday taken-for-granted 'life-world' are ordinarily unproblematic in so far as they are preinterpreted; that is, we do not see a situation and then interpret it, but see and interpret it as a single seamless activity.[9]

Matters are much more difficult, of course, if we find ourselves in an alien age or culture with whose concepts, categories, customs, and practices we are utterly unfamiliar. In such situations we are often at a loss to know *what* is being done, much less why it is or what its meaning may be. We therefore need a 'translation', which is neither more nor less than an interpretation effected by fusing that culture's horizon of meaning with ours. A good translation or interpretation is one that diminishes the strangeness of the sight, making it more familiar and accessible to an otherwise puzzled or perplexed observer. To provide such cross-cultural translations is the aim of the anthropologist, among others.

The historian of political thought often finds herself in a situation analogous to that of the anthropologist studying an alien culture.[10] The artefacts or 'texts' produced in political cultures preceding and differing from our own do not readily reveal their meanings even to the most careful reader. To read a text 'over and over again', as some advise, is no doubt necessary.[11] But it is hardly sufficient to enable us to arrive at anything like an adequate understanding of what (say) Machiavelli meant by *virtù* or what Rousseau was trying to do in devising his scheme for a *religion civile* or what Vico and Marx meant in saying that human beings 'make' their own history. To try to make sense of such puzzling terms and actions requires that we interpret their meaning. There is no understanding without interpretation, and no interpretation without the possibility of multiple (mis)understandings.

Nor is there a neutral standpoint or Archimedean point from which to interpret and appraise any text, classic or otherwise. All interpretation implies, and originates in, some vantage-point or standpoint or (to use Gadamer's term)

---

[9] A. Schutz, *Collected Papers* (The Hague, 1962), I. 7–9, 74–5.
[10] R. Rorty, J. B. Schneewind, and Q. Skinner (eds.), *Philosophy in History* (Cambridge, 1984), 6–7.
[11] J. Plamenatz, *Man and Society* (London, 1963), i. x.

'prejudice'. Every interpretation, in short, implies an interest—not simply in the sense that one is 'interested' in an author of text, but rather in the deeper (or, to speak German, the transcendental) sense that an interest provides the ground for and possibility of an interpretation—a standpoint from which enquiry can begin and interpretation proceed. These interests are, moreover, multiple and varied. One's interests can be contemporary: what (for example) can Mill still teach us about liberty? Or they may be more historical: why did Mill's arguments in *On Liberty* take the form they did? Who were Mill's main targets, and who his intended audience? Or one's interests may be more narrowly linguistic or literary: what tropes and rhetorical stratagems did Mill employ, and with what effect? What oppositions and antinomies does Mill set up ('liberty' vs. 'authority'; self- vs. other-regarding acts) and what ones does he deny or explicitly eschew ('liberty' vs. 'necessity')? Or one's interests may be logical or philosophical: is Mill's argument in *On Liberty* internally coherent and logically consistent? Are there gaps or lacunae in the argument? Does Mill construct a compelling case?

None of these interests necessarily excludes the others. But they do dictate what will count as a problem, what constitutes an interesting or important question, and what method might be most appropriate and fruitful for dealing with these matters. One would not, for example, assess the logical adequacy of Mill's argument by examining his use of tropes. Nor would one be able to answer questions posed from a historical interest or vantage-point by looking only at the logical structure of his argument.

One's method, in short, is dictated by the problem at hand and the interest that one seeks to serve. Thus all interpretations are, in a word, interest-laden. And because they necessarily answer to some interest or other, they cannot be normatively neutral or value-free. Or, to put the point more plainly, all interpretation implies appraisal; and all reinterpretation implies reappraisal. What is in these instances reappraised is not merely the text and author in question, but the adequacy or inadequacy of other interpretations that seek to satisfy a similar interest. Indeed, one's own attempts at interpretation and reappraisal typically begin in some sort of puzzlement arising in one's reading the text or in various interpretations of it.

That much, at least, seems to be fairly obvious and unproblematic. But by what means are we, as students of political theory, to interpret, criticize, and perhaps even appropriate for our own use the texts that comprise our contested canon or 'currency' or 'tradition of discourse'?[12] These are contentious questions, and one cannot pretend that the terrain on which they are addressed is anything but hotly contested. One part of the battlefield is occupied by neo-Marxists, an adjoining part by 'realists', another by assorted post-structuralists and deconstructionists, yet another by Straussians, and still another by the 'new historians' of political thought. Each takes a distinctive approach to the history of political thought, and each is highly critical of the others. Marxists interpret all political theories, past and present—save their own, perhaps—as ideological masks concealing and justifying the domination of one class by another.[13] Realists, some but not all of whom are Marxists of one or another sort, view political ideas and theories as playing a causal role in reproducing and legitimating the structures comprising the social world.[14] Poststructuralists are wont to deconstruct works by this or that author in order to show how his search for 'foundations' (in, say, 'nature' or 'human nature' or 'natural law') was actually an arbitrary construct—which, multiculturalist critics contend, contributed to oppression of one or another sort (women by men, blacks by whites, etc.). Straussians, by contrast, claim that a canon of works by Plato and a handful of other authors contains the Whole Truth about politics, a Truth which is eternal, unchanging, and accessible only to the fortunate few.[15] The 'new historians' of the 'Cambridge school', on the contrary, tend to view texts in political theory as forms of political action, grasping the point or meaning of

[12] See W. E. Connolly, *Political Theory and Modernity* (Oxford, 1988), p. vii; S. Wolin, *The Presence of the Past* (Baltimore, 1989), 1.

[13] See e.g. C. B. Macpherson, *The Political Theory of Possessive Individualism* (Oxford, 1962); N. Wood, *John Locke and Agrarian Capitalism* (Berkeley, Calif., 1984).

[14] I. Shapiro, 'Realism in the Study of the History of Ideas', *HPT* 3 (1982), 535–78.

[15] See e.g. A. Bloom, 'Leo Strauss', *Political Theory*, 2 (1974), 372–92.

which requires that one recover the intentions of the actor/author and the linguistic resources and conventions available to him or her.[16]

Such sketches do not, of course, begin to do justice to the oft-times rich and suggestive insights offered by proponents of these perspectives. But they may at least suggest something of the diversity of views and vantage-points from which we reinterpret the meaning and reappraise the value of a rich and varied heritage.

1.3 STRATEGIES OF INTERPRETATION

Various fractures and fault-lines separate the several modern theories of interpretation. One of the most obvious of these concerns the question of authorial intent. Among the most vexed in the recurring set of questions in legal, literary, and other kinds of interpretation are these: Can we identify an author's intention in writing this or that work? If we can, should we? What weight, if any, is to be assigned to an author's intentions? Have we discovered the 'meaning' of a text (or more typically a particular passage), once we discover what the author intended or meant to do in writing it? Or is the meaning to be found in (the reading of) the text itself? Or do we discount authorial intent altogether and look instead at the consequences—often the unintended consequences—of an utterance or argument or text?

These are not abstractly academic questions. For example, some American jurists and constitutional scholars contend that the discovery of the 'original intent' of the framers of the Constitution settles the matter of meaning, once and for all. And a similar argument is advanced, albeit in different ways and for different reasons, by Quentin Skinner and other Cambridge new historians. I shall argue later that the propo-

---

[16] See, *inter alia*, J. G. A. Pocock, 'The History of Political Thought: A Methodological Enquiry', in P. Laslett and W. G. Runciman (eds.), *Philosophy, Politics and Society*, 2nd ser. (Oxford, 1964), 183–202; J. Dunn, 'The Identity of the History of Ideas', *Philosophy*, 43 (1968), 85–116; Q. Skinner, 'Meaning and Understanding in the History of Ideas', *History and Theory*, 8 (1969), 3–53, repr. in J. Tully (ed.), *Meaning and Context: Quentin Skinner and his Critics* (Princeton, NJ, 1988), 97–118.

nents of 'original intent' are wrong about legal or constitutional interpretation, which in its turn differs in important
respects from interpretation in the history of political
thought.[17] Here, however, I want to defend the new historians
against an oft-heard criticism—a criticism to which they have
not, to my knowledge, offered a wholly satisfactory reply.

One criticism levelled repeatedly against Skinner and the
new historians of political thought is that the recovery of
authorial intention is unimportant or irrelevant, even if possible in principle. For, these critics contend, even if we accept
Skinner's claim that political writing is a species of action, the
fact remains that these sorts of actions—like all human
actions—produce consequences unintended, unforeseen, and
perhaps even unforeseeable by the actor/author. Hence, to
recover an author's aims or intentions, even if possible, is
beside the point.[18] The history of political thought is, or at
any rate should be, the story of the consequences of authorial
actions. It should, that is, be about the uses to which a
writer's ideas were later put by actors whose interpretation of
the meaning of a term (utterance, phrase, passage, or entire
text) may not and need not accord with the authors' own
intentions. Or, to put it another way, the historian's task is to
trace the unintended consequences of purposive political
action, in this instance the action of writing a political tract or
treatise.[19]

While it is of course true that actions, including the act of
writing, often produce unintended consequences, the claim
that intentions are irrelevant or do not matter simply does not
follow. For it is *logically* impossible to validly claim that a
certain consequence X was unintended unless one can do two
things. One must first be able to show what the author did
intend (or could conceivably have intended); and then one
must note that X differs from the end(s) that the author
(could conceivably have) intended to bring about. In other
words, the very *identification* of a consequence as 'unintended'

---

[17] See Ch. 11 below. [18] Cf. Shapiro, 'Realism'.
[19] This is also K. R. Popper's conception of the social scientist's task; see
The Open Society (London, 1969), ii, 95–6. This methodological similarity
suggests one way of effecting a *rapprochement* between political theory and
the social sciences. See J. Farr, 'Popper's Hermeneutics', *Philosophy of the
Social Sciences*, 13 (1983), 157–76.

requires that one be able to identify what the agent's/author's intentions actually are, or were. Hence, it cannot be the case that reference to an author's intention(s) is irrelevant or beside the point—particularly for anyone wishing to write the history of political thought (or problems or episodes therein) as the story of 'unintended consequences'! A good many grandiose claims about the supposed irrelevance or unimportance of intentions are wrecked on the reef of this logical common-place.

This does not, of course, mean that the historian of political thought should cease her enquiries once she has succeeded in identifying an author's ideological–linguistic context and the intention(s) it makes possible or likely. That may well show what a term or utterance, or even an entire text, 'meant' for its author, and perhaps for his or her audience; and so it may help to recover the 'historical identity' of the text;[20] but it hardly suffices to show how it was received and interpreted by subsequent reader-authors and their audiences. Here, so-called 'reception' or 'reader-response' theories of interpretation have something to offer.[21] A text is not merely an artefact produced by an author; it is also a communication received by a reader. Its meaning must in some part be the product of a 'negotiation' between the two. Gadamer's metaphor for this process—the 'fusion of horizons'—is, for me, at once illuminating and confusing. It is illuminating, inasmuch as it suggests that there is a vast distance to be bridged. But the metaphor is also confusing, in that a 'horizon' in the visual–perspectival sense is one thing, not two, and therefore not the sort of thing that could be joined or 'fused'.[22]

A more prosaic, and perhaps better, way of putting the matter has been suggested by Alan Ryan. In reading an earlier work of political theory we are, he says, tugged in two different directions at once. On the one hand, we want to know what the *author* was up to and what he or she meant in say-

[20] Dunn, 'Identity'.

[21] See S. R. Suleiman and I. Crosman (eds.), *The Reader in the Text* (Princeton, NJ, 1980); H. R. Jauss, *Toward an Aesthetic of Reception* (Minneapolis, 1982); R. C. Holub, *Reception Theory* (London, 1984).

[22] Cf. Gadamer, *Truth and Method*, 269–74.

ing something. But, on the other hand, we also have to recognize that

> Once the essay or book in which we are interested has been put before the public, it takes on a life of its own. Whatever the copyright laws, an author has only a limited control over his own writings. What he writes will have implications which he did not see—implications in the narrow sense of more or less logical inferences from what he says to the consequences of what he says. . . . Works outlive their authors, and take on lives their writers might be perturbed to see.

As 'the most obvious instance' of this process, Ryan cites 'the history of how Machiavelli's major works were read, from 1520 to the 1980s', with a sidelong glance at Marx's (mis)reading of Hegel.[23]

What Ryan refers to are in part, and once again, the manifold ways in which purposive political actions can, and typically do, produce unintended consequences. And certainly these do present problems for the historian who takes an intentionalist tack towards textual interpretation. These problems are not, however, insoluble or insurmountable, and need not pose any grave difficulty for an approach to interpretation via authorial intention. To appreciate just how and why this might be so, let us look outside the immediate purview of political theory.

Suppose I arrive home late one evening. Entering my house, I flip the light switch and several things happen. The light comes on, as I intended that it should. But the light's coming on also wakes the cat, alerts a burglar in the adjoining room, annoys a neighbour, causes the dial in the electric meter to rotate, and raises my electric bill. Flipping the switch is my 'basic action'.[24] The light's coming on is my action under an intentionalist description: that is what I was doing, or trying to do, when I flipped the switch. I did not intend, and could not have intended, to wake the cat or to frighten the burglar, since I was in no position to know that the cat was asleep or

---

[23] A. Ryan, *Property and Political Theory* (Oxford, 1984), 3–4. To Ryan's list I would add, amongst many others, later Marxists' (mis)reading of Marx; see below, Chs. 9, 10.

[24] A. C. Danto, 'Basic Actions', *American Philosophical Quarterly*, 2 (1965), 141–8.

that the burglar lurked in the adjoining room. And yet I *did*, i.e. brought about, all these things, not all of which were intended but all of which were made possible by my acting intentionally.

The performance of a political action—including the act of writing—is not unlike flipping the light switch. The basic action of putting pen to paper can be given an intentionalist description: the author was doing, or attempting to do, a certain thing—to defend or to criticize royal absolutism, to justify or decry regicide, to promote or oppose religious toleration, or any number of other things. But an author's action may well produce unintended consequences. His argument might, for example, later be used for purposes that the author did not address, and did not or perhaps could not have intended or even foreseen. The concepts used in constructing that argument, and the linguistic conventions according to which it was constructed, may well be misunderstood (or deliberately ignored) by later writers who wish to appropriate, extend, or perhaps amend what they took this earlier writer to have been doing. Some of these misunderstandings and/or rank misrepresentations may prove fruitful for other actors with their other, doubtless very different, aims and agendas. Two examples might serve to make my point.

Some modern feminists have interpreted Locke as a proto-feminist, inasmuch as he was, as they are, critical of 'patriarchalism'. Thus Melissa Butler, for one, contends that Locke's critique of Filmer's *Patriarchia* in the *Two Treatises* lays the groundwork, as it were, for modern feminist critiques of male dominion or 'patriarchy'.[25] Locke would no doubt be surprised to find himself enlisted as an early forerunner of feminism, and he might well be appalled at the prospect. But, while it would be a mistake to claim that, in criticizing Filmer, Locke meant or even could conceivably have intended to add arguments to the arsenal of modern feminists, there is nothing necessarily wrong or illegitimate in taking the view that arguments constructed for one purpose may subsequently be put to some altogether different use. And this, arguably,

[25] M. Butler, 'Early Liberal Roots of Feminism: John Locke and the Attack on Patriarchy, *APSR* 72 (1978), 135–50; and my critique, *APSR* 73 (1979), 549–50.

has happened in the case of Locke's critique of patriarchalism. Locke has, as it were, no copyright or exclusive title to his ideas and arguments. They are part of the public domain, and may be interpreted, appropriated, and applied in almost any way by any political actor who finds them congenial or useful.

My second example comes from Margaret Leslie's critique of Skinner and her defence of 'anachronistic' readings of earlier thinkers.[26] Strained analogies, and even anachronisms, may, in the hands of an ingenious writer such as Antonio Gramsci, prove to be politically persuasive when addressed to a certain sort of audience. In redescribing the Communist Party as the 'modern prince', Gramsci adapted and made creative use of what he took to be Machiavelli's notion of a ruthless and all-powerful *principe*. On Gramsci's reading, the Communist Party, like Machiavelli's prince, must be prepared to use guile, cunning, deceit, and violence to achieve worthy ends. By substituting 'Party' for 'prince', Gramsci was able to adapt Machiavelli's arguments to a more modern and distinctly different context. That Gramsci's use of Machiavelli's text was admittedly anachronistic is beside the point. As a political actor, Gramsci had, and used, the political equivalent of poetic licence.

Skinner's contention, in effect, is that no such licence is granted to historians of political thought. If we, as historians, are to understand the meaning that particular terms, utterances, claims, and arguments had for certain authors and their audiences, then surely we must, at a minimum, know something about the linguistic conventions of the day and the political concepts, languages, or idioms available to them. Thus it would in this instance be important to note, for example, that the modern concept of the 'political party', as understood by Gramsci and his audience, was not available to Machiavelli and his contemporaries.[27] One might also note that certain key concepts in Machiavelli's vocabulary, such as *fortuna*, have no place in, and are arguably at odds with, Gramsci's own rather more deterministic Marxian framework.

[26] M. Leslie, 'In Defence of Anachronism', *Political Studies*, 18 (1970), 433–47.
[27] T. Ball, 'Party', in Ball, J. Farr, and R. L. Hanson (eds.), *Political Innovation and Conceptual Change* (Cambridge, 1989).

To make these observations is of course to take nothing away from Gramsci, who wrote not as a scholar but as a political actor and activist who was in Skinner's sense an 'innovating ideologist'.[28] Gramsci, in other words, used an existing and already well-known stock of concepts and images to re-describe and lend legitimacy to an institution widely regarded as suspect. An interpretation like Gramsci's may be adjudged good (innovative, ingenious, path-breaking, persuasive, etc.) on political grounds even as it is adjudged deficient on scholarly grounds, and vice versa.

We must remember that political actors, past and present, are apt to fight dirty by, for example, misrepresenting opponents' views, constructing arguments *ad hominem*, and using almost any rhetorical weapon that comes to hand. And success in such endeavours depends, as often as not, upon one side's skill or sheer good luck in hitting upon an illuminating image or telling metaphor to make its case persuasive or at least palatable.[29] But it is also important to note that such arguments and appeals must be tailored to the tastes, standards, and outlook of the audience at which they are aimed. If one fails to take one's audience's standards into account, one runs the grave risk of having one's actions viewed as unintelligible and/or illegitimate. Both *desiderata*—intelligibility and legitimacy—are, for *political* agents, considerations surpassing importance. As Skinner notes, 'the problem facing an agent who wishes to legitimate what he is doing at the same time as gaining what he wants cannot simply be the instrumental problem of tailoring his normative language in order to fit his projects. It must in part be the problem of tailoring his projects in order to fit the available normative language.'[30] Hence,

however revolutionary the ideologist ... he will nevertheless be committed, once he has accepted the need to legitimate his behaviour, to attempting to show that some of the *existing* range of favourable

[28] Q. Skinner, 'Some Problems in the Analysis of Political Thought and Action', in Tully (ed.), *Meaning and Context*, 112.

[29] T. Ball and J. G. A. Pocock (eds.), *Conceptual Change and the Constitution* (Lawrence, Kan., 1988), 2.

[30] Q. Skinner, *Foundations of Modern Political Thought* (Cambridge, 1978), i, pp. xii–xiii.

evaluative–descriptive terms can somehow be applied as apt descriptions of his own apparently untoward actions. Every revolutionary is to this extent obliged to march backward into battle.[31]

At the same time, however, a political actor/author—particularly one on whom we (retrospectively) bestow the honorific title of political theorist—does things not only *with* language, but *to* language, in that his or her actions produce changes (sometimes intended, sometimes not) in the vocabulary available to his or her audience and to subsequent speakers of the language.[32] Through the use of argument, analogy, metaphor, and other means, he or she may be able to alter the language of description and appraisal in certain ways, perhaps by extending the meaning of a term, or even by coining a new one. But any author daring to do so is likely to proceed cautiously and perhaps even apologetically, as Locke does, for example, in the *Second Treatise*. 'It may perhaps be censured as an impertinent Criticism in a discourse of this nature', he writes, 'to find fault with words and names that have obtained in the World: And yet possibly it may not be amiss to offer new ones when the old are apt to lead Men into mistakes . . .'.[33] The concept in question is 'paternal power', which in the political–linguistic context of late-seventeenth-century England was being put to a particular political use—namely, justifying royal absolutism. Locke's refutation of arguments in favour of royal absolutism relies rather less upon the coining of new terms than upon showing that 'paternal power', as used by Filmer and other apologists, was by the logical and linguistic standards of the day contradictory and incoherent, rested on misreadings or misunderstandings of scripture, and so on. Radical as he was, Locke recognized full well that he too must proceed with caution, marching backwards into battle where necessary and couching his arguments as quarrels with contemporaries or predecessors in a language that his audience was likely to understand.

Many other examples could be offered, of course, but it seems quite clear that the history of political thought is in no

---

[31] Skinner, 'Some Problems', 112.

[32] Ball, Farr, and Hanson (eds.), *Political Innovation*; Ball, *Transforming Political Discourse* (Oxford, 1988).

[33] Locke, *Second Treatise*, ch. VI, sect. 52.

small part the story of one theorist's commentary on, or criticisms of, a predecessor or a contemporary. And among the most powerful weapons in any theorist's arsenal are arguments, like Locke's against Filmer, which purport to show that an opponent has somehow been inconsistent, incoherent, or has otherwise contradicted himself. Such Socratic questioning and criticism has been, and remains, the political theorist's stock in trade.[34] In so far as its practitioners attend closely and critically to matters of logic and language, political theory is at once a form of political action and a species of philosophical enquiry. But the latter, far from being separate from the former, is an integral part of the enterprise. And both are in turn implicated in the process of political innovation and conceptual change.[35] As Alasdair MacIntyre aptly observes:

philosophical inquiry itself plays a part in changing moral [and political] concepts. It is not that we have a straightforward history of moral concepts and then a separate and secondary history of philosophical comment. For to analyze a concept philosophically may often be to assist in its transformation by suggesting that it needs revision, or is discredited in some way. Philosophy leaves everything as it is—except concepts. And since to possess a concept involves behaving or being able to behave in certain ways in certain circumstances, to alter concepts, whether by modifying existing concepts or by making new concepts available or by destroying old ones, is to alter behaviour. A history which takes this point seriously, which is concerned with the role of philosophy in relation to actual conduct, cannot be philosophically neutral.[36]

It is in part the hybrid character of political theory that makes its history, or any particular episode therein, so difficult to interpret and so instructive to study and reflect upon.

There are, as we shall see, many different ways of interpreting and understanding what earlier thinkers were doing, and why, and what consequences (intended and unintended) followed from their actions. I now want, very briefly, to sketch the outlines of the pluralistic and problem-centred approach taken in the present volume.

---

[34] J. Farr, 'Understanding Conceptual Change Politically', in Ball, Farr, and Hanson (eds.), *Political Innovation*, 34–6.

[35] See my *Transforming Political Discourse*, ch. 1.

[36] A. MacIntyre, *A Short History of Ethics* (New York, 1966), 2–3.

1.4 MEANINGS AND CONTEXTS

In trying to understand any aspect of or episode in the history of political thought, one does not and cannot return to the scene directly. The way back has been illuminated—or littered—by an intervening history of commentary and interpretation of both the political and scholarly varieties. In reading Filmer, for example, one cannot but be aware of the uses to which *Patriarcha* (1680) was put some three decades after his death by defenders of royal absolutism, nor can one be blind to or uninterested in the criticisms that Locke levelled against these latter-day Filmerians. These subsequent uses, interpretations, and criticism have, for us, come to be *part* of what *Patriarcha* 'means' and the place it occupies in the history of political thought.[37] These are facts about an author named Filmer and a text bearing the title *Patriarcha*. That they emerged or developed only after the text's publication and well after its author's death does not detract from or impugn their status as facts: that, on the contrary, is the nature of historical fact.[38]

Consider, for example, the following statement: 'The author of *On Liberty* was born in 1806.' Is this statement true—that is, does it accurately describe a historical fact? It is certainly true that John Stuart Mill was born in 1806, and it is true that he went on to write *On Liberty*. But can we truthfully say that (someone we now know as) 'the author of *On Liberty*' was born in 1806? Yes, *we* can, even though, in the nature of the case, no one could know that in 1806. To put the point paradoxically, we might say that some facts emerge only after the fact. Or, to put it less paradoxically, we might say that facts are not fixed but are dynamic entities that emerge in time and as a consequence of subsequent developments and actions—including, in the case of texts in the history of political theory, the act of reading and interpreting them.

But no reading, as I noted earlier, is innocent or naïve; it is

[37] G. J. Schochet, *Patriarchalism in Political Thought* (New York, 1975), 268–9.
[38] The following is suggested by A.C. Danto's discussion of 'tensed sentences' in *Narration and Knowledge* (New York, 1985), 56–8.

not a direct return to the text and/or context but is filtered through, and coloured by, other readers' readings. The methodological moral to be drawn from this is that we need to be aware of the ways in which our own readings are apt to be beholden to someone else's—and not so that we can be grateful to them, but so that we can critically assess and perhaps disagree and differ with them, in the hope of overcoming the limitations that they impose upon our understanding of (say) Locke or Rousseau or Marx. We need, in short, periodically to reappraise the value and validity of the interpretations we have inherited from earlier writers.

Perhaps surprisingly, this task is in one crucial respect like that of the natural scientist. As Imre Lakatos noted, a scientific theory offers a framework for interpreting 'the data'. But these data do not exist wholly independently of the theory: which data are to count as (relevant) data are determined, in part, by the theory (or interpretive framework) itself. Even our most direct observations are impregnated with expectations generated by the theory we hold. Thus there is no neutral or natural dividing line between 'observational' and 'theoretical' statements. All observation is 'theory-laden' and involves interpretation of some kind. But if that is true, how can a scientist favour one theory or interpretation over another? Is no theory better or worse than any other? The answer, according to Lakatos, is that science is a search for truth, and this search takes the form of a 'three-cornered fight' between the data and two (or more) competing interpretations of it. Competing theories are not redundancies or luxuries, but are necessary to the enterprise of science itself.[39]

So, too, are competing interpretations of texts essential to the enterprise of political theory. We approach a text, in part, by way of other readings or interpretations of it, against which we counterpose our own or someone else's alternative reading. Out of these competing readings comes a new, and arguably better, interpretation. This process is sometimes aided by the appearance of better and more accurate versions of a particular text, and even by the discovery of new, non-

[39] I. Lakatos, 'Falsification and the Methodology of Scientific Research Programmes', in I. Lakatos and A. Musgrave (eds.), *Criticism and the Growth of Knowledge* (Cambridge, 1970), 115.

textual 'data'—such as, for example, the fact that Marx did not try to dedicate *Das Kapital* to Darwin.[40] But, these exceptions aside, we more typically begin by puzzling over a text, aided—or, we may come to believe, hindered—by someone else's attempt to make sense of the same work. And we come to reinterpret the former by taking issue with the latter.

Lakatos's three-cornered fight is characteristic of all interpretive enquiry and has indeed served as an implicit standard among political theorists for quite some time. I have alluded already to Locke's critique of Filmer—a critique necessitated by the use to which Filmer's text was then being put by proponents of royal absolutism. One could also add many other examples, including Marx's critique of capitalism, which proceeded by way of a critique of political economy, inasmuch as Adam Smith, David Ricardo, and others had supplied some of the concepts and categories in which capitalist production and distribution was redescribed, defended—and, not least, legitimated—in supposedly scientific terms.

But such three-cornered fights are fought not only by political theorists *qua* activists, but by academic political theorists as well: the form of the fight, if not the rules according to which it is conducted, are the same, whether the subject be science, political action, or political theory. For scholars the fight must be fair and be conducted, as it were, according to the academic equivalent of the Marquis of Queensbury rules. One may not, for example, deliberately misquote or misleadingly paraphrase an author; one must not conceal or suppress counter-evidence that might weigh against one's interpretation; and so on.

These rules for fighting fair do not always or necessarily apply to political actors and activists themselves. The hermeneutical battles waged by innovating ideologists are often far from fair, are rarely scholarly, and are typically conducted by almost any means available. Frederick the Great's *Anti-Machiavel* (1740) is a political tract that merits scholarly study but is not itself a work of scholarship. Much the same might be said of Locke's critique of Filmer, or Marx's reading of Ricardo, or Frau Forster-Nietzsche's selective presentation of

---

[40] See Ch. 10 below.

her brother's views on racial differences. All these were primarily political rather than scholarly works; none can be trusted as reliable guides to the thinkers about whose views they were writing. And that is simply because politics is not scholarship, nor scholarship politics. It seems to me a mistake—and an inexcusable conceit—to say, as some now do, that all scholarship is somehow 'political' or is itself politics practised by other means. That view demeans both politics and scholarship.

Now this is *not* to say that a scholar's motives must not be political, only that the methods and results of her researches must be judged according to scholarly standards, not political ones. The aim of scholarship is to seek and to tell the truth, as best one can discern it, and not to promote any particular partisan cause. Of course, if telling the truth about (say) the sources of Mill's feminism should in some way promote (say) the cause of feminism, well and good; but, *qua* scholar, one should not suppress or fail to tell the truth simply because one's cause might somehow be sullied or undermined.

One may take up a topic or a thinker out of political interest or ideological preference without thereby forfeiting one's scholarly credentials. Indeed, it is probably fair to say that most students of political theory, myself included, have been motivated by political concerns.[41] But the worth of one's work is to be judged, not according to its 'political correctness' (or lack thereof), but according to its scholarly (in)adequacy. One historian of political thought may agree with another about politics but disagree strongly about the other's use of evidence and argument.

It is just here, and on these grounds, that the three-cornered fight is waged. It may be, and often is, a friendly fight between cordial combatants. But, friendly or no, the form is always the same: one interpretation of 'the data' is challenged by another, and both are assayed according to the available evidence (textual, linguistic, historical, etc.). But, since such evidence is rarely, if ever, self-evident, it requires interpretation to tease out its meaning and significance for and bearing on the problem at hand. And for this purpose a rival interpre-

---

[41] See Ch. 2.3 below.

tation is indispensable. The second, or rival, account proceeds not only by reference to these data, but by way of a critique of the first's interpretation of it. This critique is not a distraction or an unfortunate necessity, but is instead an essential feature of the history of political thought.

This is precisely the form in which Macpherson, for example, makes his case against the interpretations supplied by commentators who paint a portrait of the tolerant, proto-democratic, 'liberal' Locke. And the critics who have tried to recover the historical identity of the *Two Treatises* have worked their way back to Locke's texts and context by way of a critique of Macpherson and other interpreters.[42] Although this is not a move advocated in the abstract methodological manifestos of the new historians, it is nevertheless one made with scrupulous regularity in their actual practice. Their programme, in practice, is not a 'fundamentalist' one eschewing any reference to an intervening history of interpretation, but is, on the contrary, one which takes off from—by taking issue with—prevailing interpretations that they deem to be defective or deficient. We see this kind of three-cornered fight even in the earlier and more militant phase of the 'new history' of political thought.

Consider, by way of example, John Dunn's preface to *The Political Thought of John Locke* (1969). His is, he says, a 'historical ... account of what *Locke* was talking about, not a doctrine written (perhaps unconsciously) by him in a sort of invisible ink which becomes apparent only when held up to the light (or heat) of the twentieth-century mind'. Dunn derides the quixotic attempts by 'a succession of determined philosophers mounting their scholastic Rosinantes and riding forth to do battle with a set of disused windmills, or solemnly and expertly flailing thin air'. Dunn's enquiry aims instead

to restore the windmill to its original condition, to show how, creakingly but unmistakably, the sails used to turn. Even at the level of preserving ancient monuments it is perhaps a service to recondition

---

[42] See, *inter alia*, J. Dunn, *The Political Thought of John Locke* (Cambridge, 1969); J. Tully, *A Discourse on Property* (Cambridge, 1980) and *An Approach to Political Philosophy: Locke in Contexts* (Cambridge, 1993); R. Ashcraft, *Revolutionary Politics and Locke's 'Two Treatises of Government'* (Princeton, NJ, 1986).

these hallowed targets. There seems little purpose in recording hits on a target that has no existence outside our own minds.[43]

Yet the interpretive principles prescribed in Dunn's drily puritanical preface actually make possible the richness, subtlety, and suggestiveness of the reading of the *Two Treatises* that follows—a reading motivated by, and mounted against, what he takes to be the misreadings offered by Macpherson and Strauss, amongst others.

Nor is Dunn alone in following this route. Quentin Skinner's manifesto of 1969, prescribing what historians of political thought ought (not) to do, proceeds by way of a critique of the ways in which historians have heretofore plied their trade. And elsewhere—for example, in his enquiry into the ideological context of Hobbes's theory of obligation—Skinner makes his case, not by eschewing intervening interpretations altogether and somehow returning directly (as though that were possible) to the original text and its context, but by way of a critique of contemporary interpretations of Hobbes's account of obligation, such as those proposed by Taylor and Warrender, amongst others. Exactly the same sort of move is made in his other historical work, including his studies of Machiavelli, More, and other seminal figures in early modern political thought.[44]

What are we to make of this? If we are to understand the pronouncements and the practices of the new historians, we must, I think, view them in much the same way that they view the writings and actions of historical actors. Their methodological prescriptions must be understood, in part, as polemics directed against a certain sort of historian or commentator. On the one side stand those 'textualists' who read a piece of political theory as a timeless text of the sort imagined and ide-

[43] Dunn, *Political Thought*, p. x. Dunn has subsequently revised his own reappraisal of Locke's relevance to our time. See 'What is Living and what is Dead in the Political Theory of John Locke?', in *Interpreting Political Responsibility* (Oxford, 1990), 9–25.

[44] Q. Skinner, 'The Ideological Context of Hobbes's Political Thought', *Historical Journal*, 9 (1966), 286–317; 'The Idea of Negative Liberty', in Rorty, Schneewind, and Skinner (eds.), *Philosophy in History*, 193–221; 'More's *Utopia* and the Language of Renaissance Humanism', in A. Pagden (ed.), *The Languages of Political Theory in Early-Modern Europe* (Cambridge, 1987), 123–57.

alized by New Critics who held that historical context and authorial intention are utterly irrelevant (indeed they claimed that to look for meaning in authorial intention is to commit something they called 'the intentional fallacy').[45] On the other side one finds 'contextualists', including conservative Namierites and radical Marxists who, despite their differences, are alike in agreeing that 'ideas' are epiphenomenal, mere flotsam floating on an eternal sea of self- or class or party or national interest.

These, then, were among the new historians' intended targets, and this the site, so to speak, from which their enterprise was launched and from which it must be understood, at least in its initial manifesto-issuing stage.

My purpose here, however, is neither to expound nor to defend the views of the new historians but to suggest several affinities between their approach and the tack taken in the present volume. Foremost among these are the following. We are alike in agreeing about the importance, indeed the indispensability, of the intellectual, political, and linguistic contexts in which political texts appear and do their work. These contexts are varied and multiple, encompassing not only the context in which a text was composed, but also the successive contexts in which it was received, read, interpreted, criticized, reread, and reinterpreted. These we might call the context of a text's composition and the subsequent contexts of its reception, respectively.

From this more complex conception of context, several implications follow. For one, authorial intentions, although important, are not in all cases all-important. For certain purposes one may wish to discover, recover, and restate an author's intentions so as to show what he was trying to do in using a certain word or phrase, or constructing a particular argument in a particular way, or even composing an entire treatise. This is especially important in those instances in which one seeks to understand an author as a political actor. But sometimes we are less interested in Locke, say, than in what subsequent author-actors made of Locke's text, and quite possibly in ways that Locke would not or even could

[45] W. K. Wimsatt and M. Beardsly, 'The Intentional Fallacy', *Sewanee Review*, 54 (1946).

not have intended, did not foresee, and almost certainly would not have approved of. Political actions—including the act of writing—often produce unintended consequences. But, as I noted earlier, it does not follow—*pace* Marxists, Namierites, New Critics, realists, and assorted deconstructionists—that intentions do not matter or need not be taken into account. And this again for the simple reason that the very identification of an outcome as unintended logically requires that we be able, first, to describe the original intention and, secondly, show that the outcome differs from the one initially intended.

More than that, we are less likely to be interested in authors, texts, and/or contexts *per se* than we are in particular *problems* that arise as we attempt to understand them. As a rule we do not come to Locke or Rousseau wanting to know all about them or their texts or their times, but because we are puzzled or troubled about something on which a certain sort of enquiry might shed some light. Did Locke really mean to defend the property rights of a rising bourgeoisie? How are we to understand the role of a *religion civile* in Rousseau's *Contrat social*? What are the probable sources of John Stuart Mill's feminist sympathies? What was the nature of Marx's debt to Darwin and what are its implications for his view of science and social theory?

Such problems can come from any source and be of almost any sort. One might be interested in Mill because one is sympathetic to or highly critical of the liberal tradition, or because one believes that liberty is under threat and that Mill might shed some light on our modern predicament. Or one might wish to assess the (in)adequacy of the Western and liberal conception of tolerance in the light of some contemporary question or issue, such as the Salman Rushdie affair, and find it both necessary and desirable to reread and reappraise Locke on toleration and Mill on liberty.[46] In short—and to borrow a distinction from the philosophy of science—the problem-driven 'context of discovery' is wide open, even as the 'context of justification' is rather more restricted.[47] The problems can come from anywhere and be addressed via a variety of strate-

[46] B. Parekh, 'The Rushdie Affair: Research Agenda for Political Philosophy', *Political Studies*, 38 (1990), 695–709.

[47] H. Reichenbach, *Experience and Prediction* (Chicago, 1961), 6–7.

gies; but the (in)adequacy of the solutions must be assessed according to more stringent scholarly criteria.

The historical study of political theory is, in sum, a problem-solving activity. It takes other interpretations as alternative solutions to some puzzle or problem, and then goes on to assess their adequacy *vis-à-vis* each other and in relation to one's own proposed solution. Interpretation is indeed a three-cornered fight. Hence we cannot but take others' interpretations into account, reappraising their adequacy and value, as I attempt to do in the studies comprising the present volume.

This process of reappraisal is not incidental to the practice of political theory but is instead an indispensable, if not indeed defining, feature of our craft. This craft is in an important sense backward-looking. Political theory, more than any other vocation, takes its own past to be an essential part of its present. Its past includes a history not only of theorizing, of great (and not-so-great) books, but of commentary on and interpretation of those thinkers and texts.[48] It is through the latter that the former are reconsidered, criticized, and re-evaluated—in short, reappraised. One might even put the point more strongly by saying that the seminal works of political theory are kept alive and vivid—keep their 'classic' status, so to speak—only in so far as they are not worshipped at academic shrines but are, on the contrary, carefully and critically reappraised.[49]

It might therefore appear that political theory, at least as regards its reappraisive function, is a benign and harmless enterprise, and the modern student of the subject a mildly curious creature in the academic zoo. Yet political theory is not without critics from various quarters, some of whom are on occasion quite vociferous. Some political scientists are apt to think of the political theorists in their midst as historians or, perhaps, philosophers. Historians, however, may not wish to claim them as colleagues, and philosophers might not understand political theorists' interest in history and, stranger still, in politics. All, moreover, are suspicious of the claim that

---

[48] D. Baumgold, 'Political Commentary on the History of Political Theory', *APSR* 75 (1981), 928–40.

[49] C. Condren, *The Status and Appraisal of Classic Texts* (Princeton, NJ, 1985).

thinkers long dead might somehow be connected with, and might in some respects illuminate, the darker recesses of our present condition.

Such suspicion sometimes erupts into open hostility. During the 'behavioural revolution' of the 1950s and 1960s, many political scientists went on the offensive against the aliens in their midst. Political theory was charged with being antiquarian, non-empirical, and, worst of all, 'normative'—that is, concerned with the 'values' or subjective preferences of this or that long-dead thinker and/or his or her present-day interpreter. This bill of indictment, as I attempt to show in Chapter 2, was predicated on a philosophy of science and a conception of cognitive meaningfulness that has long since been repudiated by philosophers of science. But academic political theorists had no sooner regained their composure and sense of dignity than they were attacked from the other side by critics who claimed that the 'classics' of political theory were the antiquated, sexist, racist, homophobic texts of 'dead white men', all sharing the aim of perpetuating and legitimating the dominance of themselves and their descendants. There was, accordingly, a call to disavow, if not eliminate from the curriculum, the 'classics', the 'canon' of 'Great Books' that, when read and taken seriously by students, can only serve to justify the unjustifiable.[50]

Since the present work is intended, in part, to be an answer to this charge, I should say that I do not think it ridiculous or entirely ill founded. There are, if not texts, then certainly ways of reading or interpreting them, that give aid and comfort to those who wish the worst for some of their fellow human beings. One need only think, for example, of the ways in which Hitler and the Nazis used (and arguably abused) the works of Nietzsche, or Stalin the works of Marx, to justify genocidal policies. But it is no less important to note that the disclosure and criticism of such (mis)understandings is itself an integral part of political theory. Far from being the sort of hagiographic exercise portrayed by some of its present-day detractors, the study of political theory is, above all, a relentlessly critical enterprise. As such, one of its essential features

[50] J. Searle, 'Storm over the University', *New York Review*, 37 (Dec. 1990), 34–42.

is its attention to the ways in which authors and texts are appropriated and used—or, as often as not, misappropriated and abused—by would-be defenders or disciples.

To enumerate and defend these and other features of my chosen vocation is not all that difficult, at least on a fairly abstract level, as I attempt to do in this and the following chapter. A second task—much more difficult, and more important by far—is to try to show how one might put these precepts into practice in particular cases. The bulk of the present work consists, accordingly, of studies or exercises of the second sort. Both, however, proceed from a particular perspective or point of view. Candour compels me to say something, if only briefly, about the perspective from which I write.

Five points merit particular mention. The first and most important, as I have noted already, is that mine is a problem-centred perspective. By this I mean that my method of interpretation varies with and is dictated by the particular interpretive problem being addressed, and not the other way round. A method is not like a stretch sock: one size does not fit all feet. Nor, by the same token, can any single method or approach—textual, contextual, Marxist, realist, Straussian, or whatever—possibly illuminate, much less resolve, every conceivable problem of interpretation.

Second, these interpretive problems can come from any source, whether historical, contemporary, literary, political, or whatever. These problems provide the interest or vantage-point from which interpretation proceeds. In the present volume my enquiries proceed not only from problems within the text, but, no less importantly, from questions raised, and interpretations advanced and defended, by subsequent commentators, often in idioms that were unavailable to the author. Charges that the theories of Plato or Rousseau were 'totalitarian' or that Bentham was a 'feminist' fall under this heading. Although anachronistic, these characterizations are not necessarily illegitimate. They may be useful and illuminating in some contexts but not in others, and a stimulus to the reinterpretation and reappraisal of a theorist and his or her work.

Third, I think it worth trying, in so far as possible and where appropriate, to place the text within two contexts, the first being the context of its composition (which necessarily includes some reference to its author's intentions), and the second being the various contexts of its reception (which may or may not take account of authorial intent).

A fourth feature of my approach is that I attempt, wherever possible, to show how an earlier theorist, and/or a subsequent interpretation, casts light on contemporary problems. The light must of necessity, I believe, be indirect or reflected—Machiavelli and Marx, for example, are not our contemporaries—but no less valuable for that. A particular way of reading Thucydides or Machiavelli, for instance, could conceivably illuminate the darker corners of our present condition as no reading of a modern self-styled 'realist' such as Henry Kissinger can.

Fifth, and finally, my aim in the present volume is not simply to say but to try to show what a pluralist and problem-driven approach to the history of political thought can (and cannot) hope to achieve. If the proof of the pudding be in the eating, then nothing is to be gained by talking about pudding in the abstract, or various recipes for pudding, or what various culinary experts—imported from France or elsewhere—have to say about the matter. Nor will a General Theory of Pudding be of much use. One must sample for oneself and, in so far as possible, trust one's own taste-buds, whether the result be retching or, as I hope, the kind of curiosity that leads one to one's own, and doubtless better, readings and reflections.

1.5 PLAN OF THE PRESENT WORK

Chapter 2 traces in rough outline selected aspects of the history, present state, and future possibilities of political theory, particularly in the North American academy. This attempt to reassess the role and present predicament of political theory begins by looking at the 'behavioural revolution' in American political science and, more specifically, its animus against 'traditional' or 'normative' political theory. Its hostility towards political theory was driven by a particular philosophy of science—Logical Positivism—which has since been discredited and abandoned by philosophers and latterly by most political scientists. The recent revival of political theory owes a good deal to the demise of its philosophical nemesis. But before we congratulate ourselves on our ostensible victory, we had better take a careful look at our vocation's increasing withdrawal from the world and its tendency to turn in on itself and to concern itself with esoterica spawned and nurtured within its own hermetically sealed hothouse. The result can only be the increasing 'alienation of political theory'.[51] I conclude by suggesting how we might resist these inward-turning tendencies and why we might want to do so.

If the studies in Part I are abstract promissory notes, those in Part II are attempts to make good on those promises. Each essay addresses a problem raised in, or prompted by, rival readings of particular texts.

Chapter 3, 'Machiavelli and Moral Change', takes issue with the conventional view that Machiavelli is the first genuinely 'modern' political theorist in that he investigates political phenomena in purely instrumental, and not ethical, terms. Taking one of these terms—*virtù*—I attempt to show that it may be understood as an attempt to resurrect a much older Homeric understanding of 'virtue' ($\alpha\rho\epsilon\tau\acute{\eta}$), which was tied to and partly constitutive of particular social or civic roles. If so, then Machiavelli was more backward- than forward-looking. Indeed, like his fictional contemporary Don Quixote, Machiavelli may be read as having attempted the quixotic feat of reviving an archaic code of conduct—a more manly alternative, as he saw it, to the effeminacy of the modern age.

If Machiavelli was not the first modern political thinker, then—so it is sometimes said—Hobbes surely was. If by 'modern' we mean something like 'scientific', then Hobbes may legitimately lay claim to the title. But before bestowing that title we had better be careful to understand what Hobbes himself meant by 'science', and by a 'civil science' in particular. In Chapter 4 I examine and criticize the claim that Hobbes was a proto-positivist precursor of the modern scientific study of politics. Against this interpretation, I argue that Hobbes may be better viewed as a thinker acutely aware of the communicative constitution of human society. In such a society,

[51] J. G. Gunnell, *Between Philosophy and Politics: The Alienation of Political Theory* (Amherst, Mass., 1986).

communicative distortion and breakdown are always possible
and the spectre of civil war an almost palpable presence. The
role of an all-powerful sovereign is accordingly to prevent, or
rather preclude, the linguistic distortion that leads to the sort
of civil dissolution that is the state of nature or 'natural condition of mankind'. Hobbes's civil science provides the under-
pinning for and justification of a new 'rhetoric of sobriety', a
scientifically sanitized language that precludes the very possibility of criticism, dissent, and revolt.

Although quite critical of Hobbes, Jean-Jacques Rousseau
shared his predecessor's preoccupation with the dangers and
possibilities of political discourse. Quite unlike Hobbes, however, Rousseau attempted to revive the lost language of
republicanism. Yet several features of Rousseau's political theorizing seem—so some interpreters have claimed—strangely at
odds with this aim. In particular, his notions of the General
Will and a dogmatic 'civil religion' appear to some modern
interpreters to have closer ties to twentieth-century totalitarianism than to classical republicanism. If recent scholarship
has done much to dispel the 'totalitarian' aura that long sur-
rounded the General Will, it has done little to clear the fog
that still surrounds the civil religion. Indeed, of all the problems perplexing Rousseau's interpreters, none has proved
more intractable than that posed by his scheme for a civil religion. While his modern critics have been quick to condemn its
ostensibly totalitarian implications, his latter-day defenders
have been rather at a loss to square it with the rest of his
work. In Chapter 5 I advance and defend a revisionist reading
of Rousseau's civil religion by attempting to answer three
questions. First, what role or place does Rousseau's scheme
for a civil religion occupy in his political theory? Second, what
were Rousseau's intentions—i.e. what was he trying to do—in
devising this scheme? And, third, how might we account for
its placement within the text of the *Social Contract*? Addressing these three questions from an external or contextual as
well as internal or textual perspective, I construct a new—and
decidedly non-totalitarian—interpretation of Rousseau's *religion civile*. The evidence is sketchy and circumstantial, but
suggestive of a possibility that has not yet, so far as I am
aware, been considered.

Chapter 6 continues the theme of a civil religion by comparing the schemes offered by two nineteenth-century thinkers, James Mill and Auguste Comte. It begins with John Stuart Mill's condemnation of Comte's Religion of Humanity and his curious failure to note that his father had advanced his own scheme for a civil religion. By comparing Comte's and James Mill's views of the civil role of religion, we can see similarities and contrasts between the former's decidedly illiberal and priestly views, and the latter's liberal and low-church conception of the role of religion in a modern and essentially secular society. The point or purpose of a civil religion, for Mill, is pedagogical: its aim is to impart civically useful knowledge and to instil a sense of civic responsibility and restraint. Such a civil religion is quite unlike its alleged Comtean counterpart, which aims to stifle criticism, manipulate the emotions, and procure assent to an authoritarian and undemocratic system of priestly rule. I conclude by considering the most probable Scottish source of Mill's conception of a civil religion.

In Chapter 7 I examine Michel Foucault's claim that 'We are less Greek than we believe', in that we dwell 'within the panoptic machine'. Foucault's master metaphor for the modern 'surveillance society' is of course Bentham's plan for a Panopticon prison. I try to show that the rationale for Benthamite prison reform offered by his chief ally and propagandist, James Mill, is—*pace* Foucault—very 'Greek' indeed. The ostensibly modern Mill reworks and recycles the argument of a 'classic' text—namely, Plato's *Republic*—and uses Plato's theory of justice and just punishment to justify and legitimate Bentham's plans for reforming penal practices. The methodological moral of this tale is that we should be wary of some modern genealogists' claims about discursive discontinuities between discrete *epistemes* or systems of thought.

But, by the same token, we should be no less suspicious of claims of intellectual ancestry and theoretical affinities across the centuries. The next three chapters examine and criticize such claims.

One can of course write the history of political thought in any number of ways and from any of several perspectives. In recent years feminism has proved to be among the most suggestive and fruitful of these theoretical vantage-points.

Feminist historians have, in their quest for forerunners, found a number of lesser known and largely unsung heroines and heroes, along with others of greater fame. In Chapter 8 I re-examine John Stuart Mill's claim to the title of feminist, with particular attention to the sources from which Mill may have drawn his then-remarkably advanced view of women. After looking closely at two candidates—Jeremy Bentham and Harriet Taylor Mill—I conclude that neither seems suited for the role assigned to them by later feminist commentators. A third, and heretofore unsuspected, thinker proves to be a much more plausible and probable source of Mill's feminist views.

The next two chapters assess claims about Karl Marx's intellectual patriomony and affinities. In Chapter 9 I consider the supposed connection between Vico and Marx, particularly as regards their claim that humans 'make' their own history. For both thinkers, this contention has an epistemic dimension: one has a special sort of knowledge of what one has made. On that much, at least, Marx and Vico agreed. I attempt to show, however, that they had very different conceptions of 'making'. Vico's view that *Verum et factum convertuntur*—that knowing and making are one—relies on a distinctly non-material or lin-guistic or communicative conception of making (as when we 'make sense' or 'make' a promise), while Marx's conception of making is decidedly materialist and concerned with the human transformation of nature through productive labour.

In Chapter 10 I re-examine the oft-heard claim that Marx's materialist conception of history owed something to, or at least shared certain affinities with, Darwin's theory of natural selection. Why else—so at any rate many commentators have claimed—might Marx have wished to dedicate *Das Kapital* to Darwin? As it happens, claims about a connection between the two thinkers, methodological or otherwise, rely on a series of mix-ups. Marx did indeed send an inscribed copy of the first volume of *Das Kapital* to Darwin; Darwin did in fact write to thank Marx; but—contrary to a long-standing myth—Marx never offered to dedicate a later volume of *Capital* to Darwin, nor did Darwin refuse his request. What actually happened, and why it matters, I discuss in some detail.

Many modern American students of political theory, it

seems to me, are rather too eager to embrace European thinkers and theories as somehow superior to or more sophisticated than their own humbler and more prosaic ancestors and contemporaries. There is, of course, nothing wrong with looking abroad—quite the contrary—but there is something wrong with ignoring or dismissing out of hand what lies in one's own back yard. The last two chapters represent a modest effort to exhibit some of the things that one can discover by digging in one's own garden. But, while the topics are American—constitutional interpretation (Chapter 11) and the myth of a distinctly American identity (Chapter 12)—they raise, I believe, questions of more universal interest and import.

Chapter 11 takes up the vexed and vexing question of legal, and more particularly constitutional, interpretation. How ought American citizens, and of course members of the Supreme Court, to read and understand the Constitution? In the law, as in political theory, rival schools supply very different answers. But, I contend, lawyers and jurists do not, or ought not, to enjoy the hermeneutical leeway that political theorists enjoy. By taking a fresh look at one theory of interpretation—'originalism' or 'original intent'—I try to show some heretofore unsuspected pitfalls awaiting anyone who adopts such a strategy. Chief among these is that a thoroughgoing originalism would require one to accept the once-credible but now-discredited or defunct theories and vocabularies within whose terms the Founders thought about politics and framed the Constitution. And this, I argue, is a retrograde move for which there is no rational justification.

The concluding chapter looks at American individualism and national identity in the light of the contemporary 'communitarian/liberal' debate. If Americans have inherited—and either eagerly embraced or vehemently rejected—a dominant myth, it is surely that of the 'American Adam'. This myth holds that America is, or was, a veritable Eden, the garden of the New World, and Americans like Adam before the Fall, fresh, innocent, and full of hope. Like all myths, this one clarifies by simplifying or ignoring a great deal (what, for example, of Native Americans or of Africans forcibly imported as slaves?). My aim here, however, is not to expose the myth's flaws and fallacies—which are notorious and legion—but to show how it pops up in quite unexpected places and is embraced by thinkers apparently unaware of its power and pervasiveness in American culture. I illustrate this claim by looking afresh at three thinkers—John Rawls, Gerard O'Neill, and Richard Rorty—all of whom would, I suspect, disavow my redescription of their respective projects. My aim here, however, is not to identify their intentions but to show how a redescription in cultural or, if you like, 'mythic' terms may call attention to and illuminate certain aspects of their work in ways that they might not recognize or agree with. No author is—or can be—aware of all possible sources of or influences on his or her thinking. Nor can one be aware of all the affinities that one's work might have with that of others, past and present. Nor, for that matter, can any author foresee all possible implications of any line of argument. And it is both daunting and humbling to reflect on the fact that this stricture also applies to the author of the present work.

2

WHITHER POLITICAL THEORY?

2.1 INTRODUCTION

The periodic reassessment and reappraisal of the value of what we have inherited from thinkers living and dead is always undertaken from the vantage-point of our own time and circumstance. We reappraise in the light of problems we encounter or choose to emphasize. And we do so with some sense of where we, as students of political theory, have been and hope to go. My aim in this chapter is to say something about where we have been, are now, and might yet go.

To supply any sort of forecast for the future direction and condition of political theory is always dangerous, if only because predictions about changing human thoughts, actions, and practices are notoriously unreliable and almost always wide of the mark. One need not be a Hegelian to appreciate the point of Hegel's warning about the dangers inherent in attempting to go beyond the world one knows and inhabits:

Whatever happens, every individual is a child of his time; so philosophy too is its own time apprehended in thoughts. It is just as absurd to fancy that a philosophy can transcend its contemporary world as it is to fancy that an individual can overleap his own age, jump over Rhodes. If his theory really goes beyond the world as it is and he builds an ideal one as it ought to be, that world exists indeed, but only in his opinions, an unsubstantial element where anything you please may, in fancy, be built.[1]

A warning well taken by the wise and prudent.

Hegel's warning notwithstanding, there is another adage that might apply to the present case: fools rush in where angels (and even Hegel) fear to tread. So, having set off on

[1] G. W. F. Hegel, *Philosophy of Right* (Oxford, 1967), 11.

what some might think a fool's errand, I propose to proceed
in the following way. Believing that the past and present may
be the best guides to (though not necessarily predictors of) the
future, I shall begin by retracing some of the steps taken by
political theory and its critics over the last three decades.
Second, having said something about where we have come
from, I want to say where I think we stand now. And, third, I
want to hazard a few half-educated guesses about where we
might be headed.

Before beginning, I should say I do not claim or pretend to
speak for anyone but myself. Many, perhaps most, of my
fellow political theorists would tell the story differently and
some—Straussians, say, or Marxists, or postmodernists—will
doubtless take exception to what I have to say. And their
objections should surely carry considerable weight. But I propose to call the shots as I see them, and to speak autobio-
graphically where it seems appropriate to do so.

2.2 THE WAY WE WERE

From the mid-1950s until the early 1970s or thereabouts, it
was *de rigueur* to celebrate (if you were a 'behaviouralist') or
to lament (if you were a 'theorist') the 'decline of political
theory'.[2] In 1953 David Easton announced the end of political
theory as it had been and, in a way that might bring the blush
of embarrassment even to the cheek of H. G. Wells, predicted
the shape of things to come. A 'normative' political theory
concerned with the structure and proper ordering of 'the state'
was at last being superseded. The 'systems' approach discarded the concept of the state and bracketed, if not eschewed
altogether, any merely normative concerns. Henceforth 'the
political system' was to be pared down and seen in proper
perspective, as one of several 'sub-systems', each having its
own characteristic 'inputs' and 'outputs'.[3] This, needless to
say, was a language far removed from the idioms in which
political theorists had been accustomed to speak.

[2] A. Cobban, 'The Decline of Political Theory', *Political Science
Quarterly*, 68 (1953), 321–37.
[3] D. Easton, *The Political System* (New York, 1953).

Easton was not, of course, the only critic of 'normative' or (as it was sometimes called) 'traditional' political theory. A veritable chorus of critics soon appeared.[4] To their voices were added those celebrating the 'end of ideology', at least in the West.[5] The major social problems had, it seemed, been resolved, or were at any rate well on the way to being resolved. A widespread normative consensus was said to pervade the Western democracies, and the United States in particular. The American 'consensus historians' showed that it had always been thus, and that the dreams, schemes, and theories of 'utopian' thinkers and ideologues were bound to come a cropper in an essentially pragmatic culture.[6] Unable (or unwilling) to forgo at least a scholarly interest in the unorthodox and the utopian, political theory was tarred with this very brush. Among the first to note, if not to celebrate, the passing of utopian thinking were, unsurprisingly, political theorists themselves.[7]

It was in this climate that Peter Laslett intoned, 'For the moment, anyway, political philosophy is dead.'[8] (A curious kind of death, this; but then political theory is a curious kind of vocation.) And even those unwilling to write its obituary were wont to lament political theory's precarious position. Sheldon Wolin prefaced *Politics and Vision* with a lamentation for the near-dead:

In many intellectual circles today there exists a marked hostility towards, and even contempt for, political philosophy in its traditional form. My hope is that this volume, if it does not give pause to those who are eager to jettison what remains of the tradition of

---

[4] See e.g. R. Dahl, 'Political Theory: Truth and Consequences', *World Politics*, 11 (1956), 89–102. For an overview of earlier disputes and a more recent survey, see, respectively, J. P. Euben, 'Political Science and Political Silence', in P. Green and S. Levinson (eds.), *Power and Community: Dissenting Essays in Political Science* (New York, 1970), 3–58; and J. G. Gunnell, *Between Philosophy and Politics: The Alienation of Political Theory* (Amherst, Mass., 1986).

[5] E. Shils, 'The End of Ideology?', *Encounter*, 5 (1955), 52–8; D. Bell, *The End of Ideology* (New York, 1960).

[6] See R. Hofstadter, *The Progressive Historians* (New York, 1969), 444–66.

[7] J. Shklar, *After Utopia* (Princeton, NJ, 1957); G. Kateb, *Utopia and its Enemies* (New York, 1963).

[8] P. Laslett, 'Introduction' to Laslett (ed.), *Philosophy, Politics and Society*, 1st ser. (Oxford, 1956), p. vii.

political philosophy, may at least succeed in making clear what it is we shall have discarded.[9]

And what was about to be discarded, on Wolin's subsequent telling, is a pearl beyond price whose value only real swine could fail to appreciate.

Not all commentators were so pessimistic. Some, such as Isaiah Berlin and John Plamenatz, held that political theory could not die, at least while its parent—politics—lived. Both, however, prefaced their accounts with apologies, albeit assertive ones. In 1960, some four years after Laslett's obituary appeared, Plamenatz wrote:

Even in Oxford, which more perhaps than any other place in the English-speaking world is the home of political theory or philosophy, it is often said that the subject is dead or sadly diminished in importance. I happen to have a professional interest in assuming that it is still alive, and as likely to remain so as any other subject as long as man continues to be a speculative and enterprising animal. I do not think that I am biased; I do not think that I need to be. The importance of the subject seems to me so obvious, and the reasons for questioning the importance so muddled, that I do not look upon myself as defending a lost or difficult cause.[10]

At about the same time, Isaiah Berlin, in a similar spirit, began an influential essay on the fate of political theory with a question. 'Is there', he asked bluntly, 'still such a subject as political theory?' Before going on to answer affirmatively, Berlin voiced an oft-heard suspicion that his opening question had posed so directly. 'This query, put with suspicious frequency in English-speaking countries,' Berlin wrote, 'questions the very credentials of the subject; it suggests that political philosophy, whatever it may have been in the past, is today dead or dying.'[11] Both Berlin and Plamenatz went on to deny that political theory was dead, or even moribund.

Who then is, or was, right—those who warned of the death or at any rate the imminent demise of political theory, or those who held that political theory was not dead and could

---

[9] S. Wolin, *Politics and Vision* (Boston, 1960), v.

[10] J. Plamenatz, 'The Uses of Political Theory', *Political Studies*, 8 (1960), 37.

[11] I. Berlin, 'Does Political Theory Still Exist?', in *Philosophy, Politics and Society*, 2nd ser. (Oxford, 1962), 1.

not die? I want to suggest that each, in their own way, was entirely right. To put my point in paradoxical terms: political theory was in some quarters dead or dying; and yet it could not die.

We can resolve the paradox if we begin by drawing (and later withdrawing) a provisional distinction between first- and second-order theorizing. First-order theorizing arises in connection with the activity of attending to the arrangements of one's society.[12] So long as people live together in communities, fundamental questions will inevitably arise. No community can long exist without addressing and answering, at least provisionally, questions of the following sort. To begin with, there are questions about justice and fairness in the distribution of duties and resources. What is due to whom, and in what order? Questions about offices and authority are also likely to arise: who is to resolve issues of common concern—all the members of the community, or only a few? If the latter, which ones and how or by whom are they to be chosen? There are, moreover, questions about conceptual-cum-political demarcation: by what criteria shall we distinguish between matters that are political or public and those that are non-political or private? These, in their turn, give rise to questions about grounds and justification: where do the aforementioned criteria come from and on what basis might they be justified (or criticized, for that matter)? Or consider questions about punishment: what shall we do with dissident or deviant members of our community—tolerate, exile, or execute them? And then there are, of course, questions about the extent and limits of obligation: does every able-bodied citizen have an obligation to fight and perhaps die for the state, if the survival of the state should seem to require it?

The list could continue to grow, but the point is perhaps clear enough: the questions in which political theorists are interested are precisely those which any civilized community must address and attempt to answer. The greatest political thinkers—an Aristotle or a Hobbes, say—have tried to elaborate theories on the basis of which such questions can be (re)framed, addressed, and perchance answered in a coherent,

---

[12] Cf. M. Oakeshott, *Rationalism in Politics* (London, 1962).

comprehensive, and systematic way.[13] But, however magnificent or mediocre the minds of those who wrestle with questions about the proper ordering of society, the fact remains that political thinking or theorizing is in this sense an important, indeed a necessary, activity. Therefore Plamenatz and Berlin were right to suggest that political theory—understood as first-order theorizing—could not die, and a more recent commentator is quite correct in deeming it indispensable.[14]

By contrast, much of what passes for political theory in the academy might, at a first cut, be termed second-order theorizing. It consists largely, though by no means exclusively, of the activity of studying, teaching, and commenting on the 'classics' of political thought. If first-order theorizing is well-nigh immortal, second-order theorizing is eminently mortal. It can die or disappear—or at least be discredited, discounted, or ignored, as happened in many departments of political science during the heyday of behaviouralism. Political theory, as practised in political science departments, was relegated to a kind of limbo, or living death: the worst kind. Many who practised second-order theorizing were made to feel unwelcome, and some were even encouraged to ply their trade in the more congenial setting supplied by departments of philosophy or history.

So, returning to the paradox posed earlier—how could political theory be both dead and alive at the same time?—we can now see that the paradox was only apparent and its resolution really quite simple. Those who, like Laslett, announced the death or imminent demise of political theory were speaking of it as a specialized academic discipline within departments of political science—as second-order theorizing, in other words. And they were at least arguably right in suggesting that political theory *in this sense* was in mortal peril, if not dead already. But Berlin and Plamenatz were no less correct in suggesting that political theory—understood as first-order

---

[13] Political theorists disagree over whether there are 'perennial questions' or whether these questions change over time. My own view is that the questions themselves change, in part because the concepts constituting the moral languages or idioms in which the questions are framed have historically mutable meanings. See my *Transforming Political Discourse* (Oxford, 1988).

[14] A. MacIntyre, 'The Indispensability of Political Theory', in D. Miller and L. Seidentop (eds.), *The Nature of Political Theory* (Oxford, 1983).

theorizing—was neither dead nor dying, nor could it be. That activity is indeed indispensable.

As it turned out, however, all reports of the death of (academic or second-order) theory proved to be premature if not perhaps wholly unwarranted in the first place. By the mid-1970s academic political theorists were wont to quote Mark Twain's remark upon reading his own obituary. 'The reports of my death', Twain cabled to his distraught editor, 'have been greatly exaggerated.' What had happened? How and why was this academic Lazarus brought back from the dead?

2.3 THE REVIVAL OF POLITICAL THEORY

Several explanations, all partial and none entirely satisfactory, help to account for the revival, indeed the astonishing resurgence, of academic political theory since the late 1970s or so.[15] The explanation often given is that political theory has prospered as, and because, its nemesis, 'behaviouralism', fell on hard times. Although an adequate history of the 'behavioural revolution'—and the larger history of political science of which it is an important part—still remains to be written, it would, at a minimum, have to include an account of the rise and demise of its philosophical foundations.[16] Although behaviouralists were wont to draw a sharp distinction between philosophy and science, discarding the former in favour of the latter, behaviouralism was in fact deeply dependent on a particular philosophy—positivism. For it was from positivism—or, as it was more commonly called, Logical Positivism or Logical Empiricism—that behaviouralism borrowed many of its key categories and distinctions.[17] For the behaviouralists, this borrowing took three important forms.

First, as an account of meaning, logical positivism

---

[15] See B. Barry, 'The Strange Death of Political Theory', *Government and Opposition*, 15 (1980), 276–88; and D. Miller, 'The Resurgence of Political Theory', *Political Studies*, 38 (1990), 421–37.

[16] See J. Farr, 'Remembering the Revolution: Behaviouralism in American Political Science', in J. Farr, J. S. Dryzek, and S. T. Leonard (eds.), *Political Science in History: Research Programs and Political Traditions* (Cambridge, 1995), ch. 8.

[17] See Euben, 'Political Science'.

distinguished three sorts of statements: 'synthetic' statements of empirical fact ('The cat is on the mat' was a favourite); 'analytic' statements of logical necessity ('All bachelors are unmarried males'); and a residual catch-all category of 'normative' utterances that neither describe some state of the world nor state logically necessary truths, but serve only to express attitudes, feelings, preferences, or 'values'. Second, this theory of meaning in its turn supplied the basis for an 'emotivist' theory of ethics which holds that ethical utterances are cognitively empty and meaningless; they are merely (in A. J. Ayer's colourful if slightly salacious term) 'ejaculations', expressive of nothing, save, perhaps, the speaker's subjective preference or state of mind. Thus the utterance 'Stealing is wrong' says nothing at all about the world, nor anything about relationships of logical entailment, but merely expresses the speaker's disapproval of stealing. And, third, as a philosophy of science, positivism provided criteria for demarcating between science and non-science.[18] Science is not about any particular subject-matter but about meaning and method. There can be a science of politics just as surely as there can be a science of chemistry or physics, provided that its statements are cognitively meaningful (i.e. synthetic) statements of ascertainable empirical fact and that its explanations conform to the requirements of the deductive–nomological (D–N) model. According to the latter, we can be said to have explained some phenomenon X if and only a statement describing X (the *explanandum*) is deducible as a conclusion from premises containing one or more general laws, along with statements of initial conditions (the *explanans*).

Philosophical positivism served, so to speak, a normative or regulative function for behaviouralism in that positivism defined for behaviouralists what 'science' is—and what political science ought to be, if it is to be a science. First, political science ought to distinguish between 'facts' and 'values'. Second, it should be 'empirical' instead of 'normative'. And, third, it ought to be explanatory in the aforementioned sense. All genuinely scientific explanation, according to positivist criteria of explanatory adequacy, depends on the discovery and

---

[18] See e.g. J. D. Moon, 'The Logic of Political Inquiry', in F. I. Greenstein and N. W. Polsby (eds.), *Handbook of Political Science* (Reading, Mass., 1975).

deployment of timeless universal 'laws'. Because most 'traditional' political theory did not conform to positivist criteria of cognitive meaningfulness and explanatory adequacy, it was dismissed as unscientific or, at best, pre-scientific and therefore destined to be superseded in due course.

But in the hands of behaviouralist critics, the positivist's scalpel cut both ways, wounding those who wielded it. It soon became clear that virtually all of what passed for 'empirical' or 'scientific' political science did not conform to those positivist criteria on the basis of which political theory had been criticized and dismissed as meaningless because 'normative'. It required no great semantic skill to show that 'values' lurked in the shadows of even the most sanitized 'scientific' statements: there were, in fact, no normatively neutral or non-theoretical descriptive statements (or 'protocol sentences', as earlier positivists had termed them).[19] Worse still, there turned out to be no 'laws' of political behaviour. None—not even the oft-touted 'laws' propounded by Michels and Duverger—could pass muster under positivist criteria.[20]

In the philosophy of science, meanwhile, the critics of positivism had carried the day, and by the mid-1970s all but the most die-hard positivists had conceded defeat. Asked by an interviewer in 1977 what the main defects of positivism had been, A. J. Ayer replied: 'Well, I suppose the most important of the defects was that nearly all of it was false.'[21] Among the many false claims that positivism had made—and that behaviouralists had borrowed—was the oft-heard chestnut that one cannot derive 'ought from is'. As it turns out, however, it is not only possible but actually quite easy to perform this purportedly impossible feat.[22]

Beholden as it had been to one particular philosophy of science, behavioural political science's fortunes could not but be affected adversely by the demise of positivism. It would,

[19] C. Taylor, 'Neutrality in Political Science', in *Philosophy, Politics and Society*, 3rd ser. (Oxford, 1967), 25–57.

[20] See J. Farr, 'Resituating Explanation', in T. Ball (ed.), *Idioms of Inquiry* (Albany, NY, 1987), 45–66.

[21] B. Magee (ed.), *Men of Ideas* (New York, 1978), 131.

[22] See G. E. M. Anscombe, 'On Brute Facts', in J. J. Thomson and G. Dworkin (eds.), *Ethics* (New York, 1968); J. R. Searle, *Speech Acts* (Cambridge, 1969), ch. 8.

however, be wrong, or at any rate one-sided and simplistic, to suggest that the resurrection of academic political theory can be traced exclusively to the declining fortunes of philosophical positivism and the allied decline of behaviouralism.

Another factor which must figure in our explanation is what Alasdair MacIntyre termed 'the end of the end of ideology'.[23] From the mid-1960s on, it became abundantly clear that ideology had not ended, nor was it likely to; on the contrary, new political movements—among students, blacks, women, anti-war activists, and others—were raising new questions and setting new agendas. However haltingly and raggedly, first-order theorizing was being done in the streets and in classrooms.[24] From the Free Speech Movement in Berkeley in 1964 to *les evénèments* of May 1968 in Paris (which very nearly toppled the Gaullist government), old orthodoxies—including the end-of-ideology thesis itself—were being questioned and unmasked as 'ideological' in their own right. In 1972 the editors of the distinguished series *Philosophy, Politics and Society*—in whose first number Laslett's obituary had appeared—acknowledged that

we were never right to think in terms of such pathological metaphors, and it is clear in any case that they are no longer applicable. It has now become a commonplace that both the intellectual movements prevailing at the time of our first introduction [in 1956], in terms of which it looked plausible for sociologists to speak of 'the end of ideology' and even for philosophers to speak of 'the death of political theory', were themselves the masks of disputable ideological positions.[25]

Any explanation of the revival of political theory would also have to include an account of the political consequences of a particular conception of the relation between social science and political practice—not in the abstract, but (to use a phrase once frequently hurled against academic political theorists) in 'the real world'. The war in Vietnam, although undeclared, was real enough. It was a war not only fought by GIs

---

[23] A. MacIntyre, *Against the Self-Images of the Age* (Notre Dame, Ind., 1971), ch. 1.

[24] J. Miller, *Democracy is in the Streets* (New York, 1987).

[25] P. Laslett, W. G. Runciman, and Q. Skinner (eds.), *Philosophy, Politics and Society*, 4th ser. (Oxford, 1972), 1.

but, more importantly, 'managed' by experts. Called 'the new Mandarins' by their critics and 'defence intellectuals' by their defenders, their claim to expertise was grounded in an instrumentalist and positivist view of social science and its relation to political practice.[26] The hope of establishing a positivistic policy science—an aspiration which can be traced back to Saint-Simon and Comte in the nineteenth century—was dealt a decisive if perhaps not mortal blow by the United States' experience in Vietnam.

But what has this to do with the rising fortunes of academic political theory? Just this: Vietnam raised anew and brought to the forefront exactly the sorts of normative questions that political theory was supposed to address—questions about the rights and duties of citizens, about one's obligation to fight for the state, about just (and unjust) wars, about active and passive resistance, and related matters.[27]

History having some connection with biography, and vice versa, I would like to pause briefly for an autobiographical aside about how I came to be an academic political theorist. To put it bluntly, I got into this line of work not so much because I was enamoured of philosophy or the history of ideas but because of the war in Vietnam. From the age of 12 until my junior year in 1965 I was certain that I wanted to be a physicist, and most of my education had been directed to that end. My interest in history and philosophy was largely restricted to the history and philosophy of science. I called myself a positivist, regarded Russell and Ayer as my heroes, and felt somewhat superior to those lesser minds labouring in lesser vineyards. I was, in short, insufferable.

But what a difference a war makes! The prospect of having to choose between going to Vietnam, going to Canada, or going to prison concentrated the mind wonderfully. The more I found out about the war, the more I believed it to be both misguided and unwinnable. Besides, it was being fought by the poor, the black, and the uneducated, few of whom had

---

[26] See my 'American Political Science in its Postwar Political Context', in J. Farr and R. Seidelman (eds.), *Discipline and History* (Ann Arbor, Mich., 1993), 207–22.

[27] See M. Walzer, *Obligations* (Cambridge, Mass., 1970), and *Just and Unjust Wars* (New York, 1977).

student deferments. That I, then a student at the University of California, did have such a deferment seemed unfair on its face. Conceding the point, the Selective Service agreed to end student deferments and inaugurate a lottery system. In the meantime, I thought, I might help to redress the unfairness by enlisting; but this would also make me complicit in a war that seemed patently unjust. Having never before faced a deep moral dilemma I had few, if any, resources upon which to draw. What should I do? Where do my duties lie? Should I support my government even when I think its policies mistaken and misguided or, worse yet, patently evil? Is there something like a duty to resist? I did not know what to do, or even how to begin to think, about such troubling questions.

So, swallowing my pride, I enrolled in a seminar in political theory—a subject I had heard about before but had dismissed as irrelevant to my interests—in which these questions were to be discussed and debated. We read Sophocles' *Antigone*, Plato's *Apology* and *Crito*, Calvin and Luther and Locke, Thoreau, Tolstoy, Gandhi, Camus, and Martin Luther King (who was then still very much alive and active, and not yet the safely dead martyr he has since become). Our discussions inside that seminar—and outside, through the wee hours of the night—had a special urgency for many of us. That seminar and those discussions did not make me decide on a course of action, although they did help to clarify the thinking that went into that decision.[28] As it turned out, my interest in political theory did not end there; it grew, it got deeper, and it became my vocation and life's work.

But enough of autobiography. I mention my own experience only because it was not, I suspect, unique—nor were such experiences unrelated to the revival of political theory through the 1970s. There were, in addition and closely related to the anti-war movement, the earlier and concurrent civil rights and women's movements.[29] Political theory prospered to the extent that it dealt with real political problems and the movements that raised and addressed them. In emphasizing the role of such extracurricular activities, however, I do not

[28] Other friends made different decisions. Two of their names are now engraved on the Vietnam Memorial in Washington, DC.
[29] S. Evans, *Personal Politics* (New York, 1979).

mean to deny or denigrate the very important contributions being made within the academy.

Political theory received a notable boost in the early 1970s with the publication of John Rawls's *A Theory of Justice* (1971). Unlike some who credit him with having single-handedly revived political theory, I do not want to exaggerate Rawls's importance, considerable though it was, and is. But I do believe that his thinking about justice had a special importance and appeal for those who had lived through, thought about, and participated in the civil rights and anti-war movements. Despite its awesomely abstract formalisms—the 'original position', the 'veil of ignorance', and the rest—Rawls's theory was nevertheless closely connected with real-world politics. It dealt incisively with pressing questions of rights, duties, and obligations; with the justification of civil disobedience; and, with his wholly original enquiry into intergenerational justice, he spoke to the concerns of the fledgling environmental movement.[30]

Although—or rather perhaps because—Rawls's theory was subjected to a good deal of critical scrutiny, commentary, and attempted refutation, its publication and reception proved to be an important factor in the revival of political theory within the academy.[31] Another, albeit rather different sort of importance must also be ascribed to the historical enquiries of Peter Laslett, John Pocock, Quentin Skinner, John Dunn, and others among the so-called 'new historians' of political thought; to the critical theory of Jürgen Habermas and the revived Frankfurt School; to the role of Ronald Dworkin and others in renewing interest in philosophy of law; and to Michel Foucault's important studies of the institutions (prisons, clinics, asylums) and other means by which modern men and women are constituted and disciplined.

The revival of political theory that began in the early 1970s

---

[30] J. Rawls, *A Theory of Justice* (Cambridge, Mass., 1971), 284–93. Cf. R. I. Sikora and B. Barry (eds.), *Obligations to Future Generations* (Philadelphia, 1978); E. Partridge (ed.), *Responsibilities to Future Generations* (Buffalo, NY, 1981); P. S. Wenz, *Environmental Justice* (Albany, NY, 1988), ch. 11.

[31] See B. Barry, *The Liberal Theory of Justice* (Oxford, 1973); N. Daniels (ed.), *Reading Rawls* (New York, 1975); R. Nozick, *Anarchy, State and Utopia* (New York, 1974).

was also aided by the appearance of new journals specializing in the subject. The first of these was *Interpretation*, a journal with decidedly 'Straussian' leanings launched in 1970. This was followed a year later—the same year that saw the publication of Rawls's *A Theory of Justice*—by *Philosophy and Public Affairs*, a journal dedicated to the proposition that issues of public concern often have an important philosophical dimension. The new journal's editors wrote that

Philosophy & Public Affairs is founded in the belief that a philosophical examination of these issues can contribute to their clarification and to their resolution. It welcomes philosophical discussions of substantive legal, social, and political problems, as well as the more abstract questions to which they give rise. In addition, it expects to publish studies of the moral and intellectual history of such problems.

The aim of this new journal, its editors concluded, was to bring the 'distinctive methods' of philosophy 'to bear on problems that concern everyone'.[32]

These new journals were joined in 1973 by *Political Theory*, a journal generally devoted to the sort of political theory done not by philosophers but by those who plied their trade within departments of political science. To review the contents of back issues of that journal is to see how political theory began to be revived and reshaped from the early 1970s on. The first issues were devoted largely, though not exclusively, to the analysis of political concepts such as 'power', 'liberty', 'equality', 'interests', even 'politics' itself. By the mid-1970s interest had shifted toward Rawls and justice, Habermas and critical theory, Marx and neo-Marxism, and other topics. One way of reading these old tea-leaves is that by the mid-1970s or thereabouts theorists had ceased to play the part of handmaid, conceptual clarifier, or 'underlabourer' to the larger discipline of political science, and that political theory was well on the way to developing an identity of its own.

But this breaking-away went unrecognized and unappreciated within many departments of political science. In a 1982 editorial, the then-editor of *Political Theory*, Benjamin Barber, observed rather peevishly that

[32] M. Cohen, *Philosophy and Public Affairs*, 1 (1973), 1.

Political philosophy continues to flourish within the discipline of political science—for which the discipline remains curiously ungrateful. For a number of years now, political theory panels have outdrawn all others at the American Political Science Association meetings by two to one, and various theory subgroups . . . continue to multiply . . . At the same time, political science seems to have lost its bearings with declining membership in the professional associations and the lost sense of purpose following the demise of the positivist project as conceived in the early 1960s . . . The discipline of political science would serve itself well if it . . . paid heed to the message found in the numbers to which it purports to pay homage.[33]

Exactly what 'message' was to be found in those growing numbers Barber did not say. But one was led to infer that political theory was back, and bolder and more popular than ever.

2.4 TOWARDS THE FUTURE

As measured by Barber's criteria, academic political theory continued to flourish through the 1980s and shows no sign of abating during the closing decade of this century. This turn of fortune is, no doubt, well deserved and long overdue. But this turn towards prosperity and respectability is also troubling in ways and for reasons that I find difficult to articulate in any satisfactory way. Lacking any better way of saying it, let me be blunt in stating a strong and growing suspicion: political theory's new-found pride may presage a fall. Indeed, I see political theory following much the same trajectory that behavioural political science followed from the mid-1950s to the early or mid-1970s. It is by no means impossible that political theory might meet with a similar fate. Several signs, it seems to me, are too obvious to miss.

The first troubling sign is to be found in political theory's increasing isolation from its own subject-matter, which it supposedly shares with political science—namely, politics. A second and closely related sign has to do with the growing specialization and professionalization of political theory. A

---

[33] B. R. Barber, *Political Theory*, 10 (1982), 491.

third danger signal is to be found in political theorists'
increasing preoccupation with questions of method and technique. And a fourth sign is discernible in our penchant for
engaging in methodological and/or metatheoretical disputes.
We are, in short, becoming the sorts of creatures we once criticized. Let me say just a bit more about each of these worries.

The best and most profound political theories have been
closely connected with politics and have generally been born
of crisis. And in today's world there are crises aplenty. But if
one takes the table of contents of successive issues of *Political
Theory* as any indication of where political theory is or might
be going, one is bound to wonder what is even remotely
'political' about political theory. Even the most careful reader
might not suspect that there was a world outside its pages,
afflicted with problems unprecedented in scope and severity.
One would not know, for example, that there is an environmental crisis of global proportions that raises troubling questions about the rights of, and our duties toward, future
generations.[34] One might instead infer that there is something
called the crisis of 'the constitution of the subject' or of the
'body' and 'desire'. Strangely self-absorbed crises for strangely
self-absorbed times. Amidst real destruction—economic, environmental, ethical—we engage in deconstruction. One does
not have to be a 'Straussian' to say of much of modern academic political theory what Leo Strauss once said of behavioural political science: 'One may say of it that it fiddles while
Rome burns. It is excused by two facts: it does not know that
it fiddles, and it does not know that Rome burns.'[35]

The isolation of political theory from politics doubtless has
a good deal to do with the dynamics of professionalization in
the American academy. Political theory shows every sign of
ceasing to be a vocation and of fast becoming a 'profession',
with all that this entails about the division of labour, the specialization of functions, and the like. Already we 'theorists'
have 'our' specialized organizations—the Foundations of

[34] The sole exception is a short note by B. Bandman, 'Do Future
Generations have the Right to Breathe Clean Air?', *Political Theory*, 10
(1982), 95–102.
[35] L. Strauss, 'Epilogue' to H. J. Storing (ed.), *Essays on the Scientific
Study of Politics* (New York, 1962), 327.

Political Thought group and the Conference for the Study of
Political Thought—and a lengthening list of 'our' journals,
including *History of Political Thought, Journal of Political
Philosophy*, and *Studies in Political Thought*. And we have
'our' panels and round tables at the American Political
Science Association and other professional meetings. Such
specialization is not altogether a bad thing; it has its advantages, but also, and no less importantly, its disadvantages.
Professionalization is a little like moving to the suburbs: one
is less likely to be mugged; but one is also less likely to meet
new people and more likely to talk only to people like oneself.
Pretty soon, the suburb becomes its own little self-contained
world—safe, secure, familiar, friendly, and utterly predictable.

In 1969 Sheldon Wolin criticized behaviouralists for their
'methodism'—that is, their preoccupation with refining their
methods of measurement, statistical techniques, and the like,
while giving short shrift to pressing political problems.[36] Now,
a quarter-century later, the same criticism might well be levelled against many political theorists. We do not, to be sure,
do very much measuring (although some of us do apparently
keep a careful count of attendance at APSA political-theory
panels); but we do, of necessity, interpret texts. And so some
of our methodological disputes tend, perhaps understandably,
to rage around methods and techniques of 'reading' or textual
interpretation.[37] Historical 'contextualists' dispute with 'textualists' of various stripes, while postmodernists turn everything—wars, revolutions, gender relations—into 'texts' to be
deconstructed. The latter seems to have gained some ground
of late. Some have welcomed this development, while others,
myself included, have doubts and reservations aplenty. The
former view is well represented by William E. Connolly, the
very able former editor of *Political Theory*. He points with
pride to 'young scholars [who] present exotic imports such
as . . . deconstruction, dialogical analysis, genealogy, or inter-
textuality, as if these orientations were part of an ongoing
conversation somewhere or other'.[38] That 'somewhere', as it
turns out, is not any politically pertinent site but is confined

[36] S. Wolin, 'Political Theory as a Vocation', *APSR* 63 (1969), 1062–83.
[37] See Ch. 1 above.
[38] W. E. Connolly, *Political Theory*, 17 (1989), 4.

to an increasingly inbred, self-important, and self-absorbed academy.

Postmodernism and other 'exotic imports' are not without their value, of course, nor do they want for critics. John Searle, for one, has said of deconstruction that 'This is the kind of philosophy that could give bullshit a bad name.'[39] One need not be as nasty as Professor Searle to have reservations about this particular import. One can even appreciate its initial appeal, at least in France, where the *lycée* system has long dictated not only what the canon is to consist of but what each of its constituent texts 'mean', sentence by sentence and word by word. If as a student I were told that—on pain of failing the *baccalauréat* examination—there is one and only one way to read or interpret Rousseau or Balzac or Victor Hugo, then I, too, would rebel. And if I had been taught, as French university students once were, that 'structure' *fait tout*—that meaning (and much else) was structurally (over)determined—then I would no doubt deconstruct and talk about 'the free play of signifiers' and such like. But I am not a Frenchman, nor did I receive a French education. Nor, for that matter, did most self-styled postmodernists among American political theorists. Which is why their way of approaching political theory has an ethereal, free-floating quality that makes it ideal for an esoteric academic hot-house but ill suits it for engagement with a world full of real political problems. For my part, I confess that postmodernism, or at least the version transplanted into the American academy, strikes me as remarkably unworldly, not to say profoundly a- or anti-political. Indeed, it seems to be a kind of intellectual autism which leads those thus afflicted to fantasize that they can dispense with discipline and remake the world in their own image. Their logic would appear to lend itself to succinct syllogistic reformulation: I have the power to interpret texts as I like; all the world's a text; ergo, the world is within my power. Right; and if wishes were horses, beggars would ride.

But this is not the place to criticize postmodernism, post-structuralism, deconstruction, or any other particular perspective. My aim here is not to say where political theory should

---

[39] J. Searle, 'On Deconstruction', *New York Review*, 30 (1983), 74–9.

not go, but where it might and perhaps should go as we prepare to enter the twenty-first century. I therefore want to conclude on a more positive note by briefly tracing three possible and complementary routes that we might follow into the next century.

First, I believe that political theory can, and should, return to its rightful role. That role is not to ape the latest fad from Frankfurt or Paris, but to draw upon all available sources in reviewing, appraising, criticizing, and perchance occasionally appreciating, the arrangements of one's own society. As it happens, we students of political theory are especially fortunate in having at our disposal an extraordinarily wide and rich range of sources. The greatest of these is, I believe—and I am well aware of the arguments against this contentious claim—the tradition of Western political thought itself. Warts and all, it is the most valuable source upon which we have to draw.

If you ask, why draw upon such a flawed source?, I can only answer: because there is no other—and certainly no perfect—alternative. There exists no Archimedean point outside our world, no Cartesian *cogito*, no ideal observer's vantage-point from which to perceive and pass judgement on our world and its inhabitants' actions and practices. We can only work with, and on, materials already at hand. It is ironic, to say the least, that, as some Westerners increasingly ignore, deny or denigrate their heritage, many non-Westerners are eager to appropriate what they can from our tradition of individual rights, of freedoms of speech, press, assembly, and the like. No doubt they have something to learn from us; but so, I think, do we have a good deal to learn from them and their aspirations—and from their attitude toward political theory, which they take to be of immediate and immense importance.

This brings me to my second hopeful route into the future. An otherwise sympathetic reader might concede that (say) the Chinese are faced with crises worthy of theoretical reflection, but that we are not so situated. Setting aside the comfortable but questionable assumption that we are as democratic as can be, there remain a number of crises which academic political theorists have, as yet, failed to recognize as worthy of theoretical attention and treatment. One that I mentioned earlier—

that interconnected series of actual and potential disasters that often goes under the name of the environmental crisis—raises a whole host of questions to which we have so far paid scant attention. It raises questions about who we are and where we belong in the order of nature; about our obligations to other people, including the members of other cultures and unborn future generations; about our conceptions of private property and profit; and about the strengths, shortcomings, and limitations of our institutions and of the moral, political, economic, and religious traditions that we have inherited from thinkers long dead. And this we need to do not merely because these matters are interesting to a few odd-ball theorists, but because they are of pressing importance to all of us, as moral agents, as citizens, and as political enquirers.[40] This is 'first-order' theorizing with a vengeance.

My third route to the future is concerned with the last of these roles. To put it simply, the questions of political theory are too important to be left to those who call themselves, or are conventionally classified as, political theorists. We theorists have no corner on wisdom or insight. If we are to speak knowledgeably about and intervene intelligently in the crises of our time, we will need at least some of the sensibilities of those among our fellow political enquirers who are conventionally classified as 'empirical' political scientists. We—and I do not use the pronoun lightly—are in desperate need of each others' talents, techniques, and sensibilities. But if we are to get together, then we must overcome a number of old obstacles, many of which are legacies of the older behaviouralism and of the anti-behaviouralist reaction. Old rifts are not bridged easily or without effort. But let me suggest one possible way of shouting across, and perchance bridging, a long-standing divide between two camps which have more in common than they might otherwise suspect.

The conventional curricular division of labour assigns to theorists the task of tracing and accounting for ideas, ideals, and beliefs, and leaves to empirical enquirers the task of describing and explaining the actual behaviour of political

---

[40] See R. E. Goodin, *Green Political Theory* (Cambridge, 1992); Wenz, *Environmental Justice*; R. Eckersley, *Environmentalism and Political Theory* (Albany, NY, 1992).

agents. This division of labour suggests that there are two quite separate domains, one of thought or 'theory' and the other of action or 'behaviour', each of which can be characterized without reference to the other. But this picture is patently false. The agent who holds certain beliefs is not separable from the agent who acts. In fact, his or her actions are not even describable without reference to his or her beliefs, and vice versa. Thus the hope of devising a science of political 'behaviour' was every bit as misbegotten as was a detached 'history of political thought'. And this, as we so often see, is a truth more readily recognizable if we look to the past. As Alasdair MacIntyre reminds us,

There ought not to be two histories, one of political and moral action and one of political and moral theorising, because there were not two pasts, one populated only by actions and the other by theories. Every action is the bearer and expression of more or less theory-laden beliefs and concepts; every piece of theorising and every expression of belief is a political and moral action.

It is only because of the peculiar 'habits of mind engendered by our modern academic curriculum', he adds, that we have arrived at the mistaken belief 'that ideas are endowed with a falsely independent life of their own on the one hand and political and social action is presented as peculiarly mindless on the other'.[41] Thus the 'ideas' or 'beliefs' studied by the theorist and the 'behaviour' studied by the political scientist are not two things, but one.

Let me give a brief example of how this might work in practice. Consider the concept of interest, which (along perhaps with power) is surely one of the central notions in the social sciences generally, and political science in particular. Political scientists and other social scientists and historians typically explain why someone acts as they do (or did) because they have or seek to satisfy certain interests. But what an actor takes to be in his or her interest depends upon beliefs about what is and is not good for or beneficial to him or her. What one believes to be in one's interest depends upon one's ideas about what human flourishing consists of and what is required to bring it about. And these beliefs can be well or

---

[41] A. MacIntyre, *After Virtue* (Notre Dame, Ind., 1981), 58.

ill-founded, valid or invalid: one can, that is, hold mistaken beliefs about what is (not) in one's interest. (This of course comes as no surprise to anyone who has read and reflected upon the exchange between Socrates and Thrasymachus in Book I of Plato's *Republic*.) But, mistaken or no, political actors interpret their situation in the light of these beliefs and ideas, and act accordingly. The social scientist in turn interprets or explains that behaviour by noting that the actor had certain interests—i.e. held certain beliefs about what is good for him or her—and acted on the basis of those beliefs.[42] Thus 'ideas' or 'beliefs' are inseparable from 'behaviour', and vice versa. It is assuredly not the case that the former are the province of the political theorist and the latter that of the political scientist. To appreciate this interdependence is to pave the way, perhaps, for a *rapprochement* between political 'theory' and political 'science'.

2.5 A CONCLUDING RETRACTION

In this spirit, then, let me conclude by reiterating and then withdrawing my earlier distinction between first- and second-order theorizing. The distinction is standardly made between those who *do* political theory and those who simply *study* or *talk about* it. In its most vulgar form, this amounts to a variation on the old chestnut: 'Those who can, do; those who can't, teach.' In its more sophisticated form, the first- and second-order distinction demarcates between actors and observers, or, to put it another way, between a particular subject-matter and its scholarly study. Even so, this more sophisticated statement of the distinction fails to do justice to what we do—or try to do—as students of political theory.

And why? Because, I believe, the distinction cuts in the wrong direction. The relevant distinction is not between first- and second-order but between first- and second-rate theorizing. We are not only scholars and students of political theory, but citizens interested in and concerned about the polity and the wider world in which we live. We therefore have reason to

[42] See my 'Interest-Explanations', *Polity*, 12 (1979), 187–201.

think critically and systematically—in short, to theorize—about that world's problems, possibilities, and prospects. This is a job, or a vocation, in which we not only want but badly need to excel, or at least to do as well as we possibly can. We therefore have reason to consult, to draw upon, and to appropriate—though not simply to imitate or slavishly duplicate—the thinking of first-rate theorists. And this we do not because we are 'second order' but because we are second-rate and trying to do better. This does not, I hasten to add, mean that one must agree with those from whom one appropriates. Far from it. One can learn more from a first-rate thinker with whom one disagrees than from a thinker who simply ratifies or reinforces what one already believes. That is why conservatives should read Marx, and Marxists should read Burke. And that, no less importantly, is why 'empirical' political scientists should heed what 'normative' theorists have to say, and vice versa.

What this amounts to can, I suppose, be restated by borrowing Wendell Berry's distinction between two types of learning: learning about and learning from.[43] Too much of modern education is concerned with learning about—that is, with acquiring 'information'. But education generally—and the study of political theory in particular—is not merely a matter of acquiring information, of 'learning about' some subject or other; it is, more importantly, a kind of *learning from*—of wrestling with, and critically appropriating, alternative perspectives that complicate and enrich one's view of the world and one's place in it by questioning conventional assumptions and conceptual schemes. And that, surely, must be foremost among the reasons for periodically reappraising the value of an intellectual inheritance whose value is forever in question and open to a variety of different interpretations and assessments.

[43] W. Berry, 'The Loss of the University', in *Home Economics: Fourteen Essays* (San Francisco, 1987), 79.

II

REAPPRAISALS

3

MACHIAVELLI AND MORAL CHANGE

> The guiding thread of Machiavelli's thought is to be
> found in the concept of 'political virtue', which is syn-
> onymous neither with 'moral virtue' nor its negation.
>
> Benedetto Croce

3.1 INTRODUCTION

It sometimes seems that there were several sixteenth-century
Florentine writers, all named Machiavelli but sharing little
else in common. The most famous, or notorious, is the
'murd'rous Machiavel' mentioned by Shakespeare and, as
'Old Nick', decried as the devil himself. An apostle of violence
and advocate of murder in the name of political expediency,
Machiavelli has been vilified and roundly condemned by critics from Frederick the Great until the present. He has been
called everything from a proto-Nazi and a 'teacher of evil' to
a misogynist.[1] But there are also other, ostensibly more
benign Machiavellis: the first 'scientific' political analyst to
focus on 'facts' while forgoing 'values',[2] the resuscitator of
republican political ideals,[3] a skilful satirist of political folly,[4]

[1] See, respectively, E. Cassirer, *Myth of the State* (New Haven, Conn.,
1946); L. Strauss, *Thoughts on Machiavelli* (Glencoe, Ill., 1958), 9; H. F.
Pitkin, *Fortune is a Woman* (Berkeley, Calif., 1984).

[2] L. Olschki, *Machiavelli the Scientist* (Berkeley, Calif., 1945);
J. Bronowski and B. Mazlish, *Western Intellectual Tradition* (New York,
1960), 30–4. Cf. Bacon: 'We are much indebted to Machiavelli, who honestly
describes what men do, and not what they ought to do' (Francis Bacon, De
augmentis scientarium, bk. VII, ch. 2).

[3] J. G. A. Pocock, *The Machiavellian Moment* (Princeton, NJ, 1975);
Q. Skinner, *Foundations of Modern Political Thought* (Cambridge, 1978), i,
ch. 6.

[4] G. Mattingly, 'Machiavelli's Prince: Political Science or Political Satire?',
American Scholar, 27 (1957–8), 482–91.

a proto-liberal who was perhaps the first to recognize the irre-ducible plurality of values,[5] a cunning deceiver and trapper of princes,[6] and many others besides.

Despite this diversity there was of course only one Renaissance writer named Machiavelli, and a great many interpretations of what he was about. These interpretations and assessments are remarkable not only for their variety but, as often as not, for their ingenuity. More remarkable still is their sheer number. And, as if to underscore the point, I pro-pose to add yet another to the long list of Machiavellis. I shall argue that one piece of conventional wisdom—that Machiavelli is (for whatever reason) a distinctly modern thinker—is somewhat doubtful, because he did not think as a thinker must if he is to be accounted 'modern'. He did not, that is, think of history in linear terms, but as a series of cycles and returns. Nor did he view morality, including politi-cal morality, as set within historically mutable moral codes or idioms which are doomed to disappear and be superseded by other ways of thinking and acting. Rather, Machiavelli saw right conduct as a matter of emulation—of imitating long-dead human models of moral rectitude and virtue whose moral codes were archaic and anything but modern.

Of course it used to be fashionable to say that Machiavelli was immoral, or at any rate amoral; but now it is more fash-ionable—and arguably more accurate—to suggest that he did in fact subscribe to a system of morality, even if there is as yet no consensus about what this code consists of. My aim here is to attempt to crack this code, or at least one part of it, and to do so in a way that has not heretofore been attempted by any of his critics or commentators. In making this attempt I hope to shed some light on Machiavelli's morals and along the way to say something about the mutability of our own moral con-cepts and convictions.

My argument takes the following form. I begin by noticing the obvious though often overlooked fact that moral concepts change over time and vary from one culture to another. The moral codes and concepts of classical Greece, of the Hopi, the

[5] I. Berlin, *Against the Current* (London, 1979), 25–79.

[6] M. G. Dietz, 'Trapping the Prince: Machiavelli and the Politics of Deception', *APSR* 80 (1986), 777–99.

Samurai, and the medieval Christian are radically different. And yet we consider them to be moral codes because they are all concerned, in their very different ways, with shaping and directing the course of human conduct. All, that is, set standards by reference to which conduct can be praised or blamed, criticized and condemned, judged and justified. It is this function, rather than their specific temporal or culture-bound content, that marks them as 'moral'. And it is for this reason that Machiavelli can be considered a moralist. For he, too, stipulates standards and criteria of virtuous conduct, not for human beings generally but (in *The Prince* at least) for princes in particular. There are, in Machiavelli's view, at least two different varieties of virtue—one for private persons, another for princes. Machiavelli's conception of princely virtue is entirely consistent with the brutal precepts and practices prescribed in *The Prince*, and for which his own and succeeding generations have roundly condemned him. My aim is to recover and re-examine Machiavelli's standards, and in particular to reconsider his central concept of princely virtue— *virtù* —and its place in his political thinking. My claim is that Machiavellian *virtù* shares some crucial conceptual affinities with the older Homeric conception of virtue ($\alpha\rho\epsilon\tau\acute{\eta}$). In attempting to resurrect and reinstate something like this archaic conception of virtue, Machiavelli's model prince rather resembles Don Quixote. For both are alike in failing to recognize the mutability of our moral concepts. From this perspective Machiavelli emerges as a misguided moralist from whose mistakes we might yet learn something about morality, and about moral change in particular.

3.2 THE MUTABILITY OF MORAL AND POLITICAL CONCEPTS

Moral and political concepts are historically mutable in two related and mutually reinforcing ways. The first is that their meanings change over time. And secondly, some concepts cease to be central to (and indeed constitutive of) our thought and action, while others become paramount before they, too, subsequently suffer the same fate. As Kierkegaard remarked,

'Concepts, like individuals, have their histories and are just as incapable of withstanding the ravages of time as are individuals.'[7] One only need think, for example, of the virtual oblivion into which the concept of virtue has passed, and the paramount place now accorded the very different concepts of obligation, right, and duty.[8]

Oddly, the mutability of our moral concepts is a theme rarely explored by philosophers. There are, to be sure, some notable exceptions. Hegel, Kierkegaard, and Nietzsche had a lively appreciation of the historicity and mutability of our moral concepts; so, in our own century, do R. G. Collingwood, Hannah Arendt, and Alasdair MacIntyre. Yet by and large these remain brilliant exceptions to the dismal rule that moral philosophers—especially of the modern Anglo–American 'analytical' variety—have tended to treat moral concepts as though they had no history, or as though their having a history was a matter of no philosophical interest or importance.

Fortunately for us, however, the myopia of the moral philosophers is at least partially compensated for and corrected by novelists and playwrights. The theme of conceptual change runs like a red thread through novels by authors as different as Lermontov and Balzac, Jane Austen and Thomas Hardy, George Eliot and Henry James, Tolstoy and Turgenev, Dostoevsky and Dickens. One need only think, for example, of Lermontov's implicit charting of changes in the concept of heroism, when he warns the reader that his hero Pechorin embodies none of the traditional virtues but, on the contrary, 'all the vices of our generation in the fullness of their development'.[9] Consider the concept of honour. The message of Böll's novel is less that Katharina Blum has lost her honour than that she lives in an age and a society in which the idea of honour itself has been lost. Her desperate defence of her honour is therefore unintelligible to her contemporaries.[10] Or consider again the concept of virtue. In *The*

---

[7] S. Kierkegaard, *The Concept of Irony* (London, 1966), 47.

[8] See S. G. Salkever, 'Virtue, Obligation and Politics', *APSR* 68 (1974), 78–92; A. MacIntyre, *After Virtue* (Notre Dame, Ind., 1981).

[9] M. Lermontov, *A Hero of Our Time* (New York, 1958), 2.

[10] H. Böll, *The Lost Honor of Katharina Blum* (New York, 1975). Cf. P. Berger, 'On the Obsolescence of the Concept of Honour', *Archives européennes de sociologie*, 11 (1970), 339–47.

Magic Mountain Thomas Mann puts into Hans Castorp's mouth the profound sense of unease and discomfort that modern men and women are apt to feel in invoking the very idea of virtue. Speaking of Settembrini, who exemplifies and embodies the classical ideals of an earlier age, young Castorp exclaims:

'What a vocabulary! and he uses the word virtue just like that, without the slightest embarrassment. What do you make of that? I've never taken the word in my mouth as long as I've lived; in school, when the book said 'virtus', we always just said 'valour' or something like that. It certainly gives me a queer feeling inside, to hear him.'[11]

This same sense of curiosity, astonishment, and incomprehension in the face of conceptual change pervades much of modern literature.

But the greatest novelistic treatment of the theme is surely Cervantes' *Don Quixote*. The Don attempts, in vain and with comic results, to follow the moral code of knight errantry in an age which thinks and speaks in an entirely different moral vocabulary. In the moral framework of the modern age, certain concepts—chivalry, for example, or courtly love, or the concept of a quest—are out of place, inappropriate, and irrelevant, if not, indeed, utterly unintelligible. It is because Don Quixote speaks, thinks, and attempts to act in accordance with these archaic notions that we—and indeed his own contemporaries—view him as a comic character and his quest (as we would say nowadays) as 'quixotic'.[12] It is Don Quixote's failure to appreciate the fact of moral and conceptual change that makes him a comic character and his quest a quixotic one.

One of Cervantes' central lessons is that our conceptually constituted moral frameworks are historically located and notoriously mutable. The fine wine of one age may prove to be the vinegar of another. Cervantes is the progenitor of a genre whose central insight is that our moral codes and concepts are forever passing away. It is a genre to which subsequent satirical and comic novelists like Mark Twain—and,

---

[11] T. Mann, *The Magic Mountain* (New York, 1966), 101.
[12] Cf. M. Foucault, *The Order of Things* (New York, 1973), 50.

more recently, Graham Greene[13]—have contributed. Twain's
A Connecticut Yankee in King Arthur's Court is Don Quixote
in reverse. Twain's hapless Yankee finds himself technologi-
cally transported back into a pre-technological, pre-utilitarian
period. He is utterly perplexed by the precepts and practices
of a courtly and chivalrous age, and so he persistently fails
to understand his new/old contemporaries, or they him.
Although he and they speak the same natural language
(namely, English), they speak very different moral languages
and live, accordingly, in different worlds. The limits of my
moral language, one might say, mark the limits of my moral
world. Communication between these different conceptually
constituted worlds requires translation, but translation of a
kind that is always difficult, often unreliable, and occasionally
impossible. Such translation is not unlike an archaeological
excavation undertaken in order to recover and reconstruct
fragmented and long-lost meanings.

3.3 THE PICARESQUE PRINCE

What has all this to do with Machiavelli? Just this: I want to
suggest that Machiavelli's model prince, like Don Quixote,
attempts, not to create a new conception of morality but, in
effect, to resurrect and revive an archaic one. Not unlike
Cervantes' hapless hero, Machiavelli's prince can be viewed as
a comic character on a serious but misbegotten mission. I hasten to add that the achievement of this comic effect was
assuredly not Machiavelli's manifest intention in writing *The
Prince*. I do not mean to suggest that Machiavelli set out to
compose a comedy (or a satire either, for that matter).[14] On
the contrary, he apparently meant to add his own unorthodox
contribution to (and perhaps the subversion or, to speak
French, the deconstruction of) the already well-established
'mirror-of-princes' genre.[15] Like other writers in this genre,

---

[13] G. Greene, *Monsignor Quixote* (New York, 1982).

[14] Mattingly, 'Machiavelli's Prince'.

[15] F. Gilbert, 'The Humanist Concept of the Prince and the Prince of
Machiavelli', *Journal of Modern History*, 11 (1939), 449–83; Q. Skinner,
Machiavelli (Oxford, 1981), ch. 2.

Machiavelli offered guidance and advice to princes, particularly to new ones who are most obviously in need of it.[16] But in Machiavelli's mirror the light of reason—*ragion di stato* or *raison d'état*, that is—is refracted and reflected in a peculiarly comedic, almost Cervantian way. Yet Cervantes knows what Machiavelli does not. Machiavelli is apparently as ignorant of the irreversibility of moral change as is Don Quixote himself. Machiavelli's advice to aspiring princes has, accordingly, a decidedly quixotic character and tenor. To the new prince Machiavelli says, in effect: if you wish to acquire and hold political power you must not think and act within the moral framework of our own age, but in that of another, earlier time. The dominant moral framework of our corrupt and effeminate age (he continues) is Christian, and its listing and ordering of the virtues is a veritable recipe for the prince's political suicide. And since no one should, morally speaking, be required to commit suicide, there is good reason to believe that the princely virtues are not identical with the virtues vaunted by the Church. A good prince, he insists, must 'learn to be not good'.[17] By this Machiavelli does not mean that the prince must learn to be evil *simpliciter*, but that he must, in his role as prince, unlearn the Christian virtues, substituting in their place virtues of another variety entirely. These distinctly political, or princely, virtues Machiavelli designates by the single word, *virtù*.

The word *virtù* recurs in Machiavelli's political writings. Indeed, one might even read his three best-known works—*The Prince*, *The Discourses*, and *The Art of War*—as explications of three varieties of *virtù*. *The Prince* explicates and illustrates the concept of princely *virtù*; *The Discourses* that of civic *virtù*; and *The Art of War* that of military *virtù*. Although one might plausibly make and defend that claim, I shall not do so here. My aim is to look in particular at princely *virtù* in order to trace its likely lineage and some of its possible implications for present-day political thought and action.

Virtù is among the most contested and controversial

[16] N. Machiavelli, *The Prince* in *The Prince and the Discourses* (New York, 1950), 6.
[17] Ibid. 56

concepts in Machiavelli's moral lexicon.[18] *Virtù*, as Machiavelli uses the term, has no exact English equivalent. Nor, for that matter, is it exactly equivalent to the Latin *virtus* from which it ostensibly derives. *Virtù* is, however, clearly connected to its Latin antecedent in at least one respect. *Virtus* derives from *vir*, or 'man' (cf. our adjective 'virile'), which however should not be understood to be a synonym for human being. *Virtus* refers, rather, to the qualities and character traits to be found in the *vir*, the free male citizen. It is indeed the possession of particular virtues—courage, temperance, prudence, and justice—which distinguishes the true *vir* from slaves or ordinary labourers or even, indeed, from women.[19] The etymological point here is that Machiavelli's concept of *virtù*, like its Latin antecedent, refers not to qualities or characteristics of human beings as such but to those qualities displayed by *viri* in filling their respective roles. *Virtù*, like *virtus*, is a role-related concept; in this the two differ radically from the Christian virtues which all human beings, regardless of role or rank, are at least potentially capable of exhibiting, especially in interpersonal or intimate interactions. The Christian virtues—humility, charity, meekness, piety, and the rest—can as well be characteristic of the attitudes and actions of women and slaves. Not for nothing did Nietzsche characterize Christianity as a 'slave morality'.[20] The Christian concept of virtue, in other words, has no necessary connection with public or political life; it is concerned primarily with private life and only tangentially, if at all, with the public realm. Political power and position are not goods to be actively sought after by the virtuous Christian but are, rather, evils inflicted upon and borne patiently by passive subjects. Christ's

[18] See, *inter alia*, F. De Sanctis, *Storia della literatura italiana* (Naples, 1870), ii; E. W. Mayer, *Machiavellis Geschictsauffassung und sein Bergriff Virtù* (Munich, 1912); J. H. Whitfield, *Machiavelli* (Oxford, 1947), 92–105; N. Wood, 'Machiavelli's Concept of *virtù* Reconsidered', *Political Studies*, 15 (1967), 159–72; I. Hannaford, 'Machiavelli's Concept of *virtù* in *The Prince* and the *Discourses* Reconsidered', *Political Studies*, 20 (1972), 185–9; J. Plamenatz, 'In Search of Machiavellian *virtù*', in A. Parel (ed.), *The Political Calculus* (Toronto, 1972), 157–78; and R. Price, 'The Senses of *virtù* in Machiavelli', *European Studies Review*, 3 (1973), 315–45.

[19] Cicero, *De officiis*, bk. I, sects. 15–18; Skinner, *Machiavelli*, 35–7.

[20] F. Nietzsche, *The Genealogy of Morals* (Garden City, NY, 1956), first essay.

resigned but resolute 'Render unto Caesar . . .' might well serve as their moral motto. Little wonder, then, that Machiavelli (like later republicans, including Rousseau) should have had such contempt for Christianity, at least in so far as its precepts might be used in guiding political practice. Whatever its other merits may be, Christianity will not suffice as a civil religion.[21]

That Machiavellian *virtù* bears scant resemblance to the Christian conception of virtue should now be clear. Less clear, perhaps, are the pronounced and profound differences between the Ciceronian–humanist concept of *virtus* and the Machiavellian concept of *virtù*. The qualities ascribed by Cicero to the virtuous statesman are not those ascribed by Machiavelli to the *virtuoso* prince. Machiavelli's prince is at least prepared to act in ways that Cicero and his humanist successors would have thought disgusting and distasteful, to say the least. Consider, for example, Cicero's acknowledgment in *De officiis* that one might on occasion achieve one's ends more efficiently by resorting to force or fraud. It might even appear to be rational to resort to such means. But the appearance, says Cicero, is misleading. To be fully rational is to be most fully human and therefore not at all 'bestial'. Force and fraud are ruled out as being 'unworthy of man' inasmuch as they are characteristic of the behaviour of beasts—force being characteristic of the lion and fraud of the fox.[22]

Machiavelli explicitly rejects the Ciceronian view that the best and most rational human action differs categorically from the behaviour of the beasts. Tweaking the Roman nose of the humanists, he says that the prince must learn to imitate both beasts by combining the cunning of the fox with the forceful courage of the lion.[23] If he is to be truly *virtuoso*, the prince must know which animal to imitate on the appropriate occasions. Clearly *virtù* is not *virtus*, at least as Cicero and later humanists used and understood that concept.[24]

With what other concept or cluster of concepts, then, might

---

[21] Machiavelli, *Discourses*, bk. I, chs. 11–14. Cf. Ch. 5 below.

[22] Cicero, *De officiis*; Skinner, *Machiavelli*, 40.

[23] Machiavelli, *Prince*, 64.

[24] *Contra* B. Wall, 'Machiavelli and the Italian Tradition', *Dublin Review*, 452 (1951), 36.

Machiavellian *virtù* be more nearly allied? My conjecture is that Machiavelli's conception of princely virtue—which encompasses lying, deceit, treachery, and so on—has obvious but heretofore unnoticed affinities with a much older conception of 'virtue'. Machiavellian *virtù*, I want to suggest, shares certain crucial conceptual affinities with the heroic conception of virtue found in the *Iliad* and the *Odyssey*. But before I can defend this claim, I must enter several caveats.

The first point to note is, of course, that our own concept of virtue did not exist in the Homeric moral vocabulary. 'Virtue' is our modern (and in many respects unsatisfactory) translation of the Greek αρετή. A better, if rather more awkward, translation of *aretē* would be 'role-related specific excellence'. *Aretē* is that quality or set of qualities which enables one to fill a particular role and to discharge its duties. From this a second point follows: *aretē* does not and cannot refer to the excellence (moral or otherwise) of man *qua* man but of man *qua* role-bearer in relation to other role-bearers. Thirdly, *aretē* need not denote specifically human qualities at all. The *aretē* of a sword, for example, is its sharpness; the *aretē* of a racehorse, its speed; the *aretē* of a guard-dog, its ferocity and loyalty to its master. Thus Odysseus' faithful dog Argos exhibits canine *aretē* by remaining fiercely loyal, by recognizing his returning master, despite his disguise, and by staying alive long enough to welcome him home before dying, his duty done, from a combination of delight, relief, and old age. Similarly, Penelope displays wifely *aretē* in remaining faithful to her husband, even though this requires duplicity and deception in her dealings with the suitors.

This brings me to a fourth, and for my purposes crucial, point: to be 'virtuous' in the Homeric sense requires on occasion that one act in ways that are, by our standards, immoral and vicious. If animal cunning and treachery are required to play one's part or fill one's role, then cunning and treachery are not only morally acceptable: they are morally required by one's role and one's specific situation. Thus Penelope's role permits, or perhaps even requires, her to deceive the suitors. Similarly, Odysseus' role requires that he do everything and anything within his power to protect his men and return them safely to Ithaca. The standards that apply to them in their respective roles do not necessarily apply to Odysseus in his. There is nothing of the Golden Rule, the Kantian categorical imperative, or the principle of universalizability in Homeric ethics. Odysseus has no scruples about ordering his men to plug their ears and lash him to the mast so that he can listen to and be tempted by the Sirens' song. Nor does he entertain any doubts about the appropriateness of deceiving the drunken Cyclops Polyphemus, and blinding him into the bargain. Nor, for that matter, does Odysseus, in his role as returning husband, hesitate to disguise himself as a beggar, the better to survey the scene, to test Penelope's loyalty, and to deceive her suitors before killing them. Such means are, in the Homeric view, justified by the ends they serve. And the ends one seeks (*telei*) are themselves set by—and are indeed constitutive of— the role one occupies. *Aretē* is the ability to discharge one's role-related functions. To display one's *aretē* in a particularly ingenious or cunning way is to enhance one's glory (*kudos*) or fame (*kleos*); to fail to exhibit these role-specific qualities is to tarnish this most precious of human possessions.[25]

If Machiavellian *virtù* has little if anything in common with either Christian virtue or Ciceronian–humanist *virtus*, it does appear to have considerable conceptual affinity with the archaic notion of *aretē*.[26] For Machiavelli's *virtuoso* prince displays his *virtù* in doing whatever his role and the necessity of his situation (*necessità*) require. If necessity requires that he act in devious and duplicitous ways, then he is, *qua* prince, morally required to act in those ways. Should he experience a failure of nerve, he will fail to fulfil his role; he will find himself unable to discharge his primary duty, which is to preserve and maintain his state, status, and station (*mantenere lo stato*—the word *stato* not yet meaning 'state' in our modern sense).[27] To seize the day, to act boldly and even ruthlessly, is

---

[25] Cf. W. Jaeger, *Paideia* (New York, 1945), i, ch. 1; L. Pearson, *Popular Ethics in Ancient Greece* (Stanford, Calif., 1962), ch. 2; and MacIntyre, *After Virtue*, ch. 10.

[26] For a different view, see H. Arendt, *Between Past and Future* (New York, 1969), 137.

[27] Cf. J. H. Hexter, *The Vision of Politics on the Eve of the Reformation* (New York, 1973), ch. 3; Q. Skinner, 'The State', in T. Ball, J. Farr, and R. L. Hanson (eds.), *Political Innovation and Conceptual Change* (Cambridge, 1989), ch. 5.

the only way in which fickle fortune (*fortuna*) can be tamed, and genuine glory (*gloria*) and lasting fame (*fama*) secured. Machiavelli's metaphor is instructive. 'Fortune', he says in a now-notorious aside, 'is a woman, and it is necessary, if you wish to master her, to conquer her by force; [for] . . . she lets herself be overcome by the bold rather than by those who proceed coldly.'[28] *Virtù* is to politics what virility is to sex: it is the congeries of qualities that make for success in the activities in which the manly man, the virile *vir*—and the *virtuoso* prince—are respectively engaged. Princely *virtù* is, in effect, Machiavelli's updated and politicized rendering of the archaic *aretē*.

3.4 OBJECTIONS AND REPLIES

Two objections will at once be raised. The first is that Machiavelli's models, examples, and illustrations are almost invariably drawn, not from Homeric Greece but from Rome; hence my 'Homeric' reading of Machiavelli's meaning must be mistaken. To this objection I can offer three replies. First, while it is true that Machiavelli's stock of examples and illustrations comes from Roman history, it does not follow that his categorial framework—his most basic concepts, categories, and criteria—is itself Roman. Clearly it is not, for the virtues praised by Cicero and other humanist writers—including, pre-eminently, the virtue of justice—are apt, in Machiavelli's view, to be vices leading to political ruin. Secondly, the copious use of Roman examples of political success and failure by an ardent Italian patriot and proto-nationalist is scarcely surprising: not only were such examples likely to be more familiar to his readers; they might also serve to remind them that Italy had once been the unified centre of the civilized world. For Machiavelli, who confesses that 'I love my native city more than my own soul',[29] this is not a neutral historical fact but a pertinent political reminder. Not for nothing does *The Prince* conclude with a call to arms and an exhortation to cast the

---

[28] Machiavelli, *Prince*, 94.
[29] Letter to Vettori, 16 Apr. 1527, in A. Gilbert (ed.), *The Letters of Machiavelli* (New York, 1961), 248–9.

barbarians out of Italy. The instrument of this exorcism is to
be the man of heroic vision and *virtù*. That man is, of course,
the prince. And because unarmed princes do not succeed in
this world, the *virtuoso* prince must resort to armed force to
gain his ends and thereby exhibit his *virtù* for all to see. This
consideration brings me to my third reply to the initial objection. It is surely significant that Machiavelli singles out for
special mention one of the heroes of the *Iliad*. Achilles was
(so Machiavelli tells us) imitated by Alexander the Great,
who was in turn imitated by Caesar.[30] Thus the *aretē* of this
Homeric hero had once served—and might again serve—as a
model and inspiration for a *virtuoso* Italian warrior-prince.
Machiavelli's moral code is, in a word, heroic; it rests upon
an archaic ethic of emulation, not upon reasoned reflection on
the right, the just, and the good.[31]

The second objection one might raise against my 'Homeric'
reading of Machiavelli is that his prince, unlike Homer's
heroes—Achilles, for example, or Odysseus—is entirely self-
serving. His prince seeks, not the good of others, but his own
'fame' and 'glory'. Thus Machiavelli appeals solely to the vanity of the upstart and usurper. This second objection is more
easily answered than the first. Homer's heroes, it will be
recalled, won honour, fame, and glory by excelling in their
respective roles. The memorableness of their deeds is attested
to by the fact that they are remembered; their stories are celebrated in song and verse, told and retold; they are held up as
models worthy of imitation; and in this way they live on long
after their deaths, thereby enjoying the only measure of
immortality of which human beings in this world are capable.
To begin a story which, so to speak, continues to unfold and
be retold after one's death is the highest human achievement.
True fame or greatness is imperishable; it is, in Thucydides'
words, not the creature of a day but a possession forever.[32]

It is just this sort of fame to which Machiavelli's model
prince aspires. Pure self-aggrandizement, unconnected to the
founding of cities, princedoms, and republics, is mere notori-

---

[30] Machiavelli, *Prince*, 55.
[31] Cf. Plamenatz, 'In Search of Machiavellian *virtù*'.
[32] Thucydides, *History of the Peloponnesian War*, trans. R. Crawley (New
York, 1951), 15.

ety; it is not genuine glory or true fame. As an example of the
former, Machiavelli cites the case of Agathocles, the tyrant of
Syracuse. At first sight Agathocles looks like the model
Machiavellian prince. Through trickery and treachery of the
basest sort he defeated his enemies, betrayed his friends, and
concentrated all power in his own hands. And yet Machiavelli
denies that Agathocles exhibited princely *virtù*. Why? Because,
he tells us, Agathocles is remembered not with the awe and
affection accorded to founders but with the disgust and
loathing reserved for wanton destroyers and tyrants. 'It cannot be called *virtù* to kill one's fellow citizens, betray one's
friends, be without faith, without pity, and without religion;
by these methods one may indeed gain power but not glory
[*gloria*].' Despite his military *virtù*, the fact remains that, as a
prince, Agathocles' 'barbarous cruelty and inhumanity, together with his countless atrocities, do not permit his being
named among the most famous men'.[33]

Not that Machiavelli has anything against atrocities or acts
of princely cruelty; but such deeds are for him morally and
politically permissible only when they are dictated by necessity,
directed against the even-crueller vicissitudes of *fortuna*, and—
most importantly—meant to create or maintain a viable body
politic. This body is, as the Greeks would have said, a civil
kosmos created out of a corrupt, pre-political *chaos* by a solitary law-giver, a Solon, a Lycurgus, or (closer to Machiavelli's
heart, perhaps) a Draco. The draconian measures to which the
prince has recourse are not freely chosen but are, on the contrary, dictated by necessity and are required of anyone who
chooses to play that particular role. And that peculiarly ruthless role is in turn called into being by time and circumstance.[34] A lone *virtuoso* in a world without civic *virtù*, the
prince makes his appearance in a society so thoroughly corrupt
that its inhabitants long ago ceased to be citizens. A people
possessing and exhibiting civic *virtù* would hardly have need of
such a prince. But a people conquered and despoiled, sunk in
dissension, depravity, and corruption, stand in dire need of his
harsh but transforming touch.[35] If this transformation is to be

---

[33] Machiavelli, *Prince*, 32.
[34] See Pocock, *Machiavellian Moment*, ch. 6.
[35] Compare Fielding's view of the England of his day: 'Do you not know . . .

more than temporary, the prince must also be a law-giver. For this task the lone *virtuoso* is peculiarly and uniquely suited. A lasting legal and political order can be created only by a singular man of princely *virtù* and vision. 'Nothing does so much honour to a newly-risen man', Machiavelli writes, 'than the new laws and measures which he introduces. These measures, when they are well based and have greatness in them, render him revered and admired . . .'[36]

Although Agathocles was not such a man, Romulus was. Agathocles had no objective other than keeping himself in power; all his dastardly deeds were directed to this end. Romulus, though he murdered Remus and acquiesced in the death of Titus Tatius, should not be censured or criticized as Agathocles deservedly is. For we must, as Machiavelli says in *The Discourses*, 'take into consideration the object which Romulus had in view in committing that homicide'. Romulus, unlike Agathocles, acted not out of a selfish regard for his own good but from a solicitous regard for the public good. A 'wise mind', he continues,

will never censure anyone for having employed any extraordinary means for the purpose of establishing a kingdom or constituting a republic. It is well that, when the act accuses him, the result should excuse him; when the result is good, as in the case of Romulus, it will always absolve him from blame. For he is to be reprehended who commits violence for the purpose of destroying, and not he who employs it for beneficient purposes.[37]

And for Machiavelli the most beneficient purpose of which any man is capable is that of founding a free republic which will outlive him. This, he insists, is the source of true glory and greatness.

The glory and greatness of an act depends upon its being remembered long after the mortal actor has left the world's stage. To found a republic is to create the conditions for such remembrance and, thus, for earthly immortality. It is, I think, a mistake to see such an act of founding as an egregiously

that this is as corrupt a nation as ever existed under the sun? And would you think of governing such a people by the strict principles of honesty and morality?' (Henry Fielding, *Amelia* (1751; New York, 1930), ii. 228).

[36] Machiavelli, *Prince*, 96.
[37] Machiavelli, *Discourses*, bk. I, ch. 9, 138–9.

egoistic act of self-stroking on the part of the *virtuoso* princely founder. This is to miss Machiavelli's point, which is that the citizen's shared remembrance of their polity's founding is a central component of civic (as distinguished from princely) virtue. Civic *virtù* is that collection of qualities required to fill the role of the free citizen of a republic. To discuss this second variety of *virtù*, as Machiavelli elaborates upon it in *The Discourses*, would take me too far afield. Here it is enough to suggest that one of the components of civic *virtù* is civic memory—that is, the stock of common memories which bind citizens together, giving them a common sense of who they are, where they have come from, and what they are collectively capable of achieving.[38] For the Romans, this *sensus communis* came in large part from the *Aeneid* of Virgil, which told the story of Rome's founding; its heroes are Aeneas, Romulus, and Numa. For the Greeks, this common sense and shared sensiblity stemmed from Homeric tales and traditions; its heroes are Achilles, Odysseus, and other exemplary figures. What we now lack, Machiavelli says in effect, is a shared civic memory; because it—and the civic *virtù* of which it is a part— does not now exist, it must be created *ex nihilo*; creation requires a creator, and to create something from nothing is bound to be a violent process. Machiavelli's *virtuoso* prince is just such a creator. The end of this process is the glory and fame he enjoys in the minds and memories of succeeding generations of *virtuosi* citizens. *Fama* is not notoriety, nor is *virtù* another name for wanton violence. If I am right, then, there is moral method in what might otherwise look like so much Machiavellian madness.

3.5 REMEMBRANCE—NOT RECOVERY—OF THINGS PAST

Why then do I consider Machiavelli's prince to be a comic character on a quixotic quest? For two reasons. The first is that his prince would have to think and act within the con-

---

[38] Cf. B. J. Smith, *Politics and Remembrance* (Princeton, NJ, 1985), chs. 1, 2; R. Dagger, 'Metropolis, Memory and Citizenship', *AJPS* 25 (1981), 715–37.

fines of a framework that is utterly foreign, not to say unintelligible, to his subjects; little wonder that their relations should be so strained and violent. Little wonder, too, that he thinks it better for a prince to be feared than loved.[39] Secondly, he is, in effect, trying to turn back the clock, to resurrect an archaic and long-lost moral framework. Despite his copious use of historical examples, Machiavelli is not a historically minded thinker. He sees the world as having its cycles, its ups and downs, its fallings-away and returns; but, because human nature remains essentially unchanged, the maxims applicable in one age are applicable in another.[40]

Machiavelli's archaic ethic of emulation is, in the end, profoundly ahistorical. For it fails to recognize that the concepts constitutive of our moral codes and practices have historically mutable meanings. The mutability of moral codes and concepts is, as I noted earlier, a pervasive theme in much of modern literature, if not in moral philosophy. It might, therefore, be instructive to conclude by contrasting Machiavelli's ahistorical ethic of emulation with the more modern view that there is nothing deader than the ethic of a bygone era, and nothing deadlier, more dangerous—or more futile—than the hope of reviving the dead and reliving the past.

My central contention here—that meaningful moral change cannot, *pace* Machiavelli and Don Quixote, be a matter of recovering a past moral system—can be underscored by considering the contrast between Machiavelli's moral sensibility and that of Thomas Hardy. To compare the views of a sixteenth-century Florentine and a late-nineteenth-century Englishman is not so absurd as it might first appear. The comparison is made possible by a point that these writers have in common—namely, that Hardy's England and Machiavelli's Italy are alike in having a Roman past:

Casterbridge announced old Rome in every street, alley, and precinct. It looked Roman, bespoke the art of Rome, concealed the dead men of Rome. It was impossible to dig more than a foot or two deep about the town fields and gardens without coming upon some tall soldier or other of the Empire, who had lain there in his silent unobtrusive rest for a space of fifteen hundred years. He was mostly found

---

[39] Machiavelli, *Prince*, chs. 17, 18.
[40] Machiavelli, *Discourses*, bk. III, ch. 43, 530.

lying on his side, in an oval scoop in the chalk, like a chicken in its shell; his knees drawn up to his chest; sometimes with the remains of his spear against his arm; a fibula or brooch of bronze on his breast or forehead; an urn at his knees, a jar at his throat, a bottle at his mouth; and mystified conjecture pouring down upon him from the eyes of Casterbridge street boys and men, who had turned a moment to gaze at the familiar spectacle as they passed by. Imaginative inhabitants, who would have felt an unpleasantness at the discovery of a comparatively modern skeleton in their gardens, were quite unmoved by these hoary shapes. They had lived so long ago, their time was so unlike the present, their hopes and motives were so widely removed from ours, that between them and the living there seemed to stretch a gulf too wide for even a spirit to pass.[41]

Machiavelli denies this. The gulf betwen past and present is not, in his view, impassable. The spirit can pass if the flesh is willing; past practices can be revived and exemplary actions emulated. The agent of this revival is to be the virtuoso prince. Thus the (re)introduction of civic virtue requires only a heroic act of princely will, supplemented, to be sure, by armed force. But the hope of forcefully turning back the clock in this way goes far beyond the most feverish dreams of the alchemists, who, after all, hoped only to turn lead into gold. Machiavelli's prince aspires to the doubly difficult, if not indeed impossible, feat of resurrecting the dead and turning the vinegar of violence into the wine of civic harmony.

Nor is Machiavelli alone in believing that such political alchemy is indeed possible. Robespierre's attempt to inaugurate a reign of 'Roman' virtue by initiating a reign of terror; Mussolini's vision of a resurrected Roman empire; Pol Pot's attempt to regain a rural paradise lost; the late Yukio Mishima's attempt to revive the Samurai code of Bushido; the late Ayatollah Khomeni's vision of an ideal Islamic order; the Moral Majority's attempt to revive patriotic and patriarchal 'moral values'—all share something with Machiavelli's quixotic hope of reviving the past and resurrecting the dead. All are alike in their failure to understand that, if indeed history repeats itself, it does so the first time as tragedy and the second time as farce.[42]

---

[41] T. Hardy, *The Mayor of Casterbridge* (London, 1960), 73–4.
[42] K. Marx, 'Eighteenth Brumaire', *MESW* 97.

4

HOBBES'S LINGUISTIC TURN

The elementary political process is the action of mind
upon mind through speech ... Even as people belong to
the same culture by the use of the same language, so they
belong to the same society by the understanding of the
same moral language. As this common moral language
extends, so does society; as it breaks up, so does society.

Bertrand de Jouvenel

4.1 INTRODUCTION

The history of momentous contests and movements is almost
invariably written by the winners rather than by the losers
and also-rans, and this is as true of philosophical as of political movements. Certainly it is, or was until quite recently, true
of positivism. Those who wrote the history of the social sciences, and of political science in particular, were as often as
not either proponents or foes of a positivistically conceived
science of society. But, friend or no, they read the history of
political thought through 'scientific' spectacles. And, as one
might expect, their interpretations contain several significant
omissions. Looking at Thucydides, ostensibly the first 'scientific' historian, or Hobbes, the first self-consciously 'scientific'
political theorist, or Hume, or Marx, or Mill, we find that certain aspects of their thinking are systematically neglected or
ignored because they cannot be grasped by the canons of
comprehension available to the methodological naturalist (or
'positivist', if you prefer). The positivists were inclined to take
as much of Thucydides and Hobbes as would fit their particular methodological mould, and to discard the rest as irrelevant. Our predecessors were thereby shown to have been
proto-positivists (or, alternatively, anti-scientific or, worse,
hopelessly muddled and 'metaphysical'). This procrustean

process of reinterpretation is not necessarily illegitimate. We do often interpret and understand our forebears not wholly in their terms, but at least partially in our own. In this sense all history is present history, and interpretation amounts (in Gadamer's phrase) to a fusion of horizons—our own and that of our predecessors.

Positivism has fallen on hard times of late. As a philosophy of science it is now quite dead. But its ghost continues to haunt our readings even now. The ghost can be exorcized only by bringing in other, alternative perspectives. My aim here is to re-examine several aspects of Hobbes's political philosophy from a perspective that may be called conceptual or linguistic. Used as a lens through which to view our predecessors and our relation to them, it enables us to restore previously ignored or discarded aspects of our intellectual ancestry. To reconsider our past is also to consider our present predicaments and future possibilities in a new light. My argument begins with a brief account of what the linguistic turn does, and does not, imply. I then go on to suggest that this turn was taken in political theory long before it was taken in philosophy and that one of the first to take it in political theory was none other than the first self-consciously scientific thinker, Thomas Hobbes, who in turn grounds his science of politics at least partly upon the conceptual-cum-political insights of the first supposedly scientific historian, Thucydides. Viewed in this way, Hobbes emerges as a richer, more interesting—and methodologically more ambivalent—thinker than the proto-positivist precursor of a naturalistic political science that he is generally presumed to be. I conclude by considering some of the political implications of Hobbes's linguistically grounded science of politics.

4.2 THE LINGUISTIC TURN

When we say that modern philosophy generally, and political philosophy in particular, has taken a linguistic turn,[1] we do not mean merely that philosophers are nowadays interested in

---

[1] See R. Rorty (ed.), *The Linguistic Turn* (Chicago, 1967).

investigating the nature and functions of language, for that has been a perennial concern (see Plato's *Cratylus*). Roughly, we might say that the linguistic turn began with the realization that our language does not merely mirror the world but is instead partially constitutive of it. Our concepts and categories are not ultimately reducible to names or labels to be affixed to independently existing phenomena or forms of life. On the contrary, reality—particularly political reality—is to a very considerable degree linguistically or conceptually constructed.[2] The materials out of which our common world is constructed are the concepts, categories, discriminations, divisions, designations, and differentiations made available to us by the language we speak. More than the lens through which we view the world, language is the medium through which we continually constitute and reconstitute our common world. And this we do by acting with, upon, and through our language. With language we perform actions and create worlds.

In hindsight, the linguistic turn appears almost as an instance of uncoordinated simultaneous discovery. Philosophers as different as Dewey and Wittgenstein, Peirce and Heidegger, argued—albeit in markedly different idioms—that our world is conceptually and communicatively constituted. Perhaps Heidegger put the point most strongly (and with uncharacteristic clarity) when he suggested that we do not have our language so much as it has us.[3] Not only philosophers, but linguists and anthropologists—Whorf and Sapir perhaps most notably—advanced and illustrated the claim that the social world is conceptually and communicatively constituted. As Dewey put it:

Society not only continues to exist ... by communication, but it may be fairly said to exist in ... communication. There is more than a verbal tie between the words common, community, and communication. Men live in a community in virtue of the things which they have in common; and communication is the way in which they come to possess things in common.[4]

[2] See e.g. M. J. Shapiro, *Language and Political Understanding* (New Haven, Conn., 1981); W. E. Connolly, *The Terms of Political Discourse* (Princeton, NJ, 1983); F. Dallmayr, *Language and Politics* (Notre Dame, Ind., 1984).

[3] M. Heidegger, *The Piety of Thinking* (Bloomington, Ind., 1976), 28.

[4] J. Dewey, *Democracy and Education* (New York, 1916), 4.

This, as we shall see, is a claim that Thucydides and Hobbes could have accepted.

4.3 HOBBES'S NEW SCIENCE OF POLITICS

Among Thomas Hobbes's many boasts, none was prouder than his claim to be the first truly scientific political thinker. Placing himself in some very impressive company, he compared his achievement with those of Galileo and Harvey. Physical science or 'natural philosophy', he continues, 'is therefore but young; but Civil Philosophy is yet much younger, as being no older than my own book *De Cive*'.[5] Hobbes's own assessment of his achievement has been widely accepted at face value. Mill's remark that Hobbes was the first to view 'the methods of physical science as the proper models for the political' anticipates the claims of later commentators.[6] According to this view, Hobbes attempted to apply the methodological canons and criteria of the natural sciences to the study of social and political phenomena. And being both a materialist and a determinist, Hobbes conceived human actions to be ultimately describable as physical matter in motion, and explainable via general laws governing the motion of all matter. Although there is no shortage of evidence to support such an interpretation, almost all of it comes from his boasts and his programmatic pronouncements and little, if any, from his actual practice. As if to underscore his contention that humans are apt to use language to mislead their unwary fellows, Hobbes often says one thing while doing something else entirely. On the one hand, he compares his science to Galileo's; but, on the other, he avers that it is the use and abuse of speech that characterizes the sentient subject-matter of civil philosophy, and this makes his science quite unlike that of Galileo or Harvey. Yet this tension goes almost wholly unrecognized and unremarked because of our penchant for

---

[5] *EW* i, p. viii.
[6] J. S. Mill, *Autobiography*, ed. J. Stillinger (Oxford, 1971), 99–100. Cf. R. S. Peters, *Hobbes* (Harmondsworth, 1967); J. W. N. Watkins, *Hobbes's System of Ideas* (London, 1965); and M. M. Goldsmith, *Hobbes's Science of Politics* (New York, 1966).

ransacking the past in search of like-minded predecessors and precursors. This results in textbook history of the simplest sort. The history of political science is supposedly the story of the forward march of science, as it progressively discards the excess baggage of philosophy and assumes a surer scientific aspect. Thus, for example, Plato's 'preference for imaginative and somewhat rigid theoretical notions drawn from brilliant fancy rather than hard fact' gives way to the 'solid good sense' of Aristotle, 'the first great behavioural scientist'.[7]

In Hobbes's case this 'progressive' move is effected by dividing his life and work into two stages. The divide is marked by Hobbes's discovery of geometry. As Aubrey relates the story:

He was . . . 40 yeares old before he looked on geometry; which happened accidently. Being in a gentleman's library . . . Euclid's Elements lay open, and 'twas the 47 *El libri* I. He read the proposition. 'By G—', sayd he (He would now and then sweare, by way of emphasis), 'this is impossible!' So he reads the demonstration of it, which referred him back to such a proposition; which proposition he read. That referred him back to another, which he also read. *Et sic deinceps*, that at last was demonstrably convinced of that trueth. This made him in love with geometry.[8]

After discovering Euclid, Hobbes discarded Thucydides; he ceased being the historically minded humanist who translated Thucydides and became the mathematically minded social scientist who wrote the *Leviathan*.[9] Against the two-Hobbeses thesis I shall suggest that he incorporated a central Thucydidean theme into his science, and that his science thereby fails to prefigure later positivist conceptions.[10]

Hobbes's translation of Thucydides' *History* in 1629 (his first published work) contains an illuminating preface in which he calls special attention to the constitutive role of speech in political affairs. It is through the medium of language that

[7] R. A. Dahl, *Modern Political Analysis* (Englewood Cliffs, NJ, 1963), 24; B. Berelson and G. Steiner, *Human Behavior* (New York, 1964), 13.

[8] J. Aubrey, *Brief Lives*, ed. O. L. Dick (Harmondsworth, 1972), 230.

[9] See, *inter alia*, Peters, *Hobbes*, ch. 1; Watkins, *Hobbes's System*, ch. 2; Goldsmith, *Hobbes's Science*, esp. ch. 7.

[10] Cf. R. Schlatter, 'Thomas Hobbes and Thucydides', *JHI* 6 (1945), 358–60; G. Klosko and D. Rice, 'Thucydides and Hobbes's State of Nature', *HPT* 4 (1985), 405–9.

societies exist and through their speech that men reason, rule, lie, command, calculate, dissimulate, deceive, justify, persuade and dissuade, accuse and excuse, commend and condemn. It is, therefore, no accident that a series of speeches should occupy pride of place in Thucydides' *History*. These speeches were not verbatim reports but were instead imaginative reconstructions in which he 'make[s] the speakers say what was in my opinion demanded of them by the various occasions'.[11] This practice has been dismissed or downplayed by some modern critics as so much window-dressing, mere literary interruptions in an ongoing causal narrative.[12]

Not so Hobbes. Thucydides' use of 'deliberative orations' is not peripheral but is in fact essential to his account. For it is through their speech that the actors reveal, and occasionally conceal, their real reasons for acting:

The grounds and motives of every action [Thucydides] setteth down before the action itself, either narratively, or else contriveth them into the form of deliberative orations ... Digressions for instruction's cause, and other such conveyance of precepts, (which is the philosopher's part), he never useth; as having so clearly set before men's eyes the ways and events of good and evil counsels, that the narration itself doth secretly instruct the reader, and more effectually than can possibly be done by precept.

'In sum,' Hobbes concludes, 'if the truth of history did ever appear in the manner of relating, it doth so in this history: so coherent, perspicuous and persuasive is the whole narration, and every part thereof.'[13] As we shall see, Hobbes's method and style are similarly inseparable; he too seeks to instruct without having recourse to explicit precepts—the political prescriptions being built, as it were, into the very structure and style of 'scientific' argumentation.

From the conventional positivist perspective, Hobbes's admiration for Thucydides is at least partially clear if not wholly transparent. For Thucydides, like his translator, allegedly

---

[11] Thucydides, *History of the Peloponnesian War*, trans. R. Crawley (New York, 1951), 14. For Hobbes's translation, see *EW*, viii. 25.

[12] See e.g. C. N. Cochrane, *Thucydides and the Science of History* (London, 1929), 25–6; W. T. Bluhm, *Theories of the Political System* (Englewood Cliffs, NJ, 1965), ch. 2.

[13] *EW* viii, p. xxi.

aspired to supply scientific explanations of political phenomena. Taking Hippocratic medicine as his model, Thucydides was in effect the Dr Harvey of Hellenic politics. Distinguishing symptoms from causes, he traces the natural course of the political disease which, like the plague at Athens, has afflicted his countrymen and must now run its natural course. Thucydides' history accordingly takes the form of a naturalistic narrative in which causes precede effects in accordance with general laws.[14] In this narrative talk is cheap; words are irrelevant; and reasons are apt to be mere rationalizations masking underlying causal processes of which the agents are unaware and over which they have little or no control. Thus the speeches of the actors are irrelevant distractions, inserted to provide literary relief from an otherwise relentless causal narrative. Thucydides' aim is supposedly to supply nomological knowledge of the appropriate causal connections, so as to enable the reader to recognize in future the symptoms of political disorder, the better to stem the most grievous excesses of the disease as it runs its natural, necessary, and inevitable course. This interpretation relies, I believe, upon a particularly deep—possibly a too-deep—reading of Thucydides' account of the plague that afflicted Athens in the second year of the war.[15] Perhaps his description of the plague is better understood as a dramatic device rather than a scientific model of a natural process.

We find in Thucydides' *History* a foreshadowing of a theme and a tension that has, in our day, become a matter for theoretical reflection. On the one side he appears to offer a straightforwardly naturalistic account of the etiology of one war, subsumed under a more general schema for analysing other subsequent conflicts. By understanding the causes of human conflict, we can in principle predict and perhaps

[14] Cochrane, *Thucydides*, chs. 3, 9; Bluhm, *Theories*, ch. 2. In *The Idea of History* (Oxford, 1946), 29, R. G. Collingwood—that most astute critic of 'scientific' history—nevertheless accepts uncritically Cochrane's 'scientific' reading of Thucydides' intentions.

[15] Thucydides, *History*, bk. II, ch. 7, 110–15; *EW* viii. 201–12. Cochrane (*Thucydides*, 27–32), Collingwood (*Idea of History*, 29–30), and Bluhm (*Theories*, 26–30) agree that Thucydides' description of the plague reveals his deep methodological debt to the Hippocratic school. For a critique, see my 'When Words Lose their Meaning', *Ethics*, 97 (1986), 620–31.

control its course. Theoretical knowledge answers to the technical interest in prediction and control. This is the 'scientific' Thucydides who is much admired by writers in the 'realist' tradition.

Yet Thucydides can be read in a different and arguably more illuminating light. What might at first appear to be natural and inevitable processes and events are themselves revealed, upon closer inspection, to be the creations—or, rather, the miscreations—of men talking past one another, failing, because of unperceived though potentially remediable distortions and misunderstandings, to communicate and thus to speak in the fraternal 'tone of expostulation' that Pericles believed to be the proper mode of address between equals and allies.[16] The appropriate contrast here is between the Athenians' earlier eloquence and the spare monotone of the later speeches, and of the Melian dialogue in particular. The speech of the Athenians—formerly so eloquent and reasonable—is, in the sixteenth year of the war, reduced to the terse formulas and ritual banalities not only of their Spartan enemies but of their earlier 'barbaric' Persian foes. All the arguments of the ill-fated Melians fall on deaf ears. Appeals to justice, and to the memory of past alliances against the Persian invaders, are summarily shrugged off. In this world, says the Athenian envoy, 'the strong do what they can and the weak suffer what they must'.[17] The Melian men are slaughtered and their women and children sold into slavery.

Even more pertinent is Thucydides' account of the revolution at Corcyra, in which the conceptual and communicative basis of political order is most fully and dramatically exemplified. When words lose their meaning, communication—and therefore community—is impossible. Conceptual confusion and political chaos are one and the same:

Words had to change their ordinary meaning and to take that which was now given them. Reckless audacity came to be considered the courage of a loyal ally; prudent hesitation, specious cowardice; moderation was held to be a cloak for unmanliness; ability to see all sides of a question inaptness to act on any. Frantic violence became the attribute of manliness; cautious plotting, a justifiable means of

[16] Thucydides, *History*, bk. I, ch. 5, 79; *EW* viii. 145.
[17] Thucydides, *History*, bk. V, ch. 17, 331; *EW* ix. 99.

self-defence. . . . To succeed in a plot was to have a shrewd head, to divine a plot a still shrewder [one] . . . Oaths of reconciliation, being only proffered on either side to meet an immediate difficulty, only held good so long as no other weapon was at hand; but when opportunity offered, he who first ventured to seize it and to take his enemy off his guard, thought this perfidious vengeance sweeter than an open one, since . . . success by treachery won him the palm of superior intelligence . . . The cause of all these evils was the lust for power arising from greed and ambition; and from these passions proceeded the violence of the parties . . . [T]he use of fair phrases to arrive at guilty ends was in high reputation. . . . The ancient simplicity into which honour so largely entered was laughed down and disappeared; and society became divided into camps in which no man trusted his fellow. To put an end to this, there was neither promise to be depended upon, nor oath that could command respect; but all parties dwelling rather in their calculation upon the hopelessness of a permanent state of things, were more intent upon self-defence than capable of confidence.[18]

Point for point, feature for feature, Hobbes's state of nature parallels Thucydides' description of the Corcyraian revolution. More striking still, Hobbes follows Thucydides' account of the essentially *conceptual* character of political conflict.

Both Hobbes and Thucydides are in effect agreed that polities are the collective communicative creations of their members. The role of Thucydides' theory is to expose, criticize, and attempt to remove the sources of blocked or systematically distorted communication. Political theory therefore answers to a 'practical' interest in human understanding rather than to a 'technical' interest in control. This is, of course, to speak in the idiom of Habermas and not of Thucydides and Hobbes, who say nothing at all about distorted communication, technical and practical knowledge-constitutive interests, and the like. And yet the hermeneutical risk seems worth taking. For it enables us to see features of their thought that are systematically obscured by an interpretation which assumes that any science worthy of the name must necessarily yield nomological knowledge and answer to a technical interest in prediction and control. An alternative reading of Hobbes suggests that the choice need not be

[18] Thucydides, *History*, bk. III, ch. 10, 189–91; *EW* viii. 348–9. Cf. J. B. White, *When Words Lose their Meaning* (Chicago, 1984), ch. 3.

between science and non-science but between two differently grounded conceptions of science.

Hobbes is hardly a closet critical theorist, nor does he reject the standard proto-positivist account of explanation via general laws. But if he sometimes seems to profess one thing while actually practising another, that is because he does not distinguish between different levels of description. Although trying his hardest to remain a reductionist, he fails miserably and magnificently. His account, like Thucydides', is too richly suggestive, too pregnant with multiple possibilities, to be confined within any austerely reductionist framework. And this is because the linguistic turn, once taken, will not permit Hobbes to take the reductionist route that he apparently wished to follow. Once viewed as speaking subjects, and not merely as material objects, human beings become self-defining creatures of convention, not of nature.

If man *qua* body is an object amenable to natural-scientific explanation, man *qua* citizen is not: 'What is to be understood about men in so far as they are *men*, is not applicable in so far as they are *citizens*.'[19] Man in the state of nature is scarcely more than a body bent upon preserving itself from annihilation; the instinct for self-preservation is natural, and shared with all other animals. 'Every man', says Hobbes, 'is desirous of what is good for him and shuns what is evil, but chiefly the chiefest of natural evils, which is death; and this he doth by a certain impulsion of nature no less than that whereby a stone moves downward.'[20] Falling stones and man *qua* body are both subject to the laws governing matter in motion. To explain a particular instance of either is merely to subsume a description of it under the appropriate general law. In this respect Hobbes does indeed appear to be the proto-positivist that he is reputed to be. Yet this apparently clear picture is quickly clouded by several further considerations. For one, Hobbes is amply aware that there are numerous and frequent counter-instances to the ostensibly general law that people act always to preserve themselves. Although their fear of violent death 'encline[s] men to Peace', they repeatedly risk

---

[19] Hobbes, *De homine* in *LW* ii, ch. 13, 116; *MC* 68.
[20] Hobbes, *De cive*, in *EW* ii. 8.

death for the sake of 'honour' and other 'trifles'.[21] Thus the natural instinct of self-preservation is occasionally overridden by vain and prideful men. At the very least it would seem that this general law would have to be restricted to the explanation of rational behaviour.

The difficulty with this move is, however, immediately apparent. For to be rational, Hobbes avers, is to have the use of speech: 'in reasoning, a man must take heed of words ...' Since without language there is no reason, only humans can be said to be fully rational.[22] But ironically it is language—the medium of reason itself—which feeds vanity and inflames the passions. To reason with loose and imprecisely defined concepts just *is* to act in inflammatory, irrational, and self-destructive ways. That we are language-using and abusing creatures makes us, unlike stones, ill-suited to be subjects of a natural science. And this difference in subject-matter dictates a difference in method.

The 'most notable and profitable invention of all other', Hobbes says, 'was that of SPEECH ... without which, there had been amongst men, neither Commonwealth, nor Society, nor Contract, nor Peace, no more than amongst Lyons, Bears, and Wolves'.[23] Language is a blessing, in that it is the medium that makes reason and science possible; but also a bane, because of our penchant for using words loosely and according to our own momentary appetites and inclinations. For every good use of language there is a corresponding abuse; and it is our penchant for abusing language—for making false statements, lying, making insincere promises, speaking metaphorically, boasting, insulting our fellows, and the like—that makes us wary and distrustful and that puts us, in short, in that 'state of Warre' that is the state of nature.

The state of nature is for Hobbes both a description of dire political possibility and an ingenious methodological device according to which 'we feign the world to be annihilated'. The world thus methodologically dissolved is the common world of mutual meanings and shared significations. The state of

---

[21] *Lev.*, ch. 13, 188; cf. also ch. 11, 164.
[22] Ibid., ch. 4, 109 and ch. 5 *passim*; cf. *De homine*, ch. 10, sect. 1, *LW* ii. 88–9; *MC* 37–8.
[23] *Lev.*, ch. 4, 100.

nature is a condition of complete communicative breakdown, a veritable Babel of mutually incomprehensible voices and tongues. Or, to speak in a more modern idiom, the tragedy of the state of nature is that, although its inhabitants are linguistically competent (in Chomsky's sense), they are not yet communicatively competent (in Habermas's sense). They have the capacity to speak, to construct and utter well-formed sentences, but still are apt to speak insincerely, self-interestedly, untruthfully, and the like.[24] Each attempts the impossible feat of speaking a private language; each tries, in Humpty-Dumpty fashion, to make words mean whatever he wishes them to mean. The upshot is that the concepts constitutive of civil order—'right' and 'justice', for example—are meaningless sounds, signifying nothing. 'To this warre of every man against every man, this also is consequent; that nothing can be Unjust. The notions of Right and Wrong, Justice and Injustice have there no place.' In this natural state there is 'no Propriety, no Dominion, no *Mine* and *Thine* distinct; but onely that to be every mans that he can get; and for so long, as he can keep it'.[25]

The natural state of humankind is, however, quite unlike the natural condition in which the other animals find themselves. And this difference is again due to our being language-using creatures. 'It is true', Hobbes acknowledges,

that certain living creatures, as Bees and Ants, live sociably with one another ... and yet have no other direction, than their particular judgements and appetites; nor speech, whereby one of them can signifie to another, what he thinks expedient for the common benefit: and therefore some men may perhaps desire to know, why Mankind cannot do the same.

Hobbes has several answers. For one, the concepts of honour, dignity, and envy are not available to ants and bees; for another, 'they want that art of words, by which some men can represent to others, that which is Good, in the likenesse of Evill; and Evill, in the likenesse of Good'.[26] Because we can

---

[24] See J. Habermas, 'Toward a Theory of Communicative Competence', *Inquiry*, 13 (1970), 360–75; *Communication and the Evolution of Society* (Boston, 1979), ch. 1.

[25] Hobbes, *Lev.*, ch. 13, 188.   [26] Ibid., ch. 17, 225–6.

speak, we can communicate our false beliefs, thereby deceiving others and, no less often, ourselves: 'man, alone among the animals . . . can devise errors and pass them on for the use of others. Therefore man errs more widely and dangerously than can other animals.' Moreover, 'because of the ease of speech, the man who truly doth not think, speaks; and since what he says, he believes to be true, he, unlike a beast, can deceive himself. Therefore by speech man is not made better but merely given greater possibilities.'[27] Thus the task of the zoologist, and indeed the natural philosopher generally, is easier and more straightforward than that of the civil philosopher or political scientist. The former need not concern himself with the linguistic and conceptual preconstitution of his science's object-domain; his subjects cannot lie, dissimulate, and mislead, for they lack the use of language altogether. The civil philosopher, by contrast, deals with a wily subject made the more canny by his capacity to acquire, to use—and above all to abuse—language. Thus civil philosophy necessarily takes a sharp turn—a linguistic turn—*away* from natural philosophy.

Hobbes's civil philosophy differs from natural philosophy in several significant respects. Natural philosophy deals in probabilities, civil philosophy in certainties; natural philosophy studies nature—the art of God—while civil philosophy studies 'the art of man'.[28] 'Since the causes of natural things are not in our power, but in [God's] . . . we . . . cannot deduce their qualities from their causes.' We can only 'demonstrate that such and such *could* have been their causes. This kind of demonstration is called *a posteriori*, and its science physics.' By contrast, 'politics and ethics (that is, the sciences of *just* and *unjust*, of *equity* and *inequity*) can be demonstrated *a priori*; because we ourselves make the principles—that is, the causes of justice (namely laws and covenants)—whereby it is known what *justice* and *equity* and their opposites *injustice* and *inequity*, are'.[29] Civil philosophy, in other words, deals with the commonwealth, that most human of creations. Our knowledge of matters political is more certain than our knowledge of natural phenomena, for we have made the for-

---

[27] *LW* ii. 90–1; *MC* 40–1 (I have slightly altered the English translation).
[28] *Lev.*, Intro., 81.   [29] *LW* ii. 93–4; *MC*, 42–3.

mer but not the latter. The creator's knowledge of his own creation is unique and privileged. And just as God has perfect knowledge of his own creation, so may man have perfect and certain knowledge of his.

It is ironic that Hobbes, who was so keenly critical of his medieval forebears, relies so heavily upon their doctrine that knowledge and creation are one. Hobbes, however, gives the medieval doctrine of *verum et factum convertuntur* a distinctly conventionalist twist.[30] Unlike (say) Aquinas, who applies the doctrine to God's creation of the material world, Hobbes the self-proclaimed materialist applies it exclusively to the non-material 'artificial' world of concepts and ideas. The language devised by Adam was lost after Babel and must now be created anew.[31] Words and concepts are our inventions and have only such meaning as we give to them. Because the world of mutual meanings and shared significations—our world—is our own creation, we can know it in a way that we can never know the world of nature.[32]

Hobbes's new science of politics takes geometry as its model, not out of a Cartesian conviction that mathematics mirrors the underlying structure of the natural world, but because it does *not*. The civil philosopher's knowledge of matters political is every bit as certain as the geometer's, and for precisely the same reason: geometry is, in Hobbes's view, the product—indeed, the very paradigm—of human art and artifice. 'Geometry, therefore is demonstrable, for the lines and figures from which we reason, are drawn and described by ourselves; and civil philosophy is demonstrable because we make the commonwealth ourselves.'[33] Because the commonwealth is created by its members, they alone can have perfect knowledge of its structure and operation.

Any science worthy of the name, Hobbes suggests, must

[30] For Vico's version of the doctrine, see Ch. 9 below.

[31] *Lev.*, ch. 4, 101. Hobbes's 'brisk wit' is especially evident in his amusing and logically astute analysis of Adam's language. 'How', he asks, 'could Adam have understood the serpent speaking of "death", whereof he, the first mortal, could have had no acquaintance and therefore no idea?' (*LW* ii. 95; *MC* 38–9 (again I have altered the translation slightly)).

[32] In this respect, at least, Hobbes's new science resembles Vico's (see Ch. 9 below).

[33] *EW* vii. 184.

yield perfect, and not merely provisional or contingent knowledge.[34] Until civil philosophy was bestowed upon mankind by Hobbes, geometry was 'the only Science that it hath pleased God hitherto to bestow on mankind . . .'.[35] The striking oddity of this claim is lessened somewhat by attending to Hobbes's distinction between two kinds of knowledge— roughly, that which we acquire through observation of 'fact' and that which we gain through deduction. And this distinction is in turn tied to the claim that we have a special sort of knowledge of what we ourselves have made:

There are of knowledge two kinds; whereof one is *Knowledge of Fact*; the other *Knowledge of the Consequence of one Affirmation to another*. The former is nothing else, but Sense and Memory, and is Absolute Knowledge; as when we see a Fact doing, or remember it done: And this is the Knowledge required in a Witnesse. The latter is called *Science*; and is Conditionall; as when we know, that, if the figure showne be a circle, then any straight line through the Centre shall divide it into two equal parts. And this is the Knowledge required in a Philosopher; that is to say, of him that pretends to Reasoning.[36]

Thus natural philosophy and civil philosophy are both scientific, but in different senses. For civil philosophy can follow, as physics cannot, the lead of the geometer. True philosophy consists of reasoning, which Hobbes contrasts with empirical observation:

Reason is not as Sense, and Memory, borne with us; nor gotten by Experience onely; as Prudence is; but attayned by Industry; first in apt imposing of Names; and secondly by getting a good and orderly Method in proceeding from the Elements, which are Names, to Assertions made by Connexion of one of them to another; and so to Syllogismes, which are the Connexions of one Assertion to another, till we come to a knowledge of all the Consequences of names appertaining to the subject in hand; and that is it, men call SCIENCE.[37]

What has heretofore passed for moral or civil philosophy has not, however, been genuinely scientific. 'What hath hitherto been written by moral philosophers, hath not made any progress in the knowledge of the truth,' says Hobbes, because

---

[34] *LW* ii. 92; *MC* 41.   [35] *Lev.*, ch. 4, 105.
[36] Ibid., ch. 9, 147–8.   [37] Ibid., ch. 5, 115.

they have not defined their terms precisely and deduced their conclusions accordingly.

For were the nature of human actions as distinctly known, as the nature of quantity in geometrical figures, the strength of avarice and ambition, which is sustained by the erroneous opinions of the vulgar, as touching the nature of right and wrong, would presently faint and languish; and mankind should enjoy such an immortal peace, that . . . there would hardly be left any pretence for war.[38]

But the pretence for civil war stems less from the crude views of the vulgar than from the pretentious and ostensibly learned opinions of the philosophers. And it is their failure to be 'scientific' that is, in Hobbes's view, the root of almost all political evils. Loose concepts, imprecisely defined terms, metaphors, tropes, and figurative speech of all sorts are the sources of sedition. And these are all the more pernicious because they purportedly derive their authority from philosophy itself. Man alone, says Hobbes, has

the privilege of Absurdity . . . And of men, those are of all most subject to it, that professe Philosophy. For . . . there can be nothing so absurd, but may be found in the books of Philosophers. And the reason is manifest. For there is not one of them that begins his ratiocination from the Definitions, or Explications of the names they are to use; which is a method that hath been used only in Geometry; whose Conclusions have thereby been made indisputable.[39]

Hobbes's complaint is not merely a methodological but a political one. The concepts bandied about by earlier philosophers—'law', 'justice', 'right'—pose a political danger of the first magnitude. In the conceptual confusions, contentions, and disagreements of the philosophers we find the first stirrings of sedition and discord. Philosophers have heretofore lived in a world of words whose meanings they refuse to define; 'and as men abound in copiousnesse of language, so they become more wise, or more mad than ordinary'.[40] Such learned madness must sooner or later affect the multitude of the vulgar who further fuel and legitimize their private appetites by appealing to ill-defined notions of justice and right. Anyone doing this 'will find himselfe entangled in

---

[38] Hobbes, *De cive*, Epistle Dedicatory, *EW* ii. 3–4.
[39] *Lev.*, ch. 5, 113–14.   [40] Ibid., ch. 4, 106.

words, as a bird in lime-twiggs; the more he struggles, the more belimed'. Traditional or unscientific philosophy is not the solution but is, politically speaking, the problem itself. Hence modern men are well advised not to 'spend time in fluttering over their bookes; as birds that entring by the chimney, and finding themselves inclosed in a chamber, flutter at the false light of a glasse window, for want of wit to consider which way they came in'. Abandon Aristotle, and Cicero, and all previous philosophers so-called, counsels Hobbes, and take the rigorous road of science. For 'in the right Definition of Names, lyes the first use of Speech; which is the Acquisition of Science: And in wrong, or no Definitions, lyes the first abuse; from which proceed all false and senseless tenets'.[41] From conceptual confusion comes political chaos.

Hobbes's fulmination against earlier philosophers pre-dates and rather resembles Keynes's oft-quoted complaint that 'madmen in authority, who hear voices in the air,' are more than likely 'distilling their frenzy from some academic scribbler of a few years back'.[42] The England of Hobbes's day, like his hypothetical state of nature, was populated by madmen, each hearing his own particular voice distilled from one or another academic scribbler. The only cure for conceptual-cum-political chaos was to be found, Hobbes thought, in civil philosophy of a more surely scientific stripe. A veritable conceptual purge, amounting to nothing less than the complete scientization of the political vocabulary, seemed the only solution. Just as geometers could not calculate without first agreeing on definitions, so citizens cannot live together without sharing a common vocabulary of concepts whose meanings are fixed in advance. To the civil philosopher, and to the sovereign who follows his lead, falls the task of purging the political and moral vocabulary of the citizenry. By fixing once and for all the meanings of the concepts constitutive of the commonwealth itself, he dampens political conflict. By linguistic art and artifice is created the great Leviathan.

The first step to be taken by Hobbes's 'mortall God' is to

[41] Ibid., ch. 4, 105–6.
[42] J. M. Keynes, *General Theory*, in *Collected Writings* (London, 1973), ii. 383. For Hobbes's version, see *Lev.*, chs. 21 (esp. 267–8), 26 (esp. 315–17), and 29 (369–70); and *LW* ii. 91–2; *MC* 40–1.

undo the damage done at Babel, when the immortal God decreed that 'every man [be] stricken for his rebellion, with an oblivion of his former language'.[43] The damage is to be undone by creating a new language, its concepts strictly and 'scientifically' defined. Thus the sovereign must purge the philosophically tainted vocabulary of his subjects: 'the Common-peoples minds, unlesse they be tainted with dependance on the Potent, or scribbled over with the opinions of their Doctors [i.e. philosophers], are like clean paper, fit to receive whatsoever by Publique Authority shall be imprinted in them.'[44] The conceptual contests fomented by all previous philosophers must be terminated by sovereign fiat, and true philosophy or 'civil science' sent to rule Leviathan-like over the children of pride. But this conceptual-cum-political purge does not end here. Besides ridding our vocabulary of the last vestiges of philosophy, Hobbes would purge it of poetry and literature as well. Hobbes, no mean poet himself (he composed his autobiography in Latin verse), vents his wrath upon metaphor and other 'abuses of speech'.[45] Into the fire go 'obscure, confused, and ambiguous Expressions, also all metaphoricall Speeches, tending to the stirring up of Passion . . .'.[46] Political science or civil philosophy offers nothing less than a political purgative.

This purge cannot be politically neutral, for science itself has an intrinsic interest in social stability and political pacification. There is indeed a symbiotic relationship between Hobbes's science of politics and the pacific polity envisioned in *Leviathan*. There can be no science, Hobbes avers, where there is no safety, and conversely no lasting security, without the aid of science, rightly understood and applied. Science promotes, and is itself part of, 'commodious living'.[47] Without a thorough cleansing of the Augean stables of philosophy men cannot live commodiously.

Hobbes's claim that we must first agree upon definitions before we can come to agreement in moral and political judgements might at first sight seem, if not normatively neutral, then at least politically innocuous. But there are several reasons for thinking otherwise. It is not only Hobbes's explic-

[43] *Lev.*, ch. 4, 101.   [44] Ibid., ch. 30, 379.   [45] Ibid., ch. 4, 102.
[46] Ibid., ch. 25, 307.   [47] *EW* i. 7–8.

itly stated premisses and his often painstakingly precise show of definitional rigour that are themselves politically charged; it is, more fundamentally, the 'scientific' mode of argument itself that, like Thucydides' exquisitely crafted narrative, 'doth secretly instruct the reader, and more effectually than can possibly be done by precept'.[48] Hobbes appeals, after all, to precision: and who but an obscurantist can doubt that precision is a virtue? Yet this virtue is not its own reward. To constrain language, to purge it of tropes and metaphors, to define its constitutive concepts tightly and precisely, just *is* to contain conflict. A sober language for a sober citizenry.

Hobbes's defence of linguistic austerity must be viewed against the background of an older rhetorical tradition in which the aim of political speech is to kindle the passions and direct the interests of the audience. Hobbes is as critical as Plato of appeals to the passions and mere 'opinions' of the masses.[49] But of course Hobbes's approach and his appeals are no less 'rhetorical'. He relies upon—indeed he virtually invents—a new rhetorical form. Hobbes appeals not to the panoply of the passions but to our fear of death and our corresponding interest in physical safety and self-preservation. This rhetoric of sobriety is not so much a result of Hobbes's civil philosophy as it is a *requirement* for it. For it is only by assuming certain sorts of interests to be 'natural' that his science acquires its intelligibility. It is by first assuming and then appealing to these natural interests that Hobbes is able to cast his arguments in ostensibly scientific form. But Hobbes's explicit epistemological and methodological presuppositions matter less than his own covertly rhetorical strategy. The persuasiveness of Hobbes's science relies a good deal less upon his definitions and deductions than upon his metaphors. What, after all, is his state of nature if not an extended metaphor in which men are beasts, life is war, war is hell, and so on? And who is the sovereign if not a secular saviour, a 'mortall god' sent not from heaven but sprung, Athena-like, from the head of the civil philosopher himself? Hobbes was always more adept at detecting the mote of metaphor in another's eye than the beam in his own.[50]

[48] *EW* viii, p. xxii. [49] *Lev.*, ch. 7, 131.
[50] See S. Wolin, *Hobbes and the Epic Tradition in Political Theory* (Los

Leaving aside Hobbes's reliance upon metaphor, analogy, allegory, and other rhetorical stratagems, there are still other reasons for viewing his science with a sceptical eye. Consider again his contention that political science must proceed by defining the concepts constitutive of political discourse. These will characteristically be what we would nowadays call operational definitions. Consider, for example, his definitions of 'law' and allied concepts like 'justice'. 'Law in generall', Hobbes says, 'is not Counsell, but Command; nor a Command of any man to any man; but only of him whose Command is addressed to one formerly obliged to obey him.'[51] Thus no law, provided that it has been duly promulgated and pronounced by the sovereign, can *ever* be *un*just. To speak of an 'unjust law' would be to contradict oneself. For sovereigns, says Hobbes, '*make* the things they command just, by commanding them, and those which they forbid, unjust, by forbidding them'.[52] 'By a good law', he says elsewhere,

I mean not a Just Law: for no Law can be Unjust. The Law is made by the Sovereign Power, and all that is done by such a Power, is warranted, and owned by every one of the people; and that which every man will have so, no man can say is unjust. It is in the Lawes of a Commonwealth, as in the Lawes of Gaming: whatsoever the Gamesters all agree on, is Injustice to none of them.[53]

From this it follows that the only operation or test by which we can determine whether a particular command is indeed a law, and therefore just, is to see whether it in fact issues from the sovereign. If it does, it is. QED

This kind of conceptual clarification through operational definition is not, needless to say, merely a verbal or semantic move having no substantive political import. By implication and inclination, Hobbes's science of politics allies itself with, and serves to legitimize, the alignment of power in the society

Angeles, 1970); N. Jacobson, *Pride and Solace* (Berkeley, Calif., 1978), ch. 3; and F. G. Whelan, 'Language and its Abuses in Hobbes's Political Philosophy', *APSR* 75 (1981), 59–75.

[51] *Lev.*, ch. 26, 312.

[52] *EW* ii. 151. Hobbes devises a 'command theory' not only of law but, more remarkably, of *justice* as well. See *LW* ii. 117–18; *MC* 69.

[53] *Lev.*, ch. 30, 388.

within which it is institutionally embedded. His science is not a neutral broom for sweeping semantic rubbish into the dustbin, but is, on the contrary, clearly prescriptive, and pregnant with a peculiar vision of the good society.

4.4 OBJECTIONS AND REPLIES

A critic might object that I am wrong in suggesting that Hobbes took a linguistic turn three centuries ago. One of the key features of the linguistic turn in modern philosophy resides in its recognition that languages (or, at any rate, natural languages) enable speakers to perform such speech-acts as making promises, excuses, agreements, and so on. But Hobbes did not take, and could not have taken, anything like a linguistic turn in our modern sense, for two very good reasons. The first is that he was the crudest kind of nominalist. He subscribed, that is, to a word-and-object conception of language and meaning, according to which words are names or labels that we, by convention, attach to independently existing objects.[54] 'All other Names, are but insignificant sounds.'[55] And, secondly, Hobbes was a metaethical emotivist who held that moral and political concepts—e.g. 'good' or 'right'—are, strictly speaking, meaningless; they serve, at most, to signal to others the speaker's state of mind. Thus to say that something is good means merely that one approves of it; conversely, to call something bad means only that one dislikes or disapproves of it. These are important objections. If they are valid, then much of my argument is undercut if not defeated outright.

Consider first the claim that Hobbes was a thoroughgoing nominalist for whom words were but names and who was, in consequence, blind to the 'performative' functions of language. This objection requires that we take at full face value Hobbes's own pronouncements about language, truth, and meaning. This we cannot do. In his actual practice Hobbes implicitly but clearly recognizes that language is the medium

[54] See J. W. Danford, *Wittgenstein and Political Philosophy* (Chicago, 1976), 43–8.
[55] *Lev.*, ch. 4, 108.

through which human beings conceive, communicate, and perform any number of linguistic actions—swearing oaths, boasting, insulting, authorizing, accusing, excusing, recalling, inciting, lying, and so on *ad infinitum*.[56] Although obscured by his earlier nominalist pronouncements, this 'performative' perspective comes clearly to the fore in *De homine* (1658). The ostensibly 'scientific' Hobbes of 1658 rather resembles the 'historical' Hobbes of 1629. His discussion of speech in the tenth chapter of *De homine* marks a turn—or rather a return—to an earlier Thucydidian theme. There Hobbes virtually abandons the crude label-and-object theory of meaning in favour of a richer and more variegated view about the ways in which language actually functions. That view, roughly speaking, focuses less upon language as a system of signs than upon *speech*, understood as the medium through which we *do* things with words. Or, to borrow a distinction from Saussure, we might say that Hobbes became progressively less interested in *langue* and more in *parole*, or language-in-use.

Three uses of speech are, Hobbes thinks, especially noteworthy. The first is that, since speech enables men to *measure*, *count*, and *number*, it makes navigation, time-keeping, and architecture possible. Secondly, 'one may *teach* another, that is, communicate his knowledge . . . he can *warn*, he can *advise*, all these he hath from speech also; so that a good, great in itself, through communication becomes even greater'. Thirdly, and most importantly, 'that we can *command* and understand commands is a benefit of speech, and truly the greatest. For without this there would be no society among men, no peace, and consequently no disciplines; but first savagery, then solitude, and for dwellings, caves.'[57] These three benefits derive directly from the performative character of human speech. An unalloyed nominalist he was not.

Consider next the objection that Hobbes was a crude meta-ethical emotivist for whom moral and political terms had no meaning other than to signify the feelings of the speaker. This

[56] See G. Parry, 'Performative Utterances and Obligation in Hobbes', *Philosophical Quarterly*, 17 (1967), 246–53; and the critique by D. R. Bell, 'What Hobbes does with Words', ibid., 19 (1969), 155–8. Unfortunately, both focus upon the *Leviathan* and take no notice of the later *De homine* (1658).

[57] *LW* ii. 90–1; *MC* 39–40 (emphasis added).

objection rests upon a misunderstanding. In the Babel of the
state of nature, the emotive theory of meaning is indeed
valid—and this is precisely what Hobbes thinks is *wrong* with
the state of nature. In that pre-civil state words like 'good'
and 'evil', 'just' and 'unjust', have no agreed-upon meaning,
other than that of signalling approval or disapproval:

> But whatsoever is the object of any mans Appetite or Desire; that is
> it, which he for his part calleth Good: And the object of his Hate,
> and Aversion, Evill; And of his Contempt, Vile, and Inconsiderable.
> For these words of Good, Evill, and Contemptible, are ever used
> with relation to the person that useth them: There being nothing
> simply and absolutely so; nor any common Rule of Good and Evill,
> to be taken from the nature of the objects themselves; but from the
> Person of the man (*where there is no Commonwealth*).[58]

Where there *is* a commonwealth, by contrast, moral concepts
do have a single fixed, agreed-upon meaning. 'What the legislator commands, must be held for *good*, and what he forbids
for *evil*.'[59] In the commonwealth, therefore, the emotivist theory no longer holds true; each moral agent speaks the same
moral language. By definitional fiat the sovereign ensures
communication, secures consent, and guarantees conceptual
continuity of meaning from person to person and from generation to generation. The sovereign supplies nothing less than
the common coin of political communication, the conceptual
currency that makes civil society possible. His primary function is to create and preserve order. And this he does by creating and maintaining meanings. Or, in a more Thucydidian
idiom, his function is to ensure that words have meanings that
they do not lose. Word and sword are two sides of the coin of
civility. Without both there can be no lasting peace.

But civil peace comes at a price. There can in Hobbes's
commonwealth be no fundamental dissent. There can be no
criticism to the effect that, for example, the sovereign is acting
illegally or that the laws he has enacted are unjust, because
there is no vocabulary in which dissent is intelligible and criticism communicable. Hobbes's model commonwealth is a conceptually closed society. Reason having been defined in terms
of discourse duly scientized, political dissent (as distinguished

---

[58] *Lev.*, ch. 6, 120 (emphasis added).   [59] *EW* ii. 150.

from complaints about individual injury) is perforce indicative of irrationality or insanity. His is a vision, not of an imaginary nightmare world but of a technocratic dream capable of coming all too true in our own time. The precursor of a conceptually sanitized and scientized society largely immune from internal criticism and deaf to dissent, Hobbes has proved to be a prescient prophet. The scientistic appropriation of the linguistic turn was, for Hobbes, an act of hope.[60] For us it stands as a warning.

[60] Compare Hobbes's high hopes for linguistic austerity with another Englishman's worst fears: 'Don't you see that the whole aim of Newspeak is to narrow the range of thought? In the end we shall make thoughtcrime literally impossible, because there will be no words in which to express it. Every concept ... will be expressed by exactly *one* word, with its meaning rigidly defined and all its subsidiary meanings rubbed out and forgotten' (George Orwell, *1984* (New York, 1981), 46).

5

ROUSSEAU'S CIVIL RELIGION RECONSIDERED

With what a salutary shock did the paradoxes of Rousseau explode like bombshells . . .

J. S. Mill

5.1 INTRODUCTION

To say that a good deal of controversy continues to surround the interpretation of Rousseau's political philosophy is merely to restate the obvious. Of all its many troubling features, however, surely none is more problematic than his scheme for a civil religion. That proposal has been controversial from the beginning. It earned for Rousseau the wrath of the authorities at Geneva, who condemned the *Contrat social* in 1762, and it has incurred its share of censure ever since. The grounds for such censure have, to be sure, changed over time and according to circumstance. In Rousseau's own day Calvinists and Catholics alike condemned it for its impiety, and atheists for its religiosity. Many modern critics claim to have exposed its 'totalitarian' implications. And so, not surprisingly, Rousseau's short chapter has been something of a burden for his latter-day defenders and admirers, and a continuing source of scholarly controversy.

I want here to suggest a new way of understanding Rousseau's *religion civile*. This I propose to do by asking and attempting to answer three questions. The first is, what place does his scheme for a civil religion occupy in his political theory? Second, what were Rousseau's intentions in formulating the idea of a civil religion; that is, what was he *doing* in devising it? And finally, how are we to account for that scheme's placement in the text of the *Social Contract*—namely, at the very end?

My argument proceeds in the following way. I shall begin by recapitulating Rousseau's argument in favour of a civil religion in book IV, chapter 8, of the *Social Contract*. I shall then canvass arguments advanced in support of the claim that Rousseau's *religion civile* is part of the 'totalitarian' teaching of the *Social Contract*. After assaying the answers given by Rousseau's critics to the three questions I posed at the outset, I examine the answers available to his defenders. As it happens, his defenders have for the most part either confessed their perplexity or have conceded the critics' claim that Rousseau's plan for a civil religion is illiberal at best and implicitly totalitarian at worst. I conclude by offering a new reading of Rousseau's *Social Contract* which, if plausible, suggests that his scheme for a civil religion may have been badly misunderstood by critics and admirers alike. A 'revisionist' reading of this aspect of Rousseau's political philosophy may, moreover, be of more than purely historical or antiquarian interest, inasmuch as the idea of a civil religion has recently resurfaced in American political discourse.[1] And, more recently still, Michel Foucault has revived the spectre of the 'totalitarian' Rousseau by pointing to the 'panoptic' aspects of his political philosophy.

5.2 THE 'TOTALITARIAN' INTERPRETATION

Rousseau's critics, particularly those who view him as a precursor of totalitarianism, have brought their bill of indictment by focusing upon four features to be found in the *Social Contract*. The first is the idea of a General Will which is 'always right' and 'cannot err'. The second is the frequency with which such sinister-sounding phrases as people being 'forced to be free' recur throughout the text. The third is the ominous figure of the omniscient god-like legislator. Finally, and most sinister of all, is Rousseau's *religion civile*, with its dogmas, oaths, religious tests, and its provisions for punishing

[1] See e.g. R. Bellah and P. E. Hammond (eds.), *Varieties of Civil Religion* (San Francisco, 1980).

unbelievers. Taken together, these four features of Rousseau's political philosophy, these critics contend, amount to a convincing case for the prosecution.

Those who have defended Rousseau against the charge that he is a proto-totalitarian, however, have had some success in showing that the General Will is not necessarily totalitarian in either its suppositions or its implications.[2] Nor do such phrases as 'forced to be free' have, when considered in context, the ominous overtones detected by Rousseau's detractors and critics.[3] But Rousseau's defenders have had much more difficulty in dealing with his account of the role of the legislator and the civil religion, and more particularly with the charge that the latter is, in the hands of the former, an instrument of political indoctrination and totalitarian rule. As a recent commentator remarks, 'Critics are apt to see in Rousseau's arguments concerning the need for a civil religion a very clear display of the totalitarian elements in his thinking.'[4]

It is easy to see why. Rousseau's *religion civile* does appear to modern—or at any rate to liberal and secular—eyes as an aberrant attempt to combine religion and politics, Church and State, in a kind of holy alliance that is almost always dangerous to individual liberties. To see just where this danger lies, let us look briefly at the arguments advanced by Rousseau in support of a civil religion.

In making his case for a civil religion Rousseau proceeds by attacking two very different targets. Against Bayle, who in his *Pensées sur la comète* (1682) had (as Rousseau rather polemically puts it) held that 'religion is of no use to a body politic', Rousseau rejoins that 'no state has ever been founded without religion as its basis'. And against Warburton's assertion that Christianity is the only firm foundation of any state,

---

[2] See, *inter alia*, W. G. Runciman and A. K. Sen, 'Games, Justice, and the General Will', *Mind*, 74 (1965), 554–62; V. Held, *The Public Interest and Individual Interests* (New York, 1970), ch. 4; R. Dagger, 'Understanding the General Will', *WPQ* 34 (1981), 359–71.

[3] J. Plamenatz, 'Ce qui ne signifie autre chose sinon qu'on le forcera d'être libre', in M. Cranston and R. S. Peters (eds.), *Hobbes and Rousseau* (Garden City, NY, 1972).

[4] N. J. H. Dent, *A Rousseau Dictionary* (Oxford, 1992), 203.

Rousseau replies that 'Christian law is at bottom more injurious than useful to the strong constitution of the state'.[5]

Christianity comes in two variants, the first being institutional 'Roman Christianity', the second the 'pure' or 'true' Christianity of the Gospels. The first undermines civic allegiance and unity, and alienates 'man' from 'citizen'. Roman Christianity provides its adherents with 'two codes of law, two rulers, two fatherlands, places them under contradictory duties, and prevents their being both believers and citizens'. But 'from a political point of view', the 'holy, sublime, and true religion' of the Gospels is no less defective. It holds that all mankind are the children of the same God and envisions a universal brotherhood composed of men of all nations, past and present, living and dead. Thus, 'this religion, having no particular connection with the body politic', Rousseau complains, 'leaves the law with no other force than its own' and thereby deprives it of an additional spiritual dimension. Worse still, 'instead of attaching the hearts of the citizens to the state', this religion distracts them from all worldly concerns, including civic ones. 'Christianity is a religion that is entirely spiritual', Rousseau asserts, and 'the fatherland of the Christian is not of this world'. Worst of all, however, is that the terms 'republic' and 'Christianity' are incompatible; 'each term excludes the other. Christianity preaches only servitude and dependence. Its spirit is too favourable to tyranny . . . True Christians are moulded to be slaves'—that is, passive subjects rather than robust and active citizens.

Rousseau then looks for a religion fit for republicans and citizens, and finds it in 'une profession de foi purement civile', whose articles are to be arranged by the sovereign 'not exactly as dogmas of religion, but as sentiments of sociability without which it is impossible to be a good citizen or a faithful subject'. The sovereign, he says, 'cannot compel men to believe' these sentiments, but 'it can banish from the state anyone who does not believe them'. The unbeliever is banished not so much for impiety as for unsociability, having shown himself

incapable of sincerely loving the laws and justice, and if need be to

---

[5] This and the following quotations are from *SC*, bk. IV, ch. 8. I rely here and throughout on *OC*; for the *Contrat Social*, see *OC* iii.

sacrifice his life to his duty. But if anyone, after having publicly agreed to these dogmas, shall behave as if he did not believe them, he is to be punished by death, for he has committed the greatest of all crimes: he has lied in the face of the law.

Rousseau's critics have been quick to seize upon several apparently slippery statements. He says, for instance, that the 'sentiments of sociability' are not exactly 'dogmas'; but then he proceeds to call them dogmas ('he does use that word, after all', notes one critic).[6]

The dogmas of the civil religion ought to be simple, few in number, precisely fixed, and without explanation or comment. The existence of a powerful, wise, and benevolent Deity who foresees and provides; the life to come; the happiness of the just; the punishment of the wicked; the sanctity of the social contract and the laws—these are its positive dogmas.

And while the sovereign cannot compel people to believe in these dogmas, it can none the less banish those who do not, and—worse yet—condemn to death anyone who, having sworn to uphold the civil religion, even acts *as if* he does not believe its dogmas (leaving it to the state, apparently, to inspect or examine the dissident's heart and mind). 'In other words', a modern critic complains,

the State has a right to conclude from a person's action—or, implicitly, from his non-action—what his *real* beliefs or opinions are, to accuse him of perjury, and to put him to death. What is this, if not the doctrine of arrest on suspicion of wrong thinking? We need take only one further step to punish people for lack of enthusiasm. The effect of such a state of affairs on people's conduct can easily be imagined from similar situations in later history.[7]

On this reading of Rousseau the civil religion is an indispensable cog in the totalitarian machinery. Without it the juggernaut could not function for long, if at all.

Rousseau's modern critics have accordingly had little difficulty in arriving at answers to the three questions I asked at the outset. To the first—what place does the plan for a civil religion occupy in Rousseau's political philosophy?—they

---

[6] L. G. Crocker, *Rousseau's Social Contract* (Cleveland, 1968), 98.
[7] Ibid. 99.

answer that it necessarily occupies a central place. For some sort of civil religion, they argue, would be indispensable to the continued functioning and legitimation of the totalitarian society envisioned in the *Social Contract*.[8] As to what Rousseau was doing, these critics answer that he was advocating a conformitarian theocracy in which all debate, dissent, and disagreement are prohibited, ostensibly on religious (though really on political) grounds.[9] Rousseau's reason for placing the chapter on the civil religion at the end of the *Social Contract* is accordingly quite clear. His concept of the General Will, his remarks about forcing people to be free, and the rest, lead logically and inexorably to just that kind of conclusion and that kind of institution. Sir Ernest Barker contends that 'It is significant that the *Contrat social* ends with the suggestion of religious persecution.' There can be no clearer proof that 'In effect, and in the last resort, Rousseau is a totalitarian.'[10] While I agree with Barker that its placement in the text is significant, I disagree that it is important for the reason to which he refers.

5.3 FROM CHARITY TO PERPLEXITY

According to the principle of interpetive charity, an author is to be assumed to be coherent and consistent until proven otherwise. Yet even the most charitable among Rousseau's readers and commentators have found it difficult if not impossible to square his scheme for a civil religion with the rest of his writings. As Alfred Cobban observes:

The object of Rousseau was to free the individual from the tyranny of a caste of priests and subject him only to those religious principles which were dictated by the nature and necessities of the state itself. But, in the end, one cannot pretend to regard the chapter on the Civil Religion as other than unfortunate: though so short, more than

---

[8] See J. L. Talmon, *Origins of Totalitarian Democracy* (New York, 1952); Crocker, *Rousseau's Social Contract*, ch. 2; R. Derathé, 'La Religion civile selon Rousseau', *ASJJR* 25 (1962), 161–80.

[9] S. Cotta, 'La Position du problème de la politique chez Rousseau', in *Études sur le Contrat social* (Paris, 1964), 177–90; Derathé, 'La Religion civile'; Crocker, *Rousseau's Social Contract*, 97–101.

[10] E. Barker, *Essays on Government* (Oxford, 1951), 115.

any other section of his political writings it helps us to understand why its author should have been so often regarded as the apostle of tyranny and an enemy to liberty in the state.[11]

F. C. Green goes even further: 'That a noble creation like the *Contrat social* should have been disfigured by such a monstrous appendage is one of the most baffling enigmas recorded in literature.'[12] Applying the principle of charity, Ramon Lemos concludes that 'Perhaps the most charitable thing that can be said about [the civil religion] is that it leaves something to be desired.'[13] R.-A. Leigh observes that 'la religion civile . . . a toujours constitué le grand scandale du *Contrat social*'.[14] Maurizio Viroli notes that 'the final chapter of the *Contrat social*, on "civil religion", casts a particularly sinister shadow over the image of the well-ordered republic'.[15] And Rousseau's most recent and very sympathetic biographer calls the chapter on the civil religion 'the most astonishing chapter in the whole book' and a 'pessimistic conclusion' to the *Contrat social*.[16]

Faced with such interpretive difficulties, Rousseau's defenders have resorted to a variety of strategies. The most common of these is simply to concede that the critics are right on this single score. 'If there is anything illiberal in Rousseau,' Asher Horowitz acknowledges, 'it is his plan for a civil religion . . .'[17] This strategy, however, opens up a further difficulty. Unlike his critics, who see Rousseau as a perfectly consistent proto-totalitarian, his defenders are left with the task of explaining the inconsistency, not to say the rank contradiction, represented by the contrast between the chapter on the civil religion and the rest of his work. Some have, accordingly,

---

[11] A. Cobban, *Rousseau and the Modern State* (London, 1964), 56.

[12] F. C. Green, *Jean-Jacques Rousseau: A Critical Study* (Cambridge, 1955), 304.

[13] R. M. Lemos, *Rousseau's Political Philosophy* (Athens, Ga., 1977), 212.

[14] R.-A. Leigh, 'Liberté et autorité dans le *Contrat social*', in *Jean-Jacques Rousseau et son Œuvre* (Paris, 1964), 258.

[15] M. Viroli, 'The Concept of *ordre* and the Language of Classical Republicanism in Jean-Jacques Rousseau', in A. Pagden (ed.), *The Languages of Political Theory in Early-Modern Europe* (Cambridge, 1987), 173.

[16] M. Cranston, *The Noble Savage: Jean-Jacques Rousseau* (London, 1991), 310, 312.

[17] A. Horowitz, *Rousseau, Nature, and History* (Toronto, 1987), 15.

advanced the thesis that there are two Rousseaus, one the champion of individual freedom and autonomy, and the other an unwitting forerunner of twentieth-century totalitarian theory and practice.[18] Frederick Watkins describes Rousseau as torn between 'liberal' and 'totalitarian' tendencies, with the latter predominating. When all is said and done, Rousseau is a 'totalitarian' or, worse, a 'totalitarian pessimist'.[19] All the offices and institutions he describes—the legislator, the general will, the civil religion—are 'strictly totalitarian in character'.[20] Invoking the liberal/totalitarian dichotomy and the distinction between means and ends, John Chapman holds that Rousseau 'is trying to achieve liberal ideas by totalitarian means'.[21] According to Ronald Grimsley, the chapter on the civil religion represented a change of mind. 'Rousseau's first intention in the *Contrat social*', Grimsley speculates, 'may have been to discuss the question of political right in purely human and secular terms, but on further reflection he was perhaps led to see that this could not be done satisfactorily without recourse to religious principles as the ultimate sanction of political laws.'[22] Grimsley's conjecture echoes those advanced earlier by P. M. Masson and Albert Schinz.[23] John Noone, by contrast, contends that the chapter on the civil religion amounts not to a change of mind but to an admission of failure—a secular republic that is both virtuous and free cannot be brought into existence, after all.[24] And John McManners attempts to explain Rousseau's apparent inconsistency by invoking an essentially psychological explanation.[25]

Noone's and McManners's interpretations are worth exploring in greater detail for at least two reasons. The first is that they attempt to answer the three questions I posed at the

[18] M. Berman, *The Politics of Authenticity* (New York, 1970); Horowitz, *Rousseau*, 15–16.

[19] F. Watkins (ed.), *Rousseau: Political Writings* (New York, 1953), pp. xxx–xxxi.

[20] Ibid., p. xxx.

[21] J. Chapman, *Rousseau, Totalitarian or Liberal?* (New York, 1956), 139.

[22] R. Grimsley (ed.), *Rousseau: Religious Writings* (Oxford, 1970), 201.

[23] P. M. Masson, *La Religion de Jean-Jacques Rousseau* (Paris, 1916), ii, ch. 5; A. Schinz, *La Pensée de Jean-Jacques Rousseau* (Paris, 1929), 364–75.

[24] J. B. Noone, *Rousseau's Social Contract* (Athens, Ga., 1980).

[25] J. McManners, *The Social Contract and Rousseau's Revolt against Society* (Leicester, 1968).

beginning. And, second, their very different interpretive strategies—Noone adopting a textual approach and McManners a
psychological one—are, besides being compatible and mutually reinforcing, both subtle and suggestive, even if arguably
mistaken.

Viewing the text of the *Social Contract* as a unified, dialecti-
cally unfolding drama, Noone attempts to account for the
appearance and the placement of Rousseau's civil religion. Its
sudden and unexpected appearance at the end of the *Social
Contract* marks a dramatically contrived moment of embarrassment, signalling that something has gone badly wrong
with Rousseau's argument up to that point. 'The Civil Creed
is an embarrassment', Noone maintains, 'not because of its
purported illiberality but because it undermines Rousseau's
original attempt to establish the conditions of a purely secular
morality.'[26] Rousseau's civil creed, on Noone's reading, 'is not
simply an afterthought; it is a counterthought', an author's
dramatic confession of failure:

Viewed dramatically, there is something very sad about the civil
creed. Up to its appearance the reader has been offered a novel theory of political obligation that is grounded in a very special type of
convention. This convention celebrates the sovereignty of man; it is a
convention that coerces man only to the extent that he voluntarily
accepts this coercion. Suddenly and without any prior indication,
Rousseau undermines the most essential principles of his theory:
consent once given is now irrevocable, and it is God, not man, that
sanctifies the contract. This is total surrender and he admits as
much.

Its author having surrendered, 'there is no sense going on, and
the *Social Contract* comes abruptly to an end'.[27] Having
begun with such high hopes for establishing the principles of
political right, the *Social Contract* thus ends in a confessional
mode with an admission of failure.

In a penetrating examination of Rousseau's 'revolt against
society', John McManners contends that the *Social Contract*
'does not fit comfortably with the rest of Rousseau's writings'.
And yet, 'In his own mind, at least, the *Social Contract* was
part of his general system of ideas.'[28] Taken as a whole, that

[26] Noone, *Rousseau's Social Contract*, 152.   [27] Ibid. 154.
[28] McManners, *Social Contract*, 3–4.

system amounts to an elaboration and defence of human freedom and autonomy. Yet the *Social Contract* abounds with
'totalitarian oddities', not the least of which is 'the Civil
Religion, [which] has the totalitarian bias that has caused so
much controversy'.[29] This of course poses a particularly difficult problem of interpretation: which is the real Rousseau—
the lover of liberty or the anticipator of and apologist for
totalitarian rule? 'His "totalitarian" passages', McManners
writes,

are so grim, and by contrast, his love of freedom was so intense,
that I cannot be satisfied that the paradox has been explained [by
other commentators]. The debate so far has fitted the *Social
Contract* into the pattern of Rousseau's thought at the expense of
pushing it out of the pattern of his genius. The full explanation is to
be found, I would maintain, in the context of his passionate,
intensely personal revolt against society.

To account for the totalitarian oddities, and 'the social-cement
religion of the *Social Contract*' in particular, we must look
more closely at the 'strange, tragic and attractive personality'
of Rousseau himself.[30]

After examining the evidence to be found in Rousseau's
corpus, and particularly in his private correspondence,
McManners concludes that 'the writer of the *Social Contract*
himself is not a totalitarian, though his book advocates totalitarian machinery', the most menacing piece of which is the
civil religion. He suggests 'that we stop trying to explain away
one or both of these facts, or to harmonize them, and that we
simply assume that Rousseau himself had no illusions. He
knew that the *Social Contract* had its sinister side: he was
telling us that this must be so.'[31] In the end McManners opts
for his own version of the two-Rousseaus thesis. On the one
hand, we have 'the revolutionary Rousseau', the bold legislator laying down the law for a republic of virtue, and, on the
other, the 'lonely Jean-Jacques', who, in revealing the 'totalitarian implications' of the institutions required to sustain it, in
effect admits that he himself would have been psychologically
unfit for life in such a society.[32] 'Like a bishop drawing up a

---

[29] McManners, *Social Contract,* 5, 13.   [30] Ibid. 5–6.
[31] Ibid. 13.   [32] Ibid. 17.

constitution for a colony of atheists, Rousseau, who has chosen another ideal from ours, writes in harsh terms to make us aware of the price we must pay.'[33]

Returning to the three questions posed at the outset, we can now see how Rousseau's latter-day defenders might answer them. To the first of these—what place does the civil religion occupy in Rousseau's political thought?—the answer is indeterminate, inasmuch as it seems so much at odds with the rest of his system. It is, in Green's phrase, a 'monstrous appendage' or, in McManners's term, an 'oddity', and a 'totalitarian' one at that. For Noone and McManners the chapter on the civil religion is something like a tocsin, serving to signal something to the attentive reader. To see exactly what signal is being sent, we need to turn to the second question: what was Rousseau doing in devising his scheme for a civil religion? Many commentators, Noone and McManners excepted, readily confess their puzzlement. Rousseau's intentions are in this instance unclear or puzzling, they say, and one might as well admit it. Advocating a closer examination of the text as a piece of political drama, Noone ventures to suggest another answer to our second question: Rousseau was admitting the failure of his, or indeed perhaps anyone's, attempt to provide a purely secular foundation for political obligation. McManners offers a rather different answer: Rousseau was warning his reader that a virtuous republic exacts an almost impossibly high price from those who would live in it. As I shall suggest in a moment, I believe that this is half right: Rousseau is indeed posting a warning, though not the one that McManners thinks he is posting. And finally, to the third query—how might we account for the placement of the plan for a civil religion at the very end of the *Social Contract*?—Noone's and McManners's answers are readily apparent. If Noone is right in claiming that Rousseau is admitting failure, it then follows that such an admission could come only at the end, after the attempt has already been made. And if McManners is correct in claiming that Rousseau is issuing a warning, he must first have described in some detail the thing against which he was warning.

[33] Ibid. 15.

It might appear, then, that, in accounting for the function and placement of Rousseau's *religion civile*, his critics have so far, and on the whole, had the better of the argument. Whatever one might think of their way of answering the three questions, they at least have answers to offer. Many, perhaps most, of Rousseau's would-be defenders readily admit their perplexity and, not infrequently, their utter bafflement as to what Rousseau's reasons might have been for introducing his scheme for a civil religion. Lacking any satisfactory alternative, they have little choice but to concede, however reluctantly, that Rousseau's critics are probably correct in their assessment of the ominous character and totalitarian implications of the civil religion. Sympathetic as they are, even Noone and McManners concede as much. I turn now to my reasons for thinking this concession unnecessary and misleading, not to say mistaken.

5.4 A BOOK AND ITS CONTEXT

The revisionist account of Rousseau's *religion civile* that I propose here rests both upon external or 'contextual' and internal or 'textual' considerations. The former considers the circumstances in which the *Social Contract* was written and rewritten; the latter concerns the relationship that Rousseau attempts to establish with the reader and the internal dialectic of the argument itself. Neither, taken alone, could possibly suffice to establish beyond reasonable doubt the validity of my, or any other, interpretation; but both, considered together, can at any rate enhance or diminish the plausibility of any particular interpretation. Lacking direct evidence of authorial intent, any conclusions to be reached must of necessity be conjectural ones inferred from reading and reflecting upon the text itself, in the light of what we know about its context and the circumstances of its composition. If this method needs a name, I suggest that we call it conjectural hermeneutics.

We know very little about the exact circumstances surrounding the composition of the *Social Contract*, save that it was originally a part of a larger work to be titled *Institutions politiques* on which Rousseau worked through the 1750s. This work, which he came to believe 'beyond my strength to complete', he finally abandoned and destroyed, except for the small portion comprising the first draft of what we now know as the *Social Contract*.[34] The latter in turn went through several drafts, none but the last of which included the chapter on the civil religion. That controversial chapter was apparently an afterthought, written with evident haste, added to the penultimate draft (the so-called 'Geneva manuscript') after it went to press in 1761, and subsequently revised.[35] This, in itself, proves nothing, of course; but it does serve to cast some doubt on his critics' claim that the chapter on the civil religion had from the beginning an integral, not to say indispensable, relation to the rest of the text—that it functions, for example, as a kind of logical conclusion to an argument whose premises the previous chapters are meant to articulate, or as the dramatic conclusion at which the author was aiming all along.

But if Rousseau's scheme for a civil religion was indeed an afterthought, why was it added? And what purpose was it intended to serve? Another piece of external evidence is sketchy but suggestive, especially in so far as it appears to link the role of Rousseau's ideal legislator to his scheme for a civil religion. The chapter on the civil religion was scribbled in some haste, not at the end of the manuscript but on the back of the sheets of the chapter on the legislator.[36] It therefore 'appears certain', says Derathé in his notes to the authoritative Pléiade edition, that, 'if Rousseau wrote the chapter on the back of the chapter on the legislator, it is because one naturally complements the other. The end of the chapter on the legislator broaches the problem of the relation between religion and politics, a problem to which the civil religion supplies a solution.'[37] I shall suggest in a moment that Derathé is, in this respect, at least half right: there is indeed a relation

---

[34] Rousseau, *Confessions* in *OC* i. 404–5, 516; *Contrat social* in *OC* iii. 349.

[35] *Political Writings of Jean-Jacques Rousseau*, ed. C. E. Vaughan (Cambridge, 1915), i. 434–5; *OC* iii. 1498.

[36] *SC*, bk. II, ch. 7.

[37] R. Derathé, 'Notes et variantes du *Contrat social*', *OC* iii. 1498.

between the two chapters, though not the one that he claims to detect.

5.5 AN ALTERNATIVE ACCOUNT

Any text—political, philosophical, poetical, legal, or literary—is an action or, rather, a series of actions. It is a species of communicative action attempted by an author and joined (or not) by a reader. Instead of asking abstractly what the text, or a particular passage within it, 'means', we should ask what action(s) an author is attempting to perform with and through it, and what sort of vocabulary was available to him or her in making this attempt.[38] As James Boyd White remarks, 'The basic question [to] ask of the texts we read, and of the particular performances within them [is], What kind of action with words is this?' And this question can in turn be 'broken down into two others: What kind of relationship does this writer establish with his language? and What kind of relationship does he establish with his audience or reader?'[39]

Few authors have been more acutely and even painfully aware than Rousseau was of the problematic character of the relation between author and audience, or more given to tracing these difficulties to the shortcomings of language itself. Again and again Rousseau complains of the imprecision and poverty of language, which should serve as a medium or bridge between people but more often functions as a barrier to communication and, hence, to communion and community.[40] And yet, as he announces at the beginning of the *Social Contract*, he is a political writer whose only medium is language. He cannot do anything by force or fiat but only by persuading with his pen. 'If asked whether I am a prince or a legislator to write about politics, I reply that I am neither; that is why I write about politics. If I were a prince or a legis-

---

[38] See Q. Skinner's methodological essays in J. Tully (ed.), *Meaning and Context: Quentin Skinner and his Critics* (Princeton, NJ, 1988), pt. II.

[39] J. B. White, *When Words Lose their Meaning* (Chicago, 1984), 6.

[40] In the *Second Discourse* (*OC* iii. 146–53) Rousseau alludes in passing to the linguistic constitution of human society, his own distinctive version of which he develops in his *Essai sur l'origine des langues* (*OC* v).

lator I would not waste my time saying what has to be done. I would do it or stay silent.' Having chosen to write rather than to remain silent, however, he cannot count on making himself understood, since language is at best an opaque medium.[41]

In attempting to render his message more persuasive and his medium more transparent, Rousseau has recourse to rhetorical strategies of several sorts. One of these is to draw distinctions between concepts whose meanings his readers are accustomed to confusing or conflating. Another is to alert the reader to the phenomenon of conceptual change (or more often, in his view, conceptual degeneration or corruption). Both strategies are evident, for example, in Rousseau's remark that

the true meaning of the word 'city' [*cité*] has been almost completely lost among modern men, most of whom mistake a town for a city and a town-dweller [*bourgeois*] for a citizen [*citoyen*]. They are unaware that houses make a town but that citizens make a city. . . . Only the French use the name citizens with complete familiarity, because they have no true idea of its meaning.[42]

Similarly, Rousseau warns repeatedly that the language he is forced to use is inadequate for his purposes. When, for example, he speaks of the necessity of 'drawing a clear distinction between the rights of the citizens and the sovereign', he addresses the reader in a footnote: 'Attentive readers, do not hasten to accuse me of contradicting myself here. I have been unable to avoid [the appearance of contradiction] in expressing myself, given the poverty of language; but wait.'[43] This combination of plea and warning recurs throughout the *Social Contract*.[44] Thus, for example, he begins the chapter 'On

[41] How one makes one's meaning, and perhaps oneself, 'transparent' through the opaque medium of language is both a persistent problem addressed by and a leitmotif running through all of Rousseau's writings. See J. Starobinski, *Jean-Jacques Rousseau, la transparence et l'obstacle* (Paris, 1957). It is just this Rousseauian ideal of 'transparency' that Foucault finds so objectionable: see Ch. 5.6 below.

[42] *SC* bk. I, ch. 6; *OC* iii. 361–2. See, further, C. Eisenmann, 'La Cité de Jean-Jacques Rousseau', in *Études sur le Contrat social*, 191–201; and G. Burdeau, 'Le Citoyen selon Rousseau', in ibid. 219–26.

[43] *SC* bk. II, ch. 4; *OC* iii. 373.

[44] Rousseau also issues similar warnings in *Émile* (*OC* iv. 345 n.) and elsewhere. In the *Jugement sur la polysynodie*, for example, he remarks rather

Government in General' by noting that the 'precise meaning of the word [government] has not heretofore been very well explained' and reminding the reader of his responsibility: 'I warn the reader that this chapter should be read carefully, and that I do not know the art of being clear for those who are unwilling to be attentive.'[45]

Rousseau's frequent lamentations about the inadequacy of the language available to him (and to the reader), his adverting to explicit definitions, his oft-times painstaking drawing of distinctions, and his repeated asides admonishing the reader represent nothing less than his attempt to construct—and to teach his reader to speak—a new political language.[46] If I read him aright, Rousseau was not simply some sort of an élitist attempting to reach an already existing audience of attentive readers.[47] He aimed instead to *create* it by teaching whoever reads him attentively to *be* that audience, and to do so for the reasons elaborated at the end of the present chapter.

From this perspective, then, Rousseau's strictures on the poverty and imprecision of language are not merely terminological or semantic complaints. He, like Hobbes, is instead reminding the reader that polities are communicatively constituted.[48] Language is the medium through which the range of

testily that 'there are many more readers who should learn to read than there are authors who should learn to be consistent' (*Political Writings*, ed. Vaughan, i. 422 n. 4).

[45] *SC* bk. III, ch. 1; *OC* iii. 395. On Rousseau's use of the term *gouvernement*, see J.-J. Chevallier, 'Le Mot et la notion de gouvernement chez Rousseau', in *Études sur le Contrat social*, 291–313.

[46] On attempts to reconstruct moral and political languages, see White, *When Words Lose their Meaning*; Pagden (ed.), *The Languages of Political Theory*; T. Ball, J. Farr, and R. L. Hanson (eds.), *Political Innovation and Conceptual Change* (Cambridge, 1989); and my *Transforming Political Discourse* (Oxford, 1988).

[47] *Contra* R. D. Masters, *The Political Philosophy of Rousseau* (Princeton, NJ, 1968), who suggests that Rousseau's asides to his 'attentive readers' indicate that the *Social Contract* 'is directed to a highly select audience, and not the general public' (306 n. 23). The audience that Rousseau is attempting to reach and influence consists, on Masters's reading, of 'ambitious politicians' and 'statesmen or potential statesmen' (pp. 309–13). For more 'democratic' or 'republican' readings of Rousseau's intentions, see J. Miller, *Rousseau: Dreamer of Democracy* (New Haven, Conn., 1984); and M. Viroli, *Jean-Jacques Rousseau and the 'well-ordered society'* (Cambridge, 1988), esp. ch. 4.

[48] See Ch. 4 below.

political possibilities is constructed. To the degree that a people's language is impoverished or otherwise inadequate, so too is their communication, and hence their community. Conversely, to the extent that their language is rich in its range of communicative possibilities, so will their common life be enriched and made more meaningful.[49] This may serve to explain why Rousseau, apprenticed as a child to a Swiss watchmaker, remained throughout his life a careful and conscientious craftsman of words if not of watches.

It is just here that the relation between the chapter on the civil religion and that on the legislator begins to come into clearer view. Rousseau's professed difficulty in communicating with his reader parallels precisely that of the legislator in constituting a new political community:

Sages who wish to speak their own language to the common people [*vulgaire*] cannot make themselves understood. There are a thousand sorts of ideas which it is impossible to translate into the language of ordinary folk. . . . Being unable to use either force or reasoned argument, he must therefore have recourse to authority of another order, which can motivate without violence and persuade without convincing.

The lack of a common moral and political language, Rousseau continues, 'is what has traditionally forced the fathers of nations to have recourse to the intervention of heaven and to attribute to the gods a wisdom that is actually their own'.[50] Citing Machiavelli's similar observation in the *Discourses*,[51] Rousseau agrees that legislators have heretofore had no other way of 'carrying along those who cannot be convinced by human prudence'.[52]

Rousseau's evident indebtedness to Machiavelli has often

---

[49] This theme, implicit throughout the *Social Contract*, is rendered explicit at the end of the *Essay on the Origin of Languages* in the chapter titled 'The Relation of Languages to Governments' (*OC* v, ch. 20). See, further, J. P. Dobel, 'The Role of Language in Rousseau's Political Thought', *Polity*, 18 (1986), 638–58.

[50] *SC*, bk. II, ch. 7; *OC* iii. 383.

[51] Machiavelli, *Discourses*, bk. I, ch. 11.

[52] *SC* bk. II, ch. 7; *OC* iii. 383–4. Cf. C. Kelly, 'To Persuade without Convincing: The Language of Rousseau's Legislator', *AJPS* 31 (1987), 321–35; S. A. Hadari, ' "Persuader sans convaincre" ', *WPQ* 39 (1986), 504–19.

been noted, of course, and some commentators have contended that the remarks about religion in the chapter on the legislator and the very idea of a civil religion is scarcely more than an extension and elaboration of Machiavelli's discussion of the central role of religion in the founding of Rome.[53] That Rousseau both admires and borrows from Machiavelli is undeniable. But we need to ask what Rousseau is *doing* in relying on Machiavelli and how what he is doing affects and shapes his relation with the reader, particularly as regards the status and point of the civil religion.

In relying on Machiavelli Rousseau appears to be attempting to do at least three things—in addition, that is, to attacking the royal author of *Anti-Machiavel*, Frederick the Great.[54] The first is to show the reader that appearances—and reputations—can be misleading. The second is to suggest several affinities between himself and 'this profound political thinker' and 'lover of liberty'.[55] And the third is once again to remind the reader of the importance of reading attentively and carefully. Machiavelli has heretofore had 'only superficial or corrupt readers'. Read aright, even *The Prince* is a book of republicans.'[56] Rousseau quotes the following remark from Machiavelli's *Discourses*: 'Truly there never was a legislator who, in introducing extraordinary laws into a country, did not have recourse to God, lest his system be rejected outright; for the knowledge of the wise man may not suffice to persuade others.'[57] Rousseau, as we saw earlier, gives a linguistic twist to Machiavelli's remark: legislators have heretofore had recourse to the trappings of religion—miracles, dogmas, revelations, and the rest—because their subjects are unable to understand the language in which the legislator himself thinks and acts.

But Rousseau then goes on to suggest that this subterfuge will no longer suffice. 'Illusions can form only a temporary bond; wisdom alone can make it endure.'[58] No new Numa can expect to found a long-lived republic by establishing a

---

[53] Derathé, 'La Religion civile', 164–5.
[54] Masters, *Political Philosophy of Rousseau*, 306–7.
[55] *SC* bk. III, ch. 6; *OC* iii. 409, 1480 n.
[56] *SC* bk. III, ch. 6; *OC* iii. 409.   [57] *SC* bk. II, ch. 7; *OC* iii. 384.
[58] Ibid.

religion. And yet, in the last chapter of the *Social Contract*, Rousseau himself has recourse to the trappings of a religion, including oaths, dogmas, and the rest. Why?

The answer is, I believe, to be found in the relationship that Rousseau is attempting to establish with the reader.[59] My conjecture is that the chapter on the civil religion serves as a test—a final examination, as it were—for the reader. Its purpose is to determine whether the reader has learnt to speak the language of the legislator, so as not to need (and indeed to be immune from) the conjuring tricks and illusions on which earlier founders had to rely. He asks, in effect: Attentive reader, do you still need this? If you do, you have not understood what has gone before. You have not yet learnt the language of the legislator. If you do not understand and speak this language, however, you are unequipped to legislate for yourself. And if you cannot legislate for yourself, you cannot be truly free, as only a citizen and member of the sovereign can be. After all, Rousseau defines freedom as 'obedience to a law which one has prescribed for oneself'. To be truly free means to be 'master of oneself'.[60]

This is a far cry from the proto-totalitarian thinker whose scheme for a civil religion proposes an 'examination [*inspection*] that bears a terrible resemblance to an inquisition'.[61] If I am right, the chapter is itself intended to function as an *inspection* in which the reader is invited, in effect, to examine him or herself to see what, if anything, has been learnt. The practice of having the reader periodically examine him or herself was not a wholly novel one. It was, in fact, a fairly common eighteenth-century literary device adopted by writers as different as Swift, Johnson, and Jane Austen.[62] That Rousseau should have adopted such a device comes as no surprise. For he saw himself as an educator and his *Social Contract*

---

[59] See R. J. Ellrich, *Rousseau and his Reader* (Chapel Hill, NC, 1969). Unfortunately, Ellrich's analysis of the *Social Contract* (pp. 35–8) is sketchy and superficial. Much more useful are M. Launay, 'L'Art de l'écrivain dans le *Contrat social*', in *Études sur le Contrat social*, 351–78; *Le Vocabulaire politique de J.-J. Rousseau* (Geneva, 1977); and *Jean-Jacques Rousseau, écrivain politique* (Geneva, 1989), esp. 402–52.

[60] *SC*, bk. I, ch. 8; *OC* iii. 365.

[61] Derathé, 'La Religion civile', 167.

[62] White, *When Words Lose their Meaning*, ch. 7.

and *Émile* (both published in the same year and meant to form a pair) as educational treatises.[63] Moreover, Rousseau's remarks on religion at the end of the chapter on the legislator is immediately followed by that 'On the People', which begins by stressing the importance of an 'examination' preparatory to legislation: 'Just as an architect, before erecting a great building, observes and tests the soil to see if it can bear the load, so does the founding sage not begin by drafting laws that are intrinsically good, but examines beforehand [*examine auparavant*] whether the people for whom they are meant are able to support them.'[64] My conjecture is that the chapter on the civil religion serves as an *examen de soi*, a self-examination by means of which the reader may determine whether he or she is able to legislate for him or herself and is therefore capable of supporting the full weight of self-government. Its point, in short, is pedagogical.[65] If I am right, then, Rousseau's *Social Contract*, considered as an educational treatise (as its companion work *Émile* assuredly is), attempts to educate and examine the reader, and in a way that might astonish us but which would scarcely have surprised an attentive eighteenth-century reader.

The evidence in support of this conjecture is, at best, circumstantial. But it does at least allow us to clear up a number of puzzles and to answer the three key questions that I posed at the outset. Before considering those questions in the light

[63] J. J. Rousseau, *Correspondence complète* (Geneva, 1969), ix. 345.

[64] *SC*, bk. II, ch. 8; *OC* iii. 384–5.

[65] A very different version of this claim is defended by Glum, who—addressing an issue of considerable importance in post-Second World War West Germany—views Rousseau's *religion civile* as an attempt to lay the groundwork for a system of democratic civic education. See F. Glum, *Jean-Jacques Rousseau: Religion und Staat* (Munich, 1956). In a similar spirit Levine suggests that, since 'the moral and intellectual capacities of the people, even of citizens of a *de jure* state, are not fully developed ... what Rousseau is proposing is a kind of transitional institution for the blind multitude emerging from the state of nature. The dogmas of civil religion, then, might just be a golden lie, a legitimating myth' (A. Levine, *The Politics of Autonomy* (Amherst, 1976), 184). Both, I believe, are right to suggest that the purpose of the civil religion is essentially educative, but wrong in claiming that Rousseau was actually proposing that it be put into practice as an agency or instrument of civic education or political socialization. The educative moves in Rousseau's argument are made in the text itself, not outside it, with the reader as active participant and dialogical partner.

of the interpretation advanced here, consider several pieces of evidence drawn from other of Rousseau's works. Towards the end of *Émile* Rousseau offers a synopsis of the *Contrat social* which, rather intriguingly, makes no mention whatever of the civil religion.[66] This could, of course, be an oversight on Rousseau's part; or it could be that he thought the civil religion insufficiently important to include in his summary. Neither of these strikes me as a satisfactory explanation. More satisfactory, perhaps—and more in line with the interpretation advanced here—is that Émile, having been educated aright, has no *need* of the civil religion or of the sort of self-examination that the chapter on the civil religion is supposed to provide. He already knows what he needs to know in order to lead a life of virtue and so, presumably, does the reader.

Consider next two further pieces of evidence. Two of Rousseau's other, later works—*Considerations on the Government of Poland* (written in 1772) and the *Constitutional Project for Corsica* (drafted in 1765)—refer repeatedly to the principles and precepts of the *Contrat social* but—again and perhaps significantly—neither makes any mention at all of any scheme for a civil religion. If Rousseau believed that some sort of civil religion was necessary for a well-ordered polity, why did he not make provision for one in the Polish and Corsican cases? One possibility immediately suggests itself: the scheme for the civil religion in the *Social Contract* is not to be taken literally, as a political prescription or constitutional requirement, but is instead meant to serve a different function altogether; it is, in effect, a means whereby the reader might examine himself to see whether he has learnt to think in the language of the legislator, so as to be able to legislate for himself.

I conclude by returning to the three questions I posed at the outset. First, what place does the civil religion occupy in Rousseau's political philosophy? It would appear to occupy a peripheral place, not because it is unimportant but because it is a literary device, a rhetorical and argumentative stratagem of a certain sort. It enables the reader to examine himself, so as to see whether, or to what extent, he has learnt the lessons

---

[66] See *Émile*, bk. V; *OC* iv. 842–8.

that the *Social Contract* has to teach. This, in turn, takes us to our second question: what were Rousseau's intentions in devising and deploying such a stratagem? We cannot say for certain, of course; but it is at least plausible to infer, on the basis of textual evidence and in the light of the admittedly scanty contextual evidence available to us, that Rousseau may have intended to supply the reader with a way of determining whether, or to what extent, he or she had learnt the language of the legislator, so as not to need a Numa to provide a chimerical foundation for the state and the loyalty of its citizens. In so doing he was posting a warning: those who have not learnt this language cannot be free, for they will lack the linguistic resources required to make, to understand, and to obey the laws under which free and sovereign citizens must live, if they are to remain both free and sovereign. And finally, why does the chapter on the civil religion come at the end of the *Social Contract* rather than, say, at the end of or immediately after the chapter on the legislator? Although arguably mistaken, my answer is at any rate simple and straightforward: where else does an examination belong, if not at the end of the course? Such an examination allows the reader to determine whether he or she has learnt the meaning and use of the concepts constitutive of free and sovereign citizenship that it is the aim of the *Social Contract* to teach.

5.6 CODA:ROUSSEAU AND FOUCAULT

The history of political thought is written, and problems posed and (sometimes) resolved, with present-day problems and perspectives in mind. It might therefore be argued that the spectre of the 'totalitarian' Rousseau (or Plato, or Hegel, or Marx, for that matter) was an artefact of the Communist spectre and the Cold War, and, with their passing, all such interpretations are now therefore *passé*.

One could of course construct a number of arguments to the contrary. For one, interpretations, or rather lines of interpretation, are historically situated but need not be *that* tightly tied to specific historical contexts. That is, I believe, a plausible objection, and one on which I have relied repeatedly throughout the present volume. But another, and I believe a better, counter-argument would, in this particular instance, take something like the form that Michel Foucault sketched toward the end of his life.

From his work on Bentham and panopticism to his last lectures, on a topic that he called 'governmentality', Foucault in effect revived the spectre of the 'totalitarian' Rousseau.[67] Rousseau, on Foucault's retelling, advanced a nightmarish vision of virtuous citizens 'normalized' and subjugated through the power of all over each. The society described in the *Social Contract* is the completest and most perfect despotism yet devised, precisely because each member wills for all, and all for each, and all think themselves free and autonomous. Everyone is constantly under the gaze of everyone else; each is subjected, as Rousseau says repeatedly, to 'examinations' and 'inspections' of the most invasive sort. Rousseau's republic of virtue is, on Foucault's reading, the forerunner of the 'carceral society' or the 'panoptic machine' in which we now largely live.[68] Rousseau, in short, paves the way for Bentham and the Panopticon:

Bentham was the complement to Rousseau. What in fact was the Rousseauist dream? . . . It was the dream of a transparent society, visible and legible in each of its parts, the dream of there no longer existing any zones of darkness [or] of disorder. It was the dream that each individual, whatever position he occupied, might be able to see the whole of society, that men's hearts should communicate, their vision be unobstructed by obstacles.[69]

Rousseau's dream of transparency was Foucault's worst nightmare.[70]

Foucault's reasons for linking Rousseau to Bentham's Panopticon and the modern mania for 'governmentality' are sketchy but suggestive. One is the idea of the general will or conception of the common good that all are obligated to seek and to uphold. This in turn requires the exercise of the sort of 'confessional' or 'pastoral power' that constitutes the thera-

---

[67] M. Foucault, *Power/Knowledge* (New York, 1980), ch. 8; 'Governmentality', in G. Burchell, C. Gordon, and P. Miller (eds.), *The Foucault Effect* (Chicago, 1991), ch. 4.

[68] See Ch. 7 below. [69] Foucault, *Power/Knowledge*, 152.

[70] J. Miller, *The Passion of Michel Foucault* (New York, 1993), 311.

peutic relationship—and that characterizes Rousseau's *religion civile*. By making statecraft into soulcraft, this ersatz religion regulates conduct by policing one's innermost thoughts and beliefs, so that nothing remains private or hidden from public view. Foucault reads Rousseau, as he readily acknowledges, through the interpretation advanced by Jean Staobinski in *Jean-Jacques Rousseau: La Transparence et l'obstacle*.[71] 'Transparency'—the public visibility of self and soul—is 'the great Rousseauist theme' to which Bentham gives actual architectural expression in the panopticon.[72]

Foucault thus provides, in effect, a post-Cold War revival of the 'totalitarian' interpretation of Rousseau's political thought, and of the *Contrat social* in particular. In this interpretation—now redubbed the 'governmentalist' view— Rousseau's civil religion resumes its central role and regains its totalitarian aura and implications. This, as we have seen, is a powerful and oft-stated criticism, and ought not be dismissed lightly—especially when advanced by a philosopher of Foucault's stature.

But, suggestive as it is, Foucault's interpretation seems to me to miss much of the power—and quite possibly the intent—of Rousseau's *Social Contract*, and the role of his *religion civile* in particular. I have tried to offer an alternative interpretation of the role and site of the self-examinations and inspections that Rousseau requires. If I am right—and I am the first to admit that I may not be—then these 'inspections' are exercises through which the reader remakes himself in ways that enhance rather than diminish his autonomy. They belong, one might say, to that set of practices that Foucault elsewhere terms *le souci de soi*, 'the care of the self',[73] but with an important political difference. Rousseau is concerned, in effect, with *le souci de soi civique*, with educating his readers in ways that will enable them to cultivate their civic selves. His much-maligned scheme for a civil religion may be understood as a means to that end.

[71] Foucault, *Power/Knowledge*, 152.

[72] Ibid., ch. 8; M. Foucault, *Discipline and Punish* (New York, 1977).

[73] M. Foucault, *The History of Sexuality*, iii. *The Care of the Self* (New York, 1986).

6

THE SURVIVOR AND THE SAVANT: TWO SCHEMES FOR CIVIL RELIGION COMPARED

> We know, and what is better we feel inwardly, that religion is the basis of civil society, and the source of all good and of all comfort.
>
> Edmund Burke

6.1 INTRODUCTION

In the preceding chapter I examined Rousseau's scheme for a civil religion. Here I want to compare and contrast two later and very different versions of civil religion, as advanced by James Mill and Auguste Comte. Like Rousseau's, Mill's civil religion is supposed to serve an essentially educative function, sharpening the citizens' critical faculties and civic capacities. Comte, by contrast, views religion rather differently. The comparison can, I think, help us to see each thinker in a new light, and to show something of the several shapes, sources, and uses to which the idea of a civil religion has been put.

It might seem odd, at first sight, to attempt to draw any parallels between two thinkers as different as James Mill and Comte. One was a Scottish protestant turned Utilitarian sceptic, the other a French Catholic turned Saint-Simonian system-builder. Their educations and political milieux differed markedly, Mill having been educated for the ministry at the University of Edinburgh at the end of the eighteenth century and Comte in medicine and mathematics at the École Polytechnique early in the nineteenth. Their theoretical vocabularies were vastly different, Mill's being associationist and Utilitarian and Comte's Positivist and Saint-Simonian. Yet

despite these differences there are, as John Stuart Mill remarked, several important affinities if not similarities between
his father's views and Comte's. My aim here is less to recount
the similarities that the younger Mill purported to see, than to
point to one that he did not detect—namely, that his father,
like Comte, advanced a scheme for what might best be termed
a civil religion. Although J. S. Mill later denounced Comte's
scheme, he did not see fit to notice, much less criticize, his
father's. Just why this should be so is one of the many minor
mysteries of that eminent thinker's career, and one on which I
shall attempt, along the way, to shed a little light. My main
purpose, however, is to make good my claim that the elder
Mill did indeed describe and defend such a scheme, and to
trace it to its probable source in Adam Smith and the social
thought of the Scottish Enlightenment.

6.2 J. S. MILL ON COMTE AND RELIGION

In his correspondence with Comte in the early 1840s John
Stuart Mill noticed several similarities between the Scottish
and the French systems of education, between the thought of
the Scottish Enlightenment and Positivism, and, more particularly, between his father's philosophy and Comte's systematic
sociology. An educated Scotsman had, he thought, more in
common with an educated Frenchman than with any Englishman, and the two could in many respects be compared, to the
distinct detriment of the English. Scotsmen and Frenchmen,
for example, were fortunately free of the atheoretical and 'too
exclusively practical' character of the English, among whom
'the true scientific spirit is very rare'—'save perhaps amongst
the Scots, whose public education has a character more
French than English'.[1] This might then serve to explain why
Comtian positivism could expect to find more adherents in
Scotland than in England.[2]

[1] J. S. Mill to Auguste Comte, 28 Jan. 1843, in F. E. Mineka (ed.), *The
Earlier Letters of John Stuart Mill*, in Mill, *CW* xiii. 566 (my trans.). For an
incisive account of 'the system of the North', see S. Collini, D. Winch, and J.
Burrow, *That Noble Science of Politics* (Cambridge, 1983), ch. 1.

[2] Mill to Comte, 5 Oct. 1844, *CW* xiii. 638–9. Mill's prediction proved to
be rather wide of the mark. Comtian Positivism was to find fewer adherents

The theoretical temper of the Scots is especially evident, the younger Mill remarked, in the great figures of the Scottish Enlightenment 'from Kaimes and Ferguson up to and including my father who died in 1836, being the last survivor of this great school'.[3] The Scottish survivor and the French savant had, he averred, quite a lot in common. Both, after all, claimed to have constructed a systematic science of society; both advanced a rudimentary version of the covering-law model of explanation; both subscribed to a 'stage' theory of human history; and both believed that religion belonged to an earlier, more primitive stage of moral and mental development and was soon to be superseded by a more enlightened scientific outlook.

The favourable comparisons drawn between his father and Comte ceased, however, when in the 1850s Comte proceeded to elaborate his grandiose scheme for a Religion of Humanity. To recount in any detail the features of this ersatz religion is not my purpose here. It must suffice to recall that Comte attempted to establish a system of social worship, or 'sociolatry', with its own rituals, saints, sacred texts, prayers, and other paraphernalia, all to be presided over by a priestly caste with himself as Pope.[4] In several respects the turn taken by Comte's later thought seems very strange indeed, especially in light of the 'law' which divides human history into three stages—the theological, the metaphysical, and the positive—with the first further subdivided into the fetishistic, polytheistic, and monotheistic phases. The Religion of Humanity that caps the Positivist stage looks in some respects like a retreat to the first, or theological stage, in that it combines fetishism with the worship of 'The Great Being' (*Le Grand Être*), now

amongst the Scots than amongst the English. Comte's English disciples—Richard Congreve, G. H. Lewes, Harriet Martineau, *et al.*—also tended to be rather less critical of the master's *système* than were such Scottish admirers as Edward Caird, Professor ôf Moral Philosophy at Glasgow. See E. Caird, *The Social Philosophy and Religion of Comte* (Glasgow, 1885). On the diffusion and reception of Comtian Positivism, see W. M. Simon, *European Positivism in the Nineteenth Century* (Ithaca, NY, 1963).

[3] Mill to Comte, 28 Jan. 1843, in *CW* xiii. 566.

[4] See, *inter alia*, Auguste Comte, *System of Positive Polity* (1854; trans. R. Congreve, London, 1877), iv *passim*, and his more popular *A General View of Positivism* (1857); trans. J. H. Bridges (New York, 1957), esp. ch. 6, and *The Catechism of Positive Religion*, trans. R. Congreve, 3rd edn. (London, 1891).

identified as Humanity itself. The critical intellect is to be subordinated to sentimental feelings of social solidarity.

This scheme the younger Mill denounced as 'the completest system of spiritual and temporal despotism, which ever yet emanated from a human brain, unless possibly that of Ignatius Loyola'. Comte, he continues,

> put[s] to an end the notion that no effectual moral authority can be maintained over society without the aid of religious belief; for Comte's work recognizes no religion except that of Humanity, yet it leaves an irresistible conviction that any moral beliefs, concurred in by the community generally, may be brought to bear upon the whole conduct and lives of its individual members with an energy and potency truly alarming to think of. The book [Comte's *Système de politique positive*] stands as a monumental warning to thinkers on society and politics, of what happens when once men lose sight, in their speculations, of the value of Liberty and of Individuality.[5]

Comte's Religion of Humanity, he concludes, is nothing less than 'an elaborate system for the total suppression of all independent thought'.[6]

The younger Mill's animus towards Comte was in due course generalized to include not only French philosophers but Frenchmen generally. Their love of 'universal systematizing, systematizing, systematizing' was part and parcel of 'the mania for regulation by which Frenchmen are distinguished among Europeans, and M. Comte among Frenchmen'.[7]

The earlier comparisons between the French and the Scots, and between Comte and the 'last survivor' of the Scottish school, are notable by their absence in Mill's *Autobiography* and elsewhere. And yet, I want to suggest, there is at least one further respect in which he might have compared his father's later speculations with those of Comte. For, like Comte, Mill in his last years elaborated his own scheme for a civil religion.

---

[5] J. S. Mill, *Autobiography*, ed. J. Stillinger (Oxford, 1971), 127–8. Cf. also *On Liberty* (Everyman edn., 1951), 101.

[6] J. S. Mill, *Auguste Comte and Positivism* (1865, Ann Arbor; Mich., 1961), 169.

[7] Ibid. 141, 153. 'The *fons errorum* in M. Comte's later speculations is this inordinate demand for "unity" and "systematization" ' (p. 141). By contrast, 'If I am asked what system of political philosophy I substituted for that which, as a philosophy, I had abandoned, I answer, no system . . .' (*Autobiography*, 97).

Before describing the main features of that scheme, however, we need to take note of several pertinent biographical details.

6.3 THE 'SURVIVOR'

Of James Mill's early years in Scotland, we know very little save the following.[8] He was born in 1773, the eldest son of James Mill (or Milne), a cobbler of Northwater Bridge in the Parish of Logie Pert in the county of Forfar. His socially ambitious mother was determined that her son should rise in the world. One of the few routes then open to young Scotsmen of a middling station was the ministry, for which the young James Mill was educated, first at Montrose Academy and later at the University of Edinburgh, thanks in part to the patronage of Sir John and Lady Jane Stuart of Fettercairn. Mill enrolled in Edinburgh in 1790, studying classics and moral philosophy (the latter with Dugald Stewart) before specializing in more narrowly theological studies. In 1797 he completed his studies in Divinity and was ordained as a minister in the Church of Scotland. Mill's career in the Kirk proved to be short-lived. Unable to secure a parish of his own, he rode the circuit as an itinerant preacher, his saddle-bags stuffed with sermons said to be learned but largely unintelligible to his simple flock. After this there followed a period of several years during which Mill made his living as a tutor before leaving for London in 1802 to make his name as an author and journalist.

Mill's first published writings show him to be both religiously orthodox and rather to the right of centre. He wrote for the conservative *Anti-Jacobin Review* and from 1802 to 1806 edited the *Literary Review*. Mill also translated Villers's history of the Reformation (1805), his notes to which are of interest for what they reveal about the religious views that Mill then held. He makes the observation—more sociological than theological—that atheism is most commonly found in Catholic countries like France and that its presence in Protestant countries can be explained as a fashionable affectation

---

[8] A. Bain, *James Mill: A Biography* (London, 1882).

amongst intellectual francophiles. 'The two most celebrated
infidels we had had in this country, Hume and Gibbon, had
spent a great part of their youth in France, and were intoxi-
cated with the vanity of imitating Frenchmen.'[9] And elsewhere
Mill denounced the 'monstrous reasonings' of those 'infidels',
Hobbes and Hume.[10] For a time after his marriage in 1804
Mill went to church, and all of his children—including the
eldest, John Stuart—were baptized and were while young
taken to church every Sunday. One visitor to the Mill house-
hold recalls the precocious John Stuart saying that 'the two
greatest books were Homer and the Bible'.[11]

It may be worth noting the difficulty of reconciling the foregoing with at least two of the younger Mill's later recollec-
tions. The first is that his father 'reject[ed] all that is called
religious belief'.[12] The second is his no less startling assertion
that he was 'one of the very few examples, in this country, of
one who has, not thrown off religious belief, but never had it:
I grew up in a negative state with regard to it'.[13] That these
two statements may reflect the later religious views of the two
Mills would be difficult to deny; but there is reason to doubt
their reliability as regards the earlier religious views of the
elder Mill.

Alexander Bain maintains that '[James] Mill's views on
Religion took their final shape between 1808 and 1810', the
former being the year in which Mill met Bentham for the first
time. 'His acquaintance with Bentham', Bain continues, must
have

hastened his course towards infidelity ... Bentham never in so many
words publicly avowed himself an atheist, but he was so in substance
... It is quite certain, however, that the whole tone of conversation
in Bentham's more select circle, was atheistic. In Mill's own family,

---

[9] Mill's notes to Charles Villers, *An Essay on the Spirit and Influence of
The Reformation*, trans. J. Mill (London, 1805), as quoted in Bain, *James
Mill*, 89–90.
[10] James Mill, *An Essay on the Impolicy of a Bounty on the Exportation of
Grain* (1804), in *James Mill: Selected Economic Writings*, ed. D. Winch
(Chicago, 1966), 47.
[11] Quoted in Bain, *James Mill*, 90.
[12] J. S. Mill, *Autobiography*, 25–6.
[13] Ibid. 27–8. On the unreliability of Mill's *Autobiography*, see
W. Thomas, 'John Stuart Mill and the Uses of Autobiography', *History*, 56
(1971), 341–59.

there is a vague tradition that his breaking with the church and religion followed his introduction to Bentham.[14]

Yet this attractively simple account of an anti-religious conversion may be rather wide of the mark in several respects. Bain, like many later commentators, credits Bentham with more intellectual influence over Mill than he actually possessed. Mill's mind had a shape of its own well before he met Bentham. Mill himself said that he 'took no man for a master' and that 'the sympathy of common opinions' first drew him to Bentham.[15] Likewise John Mill maintained that his father 'was anything but Bentham's mere follower or disciple . . . His mind and Bentham's were essentially of different construction.'[16] And, contrary to the claim that Mill became an atheist as a result of his acquaintance with Bentham, we have his son's testimony that, despite his father's scepticism, 'dogmatic atheism he looked upon as absurd'.[17] Although clearly circumstantial, such evidence casts some doubt upon the claim that Mill was in any simple sense an unbeliever.

Infidel or no, the elder Mill retained throughout his life a Scottish Protestant's hostility towards 'priestly' religions of every description. His earliest published writings contain enthusiastic endorsements of Villers's criticisms of Catholicism, along with a defence of Luther and the Reformation. His *History of British India*, begun in 1806 and completed in 1817, which is exceedingly critical of Hindu religious beliefs and practices, often reads like a thinly veiled critique of established religions and orthodoxies of any sort. Mill became increasingly critical of the Church of England, and towards the end of his life quite outspoken in opposing it.[18] Between

---

[14] Bain, *James Mill*, 88–9. Given his story of Mill's purported conversion to atheism, Bain is rather at a loss to explain why 'Mill never lost his interest in theology' (p. 206).

[15] James Mill, *Fragment on Mackintosh* (1835; 2nd edn. London, 1870), 124.

[16] J. S. Mill, *Autobiography*, 122.   [17] Ibid. 25.

[18] Such criticism still took some courage. The first quarter of the nineteenth century saw several well-publicized trials in which free-thinkers were prosecuted and convicted. In 1822 Richard Carlile, editor of the radical *Black Dwarf*, had with his wife and sister been prosecuted for 'publications hostile to Christianity'. For fear of prosecution, Bentham had been dissuaded from publishing his *Church-of-Englandism* and in 1823 the *Morning Chronicle* prudently declined to publish two pseudonymous letters by

1812 and 1835 the elder Mill wrote several articles critical of established religion, and the Church of England in particular. But his *pièce de résistance* was published in the year preceding his death. 'The Church, and its Reform', which appeared in the first number of the *London Review* in 1835, consisted of an assortment of arguments, several but by no means all of which can be construed as Benthamite. But the most notable feature of this article, for my present purposes, is that Mill in it advances his own utopian scheme for a civil religion.

6.4 RELIGION UNREFORMED

Upon its publication in 1835 Mill's 'The Church, and its Reform' caused a minor furore. 'The immediate effect of such an outspoken criticism of the Church', writes Bain, 'was to damage the circulation of the *Review*', whose apologetic editors never succeeded in effacing 'the suspicion of its irreligious tendency'.[19] Mill's article was indeed doubly offensive to orthodox Anglicans. For besides presuming to criticize the creeds and practices of the Church he also proposed to 'reform' it in several remarkably radical ways. Mill's first move was not so novel as his second. The Church had often been criticized, circumspectly if not openly, by Bentham and the other philosophic radicals. Simplifying somewhat, their criticisms—as found, for example, in Bentham's *Church-of-Englandism and its Catechism Examined* (1818) and *Not Paul but Jesus* (1823), and in George Grote's pseudonymous *Analysis of the Influence of Natural Religion on the Temporal Happiness of Mankind* (1829)—consist, in the main, of enumerating the many ways in which organized religion fails to promote, much less to maximize, human happiness.

Several of Mill's criticisms of the English Church amount to little more than variations on and reiterations of the standard Utilitarian refrain, to which Mill adds a Dissenter's disdain for creeds and rituals. 'The present ecclesiastical establishment

J. S. Mill favouring 'free publication of all opinions on religion' (J. S. Mill, *Autobiography*, 54).

[19] Bain, *James Mill*, 389.

in England', Mill writes, 'is a perfect nullity in respect to good, but an active and powerful agent in the production of evil.'[20] Mill then proceeds to advance and defend two propositions. The first is 'that the only services which are obligatory upon the Church of England clergy ... are ceremonies from which no advantages can be derived'. The second is 'that the services they might render, in raising the moral and intellectual character of the people, are not obligatory'.[21] As instances of the first Mill mentions meaningless sermons and the mind-numbing 'repetition of creeds'. None of the sermons he has ever heard (and preached?) was 'good for anything. They may be characterized as a parcel of vapid commonplaces, delivered in vague and vapouring phrases . . .'[22] As for the recital of creeds, they are at best 'purely ceremonial' and at worst 'a forced declaration of belief'.[23] Even more insidious is the idea that one ought to be rewarded for believing one way and punished for believing in other, unacceptable ways. 'To hold out rewards for believing one way, punishment for believing another way, is', says Mill, 'to suborn belief; to create . . . a habit of forcing a belief; that is, of dealing dishonestly with their own convictions'. Moreover,

as soon as a man is broken in to this mental habit, not only is the power of sound judgment destroyed within him, but the moral character does not escape uninjured. The man in whose breast this habit is created, never sees anything in an opinion, but whether it is agreeable to his interest or not. Whether it has been founded on evidence or not, he has been trained to neglect. Truth or falsehood in matters of opinion is no longer with him the first consideration.[24]

The Church's practice of punishing morally meritorious conduct, and of rewarding mindless obedience, 'poison[s] morality in the very fountain of life. The fine feeling of moral obligation is gone in a mind wherein the habit of insincerity is engendered.'[25]

Not only does the Church reward those who should be punished and punish those who should be rewarded; its system of rewards and punishments is doubly defective, being at

---

[20] James Mill, 'The Church, and its Reform', *London Review*, I (1835), 257–95, at 259.
[21] Ibid. 260.   [22] Ibid. 269.   [23] Ibid. 261.
[24] Ibid. 266–7.   [25] Ibid. 261.

once cruel and inefficient. It is cruel in that the ultimate punishment is eternal hell-fire; and it is inefficient in that punishment is neither proportional nor proximate. To use the threat
of eternal damnation as a punishment for a wide variety of
offenses is not to fit the punishment to the crime. Moreover,
the prospect of so distant a punishment, however dire, is not
sufficient to deter would-be offenders.[26] In analysing the irrational and inefficient system of religious rewards and punishment, it might appear that Mill is merely echoing Bentham.
To these Benthamite strictures, however, Mill adds a Platonic
supplement.

I have argued elsewhere that Mill's theory of punishment
and his plans for prison reform reveal a deeper debt to Plato
than to Bentham.[27] The claim can, I believe, be extended to
Mill's arguments in favour of religious reform. Just as Plato
had criticized the poets for making the gods appear to be stu-
pid, silly, and vain, so Mill criticizes the Church and its clergy
for making God seem cruel and capricious. For example, God
is said to be omniscient. And yet to tell Him 'unceasingly of
our wants, implies that He needs to be told of them'. God is
made, moreover, to appear 'imperfect both in wisdom and in
goodness'. To ask Him 'continually to do things for us,
implies our belief that he would not do them for us'. That is,
we believe 'either that God will not do what is right, if he be
not begged and entreated to do so—or that, by being begged
and entreated, he can be induced to do what is wrong'.[28] The
rituals prescribed by the Church also make God appear to be
vain. Why else should we sing His praises to please Him?
What after all, Mill asks, is the point of 'our telling the
Divine Being that he has such and such qualities; as if he was
like[ly] to mistake his own qualities, by some imperfection in
his knowledge, which we supply?'[29] Worse still, says Mill, the
Church and its clergy make God appear to be cruel. A God
who metes out 'punishments in atrocious excess' would appear
to act 'in the spirit of revenge, and to vindicate his dignity'.
Thus does the Church ascribe to the Almighty 'the character
. . . of an atrocious savage'. To maintain that 'the apprehen-

---

[26] James Mill, 'The Church, and its Reform', 267–8.
[27] See my Introduction to Mill, *PW*; also Ch. 7 below.
[28] James Mill, 'The Church, and its Reform', 262.   [29] Ibid.

sion of these punishments is a restraint on men during their lives ... is only another mode of ascribing imperfection, both intellectual and moral, to the Supreme Being'.[30] Such a God is no more worthy of being worshipped than were the gods of the Greek poets whom Plato would banish from his republic.[31] Here, as throughout Mill's writings, we can detect more than a trace of Platonism.

To offer any adequate defence of my contention that Mill is a Platonist, albeit a rather peculiar one, is well beyond the bounds of the present chapter.[32] Even so, it may be worth taking note in passing of some pieces of circumstantial evidence. Although Mill denied ever having taken any man as a master, he happily acknowledged his debt to Plato. As his son recalled, 'There is no author to whom my father thought himself more indebted for his own mental culture, than Plato, or whom he more frequently recommended to young students.'[33] The younger Mill also confessed that 'I have ever felt myself, beyond any modern that I know of except my father ... a pupil of Plato, and cast in the mould of his dialectics.'[34] Indeed, he adds, 'the title of Platonist belongs by ... right to those who have been nourished in, and have endeavoured to practise Plato's mode of investigation ...'.[35] His father's own title was acquired early on, at Edinburgh University, where, as Bain says, his studies already showed 'a dead set at Plato'.[36] Mill's early published writings include several commentaries on Plato and critiques of modern English translations of his dialogues.[37] The five volumes of his *Commonplace Books* contain copious extracts from, and comments on, the works of

---

[30] Ibid. 268.

[31] Cf. Mill's similar strictures against the Hindu gods and goddesses in his *History of British India* (London, 1818; 3rd edn., 1826), i. 291. Cf. Plato, *Republic*, 378–86, 595–600.

[32] See Ch. 7 below.   [33] J. S. Mill, *Autobiography*, 14.

[34] J. S. Mill, *The Early Draft of John Stuart Mill's 'Autobiography'*, ed. J. Stillinger, (Urbana, Ill., 1961), 48.

[35] J. S. Mill, *Autobiography*, 15.   [36] Bain, *James Mill*, 19.

[37] James Mill, 'Taylor's Translation of Plato', *Literary Journal*, 3 (May 1804), 449–61, (June 1804), 577–89; 'Taylor's Plato', *Edinburgh Review*, 14 (Apr. 1809), 187–211. Cf. Mill's fulsome praises of Plato in *Analysis of the Phenomena of the Human Mind* (1829; London, 1878), i. 271; *Fragment on Mackintosh*, 25; and the numerous references and excerpts in his *Commonplace Book* (see n. 38 below). See also Ch. 7 below.

Plato.[38] As these and other sources show, it was not Plato's metaphysics but his method—or 'mode of investigation' as his son terms it—to which Mill was attracted and which he attempted to practise. In the case of religious reform, however, Mill's Platonism takes not only a critical but a constructive or utopian turn as well.

6.5 RELIGION REFORMED

If the critical portion of Mill's article on Church reform was radical, his constructive proposals for reform were more radical still. Even his normally sympathetic biographer Bain remarks that Mill's scheme 'with all its ingenuity' and 'constructive suggestions' must, like Plato's *Republic*, be 'remanded to the list of Utopias'.[39]

That Mill in his last years should call for a state-supported church and a civil religion is at first sight surprising. He had earlier decried the connection between Church and State, believing it to be a mutually corrupting alliance, and had gone so far as to advocate their complete separation.[40] Although the Church of England 'exists for no good purpose', Mill says, it nevertheless exists for a bad purpose. It is 'a state engine; a ready and ever-willing instrument in the hands of those who desire to monopolize the powers of government'.[41] It is so structured that 'the interest of [its] clergy . . . is in direct opposition to their duty, and makes them sworn enemies of the good of their fellow creatures'. Above all, they are 'enemies of the improvement of the human mind'.[42]

In the end, however, Mill aims not to destroy this Augean stable but to clean and rebuild it. If it cannot be disestab-

---

[38] Four volumes of Mill's *Commonplace Book* are in the London Library, and a fifth in the Mill–Taylor Collection at the library of the London School of Economics.

[39] Bain, *James Mill*, 389.

[40] James Mill, 'Schools for All' (1812), repr. in W. H. Burston (ed.), *James Mill on Education* (Cambridge, 1969), 141–9, 185–7. See also 'Southey's Book of the Church', *Westminster Review*, 3 (Jan. 1825), 167–212, at 192; and 'Ecclesiastical Establishments', *Westminster Review*, 5 (Apr. 1826), 504–48, esp. 505–6.

[41] James Mill, 'The Church, and its Reform', 272.

[42] Ibid. 373–4.

lished, the Church of England might be re-established and thereby 'be converted from an instrument of evil into an instrument of much good'.[43] To this end Mill calls for the creation of 'a State religion' in which 'the whole population' is united and which is to be supported not by tithes but by taxes.[44] This church would be no less a 'state engine'; but the state it serves might thereby be made into an altogether different, and better, one than that served by the Church as presently established.

Mill describes the features of his state religion down to the minutest detail. A Minister of Public Instruction would oversee the selection and training of the clergy, who are to be recruited from 'the middle rank'.[45] Their work would in turn be scrutinized by 'inspectors' who would report directly to the Ministry of Public Instruction. It is important, Mill adds, 'not [to] over-pay' the clergy or the inspectors, who should be seen to be 'hard working' and hence morally exemplary members of the middle rank.[46]

It is, of course, no accident that Mill's model state church should be headed by a Minister of Public Instruction. His church is to be, above all, an agency of civic and moral instruction. The chief aim of a rationally redesigned religious establishment should be to build the moral character of its members. Even the Sunday sermon, earlier dismissed by Mill as so much useless ceremony, could be usefully revamped. 'We do not dispute that a discourse of the proper kind delivered . . . on the day of rest, would have happy effects.' Such a sermon would 'establish in their [the members'] minds pure ideas of the moral character of God'. This would require nothing less than undoing the damage done by earlier ecclesiastical practices. 'It is unavailing . . . to call the Almighty benevolent, when you ascribe to him lines of action which are entirely the reverse. It is vain to call him wise, when you represent him as moved by considerations [e.g. vanity] which

---

[43] Ibid. 274. [44] Ibid. 288, 279–80.

[45] Ibid. 275. By 'middle rank' Mill does not mean what we nowadays mean by 'middle class', inasmuch as 'rank' is not synonymous with 'class'. Rather, Mill uses 'rank' in the sense employed by John Millar in *The Origin and Distinction of Ranks* (London, 1806). See James Mill, 'Millar on Ranks', *Literary Journal*, 1 (1806), 624–9.

[46] James Mill, 'The Church, and its Reform', 278.

have weight only with the weakest of men.' And it is useless to call the Almighty a loving God when you attribute to him a propensity to punish offenders out of all proportion to the gravity of their offences.[47] Their theological import aside, such sermons should have a socially valuable end in view:

the object of discourses, calculated to be of real utility to the majority of those who compose congregations, would be, to make . . . as deeply as possible, all the impressions which lead to good conduct; to give strength and constancy to the kindly and generous feelings; to stimulate the desire of doing good, by showing the value of it . . . to make understood and felt the value of a good name; how much the happiness of each individual depends upon the good-will of those among whom he lives . . .

Such sermons should, in sum, 'lead us to rejoice in being the instruments of happiness to others'.[48] This lesson should be taught to parents, to spouses, to children, and—not least—to citizens.

In the setting supplied by the Sunday service 'the opportunity would be favourable for doing something to add to [the congregation's] education'. Mill is at his most schoolmasterish in drawing detailed plans for religious instruction in which social-cum-practical themes predominate. This begins with the member's manner of dress. It is 'of great importance, that all the families of a parish should be got to assemble on the Sunday—clean, and so dressed, as to make a favourable appearance in the eyes of one another. This alone is ameliorating.'[49] Once the parishioners are washed, dressed, and assembled, 'useful lectures on various branches of art and science might be delivered to them'. Thus 'workmen who make use of tools [would be] acquainted, in a general way, with the mechanical powers'. The congregation would also witness 'chemical experiments'; acquire a 'knowledge of the composition and decomposition of bodies'; and learn something of 'the science[s] of botany [and astronomy]'. All of this would, he says, 'afford a great source of interest and delight'. To these delights would be added practical 'lectures on the art of preserving the health, pointing out the mistakes which igno-

---

[47] James Mill, 'The Church, and its Reform', 267.
[48] Ibid. 269. [49] Ibid. 289.

rant people commit in the physical management, both of themselves and their children'. In these ways the parishioners would be 'deeply impressed with the importance to themselves of habits of industry and frugality'.[50] Yet, important as they are, these lessons in natural science and personal hygiene are far from sufficient. Because parishioners are not only parents but labourers and citizens as well, they therefore require civic or political instruction. It is here that the political import of Mill's scheme for a civil religion comes into clearer view.

Mill maintains that 'there is no branch of political knowledge which ought not to be carefully taught to the people in their parochial assemblies on their day of rest'.[51] They should receive instruction in 'political science' and 'political economy'. In this way they can be

made to understand the laws which determine the rate of wages—from ignorance of which rise most of their contention with their masters . . . Indeed, a knowledge of the laws of nature, by which the annual produce of the labours of the community is distributed, is the best of all modes of reconciling them to that inequality of distribution which they see takes place, and which there are people ignorant or wicked enough to tell them, is a violation of their rights.[52]

There is in Mill's model church a marriage of political economy and Platonism. From the former Mill derives the notion that political communities are first and foremost economic entities based upon a division of labour and governed by 'laws' determining production and distribution. From the latter Mill gets the idea that a just political community is one in which the members of each order or 'rank' fulfil their respective roles or perform their particular functions. As an educative institution, Mill's state church would promote justice (in the Platonic sense) by reconciling its members to the performance of those functions peculiar to their rank. In Mill's model church—as in the Lancasterian schools and in the Society for the Diffusion of Useful Knowledge in which he played an active part—members of the middle rank were to be apprised of their calling, and common labourers reconciled to theirs.

Anticipating the objection that such lessons will likely be

---

[50] Ibid. 290.   [51] Ibid. 291.   [52] Ibid.

resisted by those at whom they are aimed, Mill replies that such resistance is indicative of the presence of 'sinister interests' and that minds suitably sanitized will be persuaded by 'evidence'. 'The elements of politics', he says, 'are not abstruse.' Nor, he adds, are 'the elements of jurisprudence', which 'might be taught with great advantage'.[53] This would of course assume, in addition to ostensibly open minds, the availability of texts suitable for such didactic purposes. As it happens, Mill was the author not only of an elementary textbook on political economy, but of essays on 'Government' and 'Jurisprudence' which first appeared in the *Encyclopaedia Britannica* and were later published together in a single volume under Mill's name.[54] These may well have been the texts that Mill had in mind for Sunday sermons in his model state church.

Lest Mill's day of rest look like the most strenuous day of the week, he sounds a lighter note—although, as always, for a serious purpose. 'So much', he says, 'for the serious matters with which the minds of the people might be usefully engaged . . . on the day of rest.' The serious lessons taught on that day will, he says, sink in even more deeply if combined with certain 'amusements'. These 'social amusements . . . should be of a gentle character; harmonizing rather with the moderate, than the violent emotions; promoting cheerfulness, not profuse merriment'. Competitive games and sports, not being 'favourable to the feelings of brotherly love', should be forbidden. Mill is, however, prepared to permit 'music and dancing', but only if 'regulated'. Since dancing is a 'mimetic art', dances 'might be so contrived as to represent all the social affections, which we most desire to implant in the breasts of the people, and to call up the trains of ideas by which they are nourished'. This might be done, for example, by means of dances representing 'the parental and filial affections' and 'the fraternal affections'. Mill is quite insistent that the 'marital affections' not be represented mimetically: 'dances to represent that affection would be so apt to slide into lasciviousness, that we should be afraid to trust them.'[55]

[53] James Mill, 'The Church, and its Reform', 291.
[54] James Mill, *Essays on Government, Jurisprudence, etc.* (London, 1825).
[55] James Mill, 'The Church, and its Reform', 293.

Having spent the better part of their day of rest in listening to lectures on political economy and other sundry subjects, and having engaged in earnest dancing, Mill's model parishioners conclude the day's activities with a common meal. This they do not so much because they would by now be famished but because 'the conjunct meal' is 'a promoter of union'. These 'friendship meals' would be eminently sober affairs. Only through 'the total interdiction of intoxicating liquors' and the ready availability of large quantities of 'tea and coffee' can these friendship-meals promote social solidarity and affection.[56] Thus ends the day of rest.

The sceptical reader might be forgiven for wondering what could persuade people to attend a church such as Mill describes. To this Mill has a ready answer: once they have tried it, they will like it and prefer this to their previous forms of worship. Although some might wish to retain their membership in one or another sect, all would be required by law to belong to the state church. What the law prescribes would soon become second nature. 'Men could not long attend a worship' in this church

without acquiring attachment to it, and learning by degrees that it is the one thing needful. All would belong to this church; and after a short time would belong to no other. Familiarized with the true worship of the Divine Being, they would throw off the pseudo worship, dogmas, and ceremonies. This is the true plan for converting Dissenters. There would be no schism, if men had nothing to scind about.[57]

In this way would Mill's model church become an even more efficient 'state engine' than the Church of England had been heretofore. Its members' minds having been scientifically formed, or at any rate re-formed, by instruction received on the seventh day, Mill's state church results in a better state and a more sober citizenry.

But how are we to know whether these various lessons are being learnt and applied? Mill answers by proposing a system of incentives, negative and positive. The negative incentive is that the sermons and activities of the clergy are to be scrutinized by inspectors who report to the Ministry of Public

[56] Ibid. 294.   [57] Ibid. 288.

Instruction. This punitive stick is to be supplemented by a pecuniary carrot. Believing that the hardest-working and most successful clergymen deserve to be rewarded for their efforts, Mill proposes a system of merit pay. The state should 'give annual premiums to those ministers in whose parishes certain favourable results were manifested'. Cast in quantitative terms, these favourable results would include such things as the 'smallest number of crimes committed within the year', 'the smallest number of law-suits', 'the smallest number of paupers', 'the smallest number of uneducated children', 'the reading-rooms best attended', and so on. 'In this manner, would pretty decisive evidence be obtained of the comparative prevalence of good conduct in the different parishes, and a motive . . . applied to the obtaining of it.'[58] Mill's scheme for a civil religion is nothing if not thorough.

6.6 MILL AND COMTE COMPARED

My aim in offering the foregoing account of Mill's utopian proposal for a radically reformed religious establishment is to suggest that it appears to constitute an additional and heretofore unnoticed affinity between Mill and Comte. I do not, of course, mean to suggest that their schemes are indistinguishable, for clearly there are differences of design, detail, and emphasis. With its icons, its imagery, and its elaborate rituals, Comte's is clearly the more 'Catholic', while the relative simplicity and moral earnestness of Mill's marks his as the more 'protestant' system of social worship. Important as they are, however, these and other differences should not blind us to several genuine similarities between their schemes. Both, after all, aim at promoting social solidarity; both prescribe particular orders of worship; and both are backed by supposedly scientific arguments. One can also argue that both are paternalistic at best, and authoritarian at worst. Comte and Mill are alike not only in outlining new systems of social relations, but in proposing a religious rationale for reconciling people to it. Although Comte's is more Catholic and hierarchical, and

[58] James Mill, 'The Church, and its Reform', 289.

Mill's more protestant and ostensibly democratic, both schemes prescribe a certain social hierarchy. Comte is meticulous in prescribing a place for everyone—intellectuals, industrialists, proletarians, priests, women[59]—but so too, after his own fashion, is Mill. If his system has no high priest or pope, it does have 'the middle rank', which, as he says elsewhere, 'gives to science, to art, and to legislation itself their most distinguished ornament, and is the chief source of all that has exalted and refined human nature'.[60] It is from this rank that the clergy and the inspectorate are to be recruited; and its ideals of cleanliness, thrift, frugality, sobriety, and industriousness are the ones that the common people are to internalize through instruction received from the clergy.

At this point it is worth pausing to ask why, even as John Stuart Mill condemned Comte's scheme of social worship, he failed to mention, much less condemn, his father's scheme. Several explanations are possible, if perhaps not equally plausible. A psychohistorian, for example, might construct a 'deep' account in which Comte figures as a 'dispacement object' towards whom the younger Mill directed the subconscious hostility he felt for his father. His breaking with Comte might therefore be said to mark a symbolic break with his father.[61] The supporting evidence might include, among other things, the favourable comparison that J. S. Mill had drawn between his father and Comte, followed by his unusually vehement denunciation of the latter's 'despotism'. A less deep, and perhaps more plausible, explanation might invoke 'that filial piety which makes Mill's *Autobiography* so unreliable'.[62] Thus his failure to notice the otherwise obvious parallels between his father's and Comte's schemes for a civil religion was merely one of many instances in which the younger Mill dutifully omitted or soft-pedalled criticisms of his father's more illiberal and less defensible views.

A third, and to my mind more plausible, explanation is that J. S. Mill's mysterious omission is neither mysterious nor an omission. He never likened his father's schemes for a civil

[59] See Comte, *General View of Positivism*, chs. 2–4.
[60] James Mill, *Essay on Government*, in *PW* 41.
[61] See B. Mazlish, *James and John Stuart Mill* (New York, 1975), 251–62.
[62] See W. Thomas, *The Philosophical Radicals* (Oxford, 1979), 115.

religion to Comte's because he had no reason to do so. Moreover, had he drawn any such comparison, it would almost certainly have been in his father's favour. For one thing, Mill's scheme is devoid of the dogmas, rituals, miracles, and mysteries with which Comte's abounds. Moreover, the elder Mill's model church is meant to serve as a school in which the critical, analytical, and practical skills of the parishioners are sharpened on Sundays. He had, after all, complained that the Anglican Church and its clergy were 'enemies of the improvement of the human mind'.[63] Mill's civil religion is, accordingly, austerely cerebral and critical. By contrast, Comte's Religion of Humanity requires that its adherents not only cultivate the unreflective 'altruistic' social feelings but that they resist the 'egoistic' temptation to think critically. The 'critical spirit', he says, 'is directly contrary to that which ought to reign in scientific politics'.[64]

One can scarcely imagine either of the Mills ever endorsing such a view. Indeed, one of James Mill's main criticisms of organized religion was that its rituals tended to numb the mind even as they stirred the passions.[65] And although his son did not object to having one's passions stirred by poetry, to have them aroused and manipulated by priests of any sort was an altogether different and more dangerous matter. 'The single idea of M. Comte, on this subject', he noted, 'is that the intellect should be wholly subordinated to the feelings . . .'[66] 'The Pontiff of Positivism' requires the faithful to engage in daily 'devotional practices . . . not because his feelings require them, but for the premeditated purpose of getting his feelings up'.[67] This single-minded subordination of the critical intellect to the social feelings is the foundation on which 'the Grand Pontiff of Humanity . . . organizes an elaborate system for the total suppression of all independent thought'.[68]

Not least, both Mills shared an abiding aversion to Roman Catholicism, which for them represented every conceivable

---

[63] James Mill, 'The Church, and its Reform', 274.

[64] A. Comte, 'Plan of the Scientific Operations Necessary for Reorganising Society' (1822); repr. as an appendix to *System of Positive Polity*, iv. 574.

[65] James Mill, *Commonplace Book*, v, fo. 132.

[66] J. S. Mill, *Auguste Comte and Positivism*, 169.

[67] Ibid. 153.   [68] Ibid. 169.

vice and defect of organized religion. In James Mill's case, this aversion was articulated early on, and was in due course extended to all priestly religions, East and West. He held fast to the Dissenter's distrust of doctrinal complexity and priest-craft. The 'quakerly plainness' that Macaulay had detected in Mill's prose was not an affectation but a central feature of his thinking not only about politics, economics, and psychology, but about religion as well.[69] Mill surely spoke the truth when he confessed to being a Quaker in all but name.[70] Much the same might also be said of his son. One of the mainstays of John Stuart Mill's case against Comte consisted of pointing out the affinities between the Religion of Humanity and Roman Catholicism. In casting about for someone sufficiently despotic with whom to compare Comte, J. S. Mill invokes only one name, that of Ignatius Loyola. Moreover, he com-plains that 'M. Comte is accustomed to draw most of his ideas of moral cultivation from the discipline of the Catholic Church', although Comte, he adds, outdoes even the Church in that he attempts to transform everyone into a saint.[71] 'M. Comte is fond of borrowing the consecrated expressions of Catholicism to denote the nearest equivalents which his own system affords.'[72] Whatever other similarities it might be said to share with Comte's Religion of Humanity, James Mill's scheme for a civil religion at least owed nothing to Roman Catholicism.

More to the point, perhaps, is that James Mill's model church owed nothing to Saint-Simon, as Comte's clearly did. Despite what the younger Mill suggested, Comte's religious turn can scarcely be said to represent 'the signal anomaly in M. Comte's intellectual career'.[73] On the contrary, and as Comte himself rightly noted, the Religion of Humanity marks the culmination and completion of his own version of the sys-tem that Saint-Simon claimed (wrongly, in Comte's view) to have been the first to outline.[74] Saint-Simon's and Comte's

[69] T. B. Macaulay, 'Mill on Government', *Edinburgh Review*, 1929; repr. as appendix to *PW* 271–303, at 272.

[70] 'You are half a Quaker, and I am all but a whole one' (Mill to Henry Brougham, 15 Sept. 1831, Brougham Collection, University College, London, fo. 10764).

[71] J. S. Mill, *Auguste Comte and Positivism*, 144.   [72] Ibid. 158.

[73] Ibid. 5.   [74] Cf. Comte's Preface to his *Catechism*, 1–26.

claims to originality notwithstanding, there was in nineteenth-century France an already well-established tradition of discourse in which to talk about this or that scheme for a *religion civile*. This in turn served as a backdrop against which the civil-religious schemes of various French Counter-Enlightenment thinkers gained and enjoyed a degree of intelligibility if not plausibility or persuasiveness.[75] It is only a slight exaggeration to suggest that Voltaire's scheme represented the rationalist, and Rousseau's the romantic, variations on a single theme.[76] What Saint-Simon and Comte added, as J. S. Mill rightly said of the latter, was an unprecedented degree of rigour and systematization, or at any rate the appearance of it. At all events, Comte's *système* was never really the purely secular and scientific edifice that the younger Mill at first believed it to be. One might more plausibly argue that the elder Mill's civil religion represents rather more of an anomaly in his intellectual career than it does in Comte's—at least if we accept the account of his father's religious views offered in the *Autobiography*.

Even so, in the final analysis it is, I think, fair to say that, although both Mill and Comte advocated a civil religion, their schemes were—despite several striking similarities between them—quite different in structure, intent, and inspiration. To the younger Mill, if not to us, these differences would doubtless have been paramount. Therefore, it is perhaps unfair to expect John Stuart Mill to have compared, much less condemned, them as though they had been cut from the same cloth. It is, however, fair to ask another question: to what degree, if any, was the younger Mill justified in claiming to see similarities between eighteenth-century Scotsmen and nineteenth-century Frenchmen, and more particularly between the eminent progenitors and the unsung 'last survivor' of the Scottish school and the Positivist school of the self-annointed French savant? At the very least, the comparison seems, in retrospect, to have been strained, not to say oversimplified, overdrawn, and overdramatized.

[75] See I. Berlin, 'The Counter-Enlightenment', in *Against the Current* (London, 1979), ch. 1.

[76] P. Gay, *Voltaire's Politics* (New York, 1965), 259–72.

6.7 MILL'S SCOTTISH SOURCE

After considering the affinities and differences between Mill's and Comte's schemes for a civil religion, a larger and more intractable question remains. To what tradition of discourse does James Mill's scheme belong? I want to conclude by suggesting that besides being a curious mixture of Benthamism and Platonism, Mill's plan for a reformed church and a civil religion also belongs in some part to the Scottish 'school of the north' in which he was initially nurtured. Like Hume's and Smith's, Mill's approach to religion was less theological than sociological. If Hume was, in John Dunn's apt phrase, a 'practical atheist', James Mill was a practical theist, in that he believed misguided or mistaken theological views to have pernicious political consequences.[77] Such views stood, accordingly, in need of correction through education—precisely the sort of education that Mill's model church was supposed to supply.

Without claiming any kind of direct influence or causal connection between them, I want in conclusion to suggest that there are several striking affinities between Mill's scheme for a civil religion and the account of 'public works' to be found in Adam Smith's *Wealth of Nations*. Public works, in Smith's sense, are enterprises which serve the public good but do not come about inadvertently through the operations of the 'invisible hand'. Rather, they require the more visible hand of the state for their support. Although 'they may be in the highest degree advantageous to a great society', such public works are neither profitable nor self-supporting and must therefore be supported by the public at large. Besides 'the publick institutions and publick works necessary for the defence of the society, and for the administration of justice' and 'for facilitating the commerce of society', these public works would also include those institutions 'for promoting the instruction of the people'. Public works of this latter sort include not only

---

[77] J. Dunn, 'From Applied Theology to Social Analysis: The Break between John Locke and the Scottish Enlightenment', in I. Hont and M. Ignatieff (eds.), *Wealth and Virtue* (Cambridge, 1983), ch. 5.

schools for educating the young but the churches which over-see 'the instruction of people of all ages'.[78]

Like Mill, Smith sees the church as an educational institution. Its function is to inculcate the morals and manners promoting sociability, harmony, and commerce. Like Mill, Smith views sectarianism and enthusiasm as subversive of these ends. 'There are two very easy and effectual remedies, however, by whose joint operation the state might, without violence, correct whatever was unsocial or disagreeably rigorous in the morals of all the little sects into which the country was divided.' The first is to diffuse philosophical and scientific knowledge 'among all people of middling or more than middling rank and fortune' so that common labourers might be immunized against sectarian vices. 'Science', says Smith, 'is the great antidote to the poison of enthusiasm and superstition; and where all the superior ranks of people were secured from it, the inferior ranks could not be much exposed to it.'[79] Smith, like Mill, entrusts the 'publick work' of moral education to the enlightened and scientifically minded 'middle rank'.

But what of those gentle amusements with which Mill would leaven the rigours of the Sunday service? The second of Smith's antisectarian

remedies is the frequency and gaiety of publick diversions. The state, by encouraging . . . those who . . . would attempt, without scandal or indecency, to amuse and divert the people by painting, poetry, musick, dancing; by all sorts of dramatic representations and exhibitions, would easily dissipate, in the greater part of them, that melancholy and gloomy humour which is almost always the nurse of popular superstition and enthusiasm. Publick diversions have always been the objects of dread and hatred, to all the fanatical promoters of those popular frenzies. The gaiety and good humour which those diversions inspire were altogether inconsistent with that temper of mind, which was fittest for their purpose, or which they could best work upon.[80]

Mill might have had his reservations about carrying 'gaiety and good humour' too far; but there is little doubt that his model Sunday regimen agrees in essentials with Smith's 'publick diversions'.

[78] A. Smith, *Wealth of Nations* (Oxford, 1979), ii. 723.   [79] Ibid. 796.
[80] Ibid. 796–7.

Smith, like Mill, is as effusive in his praise of Luther as he is unsparing in his criticism of Roman Catholicism and, to a lesser degree, of the Church of England, both of which Smith compares unfavourably with the Presbyterian Church of Scotland. In the former, the clergy are overpaid and are too much given to pleasing—and not infrequently to imitating—their morally lax social superiors. 'Such a clergy,' says Smith, 'while they pay their court in this manner to the higher ranks of life, are very apt to neglect altogether the means of maintaining their influence and authority with the lower.' The Scottish Presbyterian clergy, by contrast, are models of moral rectitude. 'In all the presbyterian churches . . . it is by nobler and better arts that the established clergy in general endeavour to gain the favour of their superiors [and the respect of their inferiors]; by their learning, by the irreproachable regularity of their life, and by the faithful and diligent discharge of their duty.'[81] This they do partly out of character and moral conviction but also—and no less importantly—because their 'pay or recompense' is 'proportioned to the nature of the service' they perform:

If any service is very much under-paid, it is very apt to suffer by the meanness and incapacity of the greater part of those who are employed in it. If it is very much over-paid, it is apt to suffer, perhaps, still more by their negligence and idleness. A man of large revenue, whatever may be his profession, thinks he ought to live like other men of large revenues; and to spend a great part of his time in festivity, in vanity, and in dissipation. But in a clergyman this train of life not only consumes the time which ought to be employed in the duties of his function, but in the eyes of the common people destroys almost entirely that sanctity of character which can alone enable him to perform those duties with proper weight and authority.[82]

Mill's justification for having the state support a modestly paid clergy seems to be scarcely more than a paraphrase of Smith's arguments in support of 'publick works' and 'publick diversions'.

There are, however, at least three noteworthy dissimilarities. First, Smith—unlike Mill in his last years—remained

---

[81] Ibid. 808–9.   [82] Ibid. 813–14.

adamantly opposed to an established state church, favouring instead a competition among creeds and sects. Second, where Smith's account is detached and descriptive, Mill's is engaged and utopian. And, third, Mill's scheme for a civil religion has several 'Platonic' features that are wholly absent from Smith's discussion. These differences aside, there remain several striking similarities between Mill's plan for a radically reformed state church and Smith's analysis of religious instruction as a 'publick work'. Without wishing to claim a direct, much less a causal, connection between Smith's views and Mill's, I do want to suggest the possibility of an indirect connection. Not only had Mill read and reread Smith's *The Wealth of Nations*, first as a student and later as an aspiring political economist, but both came out of that larger eighteenth-century 'system of the north' whose members tended to view religion less from a theological than from a sociological vantage-point. Mill's scheme for a civil religion may well mark a partial return to that 'great school' of which he was indeed the last survivor.

6.8 CONCLUSION

It is, of course, altogether too easy to find Mill's and others' schemes for some sort of civil religion risible, or worse. But the problem to which they point is surely no laughing matter. The problem is, how is a society to socialize its members and legitimize its institutions? How are its less reasonable and reflective members to be led to behave in minimally decent and civil ways? By what means might a fraying social fabric be mended?[83]

Such questions were never asked in the abstract by armchair philosophers. They have always been, and still remain—now perhaps more than ever—pressing practical questions in search of some practical answer. One answer is supplied by the institution of a civil religion. Whether understood in Rousseau's or Comte's or Mill's terms may matter less, in the final analysis, than that such schemes have been proposed as a

---

[83] For a modern sociologist's restatement of the problem in eighteenth-century 'Scottish' terms, see J. Q. Wilson, *The Moral Sense* (New York, 1993).

solution to a persistent problem arising in connection with living a commodious common life.[84]

Against this more traditional way of posing the problem, one can of course invoke the names of Nietzsche and, more recently, of Foucault. Both invert the traditional order of discourse. For Foucault and Nietzsche, the very idea of a well-ordered society is itself the problem, and any means to that end—moral, religious, or educative—is to be regarded with suspicion and scorn. Morality masks and legitimizes power and privilege. Transparency is a trap and all attempts to tame the beast within every human breast are assaults to be resisted.[85] All forms of discipline—moral, religious, pedagogical, penal—must accordingly be unmasked, upended, and shown for what they are. I turn now to a consideration of Foucault's attempt to write a 'genealogical' account and critique of modern punitive practices.

[84] See M. Goldie, 'The Civil Religion of James Harrington', in A. Pagden (ed.), *The Languages of Political Theory in Early-Modern Europe* (Cambridge, 1987), 197–222.
[85] See Ch. 5.6 above.

7

BENTHAMITE DISCIPLINE AND PUNISHMENT; OR, WHAT FOUCAULT MISSED

Nous sommes bien moins grecs que nous ne le croyons.

Michel Foucault

7.1 INTRODUCTION

There are, as we have seen, many ways of thinking and writing about the history of social and political thought. One of the most common of these, the traditional—or, if you like, the old-fashioned textbook—approach stresses continuity. On this view the history of political thought is a story of change within a continuity of concerns. These 'perennial ideas' are the stuff of an ongoing conversation from one age and thinker to another. Thus, for example, Rawls's theory of justice represents the continuation of a conversation begun by earlier thinkers, including Plato and Aristotle and anyone who has since thought and written about 'justice'. Each theorist contributes a building-block to the edifice that is Western political thought. Another, and arguably newer, view stresses discontinuity—'breaks' or 'ruptures' or radical conceptual innovation and theoretical incommensurability between theories or 'paradigms' of political thinking or discursive practices.

This second story-line is borrowed from a way of thinking about the history of the natural sciences popularized by Thomas Kuhn in *The Structure of Scientific Revolutions*.[1] On this view, Newtonian physics, for example, is not a continuation and refinement of Aristotelian physics, but rather repre-

[1] T. S. Kuhn, *The Structure of Scientific Revolutions* (Chicago, 1963; rev. edn., 1974).

sents a radically new way of looking at and understanding nature. And although the two share certain concepts—e.g. 'force' and 'motion'—each understands these in very different or even incommensurable ways. The worlds thus represented—or perhaps one should say constructed—are very different indeed.

Michel Foucault's seminal studies of madness, of prisons, hospitals, asylums, sexuality, and power, proceed from the historiographical premises of this second view. Foucault follows the historian of science Gaston Bachelard (by whom Kuhn was also much influenced), who emphasizes cataclysmic change, radical breaks, ruptures, or revolutionary discontinuities between bounded and historically specific systems of scientific thought. Foucault applies this schema to the writing of the history of social and political thought. That 'genealogical' history he writes as a story of discontinuous change from one discrete system of 'discursive practices' or 'epistemes' to another. Between the pre-classical and modern epistemes there yawns a discursive divide (although Foucault is none too clear about where this is to be found). The languages or assumptions of the two are too different to be commensurable. Or, to put the point differently, each is too exclusive and self-contained to allow for any easy translation of the categories and concepts constitutive of the one into the categories and concepts of the other. Our world, the world of the 'panoptic machine' or the modern surveillance society, is constituted by a system of concepts, classifications, and discursive practices that is radically at odds with those of the Greeks, from whom we wish, misguidedly and mistakenly, to claim descent. 'We are much less Greek than we believe', if indeed we are 'Greek' at all.

This genealogical approach is brilliantly and dramatically applied in *Discipline and Punish*, in which Foucault traces the origins of our own 'carceral society' to various late-eighteenth- and early nineteenth-century humanitarians and reformers. The main villain of the piece is Jeremy Bentham, whose plan for a 'panopticon' prison provides Foucault with his central metaphor. The panopticon (from the Greek *pan-optes*, 'all-seeing') permitted a single guard in a central tower to observe all prisoners in the surrounding circle of cells at all hours of the day or night. Aware of the constant presence of 'the gaze' (*le regard*), prisoners would quickly come to internalize its presence, and begin policing themselves. While Bentham's own panopticon project was a non-starter, it nevertheless represents, for Foucault, a particularly clear-cut case—a paradigm case, as it were—with which to illustrate and sum up the unintended but nevertheless real thrust of all well-meant attempts to reform or improve human society along less cruel and more 'humane' lines. In Foucault's hands prison reform, once regarded as a humanitarian movement, comes to be seen for what it 'really' is—a veritable model and starting-point for more subtle, and markedly more efficient and economical, means by which modern society subjugates or 'normalizes' its own subjects.[2]

It is an interesting story which, in one version or another, Foucault never tired of telling. But several characters, and some important parts of the plot, are missing. Bentham is, no doubt, a central figure. Indeed he is, for Foucault, both *bête noire* and *éminence grise*. But other, ostensibly minor characters are notable by their absence from Foucault's drama. Bentham's own hero and inspiration, the crusading prison inspector and muckraking author John Howard (1726–90), is mentioned only once, and Nield and other penal reformers of the day not at all. Howard's influential *State of the Prisons* (1777), which was instrumental in exposing the evils of the English prison system, does not even merit an entry in Foucault's rather spotty bibliography.[3] These are surprising omissions for a writer who claims, as a matter of methodological principle, to eschew the pivotal role played by the Big Names in the history of Western social and political thought, preferring instead to write history 'from the bottom up' by concentrating on work done by anonymous officials, petty bureaucrats, functionaries, writers of official reports, and other ostensibly minor figures inside the system of 'capillaries' through which power circulates. But, for all his purported focus on such minor figures, Foucault fails to note the key

---

[2] M. Foucault, *Discipline and Punish* (New York, 1977).
[3] See J. Semple, *Bentham's Prison* (Oxford, 1993); 'Foucault and Bentham: A Defence of Panopticism', *Utilitas*, 4 (1992), 105–20.

role played by lesser lights, including Bentham's 'lieutenant and propagandist-in-chief', James Mill.[4]

My aim here is to insert this particular character into Foucault's tale in order to flesh it out and thereby to transform it in several important respects. My claim is that much of the shape and character of what we take to be 'Benthamite' schemes for prison reform are importantly informed not only by Bentham but also by James Mill and, more surprisingly still, by a thinker by whom Mill was much influenced—Plato. The thrust of my argument, if correct, is that a number of the 'new' developments that Foucault purports to trace may, in fact, represent recycled versions of much older theories (in this instance, of justice and punishment). Like the cat, 'classical' thinkers have many lives. So, simply put, the moral of my tale amounts to this: to ignore or downplay the importance of authors and texts conventionally characterized (and often dismissed) as belonging to 'the canon' of classical texts written by 'dead white European males'—in this instance Plato and his *Republic*—is not to be free of their influence, but is merely one particularly pernicious way of being under their spell without knowing it. *Pace* Foucault, we may well be more 'Greek' than we believe.

My route to this destination includes the following stops. I begin by considering the conventional estimate of James Mill and his relation to Bentham. I then go on to examine the elder Mill's views on punishment and penal reform, arguing that they are predicated on a decidedly Platonic theory of punishment. I contend that, so far as his premises are concerned, James Mill is rather more of a Platonist than a pure and unalloyed Benthamite. Finally, I conclude by connecting this single story to a larger concern about the way in which we ought not to write the history of political thought.

7.2 BENTHAM AND JAMES MILL

James Mill has had the misfortune to stand under doubly obscuring shadows. The first is cast by his supposed mentor,

---

[4] E. Halévy, 'James Mill', in *Encyclopedia of the Social Sciences* (New York, 1930), x. 450–1.

Jeremy Bentham, and the second by his more famous son, John Stuart Mill. The elder Mill is today remembered mainly for having been Bentham's chief propagandist and the stern teacher against whom his son later rebelled. According to the conventional account, 'Bentham gave Mill a doctrine, and Mill gave Bentham a school.'[5] On this view, Mill emerges as a minor Benthamite whose mind remained essentially empty and unformed until his meeting with the master. This did not occur until 1808—some fifteen years after Mill had graduated from the University of Edinburgh and seven years after he had left his native Scotland for London and a 'career in authorship'.[6] At the rather advanced age of 35 Mill's mind finally acquired its shape. Scratch the elder Mill wherever you wish and there you will find Bentham.

This conventional view is a caricature; and, like any memorable caricature, it contains a grain of truth. But it also obscures more than it illuminates and is misleading and mistaken in several important respects. The master–disciple view of the Bentham–Mill relationship is overdue for revising.

If indeed the elder Mill was simply an unreconstructed Benthamite, we might be better advised to go straight to the source and read the works of the master rather than those of his disciple. But this is no easy matter. As anyone who has ever tried to read Bentham knows, his prose is opaque, and dense to the point of impenetrability. He sometimes seems to speak his own private language, and his writings abound with neologisms of his own invention. And nowhere are these tendencies more evident than in his writings on prison reform. Bentham's *Panopticon; or, the Inspection-House* (1791) runs to 539 pages, 122 of which describe his 'simple idea in architecture' and the remainder are devoted to two 'postscripts' covering everything from the type of shoes to be worn by prisoners (wooden clogs) to the weight and texture of bed-linens (light and coarse).

Bentham seemed almost constitutionally incapable of writing plainly and to the point. The contemporary critic Hazlitt was more accurate than arch when he, upon hearing that

---

[5] E. Halévy, *The Growth of Philosophic Radicalism* (London, 1929), 251.
[6] A. Bain, *James Mill: A Biography* (London, 1882), chs. 1, 2; and my 'Introduction' to *PW*.

Dumont had translated Bentham into French, asked when someone would translate Bentham into English.

And that, in effect, is just what James Mill did. Where Bentham is opaque and well-nigh inaccessible, Mill is both clear and readable. He describes, much more clearly than Bentham ever did, the plan for a panopticon prison:

An idea of the contrivance may be conveyed in a few words. It is a circular building, of the width of a cell, and of any height; carried round a space, which remains vacant in the middle. The cells are all open inwards, having an iron grating instead of a wall, and, of course, are visible in every part to an eye properly placed in the vacant space. A narrow tower rises in the middle of that space, called the inspection tower, which serves for the residence of the keepers, and in which, by means of windows and blinds, they can see without being seen; the cells, by lights properly disposed, being capable of being rendered as visible by night as by day.[7]

If Mill's prose is not beautiful, it is at least clear and succinct.

But in fact Mill does much more than merely redescribe Bentham's scheme in plain prose. He supplies, as it were, a language of legitimation or justification for Bentham's plans for prison reform. And—more important still—he does so less in Benthamite than in Platonic terms. That is, Mill's language, his key concepts and justificatory arguments, are less beholden to Bentham than to Plato.

Yet most of Mill's modern readers have attended almost exclusively to Mill's ostensibly Benthamite conclusions, paying little heed to the route he followed in reaching and justifying them. Were they to do so, however, they might well be surprised. Beneath Mill's Benthamite exterior there beats, I believe, the heart of a rather peculiar Platonist. Although often cast in Bentham's idiom, Mill's major premises, his most basic concepts and first principles, derive directly or indirectly from Plato, or, at any rate, from his interpretation of Plato. Indeed, as we shall see, James Mill often deduces apparently Benthamite conclusions from decidedly Platonic premises. That he does so is not, upon reflection, wholly surprising. For in the 'quarrel between ancients and moderns', Mill tried to have it both ways. To the wisdom of the former

---

[7] Mill, 'Prisons and Prison Discipline', *PW* 199.

he hoped to add the scientific insights of the latter. Bentham, by contrast, was clearly a 'modern', and much more dismissive of the ancients. The only ancient worth his salt was Epicurus. But if Bentham was an Epicurean, Mill was rather more of a Stoic, of the stern Scots Calvinist variety. Bentham really did believe that pushpin is as good as poetry and that a pleasure is a pleasure, whatever the source and whomever the recipient.

Although Mill makes much ado about happiness, he does not equate happiness with pleasure or with pleasurable sensations of just any sort and from any source. On the contrary, Mill maintained that pleasure is not a univocal concept and that there is a hierarchy of the pleasures. The lowliest of these are the physical or bodily pleasures having to do (as his son later said) with 'the animal appetites'.[8] The highest pleasures—and the only ones connected with true happiness—are those associated with the exercise of the intellect. If Mill's elevation of the intellectual pleasures of reason and reflection can scarcely be squared with Bentham's less discriminating hedonism, it does nevertheless conform quite closely with Plato's conception of happiness, or *eudaimonia*. In this as in many other respects, James Mill was more Plato's kinsman than Bentham's.

To demonstrate this in any detail is too tall an order to fill here. I shall, therefore, focus upon a single facet of James Mill's thinking that is said to show quite clearly how deeply indebted he was to Bentham. As one commentator puts it, Mill's views on crime and punishment are 'simply those of Bentham'.[9] Against this bit of conventional wisdom I shall argue that Mill's views on punishment, and more particularly his defence of Bentham's plans for penal reform, actually reveal the extent of his indebtedness to Plato. This debt is especially evident in his essays on penology and punishment, most of which were written between 1810 and 1820. As we shall see, his defence of Bentham's proposals for prison reform incorporate insights not only from psychology and

[8] J. S. Mill, *The Early Draft of John Stuart Mill's 'Autobiography'*, ed. J. Stillinger (Urbana, Ill., 1961), 171.
[9] L. W. Sumner, 'Mill and the Death Penalty: Some Addenda', *Mill Newsletter*, 13 (1978), 13.

political economy, but, as I shall argue, from the philosophy of Plato. It is indeed Mill's use of distinctly Platonic themes and arguments which sets apart and distinguishes his views from those of Bentham and other reformers. In attempting to substantiate this claim I shall begin by briefly adverting to Mill's profuse praise of Plato. I shall then recapitulate Plato's theory of justice and just punishment and compare his theory of punishment with Mill's, showing how the former informs and undergirds the latter.

7.3 JAMES MILL'S PLATONISM

If not a thoroughgoing Platonist, James Mill was at least an ardent admirer of Plato. A formidable classicist in his own right, Mill regarded Plato as unquestionably the greatest of the Greek philosophers. There was, he admitted, 'no author more difficult to translate' than Plato, and none more commonly misunderstood.[10] Yet understanding the thinking of 'the philosopher of the most brilliant imagination' was, he averred, an absolutely necessary part of one's education. Although Plato's dialogues should 'become a general and favourite object of perusal' by men and women of all ages, it is best to begin early; for reading Plato is surely 'the most improving exercise which can engage a juvenile mind'.[11] Putting this aspect of his educational theory into immediate practice, James Mill taught his son John, at the tender and impressionable age of 3, to read Greek, for the express (though scarcely sole) purpose of reading Plato's dialogues. For it was from Plato, more than from any other single author, that the elder Mill had acquired his own 'mental culture'. As his son later remarked, 'There is no author to whom my father thought himself more indebted for his own mental

[10] James Mill, *Literary Journal*, 3/10 (1 June 1804), 578.
[11] James Mill, *Commonplace Book* (see Ch. 6 n. 38), v, fo. 49; *Edinburgh Review*, 14/27 (Apr. 1809). Elsewhere Mill writes of 'the sagacious mind of Plato' being 'far more philosophical than that of any who succeeded him' (*Analysis of the Phenomena of the Human Mind*, 2nd edn. (London, 1878), i. 271). Cf. also his *Fragment on Mackintosh*, 25, and the repeated references to Plato in his *Commonplace Book*.

culture, than Plato, or whom he more frequently recommended to young students.'[12]

Even so, the impression left by his son's *Autobiography* is that James Mill's debt to Plato was almost exclusively a methodological one. What remained with James Mill, on his son's telling, was an abiding respect for the utility of Plato's dialectical method of question and answer, conjecture and refutation. The 'title of Platonist', wrote John Stuart Mill, most rightfully 'belongs to those who have been nourished, and have endeavoured to practise Plato's mode of investigation'—namely, 'the Socratic method, of which the Platonic dialogues are the chief example . . .'.[13] Indeed, he confesses elsewhere, 'I have ever felt myself, beyond any modern that I know of except my father . . . a pupil of Plato, and cast in the mould of his dialectics.'[14] On this retelling, his father emerges as something of a methodological Platonist whose substantive doctrines owe little, if anything, to the substance of Plato's teachings. This impression I believe to be misleading.

Certainly Mill owed a large methodological debt to Plato. But, I shall argue, Mill's own substantive doctrines are also decidedly Platonic. His arguments in support of Bentham's views on discipline and punishment provide a case in point. After briefly reviewing Plato's views on these matters I shall turn to James Mill's startlingly similar arguments and conclusions.

7.4 PLATO ON PUNISHMENT

Plato drew a sharp distinction between *punishing* someone and *harming* him. To punish a wrongdoer promotes justice while harming him merely answers one unjust act with another, thereby adding to the sum of injustice. Of course by 'justice' (*diké*) Plato means each person's performing the function for which he or she is 'naturally' suited.[15] A 'just' (*dikaios*) cobbler will stick to his last, a 'just' pilot to navigation, and so on. More generally, every person, and indeed every thing, has its own specific virtue or 'particular excellence' (*aretē*). Thus

---

[12] J. S. Mill, *Autobiography* (London, 1971), 14.   [13] Ibid. 14–15.
[14] J. S. Mill, *Early Draft*, 48.   [15] Plato, *Republic*, 335b–e, 352d–354.

the virtue of a carving-knife is its sharpness, the virtue of a racehorse its speed, and the virtue of an artisan the practical knowledge and skill in pursuing his craft. To perform one's function badly—or to attempt to fill a role for which one is ill-suited—is, according to Plato, unjust. From this it follows that actions, laws, or policies which promote the performance of another's proper function are just, and those which impair or impede such functions are unjust. To harm a person is to impair his ability to perform his functionally specific role. Harm is therefore necessarily unjust. One harms—that is, acts unjustly towards—a craftsman, for example, by doing something that renders him less adept at pursuing his craft. From this Plato concludes that just punishment differs from harm, inasmuch as it is applied for the purpose of making the recipient more 'just'—that is, better able to perform his proper function. Hence, it follows that criminals from different classes should receive different punishments. For example, a craftsman afflicted with the vice characteristic of his class—namely, appetitive excess—should be made to acquire the specific excellence of his class—namely, 'temperance'.[16] A 'just' punishment thus literally 're-forms' his soul or character.

7.5 FROM BENTHAM TO PLATO

These Platonic themes and arguments re-emerge, quite clearly and distinctly, in James Mill's views on punishment, and his defence of Bentham's panopticon prison in particular. There is more than a little of the spirit of Plato in Mill's aversion to punishments which break a person's spirit and his health, thereby rendering him less able to perform his proper role in the community.

If a criminal in a prison is ever to be let out again, and to mix in society . . . nothing should be done . . . to make him a worse member of society than when he went in. There cannot be a worse quality of a punishment, than that it has a tendency to corrupt and deteriorate the individual on whom it is inflicted . . .[17]

16 Ibid. 431, and *Gorgias*, 476d–480b.
17 James Mill, 'Prisons and Prison Discipline', *PW* 204.

Punishment, properly understood, is pain inflicted upon the wrongdoer, not to harm but to help him and the community to which he belongs. The public is protected by the criminal's being kept for a time in 'safe-custody'. And the inmate is helped by being reformed, that is, fitted to fulfil his function in society.

Of course 'reform' would be quite unnecessary, if there had been no moral malformation to begin with. The individual, Mill stresses repeatedly, is not responsible for forming his own character; that task rests solely with the community.[18] Like Plato, Mill thinks it the community's duty to attend to the moral education of its members. Any community which fails to do so is itself morally defective. By this light Plato condemned Thessaly and Mill criticizes England.[19] In the best society no physical punishments would ever be needed. There would be no police, no prisons, no gaols or gallows; the internalized fear of moral censure would suffice. In punishing an offender the community is in effect making a public admission of failure; it is acknowledging that the moral education it offers its members is in some way defective. By resorting to coercive physical punishment, the community is trying to make up for two past wrongs—not merely the wrong committed by the offender, but the wrong committed by the community against the offender in having provided him with a defective moral education.

For Mill, as for Plato, punishment must be purely prospective. Intentionally to inflict pain upon someone for some offence already committed, and for which they are not exclusively responsible, is in Mill's view 'rude' and 'barbaric'; it is mere 'vengeance'.[20] But to inflict pain upon someone for the sake of 'instruction', and with an eye to improving his future conduct, is quite a different matter: only then, he believes, is punishment fully justified. This is Mill's pedagogical rendering of Plato's distinction between harming and punishing. 'Punishment' is a kind of 'instruction' oriented towards a per-

---

[18] James Mill, *Philanthropist*, 3/10 (1813), 113, 116; 4/14 (1814), 136.
[19] Plato, *Crito*, 53d; James Mill, 'State of the Nation', *Westminster Review*, Oct. 1826.
[20] James Mill, *History of British India* (London, 1818; 3rd edn., 1826), i. 217.

son's future conduct and meant to correct deficiencies in his earlier 'education' (or, in the idiom of modern social science, his 'socialization'). In Mill's view, 'punishment of the vicious when the vice has consummated itself in crime' is a pedagogical patch-job, and greatly inferior to the strategy of 'forming good characters, and letting no vicious ones be formed'. Instead of 'looking continually at punishment as its great instrument of good', government should pay more attention to 'the circumstances by which punishment may be superseded'. 'If one 40th of part of the pains which have been taken to punish crimes, were now bestowed upon the formation of [good character], how speedily, and to what an extent, would the condition of society be altered.'[21] Until society is radically reformed, however, we will have to re-form its more dangerous and depraved members.

In a quite literal sense, then, Mill regards punishment as a kind of remedial moral education. He describes Bentham's model prison as a 'school', a 'reformatory', and even—in a particularly chilling 'Foucauldian' phrase—a 'hospital for the mind'.[22] The human mind is a store of 'associations' which constitute the beliefs upon which one acts. If these associations are properly formed by a good education (in Mill's and Plato's broad sense of the term), one will act wisely and well; if not, one will act in ways that are untoward, immoral, or criminal. Behaviour of the latter sort calls for correction—that is, the re-education of the offender. This is to be accomplished not merely by changing one's behaviour but, more fundamentally, by altering one's beliefs. 'Reform' involves nothing less than the re-forming of a twisted and misguided mind.

The worst sort of moral education is inflicted upon members of the working class or, as Mill, speaking in the idiom of his day sometimes calls them, the 'lower orders'.[23] It is not surprising, therefore, that a disproportionate number of criminals come from this class. The role of the labourer is to

---

[21] James Mill, *Philanthropist*, 3/10 (1813), 116–17.

[22] James Mill, 'Prisons', *PW*; *History*, v. 532; 'Schools for All', in W. H. Burston (ed.), *James Mill on Education* (Cambridge, 1969), 139–40.

[23] Mill to William Allen, the Quaker reformer and editor of *The Philanthropist*, 17 Jan. 1811, Brougham Collection, University College, London, fo. 10,775.

labour; labour is unpleasant, not to say painful; hence, if the labourer is to fulfil his function in society, he must learn to accept his lot, to tolerate the pain of labouring, to defer present pleasures for the sake of future reward, to avoid the temptations of vice. If these lessons are not learnt naturally, they must be imposed from without. This was, of course, the aim of the Lancasterian system of education, of which Mill was a fervent supporter. 'In the streets and in the fields,' Mill laments, the children of labourers 'have implanted in them the seeds of vice and profligacy. In the Lancasterian schools they are trained in all those habits which are the foundations of virtue and worth.'[24] The best education for labourers is one that instils in them 'habits of discipline, order, and subordination'.[25] Too many labourers develop, in their early years, habits of indiscipline, disorder, and insubordination; it is these profligate proletarians who fill our prisons. They are there, says Mill, 'because they have hated labour, and have had recourse to other means than their [own] industry of attaining the supply of their wants and the gratification of their desires. People of industry, people who love labour, seldom become the criminal inmates of a prison.'[26]

The object of reformatory discipline must then be to teach labourers to 'love labour'. The point of punishing a labourer is, as Plato says, to develop in him the sorts of habits and attitudes needed to make him a better labourer. Here again Mill follows Plato's lead. 'The persons on whom reformatory discipline is intended to operate', writes Mill, 'belong to the class of those who depend upon their industry for their support,' namely, the working class. 'The grand object ... of reformatory discipline is, to create habits of useful industry.'[27] The Platonic strain in Mill's thinking is never more pronounced than it is here. Like Plato, Mill holds that each class in society performs a certain function and that the 'particular virtue' or 'specific excellence' of each is that which contributes to the performance of its specific function. Just as speed and endurance are the 'virtues' of the runner and sharpness the

[24] James Mill, 'Schools for All', 139.
[25] James Mill, *Philanthropist*, I/11 (1811), 75.
[26] James Mill, 'Prisons', *PW* 204.
[27] Ibid. 215; *Philanthropist*, I/1 (1811), 75.

virtue of the carving-knife, so 'industry' and 'love of labour' are the virtues of the labourer.[28] Once these virtues become behaviourally imprinted 'habits', they enable the labourer to do what he does best, and thereby to contribute to his own well-being and to that of the community as well.

But, if prisons are pedagogical institutions, they are not at present, Mill maintains, very useful or effective ones. They are scarcely more than 'universities' in which criminals merely learn how to be better criminals.[29] As proponents of 'scientific' penology, Mill and Bentham believed it possible to turn prisons into reformatories for misguided minds and misshapen characters. Labourer-inmates should somehow be made, as Mill put it, to love labour. This lesson is not, at present, one that inmates learn; on the contrary, in unreformed prisons they learn to despise it all the more. For this unhappy and unproductive situation Mill proposes a diagnosis and a cure.

According to the conventional view, punishments should consist of something that the prisoner finds painful. Since criminals find labour especially painful, why not use hard labour as a punishment? This answer, says Mill, is simple, obvious—and utterly mistaken. It reflects an inadequate understanding of associationist psychology:

One thing . . . is pretty certain, that men seldom become in love with their punishments. If the grand cause of the crimes which have brought a man to punishment is his having not a love but [rather a] hatred of labour; [then] to make labour his punishment, is only to make him hate it the more. If the more a man hates labour, the more he is likely to act as a bad member of society; to punish a man with labour, and then to turn him out upon society . . . savours not of the highest wisdom.[30]

Not only does the labour-hating inmate come to despise labour even more: the honest workingman outside the prison walls, seeing labour like his own being employed as a means of punishment, comes to think less of his honest toil. 'In treating labour as an instrument of punishment,' Mill asks, 'what sort of lesson do you teach to the industrious and laborious

---

[28] James Mill, 'Prisons', *PW* 204; cf. 'Education', *PW* 185.
[29] James Mill, *Philanthropist*, 2/8 (1812), 360.
[30] James Mill, 'Prisons', *PW* 204.

class, who form the great body of your people? to those whose lot is labour ... harder than any which it is in your power to impose?' He concludes that, as 'an instrument of punishment, hardly any thing can be conceived more exceptionable [than labour]. That which is the source of all that mankind enjoy, that which is the foundation of every virtue in the most numerous class of the community, would you stamp with ignomy and dishonour, by inflicting it as a punishment upon the worst and basest of your people?' And finally, Mill adds, labour is ill-suited as a means of punishment for still another reason. If punishment is to be fair, it must be meted out equitably; two criminals imprisoned for the same offence should, ideally, be made to suffer equally. But labour 'operates with more inequality than almost any other instrument of punishment ... The same degree of labour would kill one man, that to another would be only a pastime.'[31]

These considerations lead Mill to doubt the value of labour as a source of pain and an instrument of punishment. Yet Mill is not prepared to abandon labour as an instrument of reform. On the contrary, he thinks that labour, properly used, might prove a most valuable instrument. His solution is one of which some modern behaviourists might well approve.

An inmate is in prison in the first place, Mill avers, because he despises labour. He hates labour, moreover, because he 'associates' the idea of labour with the 'painful sensations'. If his mind is to be re-formed, some way must be found to make him associate labour with the pleasurable sensations. 'What is desired', Mill writes, is 'to create a habit of doing useful acts, break the habit of doing hurtful acts.' These habits are created (or destroyed, as the case may be) by 'making the individual in question perform certain acts, [and] abstain from the performance of certain other acts'. This can be accomplished either by punishment or by reward. But, since we wish to instil a 'love of labour' in the inmate, we cannot use labour as a source of pain to him, lest he come to despise it all the more. 'Labour', says Mill, should 'be regarded as the foundation of all reformatory discipline. But as the object of this discipline is to train the man to love, not to hate labour, we

---

[31] James Mill, 'Prisons', *PW* 204.

must not render the labour any part of his punishment. The labour must, for this important purpose, be a source of pleasure, not of pain.' Labour produces pleasurable consequences in prison in exactly the same way as it produces pleasure outside: 'Advantages must accrue from the performing of it.' And in the closed society of the prison it is especially 'easy to prevent the attaining of any pleasure, except through the medium of labour'.[32] There one can withhold the amenities of life—soap, sweets, tobacco, and the like—from those who will not work for them. By rewarding his labours with these 'indulgences' one can establish in the inmate's mind the 'association' between present pain and future pleasure, i.e. between labour and reward. When that association is firmly established, the inmate is then said to be reformed. Now equipped with the particular virtue of the labourer—'industry' or 'love of labour'—he is at last fit to re-enter society and to perform his proper function. Thus does Mill, in effect, advocate the application of associationist means for the achievement of Platonic ends.

But why Plato? Why would Mill turn to this ancient author to lend legitimacy to schemes for penal reform advanced by a distinctly modern (and decidedly anti-Platonic) political thinker? There are, I believe, two possible (and interconnected) reasons. The first is that Mill was by education and inclination wont to redescribe many modern problems and phenomena in 'Platonic' terms. Such platonizing came quite naturally to him.[33] But this penchant was by no means unique to Mill. A ready recourse to Plato and the ancients was instead part of the culture of political argument in nineteenth-century Britain. The Tories and the Whigs each had 'their' Plato, and the Philosophic Radicals theirs; but the important point to note is that they argued against each other 'in Greek', as it were, with Platonic and other arguments always available and at the ready.[34] Little wonder, then, that Mill should have turned so easily and so readily to Plato in order

[32] Ibid. 210–11.
[33] On Mill's Platonist leanings, see W. Thomas, *The Philosophical Radicals* (Oxford, 1979), ch. 3.
[34] See F. M. Turner, *The Greek Heritage in Victorian Britain* (New Haven, Conn., 1981).

to redescribe and legitimize what might otherwise appear to be too-radical—not to say hare-brained—Benthamite schemes for penal reform. To redescribe such schemes in familiar and perhaps even comfortable 'classical' terms was, in the discourse of the day, to present them in a more favourable and legitimate light.

7.6 WHAT FOUCAULT MISSED

My interpretation, if correct, should cast some doubt upon the conventional view of James Mill as Bentham's mere mouthpiece and disciple. Taking one small corner of his social and political thought—his views on punishment—I have tried to show that Mill's ideas are not simply borrowed from Bentham. To be sure, there is, on the surface, a considerable and effusively acknowledged debt to Bentham's thinking on these matters.[35] But, looking beneath the surface to the structure of the arguments he employed to 'translate' and legitimate Bentham's schemes, we detect the brooding presence, not only of Bentham, but of Plato as well. It thus appears that John Stuart Mill was quite correct on at least two counts. First, his father was indeed 'a pupil of Plato, and cast in the mould of his dialectics'. And, secondly, James Mill was, as his son rightly remarked, 'anything but Bentham's mere follower or disciple . . . His mind and Bentham's were of essentially different construction.'[36] A closer look at James Mill's supposedly Benthamite theory of punishment appears to bear this out.

What then is the upshot of this discovery? Just this: Mill,

---

[35] For example, Mill concludes 'Prisons' with this too-modest disclaimer: 'There is not, we believe, an idea [in this essay] which did not originate with Mr. Bentham, whose work ought to be the manual of all those who are concerned in this material department of public administration' (*PW* 224). Bentham expected such praise from his followers, and perhaps especially from Mill, whose meagre livelihood was supplemented by Bentham's largesse. In his private correspondence Mill complains repeatedly of the testiness and garrulousness of 'the old philosopher' and of their frequent quarrels. After the literary and financial success of his *History of British India* (1818), Mill ceased to sing Bentham's praises and the two soon parted with some bitterness on both sides.

[36] J. S. Mill, *Autobiography*, 122.

like Plato and Bentham, believed that expert knowledge, rightly applied by experts, would render society safer, saner, and more just. All believed that the good society could only come about through the therapeutic interventions and minis-trations of an élite corps of selfless and dedicated doctors of the sick society. It is against this backdrop that Mill's 'Platonic' theory of punishment comes into clearer view. However noble his intentions, there should be no mistaking their essentially manipulatory character: by 'reform' Mill quite literally meant the re-forming of men's minds and characters. Like Bentham, Mill averred that manipulative penal practices ought not be confined solely to prisons. In Mill's scheme of social reformation, the efficient and well-run prison emerges as a microcosm or model of the good society itself. It is within prison walls that men's characters can be most readily and expertly reformed. Such enlightened expertise should also be applied, Mill believed, not only to the reformation of crim-inals but to the initial formation of all men's and women's minds and characters. Their minds being formed to know the good, they would have no choice except to do good. Fitted to perform their proper function, they would perform it without disagreement or dissent. A society whose members were thus properly educated would have no use for prisons. This, at least, was Mill's ideal. But in the final analysis his ideal may admit of a different and more frightening Foucauldian description: only when society itself has become a prison would prisons become superfluous.

That, at any rate, is how Foucault might have deepened and strengthened his story, had he included James Mill in the telling. But to include Mill would perforce require him to rec-ognize the part played by Plato in Mill's thinking about disci-pline and punishment. It would require bringing the 'Greeks' back in, and giving Plato his due.

7.7 TEXTBOOK VS. GENEALOGICAL HISTORIES

What larger lessons might lurk in the revisionist tale I have told here? If that tale is true—or at any rate plausible—we can, I believe, learn at least two things from this episode. The first and most general of these is that we should be wary of traditional intellectual historians who retrospectively construct monolithic 'traditions' and seamless 'schools' of thought into which supposedly similar thinkers can be forced, Procrustes-like, against their will and against readily available evidence to the contrary. Whatever its attractions, the textbook picture of the history of political thought as an ongoing intergenerational conversation about perennial ideas and timeless truths is deceptively simple and sometimes simply wrong. Nor should we succumb to the temptation to think of that history as a cumulative process, with each thinker adding a building block to a growing and ever more magnificent edifice. We should, as Foucault rightly reminds us, be sensitive to the possible presence of discontinuities, of conceptual revolutions and radical innovations, in social and political thinking.[37]

The second moral of my tale is that we should be no less wary of modern genealogists who purport to find discontinuities or breaks between early or 'classical' and modern 'epistemes' or discursive 'grids' or 'systems of thought'.[38] Important features of what Foucault believes to be distinctively and discontinuously modern ideas are actually arguments that modern thinkers (in this case Mill) have reworked or recycled from distant forerunners (in this instance Plato). And in this crucial respect the history of political thought is not at all like the history of the natural sciences, as Bachelard and Kuhn would have us write it. It is unlikely, not to say inconceivable, that bits of (say) Aristotelian physics could be borrowed and put to use by a modern theoretical physicist. But it is just here that the natural sciences depart, quite dramatically and in principle, from political theory. Old arguments from earlier *political* thinkers can be, and often are, adapted or retrofitted for use by later political thinkers. Foucault's borrowing of the Bachelardian model for writing histories of the human sciences blinds him to this ever-present possibility.

Of course, to criticize Foucault is not to deny his power as

[37] M. Foucault, 'Nietzsche, Genealogy, History', in *Language, Counter-Memory, Practice* (Ithaca, NY, 1977), 139–64.
[38] It may bear mentioning that Foucault's formal title at the Collège de France was Professor of the History of Systems of Thought.

a political theorist or a historian of the human sciences. From its grisly opening scene through its detailed descriptions of the mechanisms of surveillance to its deeply disturbing conclusion, *Discipline and Punish* is a most remarkable book. In Foucault's hands, the panopticon becomes a powerful and memorable metaphor. One can only marvel at what Bentham, that curmudgeonly critic of all metaphor, might have made of the panopticon's passage from stone and steel into something as airy and insubstantial as a metaphor for the modern surveillance society. Yet the view from any tower, be it of stone or ivory, is necessarily partial and incomplete. Foucault, overseer-nemesis of guards and guardians, missed or misinterpreted much of what came under his powerful gaze. There is, as Norwood Russell Hanson liked to say, 'more to seeing than meets the eyball'.[39] All observations, including those made by historians of social and political thought, are in some sense 'theory-laden'. In Foucault's case, the theory is a historiographical one that stresses discontinuities, 'breaks', and 'ruptures' between discrete *epistemes*. I have argued that such a theory, when put into interpretive practice, and perhaps particularly in political theory, yields results that are more apt to be dramatic than historically accurate.

[39] See N. R. Hanson, *Patterns of Discovery* (Cambridge, 1965), 7.

8

UTILITARIANISM, FEMINISM, AND THE FRANCHISE

> In the government of the physical world it is observable
> that the female in point of strength is, in general, inferior
> to the male. This is the law of Nature ... But not con-
> tent with this natural preeminence, men endeavour to
> sink us still lower, merely to render us alluring objects
> for a moment.
>
> Mary Wollstonecraft

8.1 INTRODUCTION

If nothing else, the preceding studies have shown something of
the variety of interpretive standpoints from which one may
reread and reappraise the works of earlier political theorists.
One of the newest and most suggestive of these standpoints is
supplied by feminist theory. And yet to reread the history of
political thought from a feminist perspective is to be struck by
the extent to which the legal and political status of women
was long considered to be a subject unfit for theoretical treatment. The neglect of women in the history of Western political thought is (to speak French) an 'absence' or 'silence' that,
to modern ears, is deafening. To this dismal rule there are,
however, several apparent (though arguably anachronistic)
exceptions: Plato challenged the complacent view (reiterated
by Aristotle) that women are unfit to rule or even to take part
in public life; Locke challenged Filmer's patriarchal doctrine;[1]
Mary Wollstonecraft extended Paine's views on the rights of
man to include women as well; and, not least, 'the majority of

---

[1] For two sharply contrasting views of Locke and women, see M. Butler,
'Early Liberal Roots of Feminism: John Locke and the Attack on Patri-
archy', *APSR* 72 (1978), 135–50; and C. Pateman, *The Sexual Contract*
(Stanford, Calif., 1988), esp. ch. 2.

the Utilitarian Radicals, with Bentham at their head', were 'feminists'.[2] Bentham, indeed, was 'the father of feminism',[3] and John Stuart Mill its 'patron saint'.[4] The odd man out was James Mill. For it was he who, in the course of the debate preceding the 1832 Reform Act, contended that women can 'without inconvenience' be denied the right to vote, inasmuch as their interests are 'included in' those of their husbands and fathers. In the annals of political thought there is surely no more blatant expression of sexist sentiment, and James Mill has been duly classified and condemned as an ardent antifeminist from whose views his son somehow escaped.

That, at any rate, is the conventional view. Matters are not, however, so simple; the case of the Philosophic Radicals, and of the two Mills in particular, is rather more complex, convoluted, and interesting than anyone has heretofore supposed. My aim here is to challenge the conventional view from several different angles. My initial point of entry is provided by James Mill's proposed exclusion of women from the franchise. I begin by showing how James Mill's ostensible opposition to women's suffrage is inconsistent with his view of women in his *History of British India*. By comparing his *History* with his *Essay on Government* we can see that the former has 'feminist' implications denied by the latter. Considered in the round, Mill's view of women's roles and rights is not so straightforwardly male-supremacist as has been supposed. I next examine the oft-heard claim that Bentham was a feminist and, indeed, the main source of J. S. Mill's enlightened view of women. A close analysis of Bentham's writings suggests that he is not the feminist he is widely believed to be; on the contrary, his views on the roles and rights of women are every bit as benighted as James Mill's are reputed to be, and possibly more so. This in turn casts doubt upon the conventional view that J. S. Mill's feminist views are traceable to Bentham's. I then go on to consider the claim that J. S. Mill's feminist convictions owe a good deal to his wife, Harriet Taylor Mill, or, alternatively, to T. B. Macaulay. I conclude by arguing that

[2] E. Halévy, *The Growth of Philosophic Radicalism* (London, 1929), 20.
[3] L. C. Boralevi, *Bentham and the Oppressed* (Berlin, 1984), 22–6.
[4] M. Williford, 'Bentham on the Rights of Women', *JHI* 36 (1975), 167–76.

the younger Mill's feminism owes little, if anything, to these thinkers, and rather a lot to two previously unsuspected sources. By means of this critique I hope to undermine the conventional interpretation of the Philosophic Radicals' relation to modern feminism, the two Mills' relation to each other and to modern feminism, and to lay the groundwork for a new interpretation.

8.2 JAMES MILL'S TWO POSITIONS

In the midst of writing his article on 'Government' for the *Encyclopaedia Britannica*, James Mill attempted to reassure his nervous editor: 'You need be under no alarm about my article Government. I shall say nothing capable of alarming even a whig . . .'[5] As it turned out, Mill was quite mistaken. His *Essay on Government* alarmed almost everyone, Whigs, Tories, and those among his fellow Philosophic Radicals who (like his son) regarded themselves as feminists. For the latter, the most alarming statement in that controversial essay was this:

One thing is pretty clear, that all those individuals whose interests are indisputably included in those of other individuals, may be struck off without inconvenience. In this light may be viewed all children, up to a certain age, whose interests are involved in those of their parents. In this light, also, women may be regarded, the interest of almost all of whom is involved either in that of their fathers or in that of their husbands.[6]

Abandoning his penchant for understatement, J. S. Mill later termed this paragraph from his father's *Essay* 'the worst . . . he ever wrote'.[7] Mill's other critics, as we shall see, were no less aghast. The antifeminist tone and implications of this paragraph are patent: politically speaking, a woman is like a

---

[5] James Mill to Macvey Napier (10 Sept. 1819), BL Add. MSS 34612, fos. 287–8.

[6] James Mill, 'Government', *PW* 27.

[7] J. S. Mill, *The Early Draft of John Stuart Mill's Autobiography*, ed. J. Stillinger (Urbana, Ill., 1961), 98. This remark was, however, excised from the final draft of the *Autobiography*. (Note: I have referred throughout the present chapter to the more complete *Early Draft*, noting, as here, any differences between the early and the final versions.)

child, but with this difference—children (or at least male children) grow up to assume the mantle of citizenship, while women do not. Mill's position *vis-à-vis* women is clearly a condescending and paternalistic one.

If Mill's *Essay* represented his first and last words on the subject, he would doubtless deserve the contempt that feminist critics have heaped upon him. Yet their harsh judgement may be mitigated somewhat if we turn from the *Essay* to the work of which he was proudest, his massive *History of British India*. The position taken in the latter differs markedly from—and arguably contradicts—that taken in the former. A comparison of these two works reveals an ambivalent and clearly contradictory region in an ostensibly rigorous and generally consistent political philosophy.[8]

Mill's multi-volume *History* stands in stark contrast to the brief *Essay*. The *Essay*, he remarked, was nothing more than a 'comprehensive outline', a sketch or 'skeleton map' in which 'the principles of human nature' and their political implications were briefly and boldly exhibited.[9] His *History*, by contrast, was meant to portray in copious detail the operation of these principles.[10] For this reason his *History*, Mill boasted, 'makes no bad introduction to the study of civil society in general'.[11] India was for Mill and his fellow Utilitarians a laboratory in which to conduct reformist experiments. His is accordingly a 'critical' or 'judging history' in which India's past and present were judged by Utilitarian criteria and found wanting.[12] If Mill criticized and condemned Indian customs and practices, that was only because he believed it necessary to pave a path towards a more 'progressive' future.[13] Significantly, Mill's criticism and condemnation of Hindu

---

[8] For a brief overview of James Mill's political philosophy, see my Introduction to *PW*.

[9] James Mill to Napier (11 May 1820), BL Add. MSS 34612, fo. 354; James Mill to Dumont (8 June 1821), MSS Dumont, Bibliothèque Publique et Universitaire (Geneva), MS 76, fo. 21.

[10] James Mill, *History of British India* (London, 1818), i. x–xii.

[11] James Mill to Ricardo (19 Oct. 1817), in David Ricardo, *Works and Correspondence*, ed. P. Sraffa (Cambridge, 1962), vii. 195–6.

[12] James Mill, *History*, i, p. x.

[13] See D. Forbes, 'James Mill and India', *Cambridge Journal*, 5 (1951), 19–33; E. Stokes, *The English Utilitarians and India* (Oxford, 1959), 48–57.

practices includes an implicit, and even impassioned, defence of the rights of women.

The history of India, Mill told Ricardo, 'afforded an opportunity of laying open the principles and laws of the social order in almost all its more remarkable states, from the most rude to the most perfect . . .'.[14] In the *History* Mill takes 'the condition of women' to be

> one of the most decisive criterions [*sic*] of the stage of society at which [a nation has] arrived. Among rude people, the women are generally degraded; among civilized people, they are exalted . . . The history of uncultivated nations uniformly represents the women as in a state of abject slavery, from which they slowly emerge, as civilization advances.[15]

Following John Millar and the Scottish school, Mill explains this moral and social advancement partly in 'materialist' terms.[16] The moral 'state of society' depends, in Mill's view, upon economic and technological conditions. In backward or 'rude' societies, a premium is placed upon sheer physical strength; the strong are exalted over the weak because their physical strength is the society's means of wresting a living from a recalcitrant nature. Women being in general physically weaker than men, they are subservient to them. Once this subsistence stage is transcended, however, physical strength comes to count for less; other qualities—'qualities of mind'—begin to be recognized and developed.

> In proportion as society . . . advances into that state of civilization, in which . . . the qualities of the mind are ranked above the qualities of the body [says Mill], the condition of the weaker sex is gradually improved, till they associate at last on equal terms with the men, and fill the place of voluntary and useful copartners.[17]

Taking the 'condition of women' as a 'decisive criterion'— the same criterion, incidentally, later used by J. S. Mill in *The Subjection of Women*[18]—Mill passes a harsh judgement on Hindu society. There is, in his view, no more primitive or rude society than that of the Hindus, if we are to judge by

---

[14] Ricardo, *Works*, vii. 195.   [15] James Mill, *History*, i. 293.
[16] J. Millar, *Inquiry into the Distinction of Ranks* (Edinburgh, 1806); J. Mill, 'Millar on Ranks', *Literary Journal* (June 1806), 624–9.
[17] James Mill, *History*, i. 293–4.   [18] See Ch. 8.4 below.

their treatment of women: 'A state of dependence more strict and humiliating than that which is ordained for the weaker sex among the Hindus cannot easily be conceived.'[19] With the arrival of the British and the introduction of advanced Western technology, this mistreatment of women loses whatever material-productive basis and justification it might once have had. The continued supremacy of men and subservience of women is wholly lacking in rational economic justification, and its sole source now resides only in archaic Hindu religious beliefs and practices. By way of illustration Mill cites several passages from the *Institutes of Menu*, the Hindu holy book:

'Day and night', says Menu, 'must women be held by their protectors in a state of dependence'. Who is meant by their protectors is immediately explained: 'Their fathers protect them in childhood; their husbands protect them in their youth, their sons protect them in old age: a woman', it is added, 'is never fit for independence ... In childhood must a female be dependant [*sic*] on her father; in youth, on her husband; her lord being dead, on her sons: a woman must never seek independence'.[20]

Another Hindu holy text, the *Hetopadesa*, contains a similar commandment: 'In infancy the father should guard her, in youth her husband should guard her, and in old age her children should guard her; for at no time is a woman fit to be treated with liberty.'[21] Such commandments, Mill maintains, are outmoded relics of a bygone era, and ought now be discarded. 'Nothing', he says, 'can exceed the habitual contempt which the Hindus entertain for their women. Hardly are they ever mentioned in their laws, or other books, but as wretches of the most base and vicious inclinations, on whose nature no virtue or useful qualities may be grafted.'[22] Worse still, Mill adds, is the Hindu's failure to recognize, much less develop, the moral and religious 'qualities of mind' that women share with men—witness, for example, their practice of excluding unmarried women from religious observances. Mill thinks it a mark of 'extreme degradation' that women 'are not accounted worthy to partake of religious rites but in conjunction with their husbands'.[23]

[19] James Mill, *History*, i. 294.
[20] Quoted in ibid. 294.
[21] Ibid. 295.
[22] Ibid. 295.
[23] Ibid. 296.

Ironically, the trap that Mill sets to catch the Hindu seems to ensnare Mill as well. The 'decisive criterion' that he applies to Indian society is not applied to English society. It is curious that Mill, who in his *History* thought it a sign of 'extreme degradation' that Hindu women 'are not accounted worthy to partake of religious rites but in conjunction with their husbands', was nevertheless prepared to exclude English women from that pre-eminently political rite—voting—on the ground that their husbands may speak in their stead.[24] Is the latter position, as advocated in his *Essay*, not tantamount to keeping women 'in a state of dependence'? In identifying a girl's interest with her father's, and a woman's with her husband's, is Mill not in effect endorsing the Hindu maxim that 'Their fathers protect them in childhood; their husbands protect them in their youth . . .'? And is this not in turn tantamount to saying, with Menu, that 'a woman must never seek independence . . . at no time is a woman fit to be trusted with liberty'? In short: is not Mill's exclusion of women from the franchise merely an anglicized and politicized version of the very practices for which he condemns the Hindus?

We must, I think, answer all these questions in the affirmative. Mill does indeed appear to stake out and defend two mutually contradictory positions. When prescribing for the Hindu, Mill assumes one position—his missionary position, as it were—but when prescribing for his countrymen, he appears to adopt quite another. The first has profeminist implications overlooked by his critics; the second has antifeminist implications which his critics have been quick to seize upon. It is this latter position for which Mill is today remembered and roundly condemned. Yet this condemnation may be less than just, if we take the former or 'feminist' passages of his *History* into account.

To the question, which of these represents Mill's 'real' position?, I can give no satisfactory answer—nor, I suspect, could Mill himself. He appears never to have seen the contradiction between the *Essay* and the *History*.[25] For a thinker less logical

[24] James Mill, 'Government,' *PW* 27.
[25] James Mill left unchanged his discussion of women in the second edition of his *History* (1820), which appeared in the same year as the *Essay on Government*.

than Mill, such a contradiction might occasion little surprise; but in Mill's case the presence of such a contradiction is, to say the least, perplexing.

The perplexity might be mitigated somewhat, if we accept the view taken by J. S. Mill and, more recently, by William Thomas, that the *Essay on Government* was less a logically rigorous 'scientific treatise on politics' than a partisan political 'argument for parliamentary reform'.[26] James Mill spoke truthfully when he told his editor that he did not want to alarm even a whig. And one of the surest ways to offend a great many readers would be to propose the enfranchisement of women. Thus Mill, for political reasons, pulled his punches and played down the radical implications of reform along the lines favoured by the Philosophic Radicals. Hence the contradictions and logical lacunae in his *Essay on Government*. And it bears mentioning, in support of such an interpretation, that—as the younger Mill himself notes—James Mill says only that women '*may* be' excluded from the franchise, and not that they *must* or *should* be 'struck off'.[27]

But this exculpatory interpretation may well carry the principle of interpretive charity too far. For, in the first place, James Mill did not draw a distinction between a 'scientific treatise on politics' and a coherent and compelling political argument in favour of 'parliamentary reform'. Nor, secondly, could he do so, since he held that the best political arguments just *are* scientific and that any reforms that were workable and worth having could only be based on an adequate scientific theory of society. The *Essay on Government* was meant to be both, if only in brief outline, and his *History* was also, although at much greater length. Yet, all the talk about 'science' and the show of logical rigour notwithstanding, there does appear to be a tension, if not a contradiction, between the view of women advanced in these works. When all is said and done, we must, I think, recognize that Mill was a man of his time whose views regarding the role and rights of women,

---

[26] J. S. Mill, *Early Draft*, 134; see further, W. Thomas, 'James Mill's Politics: The Essay on Government and the Movement for Reform', *Historical Journal*, 12 (1969), 249–84; and 'James Mill's Politics: A Rejoinder', ibid. 14 (1971), 735–50.

[27] James Mill, 'Government', *PW* 27; J. S. Mill, *Early Draft*, 98.

although clearly quite advanced in certain respects, are in the final analysis ambivalent at best. But James Mill's views are no less ambivalent, as we shall see, than those of Jeremy Bentham.

8.3 BENTHAM'S AMBIVALENT ANTIFEMINISM

Jeremy Bentham has long been regarded as an ardent defender of women's rights. No less an authority than Halévy maintains that 'the majority of the Utilitarian Radicals, with Bentham at their head,' were 'feminists'.[28] A modern feminist historian agrees that 'Bentham was a feminist' with a marked 'enthusiasm for women's rights'.[29] Another suggests that Bentham was a 'feminist', albeit a 'covert' one.[30] And more recently Lea Campos Boralevi has called Bentham the 'father of feminism'.[31] But was Bentham really a feminist, or even, for that matter, a distant forerunner or 'father' of modern feminism? After briefly examining the reasons most commonly advanced for supposing Bentham to be a feminist, I shall argue that he almost certainly cannot be so described in any simple or straightforward way.

Bentham's reputation as a feminist derives from several sources. He was, for example, an outspoken critic of laws pertaining to marriage, going so far as to advocate divorce, inasmuch as a union from which there is no possibility of escape constitutes a kind of 'slavery'.[32] But Bentham's privileged position in the feminist pantheon is usually traced to two other considerations. The first is his supposed defence of women's suffrage, developed in part in his dissent from the antifeminist stance taken in James Mill's *Essay*; the second has to do with his supposed influence upon the younger Mill's feminist views, particularly as expounded in *The Subjection of Women*. Both considerations are, however, chimerical.

According to his biographer, Bowring, Bentham counted

---

[28] Halévy, *Growth of Philosophic Radicalism*, 20.
[29] Williford, 'Bentham on the Rights of Women', 168.
[30] M. P. Mack, *Jeremy Bentham* (London, 1962), 112.
[31] Boralevi, *Bentham and the Oppressed*, 22–6.
[32] Bentham, *Works*, i. 352–5.

among the elder Mill's 'heresies' his 'abominable opinion' of women.[33] Bentham, moreover, took strong exception to Mill's proposed exclusion of women from the franchise. In a set of unpublished notes he criticized Mill's *Essay* for its exclusionist 'position, the object of which is to place all females under the absolute dominion of all males . . . Reasons for the exclusion none.'[34] Bentham develops this objection at greater length in his *Constitutional Code*: 'If a man who calls for the right of suffrage to be given to any one human being, calls for its being refused to any other human being, it lies upon him to give a particular reason for such refusal.' If we are to exclude anyone from the franchise, we must enumerate those 'disqualifying circumstances' which, taken together, would tip the balance against the presumption of their being eligible to vote.[35] In the case of children, the balance is easily tipped; they are excluded only temporarily, on the ground that they are 'not yet competent to the management of [their] own affairs . . .'. But, adds Bentham, 'the exclusion thus put on the ground of age, is not like the exclusion put on the ground of sex', because gender, unlike age, does not change. 'Why', Bentham asks, 'exclude the whole female sex from all participation in the constitutive [i.e. electoral] power?' For, he continues, 'On the ground of the greatest happiness principle, the claim of this sex is . . . at least . . . as good as that of the other. The happiness and interest of a person of the female sex, constitutes as large a portion of the universal happiness and interest, as does that of a person of the male sex.' There is, Bentham maintains, 'no reason . . . why a person of the one sex should as such have less happiness than a person of the other sex'. Warming to his subject, Bentham goes further still: since women are subject to physiological pains unique to their sex—'such as pains of gestation, of parturition, labour of nurturition, periodical and casual weaknesses, [and] inferiority in

---

[33] Bentham, *Works*, x. 450. The veracity of this, and other, remarks attributed to Bentham by Bowring, was questioned by J. S. Mill: see A. Bain, *James Mill: A Biography* (London, 1882), 461–3.

[34] Bentham MSS, UCL, box 34, folder 12, fos. 302–3.

[35] Bentham, *Works*, ix. 108. Bentham subscribed to the 'presumptivist' view that people are to be treated alike unless a 'relevant difference' between them can be established: cf. I. Berlin, 'Equality', in *Concepts and Categories* (London, 1978), 81–102.

all physical contests with the male sex'—their claim to happiness from other, non-physiological sources is greater than men's. It can, therefore, be argued that women should have a correspondingly greater share of electoral or 'constitutive' power. In this regard, 'the principle of equality affords another reason, not merely for admitting the female sex to an equal share in the constitutive, but even to a greater share than in the case of the male'. No less important is women's need to make up in political power what they lack in physical power. For example, 'in domestic concerns, males derive greater power from physical force: here, then, is a means of injury: for security against it, if in respect of political power, there should be a difference, it should rather be in their favour than in the favour of males'.[36]

Bentham's case for giving women the vote comes to this: everyone has an equal interest in happiness. But it does not follow from this that women's interests are wholly included in those of their husbands or fathers. On the contrary, since happiness is nothing more than the sum of its elements, and the composition and nature of those elements is in part sexually determined and gender-specific, then men and women may have very different interests. Indeed, their respective interests may not only be different, but antithetical. For example, if a man's interest in happiness is served by his regularly beating his wife, it does not follow that her interest in happiness is 'included in' that of her husband; on the contrary, her pain being the source of his pleasure, her interest is diametrically opposed to his. Women are, moreover, subject to certain kinds of pain—e.g. the physical and psychic pain of rape—to which men are not similarly subject. If women are to have a say in the passage of legislation affecting their happiness, it follows, Bentham argues, that they must have a hand in electing legislators. Their enfranchisement is consistent with—indeed, required by—the Utilitarians' greatest-happiness principle.[37] Granted that the principle is sound, he asks: 'Can [any] practical good . . . [come] from admitting the female sex into a participation of the supreme constitutive power [i.e. the electorate]?' He answers: 'Yes. The affording increased proba-

---

[36] Bentham, *Works*, ix. 108.   [37] Ibid. 106–8.

bility of the adoption of legislative arrangements, placing sexual intercourse upon a footing less disadvantageous than the present to the weaker sex.'[38] The enfranchisement of women is thus justified in principle as well as in practice.[39]

From the foregoing it would appear that Bentham is indeed the feminist that he is reputed to be. The appearance may, however, be misleading. What Bentham gives with one hand he sometimes takes away with the other. After a lengthy consideration of the reasons for enfranchising women, Bentham nevertheless concludes that they should, after all, be denied the right to vote. He justifies this rather surprising conclusion on grounds of practicality and of principle, and on both counts contradicts himself.

Bentham's 'practical' argument for exclusion runs as follows. He does not 'think it at present expedient to propose a set of legislative arrangements directed to this end' because 'the contest and confusion produced by the proposal of this improvement would entirely engross the public mind, and throw improvement, in all other shapes, to a distance'.[40] Returning, then, to his original question—'Why exclude the whole female sex from all participation in the constitutive power?'—he answers: 'Because the prepossession against their admission is at present too general, and too intense, to afford any chance in favour of a proposal for their admission.'[41] Taking this 'practical' objection as decisive, Bentham

---

[38] Ibid. 109.

[39] In a model constitution drafted for (but ignored by) the French revolutionaries, Bentham asks, 'Why admit women to the right of suffrage?' He answers: 'Why exclude them?' To the objection that their political duties would 'call them oft from their domestic duties', he replies: 'The men have their domestic duties as well as the women ... It is not more necessary that women should cook the victuals, clean the house, and nurse the children than it is that the greater part of the male sex should employ an equal share of their time in the labours of the workshop or the field' (Bentham MSS, UCL, box 170, folder 7, fos. 144–5). Before concluding that Bentham was an ardent feminist one should consult 'L'Essai sur la représentation', written for the French National Assembly in 1788. There Bentham says that, although everyone has an equal desire for happiness, some people—namely 'minors, the insane, and women'—are 'utterly lacking in the capacity of judging' what is, or is not, conducive to their happiness: extracted in E. Halévy, *La Formation du radicalisme philosophique* (Paris, 1904), i, app. IV, 429–430 (my trans.). This and other important appendices are unfortunately omitted from the English translation.

[40] Bentham, *Works*, ix. 109.   [41] Ibid. 108.

proceeded to draw up a less-than-radical *Radical Reform Bill* in which women were pointedly excluded from the franchise. In that proposal he stipulates that the suffrage, if it is to be at all meaningful, must be both universal and equal. But then he adds: '*Universality* we say for shortness, instead of *Virtual Universality*. No man means that children that can but just speak, should vote [nor] that females should vote.'[42] What then of equality? 'By *equality of suffrage*', Bentham explains, 'is meant equality . . . between the suffrage of one man and the suffrage of another.'[43] Nor does Bentham mean 'man' in the generic sense. The electors comprise 'every male person' who meets residence, literacy, and other requirements.[44]

Bentham's 'practical' argument for exclusion is remarkable in two respects. In the first place, he reaches—albeit by a different route—the exclusionist position enunciated in Mill's *Essay on Government*. Considered in this light, Bentham's purportedly profeminist critique of Mill loses much of its force and, indeed, its credibility. Secondly, the very mode of argument by which Bentham reaches his 'practical' conclusion is— by his own standards—an illegitimate one, inasmuch as he commits two of the 'fallacies of Delay' enumerated in his *Book of Fallacies*. The first fallacy of delay is to be found in 'The Procrastinator's Argument', to the effect that proponents of reform should 'wait a little, this is not the time'. This 'instrument of deception', he says, is 'employed by those who, being in wish and endeavour hostile to a measure, are afraid or ashamed of being seen to be so. They pretend, perhaps, to approve of the measure—they only differ as to the proper time of bringing it forward.' In this 'practical' ploy is concealed their 'wish . . . that it should remain excluded for ever'.[45] Bentham then hoists himself on his own petard: 'Which is the properest day to do good?—which is the properest day to remove a nuisance? Answer: The very first day that a man can be found to propose the removal of it; and whoso-

---

[42] Bentham, *Works*, iii. 559.   [43] Ibid. 561.   [44] Ibid. 564.

[45] Ibid. ii. 432. Bentham does, however, leave himself an escape hatch: 'True it is, that, the measure being a measure of reform or improvement, an observation to this effect may be brought forward by a friend of the measure: and in this case, it is not an instrument of deception, but an expedient of unhappily necessary prudence.'

ever opposes the removal of it on that day will, if he dare, oppose the removal on every other.'[46] Bentham's practical objection relies, moreover, upon a second fallacious argument—the 'snail's-pace argument'—which admonishes, 'One thing at a time! Not too fast! Slow and sure!'[47] Both forms of argument, he holds, are fallacious. And yet, with respect to the enfranchisement of women, Bentham's 'practical' argument for their exclusion relies implicitly upon the two aforementioned fallacies of delay.

Bentham's objections to women's suffrage are not, however, exclusively 'practical' ones resting upon political expediency.[48] Some of his objections are based explicitly or implicitly upon 'principle'. Of his scheme for 'virtual universality' of suffrage—in which all women are excluded—Bentham says that it is 'defensible on principle'.[49] Now, whenever Bentham speaks of 'principle', he invariably means the principle of Utility, or at least to some lesser principle subsumable under it. The enfranchisement of women must then somehow contravene the principle of Utility. But how, in the light of his arguments in the *Constitutional Code*, is such a view even conceivable, much less defensible? For the answer to that question we must turn to Bentham's *Introduction to the Principles of Morals and Legislation*. There Bentham draws a distinction between learnt and innate differences between the sexes—or, as we would say nowadays, between 'nurture' and 'nature'. Differences of the first sort stem from education and environment; differences of the second from 'primitive modifications of the corporeal frame', i.e. anatomical differences. The former can be eliminated, or at least modified, through education; the latter, being innate, cannot.

To which category, then, do the *politically* relevant differences between the sexes belong? Bentham answers that they belong, in the main, to unchangeable nature. A woman's nature, he maintains, is so constituted as to render her

---

[46] Bentham, *Works*, ii. 432. [47] Ibid. 433.

[48] *Pace* Mack, *Jeremy Bentham*, 323, 416; Williford, 'Bentham on the Rights of Women', 169–70; Boralevi, *Bentham and the Oppressed*, 25; and D. Baumgardt, *Bentham and the Ethics of Today* (Princeton, NJ, 1966), 467, all of whom hold that Bentham's objections are based solely on 'practical' considerations.

[49] Bentham, *Works*, iii. 599.

virtually unable to make rational political judgements—that is, decisions based upon the principle of Utility. This is so, he declares, because 'the female is rather more inclined than the male to superstition; that is, to observances not dictated by the principle of utility . . .'. This difference between the sexes, he adds, 'may be pretty well accounted for' by innate inclinations, that is, by 'the primitive modifications of the corporeal frame' that 'influence the quantum and bias of sensibility'.[50] A woman's 'sympathetic biases', Bentham continues,

> are in many respects different: for her own offspring . . . her affection is commonly stronger than that of the male. Her affections are apt to be less enlarged: seldom expanding themselves so much as to take in the welfare of her country in general, much less that of mankind, or the whole sensitive creation: seldom embracing any extensive class or division, even of her own countrymen, unless it be in virtue of her sympathy for some particular individuals that belong to it.

Women, in other words, are scarcely capable of thinking about, much less promoting, the greatest happiness of the greatest number; their 'sympathetic biases' rarely, if ever, extend beyond an immediate and intimate circle comprised of family and friends. 'In general', Bentham concludes, a woman's 'antipathetic, as well as sympathetic biases, are apt to be less conformable to the principle of utility than those of the male . . .'[51]

The political implications are both clear and astounding: A Utilitarian polity could not enfranchise women without subverting itself. To permit women to vote would be to open the door to 'superstition' and other forces hostile to the principle of Utility.[52] Considered in this light, Bentham's justification of 'virtual universality' of suffrage as 'defensible on principle' comes into clearer view. Politically speaking, biology—'primi-

---

[50] J. Bentham, *Introduction to the Principles of Morals and Legislation* (1789), in Bentham, *CW* i. 64.

[51] Ibid. 64–5.

[52] Contrast the analysis of sexual differences in Bentham's *Introduction to the Principles of Morals and Legislation* (1789), and in his model French constitution, written in the same year. Apparently Bentham, like Mill, was not above assuming his own 'missionary' position when dealing with the affairs of other nations. In any event, the *Introduction*'s account of sexual differences was retained unchanged in the 1823 edition, and so presumably reflects Bentham's final considered opinion.

tive modifications of the corporeal frame'—is destiny, and women are destined to be excluded from participation in Utilitarian politics. Their exclusion is predicated upon the principle of Utility itself.

To the degree that biology is destiny, education is, if not superfluous, of strictly limited value. This view is implicit in Bentham's *Introduction to the Principles of Morals and Legislation*, and explicit in his treatise on education, the *Chrestomathia*. Although 'female children' are to be admitted to Bentham's model Chrestomathic School, they—unlike the boys—are to receive instruction in 'needle-work' and other aspects of 'domestic economy'.[53] In any event, to instruct young women in the political arts would be to waste precious pedagogical resources. For, Bentham holds, not only should women be excluded from the franchise; they should also be excluded from serving on juries, holding public office, and even from attending parliamentary debates.[54] The two latter exclusions provide important clues to Bentham's thinking, and bear closer examination.

Considering that Bentham would in the end exclude women from voting, it is hardly surprising that he would likewise bar them from holding public office. But if this conclusion is not surprising, his reasons for reaching it are: 'The reciprocal seduction that would ensue in the case of a mixture of the sexes in the composition of a legislative or executive body, seems a conclusive reason against admitting the weaker sex into a share in those branches of power: it would lead to nothing but confusion and ridicule.' Bentham does not necessarily mean 'seduction' in a sexual or physical sense. He refers, rather, to the tendency of each sex's tendency to flatter and please the other in order to have its way—an art in which women are much more skilled than men. Their natural seductiveness, combined with 'the comparative inaptitude of the female sex, with reference to the legislative and executive functions,' is, Bentham believes, sufficient reason for barring women from public office. This apparent 'infringement on equality', he concludes, is 'necessary'.[55] Thus only men may hold political office.[56]

[53] Bentham, *Works*, viii. 56.   [54] Ibid. ii. 127.   [55] Ibid. ix. 108.
[56] Ibid. iii. 566.

Still it might be objected, Bentham acknowledges, that women have, after all, sat on the throne of England: why, then, should they not hold lesser public office? This 'practice of vesting political power in the softer sex', Bentham replies, is merely an artefact of a hereditary system of monarchy which will in due course disappear with the advancement of democracy.[57] To the further objection that women have served with distinction on the Directory of the East India Company, Bentham replies that the Company governs in an 'aristocratic', not a democratic, manner.[58] True, but irrelevant: Bentham, it will be observed, shifts the ground of his argument away from the 'reciprocal seduction' view previously advanced. If he were consistent, he would presumably be committed to the view that such mutual seductions have occurred between male and female directors of the East India Company. But he does not. Here Bentham's logic appears to be less impeccable than his decorum.

To the foregoing list of exclusions Bentham adds yet another: women ought not be allowed to attend parliamentary debates. In support of this exclusion Bentham argues as follows. The 'sinister interest' of the few is served by secrecy; the public interest of the many is served by 'publicity'—that is, by the public airing and critical examination of political positions and issues. A free press serves this critical function; so, too, does the practice of admitting visitors to parliamentary debates. Yet there must, Bentham adds, be some restrictions placed upon who is to be admitted. Clearly, anyone whose presence would disrupt the proceedings should be denied admission. Thus rowdies, drunks, and madmen ought to be excluded. But, Bentham asks,

Ought females to be admitted? No. I have hesitated, I have weighed the reasons for and against. I would repudiate a separation, which appears an act of injustice and contempt. But to fear [women] is not to despise them. Removing them from an assembly where tranquil and cool reason ought alone to reign, is avowing their influence, and it ought not to wound their pride.

Bentham does not say why this would leave women's pride intact. On the contrary, he goes on to add insult to injury by

[57] Bentham, *Works*, viii. 463.   [58] Ibid. 463.

arguing that their influence upon political debate and deliberation is wholly deleterious:

The seductions of eloquence and ridicule are most dangerous instruments in a political assembly. Admit females—you add a new force
to these seductions ... All the passions touch and enkindle each
other reciprocally. The right of speaking would often be employed
only as a means of pleasing; but the direct method of pleasing
female sensibility consists in showing a mind susceptible of emotion
and enthusiasm. Everything would take an exalted tone, brilliant or
tragical—excitement and tropes would be scattered everywhere; it
would be necessary to speak of liberty in lyric strains, and to be
poetic with regard to those great events which require the greatest
calmness.

Bentham concludes by praising the English House of
Commons for showing rare good judgement in banishing
women from parliamentary debates:

Among the English, where females have so little influence on political affairs—where they seek so little to meddle with them—where the
two sexes are accustomed to separate for a time, even after familiar
repasts—females are not permitted to be present at the parliamentary debates. They have been excluded from the House of Commons,
after the experiment has been tried, and for weighty reasons. It has
been found, that their presence gave a particular turn to the delibera-
tions—that self-love played too conspicuous a part—that personalities were more lively—and that too much was sacrificed to vanity
and wit.[59]

Bentham never considers the possibility that his 'weighty reasons' might have rather more to do with the silliness of men
than the seductiveness of women.

   In his proposals for depriving women of any distinctively
political rights and roles, Bentham considerably outdistances
James Mill. Mill, after all, merely suggested that women could
be excluded from the franchise. Bentham would deprive them
not only of the right to vote, but to serve on juries, hold public office, and attend parliamentary debates. Women are
consigned by Bentham to a kind of permanent political unemployment. Women's natural sphere of operation, he suggests,
is centred on home and hearth. And yet, when we enquire

[59] Ibid. ii. 327.

into his views concerning the familial microcosm, we find that women fare little better than they do in the wider political macrocosm.

There is, says Bentham, a 'fundamental law, which subjects the wife to the authority of the husband'.[60] This fundamental law, upon inspection, turns out to be the law of the strongest:

Between the wishes of two persons who pass their life together, there may at every moment be a contradiction. The benefit of peace renders it desirable that a pre-eminence should be established, which should prevent or terminate these contests. But why is the man to be the governor? Because he is the stronger. In his hands power sustains itself. Place the authority in the hands of the wife, every moment will be marked by revolt on the part of the husband.[61]

It is worth noting, in this connection, yet another difference between Bentham and James Mill. Bentham conceives this 'fundamental law'—that the weaker sex should be subordinated to the stronger—as a 'general law' valid for all times and places. The elder Mill, by contrast, links this law to the early stages of social and economic development, when such 'qualities of the body' as physical strength count for more than those 'qualities of the mind' shared by men and women alike. As these latter qualities are developed, men and women 'associate at last on equal terms' and become 'voluntary and useful copartners'.[62] In other words, Mill's analysis of sexual inequality has a *historical* dimension that is wholly absent in Bentham's analysis. Sexual equality is, for Mill, a historical possibility.

If Mill believes that husband and wife might one day be equals, Bentham does not. 'Master of the wife as to what regards his own interests,' the husband, Bentham says, 'ought to be guardian of the wife as to what regards her interests'.[63] The husband alone has the 'aptitude' for judging his wife's interests, and the 'authority' to enforce his judgements. 'This being the case, it is manifest', says Bentham, 'that the legal relation which the husband will bear to the wife will be a complex one: compounded of that of master and that of guardian.' Therefore, 'the condition of a husband', he adds,

[60] Bentham, *Works*, viii. 356. [61] Ibid. 355.
[62] James Mill, *History*, i. 294. [63] Bentham, *Works*, i. 355.

'stands upon the same footing as that of a parent', but with one difference: a husband is empowered to command 'certain reciprocal services' of a sexual nature which a parent may not command from a child.[64] Between husband and wife 'there subsists a legal obligation for the purpose of . . . a sexual intercourse to be carried on between them', in addition to 'the indiscriminate train of services at large which the husband in his character of master is impowered [*sic*] to exact . . .'.[65] Even so, Bentham admonishes, 'it is not proper to make the man a tyrant, and to reduce to a state of passive slavery the sex which, by its weakness and gentleness, has the greatest need of protection. The interests of females have too often been neglected.'

From this dismal history of neglect Bentham derives a moral: men should not cease to be masters but should strive to be better masters. One should at all costs avoid the 'dangerous snare' of 'absolute equality' between the sexes:

those who, from some vague notion of justice and of generosity, would bestow upon females an absolute equality, would only spread a dangerous snare for them. To set them free, as much as it is possible for the laws so to do, from the necessity of pleasing their husbands, would be, in a moral point of view, to weaken instead of strengthen their empire.[66]

These arguments against 'women's liberation' have, to modern ears, an oddly familiar ring.

Bentham's reputation as a feminist, or even as 'the father of feminism', is, to say the least, somewhat exaggerated. But old myths die hard. This particular myth got an early start and has gained credence over time. Bentham's enlightened views of women were contrasted, in his own day as in ours, with the benighted views of his two eminent followers, James Mill and Étienne Dumont. Exactly why Mill and Dumont should agree with Bentham about everything except women's rights has never been satisfactorily explained. I should like to suggest that there is nothing to explain, inasmuch as there is no gap to be bridged: Bentham is every bit as benighted as his two

---

[64] Bentham, *Introduction*, in Bentham, *CW* i. 255.   [65] Ibid. 254–5.
[66] Bentham, *Works*, i. 355.

disciples, and is, indeed, the most likely source of some of the views for which they have received all the blame.

The idea that Bentham differed from his two chief disciples over the political rights of women goes back a long way and has a number of sources. One of these was Bentham himself. After a serious falling-out with Mill in 1818 or so, Bentham scarcely had a good word to say for, or about, his former follower. Although their differences were personal rather than political, they coloured Bentham's assessment of Mill's subsequent work, and the *Essay on Government* in particular.[67] In his spite Bentham was not always consistent. Thus, in his notes on Mill's *Essay*, he criticized Mill for taking a position—that women may be excluded from the franchise—that Bentham himself took.[68] Much of Bentham's work remained unpublished in his own lifetime. Critics and admirers had little to criticize or to admire, and had in the main to rely on Dumont's French translations of Bentham's few finished works. Curiously, however, Bentham's antifeminist views passed unnoticed even by feminists. William Thompson provides a case in point.

Thompson was among the first to detect a rift between Bentham's enlightened view of women and the allegedly antifeminist views of Mill and Dumont. Indeed, Thompson wrote an entire book to refute a single paragraph in Mill's *Essay on Government*. After quoting the 'infamous paragraph' in Mill's *Essay*, Thompson comments:

Thus cavalierly are dealt with by this philosopher of humanity, the interests of one half the human species! Not so Mr. Bentham, whose disciple he is: the philosophy of that enlightened and benevolent man, embraces in its grasp every sentient human being, and acknowledges the claim of every rational adult, without distinction of sex or colour, to equal political rights. Is the authority of the disciple above that of the master?[69]

He is no less critical of Dumont:

Mr. Mill is not the only one of the new school of Utility who has misapplied the principle to the degradation of one half the human

[67] See Bain, *James Mill*, 461–3.

[68] Bentham MSS, UCL, box 34, folder 12, fos. 302–3.

[69] W. Thompson, *Appeal of One Half the Human Race* (London, 1825), 9–10.

race. Another philosopher of the new school, Mr. Dumont of Geneva, another retrograde disciple of the great master of Legislation, though the collator and editor in French of Mr. Bentham's manuscripts, unites with the author of the 'Article on Government' in his contemptuous exclusion of women. In the 'Tactiques des Assemblées Législatives' . . . this lover of equal justice recommends, *with great sorrow*, the exclusion of women from even listening to legislative debates; as is sagely done by . . . British Legislators . . . lest female blandishments should distract the young orators! Such is the wisdom of Mr. Dumont on the subject of women. Does Mr. Bentham approve of such puerilities?—He laughs at them.[70]

In both cases, however, Thompson is quite mistaken.

In the first place, Thompson errs in opposing Mill's exclusionist position to Bentham's; for, as we have seen, they both approve of excluding women from the franchise. Indeed Bentham goes even further than Mill by excluding women from all aspects of political life, including attending parliamentary debates. In the second place, Bentham does not 'laugh at'—he *agrees with*—Mill's and Dumont's antifeminist views. In fact, in Dumont's case, Bentham is the *source* of these 'puerilities'. After all, Dumont's *Tactique des assemblées législatives* is not his own work but Bentham's *Essay on Political Tactics*, faithfully rendered into French.[71] It was Bentham, not Dumont, who first proposed excluding women from legislative debates. Thus Thompson is quite mistaken, on both counts. Bentham could not laugh at Mill and Dumont without laughing at himself (which, on other occasions, he did, albeit rarely).

Thompson's Manichaean view of Bentham's relation to his foremost disciples rests upon a misunderstanding that subsequently became widespread. Even John Stuart Mill himself contributed to the myth that Bentham was a feminist. In his *Autobiography* the younger Mill wrote 'that every reason which exists for giving the suffrage to anybody, imperatively requires that it be given to women. This was also the general opinion of the younger proselytes: and it is pleasant to be able

[70] Ibid., pp. viii–ix.
[71] One can see just how faithful the translation is by comparing E. Dumont, *Tactiques des assemblées legislatives* (Geneva, 1816), i, 258–9, and Bentham, *Works*, ii. 327.

to say that Bentham, on this most important point, was wholly with us.'[72] But here, as so often in his *Autobiography*, his recollection is faulty.[73] Bentham, as we have seen, considers the reasons for *and against* enfranchising women, and concludes, on grounds of both practicality and principle, that women should not be granted the right to vote—nor, indeed, any other political or civil rights. If on some occasions Bentham was an ambivalent feminist, he was, on many more, an ardent antifeminist, at least by modern lights. There can be little doubt that, by the standards of the day, both Bentham and James Mill were well ahead of their time as regards the rights of women. But by contemporary criteria they not only fail to meet but fall, quite unsurprisingly, far short of even the most minimal standard of anything like a 'feminist' sensibility.

Bentham's reputation as a feminist, or at any rate a forerunner of modern feminism, rests upon the oft-heard claim that he dissented from the antifeminist position staked out in Mill's *Essay*. That claim, as we have seen, is mistaken; it rests upon a too-hasty and partial reading of Bentham's political writings, and cannot withstand close critical examination. That being so, we are now in a position to look critically at a second claim: that John Stuart Mill's feminist views were formed under Bentham's influence.

'Perhaps the most significant contribution of Bentham to the women's movement', writes Miriam Williford, 'was his influence on John Stuart Mill.' This 'patron saint of the women's movement' was led by 'Bentham's influence . . . to his initial interest in the condition of women'. John Stuart Mill 'took issue with [his father's] *Essay on Government* [and] accepted Bentham's view of women . . .'.[74] Having already examined 'Bentham's view of women', we can see how profoundly it differs from that advanced and defended in *The Subjection of Women*.

But if Bentham was not the source of J. S. Mill's feminist views, who was? Alice Rossi suggests one possibility. Mill's

---

[72] J. S. Mill, *Autobiography*, 99.

[73] For the points on which J. S. Mill's *Autobiography* serves as an unreliable guide, see W. Thomas, 'John Stuart Mill and the Uses of Autobiography', *History*, 56 (1971), 341–59.

[74] Williford, 'Bentham on the Rights of Women', 174–5.

feminist sensibilities, she claims, originated in and were deepened by his association with and subsequent marriage to Harriet Taylor. Harriet Taylor Mill was quite clearly 'a central figure in Mill's intellectual and personal life', and can be credited with Mill's conversion to feminism. 'It is doubtful', Rossi contends, 'that *The Subjection of Women* would ever have been written if it were not for Mill's twenty-eight-year relationship with Harriet Taylor.'[75]

Certainly it is true that John Stuart Mill set great store by his wife's views and opinions on this and many other matters. And certainly he was often extravagent in his praise, crediting her with inspiring and influencing much of his later work, especially his *Principles of Political Economy* (1848) and *On Liberty* (1859). But Mill explicitly denied that his feminist convictions were the product of his relationship with Harriet Taylor. Rossi notes Mill's denial, but dismisses it as 'curious'.[76] There is, in fact, nothing curious about it, as all the available evidence clearly attests.

In the first place, as Mill notes at the beginning of *The Subjection of Women*, his view that women are men's moral and political equals is 'an opinion which I have held from the very earliest period when I had formed any opinions at all on social or political matters'.[77] And, as he tells us in his *Autobiography*, this and other opinions were formed very early indeed. By the age of 12 his most fundamental opinions were already moulded, and at the age of 18 he was writing articles and essays on political subjects, several of them touching on the status of women. At the age of 19 he was arrested for making information about birth control available to married women. The younger Mill was quite clearly committed to the emancipation of women well before he met Harriet Taylor. They did not meet until 1830, when he was 25 (and unmarried) and she 23 (and married). As he remarks in his *Autobiography*, he was initially attracted to Harriet Taylor, and she to him, because both had already arrived at similar convictions on several subjects, including the rights of

[75] A. Rossi, 'Introduction' to J. S. Mill and H. T. Mill, *Essays on Sex Equality* (Chicago, 1970), 6.

[76] Ibid. 20.

[77] J. S. Mill, *The Subjection of Women* (London, 1869), 1.

women.[78] It would be 'curious' to the point of inexplicability if Mill had claimed otherwise.

Having now canvassed the conventional views about the origins of John Stuart Mill's feminism, we can see that none appears able to withstand close critical scrutiny. Against the foregoing interpretations I should like to offer, by way of conjecture and educated guess, two rather surprising possibilities. John Stuart Mill's enlightened view of women may be traced, in the first instance, to the influence of his father—not simply by way of his negative reaction to James Mill's *Essay on Government* but, more positively, to the profound impact that his father's *History of British India* had on his thinking. My second conjecture is that the younger Mill's feminist impulse was quickened by, but did not originate with, William Thompson's critique of the elder Mill's *Essay*. The first possibility I shall discuss straightaway, leaving the second for the section following.

8.4 THE FEMINIST AND HIS FATHER

I have tried to show that the elder Mill was not quite the unabashed antifeminist that he is reputed to be. His unsavoury reputation rests entirely upon a single short paragraph in his *Essay on Government*, and is belied by his much more extensive discussion of women in his *History of British India*. My analysis, if correct, should cast some doubt upon the validity of Packe's contention that John Stuart Mill's interest in women's rights was 'independently acquired as his father cared nothing for it'.[79] Packe and Williford are surely correct in suggesting that the younger Mill's feminist outlook was to some degree grounded in his reaction against his father's *Essay on Government*. Both, however, overlook the possibility that the son's feminist perspective might owe something to his father's other works, and more particularly to his *History of British India*. No one, so far as I am aware, has recognized or appreciated the extent to which J. S. Mill's defence of

[78] J. S. Mill, *Early Draft*, 196–7.
[79] M. St J. Packe, *Life of John Stuart Mill* (London 1954), 63.

women's rights may be traced in part to his father's influence. A reconsideration of their relationship is long overdue.[80]

In *The Subjection of Women* John Stuart Mill maintains that

the principle which regulates the existing social relations between the two sexes—the legal subordination of one sex to the other—is wrong in itself, and now one of the chief hindrances to human improvement; and that it ought to be replaced by a principle of perfect equality, admitting no power or privilege on the one side, nor disability on the other.

This, he adds, is 'an opinion which I have held from the very earliest period when I had formed any opinions at all on social or political matters ...'.[81] And, as readers of his *Autobiography* will recall, his opinions on social and political matters were formed at a remarkably early age, and under his father's stern tutelage.

J. S. Mill and the *History of British India* were conceived in the same year (1806) and quite literally grew up together. 'Almost as soon as I could hold a pen', he writes, 'I [wanted to] write a history of India too.'[82] For twelve years James Mill toiled over his *History*, as his son, seated beside him, laboured over lessons in Latin, Greek, and political economy. That experience, and the end result—*The History of British India*—had a profound and formative influence upon the younger Mill:

A book which contributed very much to my education was my father's History of India ... During the year [preceding its publication] I used to read ... the manuscript to him while he corrected the proofs. The number of new ideas which I received from this remarkable book, and the impulse and stimulus as well as guidance given to my thoughts by its criticisms and disquisitions on society and civilization in the Hindoo part ... made my early familiarity with this book eminently useful to my subsequent progress. And though I can perceive deficiencies in it now as compared with a perfect standard, I still think it the most instructive history ever yet written, and one of

---

[80] On J. S. Mill's intellectual debt to his father, see J. C. Rees, *John Stuart Mill's 'On Liberty'* (Oxford, 1985), chs. 1, 2.

[81] J. S. Mill, *Subjection*, 1.   [82] J. S. Mill, *Early Draft*, 43.

the books from which most benefit may be derived by a mind in the course of making up its opinions.[83]

Unfortunately John Stuart Mill does not tell us exactly how his mind 'benefit[ed] . . . in the course of making up its opinions'. But one possibility immediately suggests itself. Among his father's 'criticisms and disquisitions on society and civilization in the Hindoo part' was—as I noted earlier—a historical explanation and moral critique of the debasement of women.[84] In particular, James Mill takes a society's treatment of women as a 'decisive criterion' for judging its level of material and moral development.[85] Turning to *The Subjection of Women* we find his son likewise taking the 'elevation or debasement [of women] as on the whole the surest and most correct measure of the civilization of a people or an age'.[86] The elder Mill envisions sexual equality not merely as an ideal but as a genuine historical possibility.[87] So, too, does the younger Mill: 'Through all the progressive period of human history, the condition of women has been approaching nearer to equality with men. This does not of itself prove that the assimilation must go on to complete equality; but it assuredly affords some presumption that such is the case.'[88] No less striking is James Mill's stress upon the 'qualities of mind', shared by men and women alike, that come to the fore and are developed in 'advanced' societies.[89] This emphasis is equally apparent throughout his son's *Subjection of Women*.[90] Moreover, just as the elder Mill criticizes the Hindus' debasement of women as a historical anachronism, so the son likewise contends that 'The social subordination of women . . . stands out as an isolated fact in modern social institutions; a solitary breach of what has become their fundamental law; a single relic of an old world of thought and practice exploded in everything else, but retained in the one thing of most universal interest . . .'[91] Finally, James Mill's criticism of exclusionist *religious* practices is extended by his son in a distinctly *political* direction. The elder Mill thought it a sign of 'extreme

[83] J. S. Mill, *Early Drafts*, 50.
[85] Ibid. 293.
[87] James Mill, *History*, i. 293–4.
[89] James Mill, *History*, i. 294.
[91] Ibid. 36.

[84] James Mill, *History*, i. 293–5.
[86] J. S. Mill, *Subjection*, 38.
[88] J. S. Mill, *Subjection*, 38.
[90] J. S. Mill, *Subjection*, esp. ch. 3.

degradation' that Hindu women 'are not accounted worthy to partake of religious rites but in conjunction with their husbands'.[92] So, too, the younger Mill thought it degrading that women were excluded from sharing the rights and participating in the rites of political life.[93] Upon the right to vote, said J. S. Mill, everything else depends: 'When that has been gained, everything else will follow.'[94] And on this final matter the author of the *Essay* parted company with his son. What is striking, however, is not this well-publicized difference between them, but the many remarkable similarities between the view of women advanced in James Mill's *History* and that put forward in his son's *Subjection of Women*.

John Stuart Mill's debt to his father was two-sided. On the one side, he owed a considerable, if only obliquely acknowledged, debt to his father's *History*; on the other side, he owed a rather more negative debt to James Mill's *Essay on Government*. As he notes in his *Autobiography*, J. S. Mill could not rest until he had come to grips with all the more troubling aspects of his father's *Essay*. These included, in addition to troubling epistemological and methodological issues,[95] vexing moral questions about the political and legal status of women. The younger Mill could not accept his elder's view that the interests of women were somehow 'included in' those of their husbands and fathers. He did not, however, reach, much less defend, his view in an intellectual vacuum. He had the help of his father's *History*, as I have suggested already; he also had the help of others who were outspoken in their criticisms of James Mill's *Essay* and in particular its proposal to exclude women from the franchise. Foremost among these critics were William Thompson and Thomas Babington Macaulay.

8.5 THOMPSON AND MACAULAY

William Thompson was an Irish radical, self-described socialist, fellow-travelling Utilitarian, and an outspoken defender of

---

[92] James Mill, *History*, i. 296.

[93] J. S. Mill, *Subjection*, 95–7; *Early Draft*, 98–9.

[94] Quoted in Packe, *Life*, 500.

[95] Most notably, Macaulay's critique of James Mill's 'geometric' conception of political analysis: see J. S. Mill, *Early Draft*, 134–6; *System of Logic* (London, 1906), vi. 578–615.

women's rights. His *Appeal of One Half the Human Race*, directed explicitly and at length against that single 'infamous paragraph' in James Mill's *Essay*, created a minor sensation when it was published in 1825 and was almost as quickly forgotten. The book, and its author, evidently left their impression upon the younger Mill. In his *Autobiography* J. S. Mill mentions 'a very estimable man with whom I was well acquainted, Mr. William Thompson of Cork, author of . . . an Appeal in behalf of women against the passage relating to them in my father's Essay on Government'.[96] That the younger Mill's interest in feminism was quickened by his acquaintance with Thompson seems highly probable. Their meeting 'in the early part of 1825', when Mill was 19, coincided with the publication of Thompson's *Appeal*. Thompson was, moreover, effusive in his praise of Anna Wheeler, whom he credited with inspiring and deepening his feminist views.[97] One could plausibly conjecture that Thompson's chaste and cerebral relationship with Mrs Wheeler provided a model for John Stuart Mill's subsequent relationship with Harriet Taylor; but, lacking testimonial evidence to that effect, we must leave it at that. We are on somewhat firmer ground in suggesting that the arguments in Thompson's *Appeal* prefigure those advanced nearly half a century later in *The Subjection of Women*.

Against James Mill's proposed exclusion of women from the franchise Thompson raises a factual and logical question: 'Does an identity . . . of interest, in point of fact and necessity, exist between women and men?'[98] Thompson replies that any answer to the first, or factual, part of the question presupposes a judgement—specifically, a judgement as to *what* is in *whose* interest. And this, in turn, raises a further question: *who* is to judge? In staunch Utilitarian fashion, Thompson maintains that each of us is the best—indeed, the only—judge of what is, or is not, in our own interest. Mill (and, unbeknownst to Thompson, Bentham) begs the question entirely, by leaving it to 'one half the human race'—men—to judge

[96] J. S. Mill, *Early Draft*, 111.
[97] See Thompson's 'Introductory Letter to Mrs. Wheeler' (*Appeal*, pp. v–xiv); and R. Pankhurst, *William Thompson* (London, 1954), ch. 8.
[98] Thompson, *Appeal*, 25.

what is, or is not, in the interest of the other half. Thompson then goes on to raise a powerful logical objection: does not Mill begin by assuming that all human beings are rapacious and self-interested? Does it not then follow that, since men are human beings, their judgements of women's interests will 'in point of fact' be judgements as to what is in their *own* interest, and *not* in the women's? 'The general argument' of Mill's *Essay*, he writes, 'is founded on the universal love of power of all human beings over all their fellow creatures, for selfish purposes. This is stated to be the grand governing law of human nature.' And yet Mill proposes to allow men to judge, on women's behalf, what is in women's interest. Mill thereby exempts all men from this 'grand governing law of human nature'. What then, Thompson asks, 'becomes of the law itself and the arguments founded on it?'[99] 'This exception of one half from the influence of the general rule', Thompson says sarcastically, 'is certainly a pretty large exception . . . In any other hands, so large an exception would . . . destroy the rule.'[100] So 'even if [Mill's] facts were true', his 'inferences [are] controverted'.[101] In this way Thompson, in a dialectical *tour de force*, turns Mill's own argument against him. James Mill's exclusionist argument collapses from within.

Thompson's *Appeal* goes far beyond its author's avowed purpose of criticizing James Mill's *Essay*. It analyses at some length the causes and consequences of the subjugation of women in even the most 'civilized' societies. Thompson concludes that the 'civil and domestic slavery' in which women live has, at bottom, a single *political* cause: their continued exclusion from political life. If women had a hand, as voters and as legislators, in making the laws that affect their happiness, so-called 'civilized' society would at long last become truly civilized. Laws which debase and subjugate women likewise demean men. In playing the part of master, however kind and benign, a man 'surrenders the delights of equality, namely those of esteem, of friendship, of intellectual and sympathetic intercourse, for the vulgar pleasure of command'. In this way 'the whole moral structure of the mind of *man* is perverted' by the 'domestic despotism' of which he believes himself the

---

[99] Ibid. 1, 2–10.   [100] Ibid. 7.   [101] Ibid., p. ix.

beneficiary.[102] If women were to be granted the political rights to vote and hold office, the entire condition of society and its members—male and female alike—would be altered in a more humane and egalitarian direction. The enfranchisement of women, Thompson holds, is the *sine qua non* of all further progress—a judgement in which J. S. Mill whole heartedly concurred.[103]

Thomas Babington Macaulay's critique of Mill's *Essay*, published four years after Thompson's *Appeal*, raised exactly the same objections, albeit for different reasons. As a Whig, Macaulay certainly did not share Thompson's radical views. But he borrowed extensively from Thompson's *Appeal*, and found in its critique of Mill's logic a most useful and congenial weapon with which to attack the Utilitarians, and Mill in particular.

'Mr. Mill', writes Macaulay, 'recommends that all males of mature age, rich and poor, educated and ignorant, shall have votes. But,' he asks, 'why not the women too? This question has often been asked in parliamentary debate, and has never, to our knowledge, received a plausible answer.' Nor does Mill supply any answer: 'Mr. Mill escapes from it as fast as he can.' Pausing 'to dwell a little on the words of the oracle', Macaulay quotes the notorious paragraph from Mill's *Essay*. Then, without so much as a mention of Thompson, Macaulay continues:

Without adducing one fact, without taking the trouble to perplex the question by one sophism, he placidly dogmatizes away the interest of one half the human race. If there be a word of truth in history, women have always been, and still are, over the greater part of the globe, humble companions, playthings, captives, menials, beasts of burden. Except in a few happy and highly civilized communities, they are strictly in a state of personal slavery. Even in those countries where they are best treated, the laws are generally unfavourable to them, with respect to almost all the points in which they are mostly deeply interested.[104]

After noting—again without mentioning Thompson—the logical contradiction between Mill's 'law' that all human beings

---

[102] Thompson, *Appeal*, 70–1.　　　　[103] J. S. Mill, *Subjection*, 95–104.
[104] T. B. Macaulay, 'Mill on Government', *Edinburgh Review* (1829); repr. in Mill, *PW* 291.

are by nature self-interested, and his proposal to exclude one half the human race from the purview of that law, Macaulay goes on to question Mill's identity-of-interest thesis:

Mr. Mill is not legislating for England or the United States; but for mankind. Is then the interest of a Turk the same with that of the girls who compose his harem? Is the interest of a Chinese the same with that of the woman whom he harnesses to his plough? Is the interest of an Italian the same with that of the daughter whom he devotes to God?

Clearly not, Macaulay believes. But at this point Macaulay proceeds to controvert Mill's 'law' and, by implication, to agree with his exclusionist position:

The interest of a respectable Englishman may be said, without any impropriety, to be identical with that of his wife. But why is it so? Because human nature is *not* what Mr. Mill conceives it to be; because civilized men, pursuing their own happiness in a social state, are not Yahoos fighting for carrion; because there is a pleasure in being loved and esteemed, as well as in being feared and servilely obeyed. Why does not a gentleman restrict his wife to the bare maintenance which the law would compel him to allow her, that he may have more to spend on his personal pleasures? Because, if he loves her, he has pleasure in seeing her pleased; and because, even if he dislikes her, he is unwilling that the whole neighbourhood should cry shame on his meanness and ill-nature. Why does not the legislature, altogether composed of males, pass a law to deprive women of all civil privileges whatever, and reduce them to the state of slaves? By passing such a law, they would gratify what Mr. Mill tells us is an inseparable part of human nature, the desire to possess unlimited power of inflicting pain upon others. That they do not pass such a law, though they have the power to pass it, and that no man in England wishes to see such a law passed, proves that the desire to possess unlimited power of inflicting pain is not inseparable from human nature.

The 'identity of interest between the two sexes' in England, says Macaulay, arises from the Englishman's 'pleasure of being loved, and of communicating happiness'.[105] The Englishman's character and his country's institutions combine to make him a breed apart from other, less enlightened men.

[105] Ibid. 291–2.

Macaulay's critique differs from Thompson's in one crucial respect. Whereas Thompson uses Mill's 'law' to controvert his identity-of-interest thesis, Macaulay uses Mill's identity thesis to controvert his 'law'. The upshot of Macaulay's reasoning is 'chauvinistic' in both the older nationalist, and the newer sexual, senses of the term. The exemplary behaviour of Englishmen, Macaulay concludes, falsifies Mill's 'law' even as it justifies his exclusionist position. This rather self-congratulatory conclusion differs markedly from the self-critical positions taken by Thompson in the *Appeal*—and by J. S. Mill in *The Subjection of Women*.

Mill writes in his *Autobiography* that Macaulay's 'famous attack' on his father's *Essay* 'gave me much to think about'.[106] But the thoughts inspired by Macaulay were about epistemological and methodological matters—and *not* about the position of women. Packe is quite mistaken, therefore, in suggesting that, of all the many remarkable passages in Macaulay's critique,

The passage about the position of women struck [J. S. Mill] particularly hard: throughout his life, that question was so much a passion with him that he often made it the final issue, the test on which depended his acceptance or rejection of a philosophic system. In this case, it was the means of doubling the gap between his father and himself; and . . . he incorporated unconsciously and without acknowledgement [Macaulay's] two striking concepts—that the interests of women were no more identical with that of their husbands than the interests of subjects with their kings, and that the denial of rights to women was the enslavement of one half of the human race—almost word for word into the groundwork of all his future dissertations.[107]

Packe's attribution of influence is mistaken in several respects. First, John Stuart Mill was struck particularly hard not by the passage about women's rights (which he never mentions) but by Macaulay's methodological critique of the elder Mill's *Essay*.[108] Secondly, the younger Mill's making 'the position of women' a 'test on which depended his acceptance or rejection of a philosophic system' was inspired not by Macaulay's attack but apparently—as we have noted

---

[106] J. S. Mill, *Early Draft*, 134.   [107] Packe, *Life*, 90.
[108] J. S. Mill, *Early Draft*, 134–6.

already—by his father's *History*. Thus, thirdly, it cannot be true that J. S. Mill's criterion of acceptability 'was the means of doubling the gap between his father and himself'. On the contrary, it was, if anything, a means of narrowing the gap between them. Fourthly, Packe attributes to Macaulay 'two striking concepts', which, as we have just seen, he took great pains to *deny*: his critique is anything but a feminist tract. The 'two striking concepts' derive not from Macaulay but, more probably, from Thompson's *Appeal*. And, finally, it was Thompson's views, not Macaulay's, which the younger Mill 'incorporated unconsciously and without acknowledgement . . . almost word for word into the groundwork of all his future dissertations', or at any rate into *The Subjection of Women*.

The conventional view about the sources of John Stuart Mill's feminism appears to be mistaken. He owes little, if anything, to Bentham or (initially, at least) to Harriet Taylor Mill, still less to Macaulay, and rather a lot to heretofore unsuspected sources—James Mill's *History* and William Thompson's *Appeal*. Thompson has only recently, if rather belatedly, been recognized as an important figure in the history of feminist theory.[109] James Mill has, as yet, received no such recognition but has, on the contrary, been roundly excoriated for his supposedly antifeminist views, which are in turn invariably contrasted with the more enlightened outlook of Bentham and of his eldest son. I have tried to suggest that matters are not quite so simple and that some aspects of the intellectual and political relationships within Bentham's circle and between the two Mills have long been misunderstood. Having, as I hope, cleared up at least some of these misunderstandings, the way may now be prepared for a reinterpretation and reappraisal of their respective places in the history of political thought, and of feminist theory in particular.

[109] Thompson's *Appeal* has been reprinted with an Introduction by R. Pankhurst by Virago Press (London, 1983); cf. S. M. Okin, *Women in Western Political Thought* (Princeton, NJ, 1979), ch. 9.

9

VICO AND MARX ON 'MAKING' HISTORY

Men make their own history . . .

Karl Marx

9.1 INTRODUCTION

In their eagerness to discover intellectual influences upon, and theoretical connections between, thinkers of different ages, commentators too often mistake passing references or resemblances for the real thing. This is notoriously the case with Marxists and Marxologists who attempt to trace the sources of Marx's ideas. As often as not, old myths—that Marx was, for example, a socialist Darwinist whose concept of class struggle stemmed from Darwin's 'struggle for existence'—have merely been perpetuated and embellished instead of being critically reconsidered. I shall in Chapter 10 attempt to expose the errors and exaggerations of a 'Darwinian' reading of Marx; here I shall suggest why a Vichian reading of Marx, or a Marxian reading of Vico, is equally unsatisfactory. Marx and the Marxists—like so many others—have in certain respects misappropriated Vico. This misappropriation rests, I believe, upon a misrepresentation, or at any rate a misunderstanding, of Vico's views and in particular of his central doctrine that we have a special sort of knowledge of what we ourselves have made.

In working my way towards this conclusion I shall make use of a series of intertwining arguments. I shall begin by examining, and distinguishing between, several sorts of supposed 'connections' between Vico and Marx.[1] Then I shall

---

[1] For a richly variegated defence of the claim that there are 'affinities'—as well as 'contrasts'—between the two thinkers, see G. Tagliacozzo (ed.), *Vico and Marx: Affinities and Contrasts* (Atlantic Highlands, NJ, 1983).

consider some of the more obvious, though often overlooked, differences between the two thinkers. This, in turn, leads me to enquire into a non-obvious but, I believe, crucial difference between Vico and Marx—namely, their very different conceptions of what is involved in 'making' history and human society. Vico's doctrine that we can know civil society because we ourselves have made it rests, I contend, upon a communicative conception of making (as when we 'make' an agreement or 'make sense'), while Marx's version of this doctrine relies upon 'making' in the technical-productive sense of fabrication or manufacture and applies, moreover, not only to human society but to nature as well. The upshot of my several arguments is that the distance between Marx and Vico is vaster than has heretofore been believed.

9.2 MARX DISCOVERS VICO

The idea that Vico was something of a proto-Marxist, or Marx a latter-day Vichian, appears to owe more to later Marxists than to Marx himself. Marx seems not to have read Vico before 1862 or thereabouts, well after the groundwork of his system had been laid, and even then he made remarkably few references to 'the old Neapolitan'.[2] Marx's 'favourite occupation', he confessed, was 'book-worming';[3] and it was apparently in the course of pursuing this occupation that he came across Vico's *New Science*, immediately read—or, rather, devoured—it, and thereupon recommended it enthusiastically to Ferdinand Lassalle. Warning that the original would be hard going, not merely because it was written in Italian but, worse yet, in the 'very tricky Neapolitan idiom' (*sehr verzwicktem neapolitanischen Idiom*), Marx accordingly

---

[2] Marx to Engels, 28 Apr. 1862, in *MEW* xxx. 228. See also E. Kamenka, 'Vico and Marxism', in G. Tagliacozzo and H. V. White (eds.), *Giambattista Vico: An International Symposium* (Baltimore, 1969), esp. 138; H. Aronovitch, 'Vico and Marx on Human Nature and Historical Development', and M. Jay, 'Vico and Western Marxism', in G. Tagliacozzo (ed.), *Vico: Past and Present* (Atlantic Highlands, NJ, 1981), ii. 47–57 and 195–212, respectively.

[3] Quoted in D. McLellan, *Karl Marx: His Life and Thought* (London, 1973), 457.

recommended the 1844 French translation, from which he quotes several snippets 'to whet your appetite'.[4] He adds that he has tried but failed to find Vico's juridical writings.[5]

Like most of Vico's readers, Marx was impressed by Vico's originality and erudition, and half-amused by his more bizarre flights of philological fancy.[6] But one aspect of Vico's thought impressed Marx greatly: the idea, namely, that human beings make their own history and can, accordingly, know it in a way that they do not—indeed, cannot—know what they have not made. In an 'important footnote'[7] to *Capital I* Marx writes:

Darwin has interested us in the history of Nature's Technology, i.e. in the formation of the organs of plants and animals, which organs serve as instruments of production for sustaining life. Does not the history of the productive organs of man, of organs that are the material basis of all social organization, deserve equal attention? And would not such a history be easier to compile, since, as Vico says, human history differs from natural history in this, that we have made the former, but not the latter?[8]

Marxists and Marxologists have made much—indeed perhaps too much—of this passage. A mere three sentences, tucked away in a single footnote in a book of 800-plus pages, and appearing to occur almost as an afterthought or embellishment to the text, hardly suffices to show that Marx owed a great intellectual debt to Vico. And yet Marxists and Marxologists have, for more than a century, insisted that Marx's reference to Vico points to a profoundly important connection between the two thinkers.

Claims about the existence of such a connection generally take one of two forms, some commentators contending that the link is one involving direct influence, and others making the less precise claim that there are deep-seated thematic affinities between Vico and Marx. A claim of the former sort is advanced by Maximilien Rubel, who maintains that Marx's 'Promethean vision of history' derives in large part from his

---

[4] Marx to Lassalle, 28 Apr. 1862, *MEW* xxx. 622.   [5] Ibid. 623.
[6] Marx to Engels, 28 Apr. 1862, *MEW* xxx. 227-8.
[7] M. H. Fisch, 'Introduction' to the *Autobiography of Giambattista Vico* (Ithaca, NY, 1963), 104.
[8] K. Marx, *Capital* (New York, 1967), i. 372.

reading of Vico.[9] Such a claim seems scarcely credible, considering that Marx arrived at his vision of history well before he had read Vico and that Hegel, in any event, lay closer to hand. Nor is Rubel alone in insisting that such a connection exists. Christopher Lasch, who takes the title of his book, *The World of Nations*, from Vico, writes that 'Vico's principle [that we can understand the world of nations because we ourselves have made it] provides an indispensable support for the Marxian critique of political economy'.[10] Yet Lasch's claim is no more plausible than Rubel's, and again for much the same reason: the main lines of Marx's critique of political economy were laid down in the *Grundrisse* of 1875–8—that is, five years *before* Marx's book-worming led him to Vico's *New Science*. The real or imagined 'support' provided by Vico was, though doubtless welcome, hardly 'indispensable'. Otherwise Vico would, one might think, merit more than a minor footnote in Marx's *magnum opus*.

If claims about direct Vichian influences are easily countered, another sort of claim is difficult to formulate precisely, much less to criticize or confute. I mean, of course, the claim that there are affinities, elective or otherwise, between the two thinkers, and that the historian of ideas has only to point these out. Doubtless there are parallels and resemblances, some of them quite striking, between Vico and Marx. But these do not, I think, go very deep, nor are they especially impressive when considered in the light of the vast and profound differences between the two thinkers. This sweeping claim I cannot hope to substantiate here. Instead I shall, more modestly, focus upon several striking differences. I want to focus, in particular, upon Marx's and later Marxists' understanding—or rather, as I maintain, their misunderstanding—of Vico's view that we can know human history because we ourselves have made it. It is this Vichian doctrine, more than any other, that Marx and later Marxists—including Marx's son-in-law Paul Lafargue, Georges Sorel, Antonio Labriola, and Leon Trotsky—seized upon and interpreted as an anticipation of the materialist conception of history.[11]

[9] M. Rubel, *Karl Marx: Essai de biographie intellectuelle* (Paris, 1957), 315.
[10] C. Lasch, *The World of Nations* (New York, 1973), 312.
[11] P. Lafargue, *Karl Marx: His Life and Work* (New York, 1943), 15, and

Consider the case of Sorel. His study of Vico led him to embrace a peculiarly Vichian version of Marxism in the waning years of the nineteenth century.[12] Two Vichian doctrines he found especially attractive. The first was the notion of *ricorsi*, those periodic revivals of ethical energy and enthusiasm which precede and announce new epochs. The second— and for our purposes more pertinent—is Vico's notion that men make their history. An engineer by profession, Sorel was particularly impressed by the idea that man makes the social world no less than the engineer constructs bridges and dams. These two elements he brings together in a peculiar and novel way. The next *ricorso* would, he hoped, be brought about by, and reveal, a new kind of hero uniquely suited to the peculiarities and possibilities of a new age. For Sorel, as Stuart Hughes remarks, 'craftsmen and technicians—the heroes of the machine age—offered the loftiest contemporary examples of morality'.[13] In Sorel's hands the Durkheimian notion of 'mechanical solidarity' receives, as it were, a quite literal twist. He believed, as Berlin observes, that 'Machinery is a social cement more effective ... than even language' and that 'the factory should become the vehicle of the social poetry of modern producers'.[14] (There are echoes here of Marx's celebration of the factory as the schoolroom of revolution.[15]) Sorel ranks, in Berlin's judgement, as 'one of the few perceptive readers [of Vico] in the nineteenth century'.[16] Doubtless this is, in some respects, entirely correct. But it is, I believe, apt to be misleading in another, long-overlooked sense. For, I shall argue,

Le Déterminisme économique de Karl Marx (1907; 3rd edn., Paris, 1928), ch. 3, 'Lois historiques de Vico'; G. Sorel, 'Étude sur Vico', *Devenir social*, 2 (Oct.–Dec. 1896), 787–817, 906–41, 1013–46; A. Labriola, *Essays on the Materialist Conception of History* (1896; New York, 1966), 120–1, 163, 215–18, 232–3; and L. Trotsky, *My Life* (New York, 1970), 119, 122, for an account of the impact of Labriola's *Essays*, which Trotsky read in a French translation during his first imprisonment in 1898.

[12] Sorel, 'Étude sur Vico'. Cf. G. Lichtheim, *From Marx to Hegel* (New York, 1971), 101, 111; H. S. Hughes, *Consciousness and Society*, rev. edn. (New York, 1977), ch. 5, esp. 171–2; I. Berlin, 'Georges Sorel', in his *Against the Current* (New York, 1979), 296–332; and J. R. Jennings, 'Sorel, Vico, and Marx', in Tagliacozzo (ed.), *Vico and Marx*, 326–41.

[13] Hughes, *Consciousness and Society*, 172.

[14] Berlin, *Against the Current*, 308.

[15] In the *Communist Manifesto*. See *MESW*, 43-6.

[16] Berlin, *Against the Current*, 301.

Sorel—like Marx before him—had in one crucial respect mis-read Vico and, having misunderstood his meaning, went on to misinterpret him as something of a proto-Marxist.

Very simply, both Sorel and Marx misunderstood what Vico meant in saying that we make the social world. They understood Vico to mean 'making' in the technical sense of construction, fabrication, production, or manufacture; but in fact, as I shall argue, Vico harks back to the classical distinction between the *techne* of the craftsman and the *praxis* of communicating members of historically situated communities. The sort of 'making' to which Vico refers is not the technical-productive activity of *homo faber* but the 'practical' creativity of communicating citizens. Before making (*sic*) this argument regarding a non-obvious difference between Vico and Marx, however, I should first like to bring out some of their more obvious differences.

9.3 MARXIAN MONISM VS. VICHIAN DUALISM

Two differences between Vico and Marx are crucial, and too obvious to be missed. The first is that Vico was a devout Christian and Marx an atheist.[17] Anyone wishing to connect Marx's thought to Vico's must somehow bridge this chasm between them. Some commentators have accordingly sug-gested that Vico was not such a devout Christian after all; that he kept God in his system only because he feared the fires of the Inquisition; and that his references to divine provi-dence are merely metaphorical. Thus James Morrison, for example, maintains that 'The idea of divine providence is for Vico simply a metaphor for the irony of history.'[18] And

[17] Interestingly, Marx denied that he was an atheist, inasmuch as atheism is, strictly speaking, the denial of something unreal, i.e. God. See K. Marx, *The Economic and Philosophic Manuscripts of 1844* (New York, 1964), 145–6. Suffice it to say that he was at any rate an unbeliever.

[18] J. C. Morrison, 'How to Interpret the Idea of Divine Providence in Vico's New Science', *Philosophy and Rhetoric*, 12 (1979), 256–61, at 259. For another argument to the effect that Vico did not actually mean what he said, see F. Vaughan, *The Political Philosophy of Giambattista Vico* (The Hague, 1972). Dr Vaughan, a disciple of the late Professor Leo Strauss, follows his mentor in elevating the mere possibility that an author who feared persecu-tion might write cautiously and circumspectly, into an all-pervasive principle

Edmund Wilson says that 'In the Catholic city of Naples, in
the shadow of the Inquisition, Vico had to keep God in his
system,'[19] the implication being that he would, if he dared,
remove Him entirely—as though Vico could say of God, as
Laplace did, 'Je n'ai pas eu besoin de cette hypothèse.'[20] If
Vico were the secular thinker that Morrison and Wilson portray, it would of course be easier to reconcile his thought with
Marx's. But Vico was not a secular thinker. God was not, for
Vico, a hypothesis, much less a dispensable one, nor were his
references to divine providence merely metaphorical. As
Professor Fisch remarks, Vico's theory of divine providence 'is
not merely a presupposition of [his] science but an integral
part or "principle aspect" of it'—an 'article of faith', in short,
which animates his thinking and gives coherence to his system.[21]

A second important difference between Vico and Marx can,
I believe, be traced to the first. Marx is a monist and Vico a
dualist—as much of a dualist, indeed, as his *bête noire*
Descartes ever was, although, as Berlin notes, his dualism
'stretches across a different part of the metaphysical map'.[22]
As an atheist and an avowed opponent of all dualisms, Marx
could hardly have accepted Vico's version of the doctrine that
we know what we ourselves have made. This epistemological
doctrine, as Vico formulates it, points to an irreducible ontological dualism—to a division, that is, between that which
God has made and that which humans have made. 'Natural
history' is the story of what God has made—namely, nature—
and 'human history' the story of what human beings have
made—namely, civil society or 'the world of nations'. Because
one has a special knowledge—knowledge *'per caussas'* (*sic*),
'through causes'—of what one has made, God alone has an

---

of textual interpretation. See L. Strauss, *Persecution and the Art of Writing*
(Glencoe, Ill., 1952).

[19] E. Wilson, *To the Finland Station* (New York, 1953), 467.

[20] Legend has it that this was Laplace's reply when Napoleon asked where
God belonged in his *Système du monde* (1796): A. Koyré, *From the Closed
World to the Infinite Universe* (Baltimore, 1957), 276.

[21] M. H. Fisch, 'Introduction' to *NS*, p. xxxii. The author of the *Scienza
nouva* was, as Berlin notes, 'a pious if peculiar Christian' (*Vico and Herder*
(New York, 1976), 70).

[22] Berlin, *Vico and Herder*, 121.

intimate 'maker's knowledge' of nature.[23] Such a knowledge of nature is not open to mere mortals, for we take nature as we find it; because we did not create it, nature remains opaque and not fully accessible to our intelligence. It is, however, quite a different matter with human society; for, since humans have made it, they have a quasi-divine knowledge of its structure, purpose, and operation. In a famous and oft-quoted passage Vico is quite explicit about the divine origin of this ontological and epistemological dualism:

But in the night of thick darkness enveloping the earliest antiquity, so remote from ourselves, there shines the eternal and never failing light of a truth beyond all question: that the world of civil society has certainly been made by men, and that its principles are therefore to be found within the modifications of our own human mind. Whoever reflects on this cannot but marvel that the philosophers should have bent all their energies to the study of the world of nature, which, since God made it, He alone knows; and that they should have neglected the study of the world of nations, or civil world, which since men had made it, men could come to know.[24]

This arresting passage contains the most succinct statement of Vico's version of the medieval doctrine (traceable to Aquinas and, earlier still, to St Augustine) of *Verum et factum convertuntur*—that knowledge and creation are one.[25] Just as God can know nature because He has made it, so men can know civil society because they have made it.

I turn now to the central contention of this chapter: that Vico and Marx meant very different things by 'making'; that

---

[23] See J. Hintikka, 'Practical vs. Theoretical Reason—An Ambiguous Legacy', in S. Körner (ed.), *Practical Reason* (Oxford, 1974), ch. 3. A. Harrison (*Making and Thinking* (London, 1978), 152) mistakenly attributes the phrase (if not the idea of) 'maker's knowledge' to Vico. Unfortunately, both Hintikka and Harrison—like most modern writers, including Marx—confuse and conflate the 'practical' knowledge of the actor (or doer) with the 'technical' knowledge of the producer. The result, so far as their reading of Vico is concerned, is quite misleading. Hintikka, like Marx, maintains that men have an ever-increasing 'maker's knowledge' of nature—a view rightly attributable to Marx but not (*pace* Hintikka, 87–8) to Vico.

[24] *NS* 331.

[25] See K. Löwith, ' "Verum et factum convertuntur": Le premese teologiche de principio di Vico e le loro consequenze secolari', in A. Corsano *et al.*, *Omagio a Vico* (Naples, 1968), 73–113.

Vico meant making in a communicative sense, while Marx referred to making in the nature-transforming technical sense of fabrication, production, or manufacture; and that in terms of the classical distinction, drawn by Aristotle, between acting (or doing) and making, Vico relies implicitly upon the former and Marx explicitly upon the latter.[26] I shall begin with a digression upon the distinction drawn by 'the master of them that know'.[27]

9.4 TWO KINDS OF MAKING

Aristotle drew a distinction between *theoria, poiesis,* and *praxis,* linking these with three categorially distinct kinds of knowledge and three corresponding ways of life (*bioi*).[28] *Theoria* is the activity of contemplating what is immutable, eternal, and divine; 'theoretical knowledge' is the certain knowledge of these unchanging objects and relations, and the *bios theoretikos* the way of life devoted to this solitary pursuit. *Poiesis* is the productive activity of the craftsman or artisan; his knowledge is 'technical' and is shown in the particular skill or *techne* with which he transforms natural materials into humanly useful objects or artefacts. *Praxis* is the communicative activity of the citizen; his 'practical' knowledge (*phronesis*) is the knowledge of people like himself—of their thoughts, ambitions, and aspirations, their hopes and their fears—and is acquired in and through his actions and interactions with them. Unlike the craftsman, who works with tangible materials, those who pursue the *bios politikos* 'work' with words: speech (*lexis*) is their medium and rhetoric their art. Rhetoric, the political art *par excellence,* appeals quite literally to common sense—that is, the sense and sensibilities shared in com-

---

[26] *Pace* Berlin's claim that Vico 'does not distinguish, as Aristotle did, between "doing" [or acting] and "making"; nor, for his purposes, was this necessary' (*Vico and Herder,* 107 n. 1).

[27] *'Imaestro di color che sanno*: Dante's paean to Aristotle (*Inferno,* Canto IV, 130–1). On the connection between Vico and Dante, see G. Cambon, 'Vico and Dante', in Tagliacozzo and White (eds.), *Giambattista Vico,* 15–28.

[28] See e.g. Aristotle, *Nichomachean Ethics,* bk. VI, sects. 4–5. Cf. N. Lobkowicz, 'On the History of Theory and Praxis', in T. Ball (ed.), *Political Theory and Praxis* (Minneapolis, 1977), 13–27.

mon by an assembly, or indeed a whole people, that the Romans later termed the *sensus communis*.[29]

In the transition from pagan *polis* to Christian *cosmopolis*, however, several significant changes were wrought in Aristotle's distinction. The most important of these, for our present purposes, concerns the curious conflation of 'practical' and 'productive' activities (so that one could, for example, henceforth speak of making a pot as a 'practical' task). The case of Aquinas is perhaps especially instructive. St Thomas was certainly well acquainted with the distinction between *poiesis* and *praxis*, and when commenting on Aristotle he renders these as *factio* and *actio*, respectively. But, as Lobkowicz notes,

when he is not commenting on Aristotle and speaks in general about human actions, he continually illustrates *actio*, the medieval counterpart to *praxis*, by activities of production. This is more than a conceptual sloppiness, of which St Thomas can hardly be accused. It is a consequence of, among other things, the idea, which is foreign to the Greeks, that God has created the world and, to that extent, can be understood *mutatis mutandis* as producer ... this leads to an immense increase in the value of *poiesis* and eventually to a disappearance of the distinction between *praxis* and *poiesis*.[30]

In Marx's writings, as I shall suggest presently, this distinction disappears completely—so completely, indeed, that *praxis*, as he uses the term, refers to the technical transformation of nature through productive labour. In Vico's *New Science*, by contrast, the classical distinction between *poiesis* and *praxis* is obscured but not obliterated.

The classical distinction between acting (or doing) and making is obscured in Vico's *New Science* in much the same way, and for much the same reason, I suspect, as it is obscured in Aquinas. If man is god-like in his ability to know what he has made, and if God's creation of the natural world falls under the heading of *factio* (the medieval counterpart of *poiesis*), then man's creation and knowledge of the civil world must likewise be technical or 'poetic' in character. And indeed Vico

[29] See *NS*, 142, 145, 311. On the idea of a *sensus communis*, particularly for Vico, see H.-G. Gadamer, *Truth and Method* (New York, 1984), esp. 19–29; and J. M. Krois, 'Vico's and Peirce's "Sensus Communis" ', in Tagliacozzo (ed.), *Vico: Past and Present*, ii. 58–71.

[30] Lobkowicz, 'On the History of Theory and Praxis', 22–3.

is etymologically explicit on this score. The wisdom of our distant ancestors he terms 'poetic', not merely because their metaphysics—their attempt to understand the world—was couched in the language of poetry but because those who made it 'were called "poets", which is Greek for "creators" '.[31] The *word* to which he refers is clearly *poiesis*, or making; but, I want to suggest, the *concept* to which he implicitly refers is not *poiesis* but *praxis*.[32]

Poiesis originally referred, as we have seen, to the class of technical-instrumental activities aimed at producing tangible objects like pots and chairs, while *praxis* had to do with the intangible but socially indispensable 'practical' activities of communicating and making sense together. Yet 'poetic' knowledge or wisdom, as Vico understands it, has no connection with *poiesis* in the classical sense, for it is not concerned with the transformation of natural substances into tangible objects or artefacts. Poetic metaphysics is an attempt not to 'make' in the sense of fabrication or manufacture, but rather to create meaning and to make sense of an otherwise puzzling world.

In our collective attempt to make sense together, we create the world in which we live—the 'world of nations', in Vico's famous phrase. Societies are the communicative creations of their members, past and present.[33] Political systems and codes of law, like epic poems, are not the inventions or fabrications of any individual but are instead the communicative creations of an entire people. They arise from the daily discourse of a people seeking some sense of shared meaning; and, being unable to credit their own collective genius, they conceive of these ingenious creations as the 'products' of heroic and god-

---

[31] *NS*, 376.

[32] Other interpreters have also suggested that Vico does not mean 'making' in the technical-instrumental sense: B. A. Haddock, 'Vico on Political Wisdom', *European Studies Review*, 8 (1978), 181; Berlin, *Vico and Herder*, pp. xvi, 107; and Fisch, 'Introduction' to *NS*, p. xi. None, however, follows this up in the way I attempt to do in Ch. 9.4 below.

[33] Cf. Dewey's observation that 'Society not only continues to exist . . . by communication, but it may fairly be said to exist in . . . communication. There is more than a verbal tie between the words common, community, and communication. Men live in a community in virtue of the things which they have in common; and communication is the way in which they come to possess things in common . . .' (J. Dewey, *Democracy and Education* (New York, 1916), 4–5).

like individuals—of Homer, of Solon and Lycurgus, of Romulus.[34] But in fact it is an entire people, speaking and acting together, who create poems and polities. It is they, Vico suggests, who have (or rather can have) a special insight into and knowledge of their own creation and who are in this respect god-like.

Two questions arise here. First, how can a person or a people be said to 'make' or 'create' anything 'communicatively'? And, secondly, in what sense is such a creation, and their knowledge of it, god-like? Surely, it will be objected, God did not create the world of nature as man creates the world of nations—that is, by communicating or interacting with other creatures like Himself. Or, to put it another way: if *praxis* refers to communicative action or interaction among equals, then surely God—who is unique and therefore without equals—does not, and indeed cannot, engage in *praxis*. He can, however, engage in *poeisis*, which involves no other beings like Himself. I shall consider the second question first.

First, God did create the world of nature in a distinctly 'communicative' sense. For he created it *ex nihilo* and—more significantly still—by the Word. 'In the beginning was the Word, and the Word was with God, and the Word was God. ... All things were made by Him'—and made, moreover, by the spoken word: 'And God said, Let there be light: and there was light.'[35] And God in this way created the world of nature—the sun, the moon and the stars, dry land and oceans, plants and animals. Finally he created 'in his own image' a communicating creature: man.

Now just as the Word of God created the world of nature, so do the words of man create the world of nations. The creators of this world are also god-like, inasmuch as they create it *ex nihilo* and by the word. We live, after all, in a world of words: these are the 'materials' from which society is 'made'. Vico, whose academic speciality was jurisprudence, was greatly impressed by the creative power of language. By their utterances men create their world—as when we 'create' obligations by 'making' promises.[36] By means of language we not

---

[34] *NS*, bk. III, esp. sect. II; 414–17, 423, 469, 561–2, *et seq.*
[35] John 1: 1–3; Gen. 1: 1–27.
[36] It is perhaps significant that we do not speak of (say) promising in the

only name, denote, or describe; we also perform the actions and perpetuate the practices upon which society depends.[37] So powerful and pervasive is this feature of language that our ancestors were led to believe that the very words used in performing actions—promising, blessing, forgiving, etc.—were themselves magical.

Because the world of nations is conceptually and communicatively constituted, it differs radically from the world of nature, and the human sciences must perforce differ in principle from the natural sciences. The natural scientist may in some (admittedly problematic) sense refer to or describe a pre-existing world: stars and galaxies, for example, existed before the concepts of 'star' or 'galaxy' existed. But our social and political concepts do not describe or denote or refer to a pre-existing world; they actually help to constitute that world. Promises and obligations did not exist before the concepts of 'promise' and 'obligation'. Our social and political concepts are themselves constitutive of social reality; they figure in the creation and maintenance of the world in which we live and act. If shared meaning and social order are conceptually or communicatively constituted, then they cannot, Vico reasoned, be imposed from without; they cannot, that is, be the product of a solitary lawgiver—a Solon or a Lycurgus or a Draco—whose laws and precepts would quite literally be incomprehensible and meaningless unless couched in the terms of an already existing common sense—that is, the communicatively

'technical' idiom: we speak of making, but not of manufacturing or producing, promises and obligations. We should hardly know what to think of someone who purported to 'fabricate' or 'manufacture' promises. This is not mere word-play; it provides a conceptual clue and serves—in the truest Vichian sense—to remind us of a truth so obvious as to be overlooked. We can only begin to understand the sense in which 'making' promises and 'creating' obligations differs from other sorts of making by noting what we do (and do not) ordinarily say. Ordinary language is a repository of common or communal sense. The main modern resuscitator of this view is, of course, Wittgenstein. See E. Riverso, 'Vico and Wittgenstein', in G. Tagliacozzo and D. P. Verene (eds.), *Giambattista Vico's Science of Humanity* (Baltimore, 1976), 263–73; and S. Hampshire, 'Vico and the Contemporary Philosophy of Language', in *Giambattista Vico: An International Symposium*, 475–81.

[37] Cf. Berlin, *Vico and Herder*, 50–1; and H. Arendt, *The Human Condition* (Chicago, 1958), 236–47. Arendt, in particular, stresses the socially constitutive character of such 'performative' utterances as promising and forgiving. Cf. Ch. 4 above.

constituted *sensus communis*.[38] The 'master key' of Vico's new science is to be found in tracing the modifications of the human mind, so as to dispel the myths and mystifications which prevent our seeing our own creations for what they are. Human history is the history of our changing concepts or ideas; it is the story of the human mind's successive self-modifications. The secrets so long kept from ourselves can be unlocked and revealed, to be sure, but only with great difficulty. For this a special method is required. The method, unique to the human sciences, is imaginative reconstruction—*fantasia*—or simply, as he says elsewhere, 'reflection'.[39] It is only by reflection or imaginative re-creation that we are able to acquire knowledge *per causas* of our own collective creation.

Our god-like character is revealed only in our communicative creations—that is, in our *praxis*. Our technical transformations of the natural world, by contrast, yield no special or privileged knowledge. The secrets and the essential structure of nature must remain forever opaque to us. The world of nature, being God's creation, is fully knowable and meaningful only to Him. The world of nations, by contrast, is our own collective creation and is, accordingly, as accessible and meaningful to us as nature is to God.

In thus distinguishing between natural history and human history, Vico renders unto God what is God's and unto man what is man's. And never the twain shall meet. This, as we shall now see, is a far cry from Marx's conception of 'making' history and his monistic view of the relation between man and nature.

9.5 TWO CONCEPTS OF NATURE

Human history is for Marx the story of the self-transformation of the human species, of the unfolding and development of

---

[38] Vico (*On the Study Methods of Our Time* (Indianapolis, 1965), ch. 7) rebukes Descartes—with his 'theoretical' notion of solitary dispassionate and disconnected egos—for his lack of 'common sense'. Cf. Arendt, *Human Condition*, 283; and J. Habermas, *Theory and Practice* (Boston, 1973), 43–6.

[39] *NS* 338, 378, 236.

dormant human powers through the nature-transforming medium of man's own labour. 'The writing of history', says Marx, 'must always set out from these natural bases [*natür-lichen Gründlagen*] and their modification in the course of history through the action of men.'[40] The 'modification' to which Marx refers is not Vico's 'modifications of our own human mind',[41] but rather our successive modifications of the natural environment and, in consequence, of our social organization and our ideological self-conceptions. Thus by 'the actions of men' (*Aktion der Menschen*) Marx understands, not action or *praxis* in the classical communicative sense, but *poiesis*—that is, nature-transforming labour or 'production'.[42]

Ironically, the assimilation of 'practical' to 'productive' activities begun by the Christian Schoolmen was carried by Karl Marx to its logical conclusion. For Marx *praxis* becomes synonymous with material and thence mental 'production'. 'Men', says Marx, 'begin to distinguish themselves from animals as soon as they begin to produce [*produzieren*] their means of subsistence,' and their 'mode of life' is determined or shaped (*bedingt*) by the requirements of material production. 'What they are, therefore, coincides with their production, both with what they produce and with how they produce. The nature of individuals thus depends on the material conditions determining their production.'[43] In the course of producing their material means of subsistence, men unwittingly 'produce' conceptions or ideas, e.g. political theories, laws, morality, religion, and metaphysics—'ideologies', in short—which serve to explain and justify successive social formations as natural, normal, and necessary.[44] The ideology of primitive producers assumes the form of 'natural religion', or nature-worship, in which the powers of nature are personified as alien divinities, whimsical, capricious, and cruel. Like Vico's *grossi bestioni*, Marx's primitive producers stand in awe of an alien nature,

---

[40] K. Marx and F. Engels, *The German Ideology* (New York, 1963), 7.

[41] *NS* 331.

[42] See e.g. Lobkowicz, 'On the History of Theory and Praxis'; K. Axelos, *Marx, penseur de la technique* (Paris, 1969), esp. ch. 7; Arendt, *Human Condition*, ch. 3; Habermas, *Theory and Practice*, ch. 1, and *Knowledge and Human Interests* (Boston, 1971), ch. 3.

[43] Marx and Engels, *German Ideology*, 7.   [44] Ibid. 14.

which they try to render less alien and more comprehensible by anthropomorphizing it.[45]

Marx's account of primitive ideology bears, at first glance, a striking resemblance to Vico's account of poetic wisdom. On closer inspection, however, the resemblance proves superficial if not illusory. For whereas nature is, in Vico's view, rendered (illusorily) comprehensible via anthropomorphic concepts and categories, it is, on Marx's account, rendered actually comprehensible. And, as men work to transform nature, it becomes less and less alien to them; they begin, haltingly at first, and later in an almost torrential rush of human invention and technological innovation, to dominate nature, to harness its powers for human ends. Nature ceases to be alien; it becomes 'humanized nature'. Nature 'in itself' (*an sich*) ceases to exist, and is replaced by a humanized nature existing 'for man'. Nature—and man himself—become at last a human creation, and God is revealed as an outworn and outmoded ideological fiction. The truth, disclosed to human beings as through a glass darkly, though with increasing clarity, is that man is the active subject and nature the passive predicate, the inert material upon which man stamps the unique and unmistakable mark of his own personality (a relationship still obscured, admittedly, under the conditions of capitalist production). In Marx's view, 'the entire so-called history of the world is nothing but the creation of man through human labour, nothing but the emergence of nature for man, so he has the visible, irrefutable proof of his birth through himself, of the process of his creation'.[46] So complete is this humanization of nature, says Marx, that man can no longer be 'considered to be distinct from nature. For ... nature, the nature that preceded human history, is not by any means the nature in which Feuerbach lives, nor the nature which today no longer exists anywhere (except perhaps on a few Australian coral islands of recent origin).'[47]

The Vichian distinction between man and nature, between 'human' and 'natural' history, is for Marx scarcely more than a convenient figure of speech. Nature can hardly have been

[45] Ibid. 19.
[46] Marx, *Economic and Philosophic Manuscripts of 1844*, 145.
[47] Marx and Engels, *German Ideology*, 37.

created by God, for God does not exist; or rather, He exists only as a human creation, a projection on to the heavens, as it were, of man's heretofore alienated powers.[48] As man comes to dominate nature, to remake it in his own image, he becomes increasingly aware of his own human powers, until at last he recognizes that the nature he knows is his own creation. 'Man is the supreme being for man.'[49] 'Naturalism' and 'humanism' then become interchangeable expressions, and 'natural science' identical with 'the science of man'. 'History itself', says Marx, 'is a real [actual, *wirkliche*] part of natural history—of nature developing into man. Natural science will in time incorporate into itself the science of man, just as the science of man will incorporate into itself natural science: there will be one science.'[50]

The distance between Marx's views and Vico's could hardly be greater. Whatever else they might have been, Vico was no proto-Marxist, and Marx no latter-day Vichian.

---

[48] An idea borrowed from Feuerbach. See Ludwig Feuerbach, 'Preliminary Theses on the Reform of Philosophy' (1842) in *The Fiery Brook: Selected Writings of Ludwig Feuerbach* (New York, 1972), 153–73, and *The Essence of Christianity* (New York, 1957), 274–5.

[49] K. Marx, *Critique of Hegel's 'Philosophy of Right'* (Cambridge, 1970), 137.

[50] Marx, *Economic and Philosophic Manuscripts of 1844*, 143. Marx's remarks should not, however, be interpreted in the light of the later—and in many respects antithetical—'unity of science' programme propounded by the Logical Positivists, whose views are closer to Engels's than Marx's: J. Farr, 'Marx and Positivism', in T. Ball and J. Farr (eds.), *After Marx* (Cambridge, 1984), ch. 10.

10

MARX AND DARWIN: A RECONSIDERATION

Just as Darwin discovered the law of development of organic nature, so Marx discovered the law of development of human history.

Friedrich Engels

10.1 INTRODUCTION

Having in the preceding chapter considered the Marx–Vico myth, I turn to an even more pervasive Marxian myth. For more than a century the names of Karl Marx and Charles Darwin have been linked in an apparently indissoluble union. That union, I shall argue, is almost wholly chimerical. It derives from a myth created after Marx's death by Friedrich Engels, disseminated by later Marxists as evidence for their theory's 'scientific' status, and given considerable credence and support by the discovery of two letters written by Darwin to Marx. As we shall see, the first of these letters is authentic; so too is the second—except that the addressee was not Karl Marx. And thereby hangs a tale. The myth of a connection, methodological or otherwise, between Marx and Darwin rests upon a series of mix-ups. This veritable comedy of errors is at once instructive, amusing, and—in so far as it hastened Marxian theory's ossification into scientistic dogma—tragic.

10.2 SOCIALIST DARWINISM

The Marx–Darwin myth began innocently enough. In his speech at Marx's graveside in 1883, the distraught but ever-respectful Engels paid his old friend the high compliment of comparing his achievement with Darwin's. 'Just as Darwin discovered the law of development of organic nature,' said Engels, 'so Marx discovered the law of development of human history.' Engels's remarks were published the following week in *Der Sozialdemokrat*.[1] Five years later Engels again drew the comparison in his preface to the 1888 English edition of the *Communist Manifesto*. This was followed in 1895 (the year of his death) by Engels's 'Darwinian' interpretation of human history, *The Part Played by Labour in the Transition from Ape to Man*.[2] Since Engels was Marx's life-long friend, confidant, and literary executor, his comparison bore the stamp of authenticity.

The putative parallel between Marx's theory and Darwin's was quickly picked up by Marxists throughout Europe and was thereafter repeated almost ritualistically whenever Marxism's 'scientific' character was called into question. In Italy Engels's comparison was enthusiastically seconded by Filippo Turati, who in an 1892 polemic called Marx 'the Darwin of social science', a judgement later reiterated by Antonio Labriola.[3] In Russia a still-obscure revolutionary, V. I. Lenin, drew the parallel between Marx and Darwin in his 1894 essay, 'What the "Friends of the People" Are', and the parallel later became a firmly established feature of Soviet orthodoxy.[4] In England the 1897 *New Century Review* carried an article by Edward Aveling, Marx's son-in-law, entitled 'Charles Darwin and Karl Marx: A Comparison', German and French translations of which were published simultaneously on the Continent.[5] In 1894 Ludwig Büchner published his *Darwinismus und Sozialismus*. This was followed in 1899 by Ludwig Woltmann's *Die Darwinsche Theorie und der Sozialismus* and still later, in 1906, by Karl Kautsky's influen-

[1] Engels, 'Speech at Marx's Graveside', in *MESW* 429; repr. from *Der Sozialdemokrat*, 22 Mar. 1883, in *MEW* xxx. 335.

[2] *MESW* 354–64; *MEW* xx. 444–55.

[3] F. Turati, in *Critica sociale*, 2 (1892), 135; A. Labriola, *Saggi sul materialismo storico* (1895; Rome, 1964), 236.

[4] V. I. Lenin, 'What the "Friends of the People" are and How they Fight the Social Democrats', in Lenin, *Selected Works* (London, 1939), xi. 421–2.

[5] E. Aveling, 'Charles Darwin and Karl Marx: A Comparison', *New Century Review* (Mar.–Apr. 1897), 232–43; 'Charles Darwin und Karl Marx—Eine Parallele', *Die Neue Zeit*, 2 (1897), 745–57; 'Charles Darwin et Karl Marx', *Devenir social* (1897).

tial *Ethik und materialistische Geschichtsauffassung*.[6] All shared the common conviction that Marx's method and his intentions paralleled Darwin's and that human history should, moreover, be regarded merely as a branch of natural history. Purpose, intention—teleology—was out, 'evolution' via 'natural selection' in. All were alike in subscribing to a leftist version of Social Darwinism—a socialist Darwinism, as it were. None was aware that such a view contrasted sharply with Marx's own rather more sceptical view of Darwin's relevance to the study of human history.

10.3 MARX ON 'HUMANIZED NATURE'

In spite of their long friendship and obvious political affinities, it must be remembered that Marx and Engels were, after all, two men and not one. Each had his own predilections, preferences, and peculiarities. (Marx, for example, could never quite understand Engels's fascination with military history, nor could Engels comprehend Marx's fondness for higher mathematics.) Foremost among their differences were their contrasting views of nature. Marx was rather more inclined than Engels to view 'nature' in 'human' terms. Nature began to exist 'for man', Marx believed, only with the advent of active human intervention in natural processes.[7] Nature, as we know it, is nature as it has been fitted to human purposes

---

[6] F. C. C. L. Büchner, *Darwinismus and Sozialismus* (Leipzig, 1894); Ludwig Woltmann, *Die Darwinsche Theorie und der Sozialismus: Ein Beitrag zur Naturgeschichte der Menschlichen Gesellschaft* (Dusseldorf, 1899), ch. 1 and 177–85; Karl Kautsky, *Ethik und materialistische Geschichtsauffassung* (1906; 2nd edn., Berlin and Stuttgart, 1922), esp. 79–82, where Kautsky maintains that 'the organism of human society [*der Organismus der menschlichen Gesellschaft*]' gradually 'evolves' like any other organic species. Hence one can—as the subtitle of Woltmann's book suggests—speak of 'the natural history of human society'. Kautsky first enunciated this 'evolutionist' doctrine in his debate with Cunow in *Die Neue Zeit*: see H[einrich] C[unow], 'Darwinismus und Marxismus', *Die Neue Zeit*, 13 (1890), esp. 709. In the 1890s the Marx–Darwin connection was a lively topic of debate within the German Social Democratic Party (see Woltmann, *Die Darwinsche Theorie*, ch. 2). With the disclosure of the Marx–Darwin 'correspondence' the debate ended and an 'evolutionary' socialist Darwinism became the SPD orthodoxy.

[7] See e.g. K. Marx, *Economic and Philosophic Manuscripts of 1844* (New York, 1964), 191; *The German Ideology* (New York, 1963), 35–7.

through invention, technology, and industry. The idea (later espoused by Engels) that we can know the nature that exists independently of, and prior to, human efforts to transform it is utterly foreign to Marx's radical humanism.[8]

Marx's humanism is 'radical' in three senses. I shall call these the etymological, the teleological, and the epistemological senses. Etymologically, his pun in the *Contribution* to the *Critique of Hegel's 'Philosophy of Right'* is instructive: 'To be radical is to grasp matters at the root. But for man, the root is man himself.'[9] The Delphic injunction, 'Know thyself', can be carried out only by way of a radical enquiry into human powers and potentials, which are in turn known only through their exercise and actualization through the nature-transforming activity of labour.

Marx's humanism is radical in a second, teleological sense: human beings transform nature—and thereby, indirectly, themselves—according to their own designs and purposes. The only 'purpose' to be found in nature is that which is supplied by human beings. It is this teleological aspect of human consciousness that separates humans from the lower animals and human history from pre-human natural history.[10] This humanistic view, first advanced in the early *Economic and Philosophical Manuscripts* of 1844, is reiterated in the capstone of Marx's mature work, *Capital I*. There Marx acknowledges that 'a bee puts to shame many an architect in the construction of her cells. But what distinguishes the worst architect from the best of bees is this, that the architect raises his structure in imagination before he erects it in reality.'[11] (Marx's aside was almost certainly a slap at Bernard Mandeville's *Fable of the Bees*, in which the activities of bees and men are compared and Nature is shown to be operating benevolently

[8] On Marx's and Engels's differing conceptions of nature and the natural sciences, see A. Schmidt, *The Concept of Nature in Marx* (London, 1971); P. Thomas, 'Marx and Science', *Political Studies*, 24 (Mar. 1976), 1–23; J. Farr, 'Marx and Positivism' and my 'Marxian Science and Positivist Politics', in T. Ball and J. Farr (eds.), *After Marx* (Cambridge, 1984), chs. 10, 11.

[9] K. Marx, *Critique of Hegel's 'Philosophy of Right'* (Cambridge, 1970), 137.

[10] On the human capacity of 'projective consciousness', see J. McMurtry, *The Structure of Marx's World-View* (Princeton, NJ, 1978), 23–39.

[11] K. Marx, *Capital I* (New York, 1967), 178, 372 n. 3.

according to an unseen Higher Law.) Human history is, therefore, teleological in a way that natural history cannot be. Citing Vico, Marx avers that 'human history differs from natural history in this, that we have made the former, but not the latter'.[12]

Thirdly, and finally, Marx's humanism is radical inasmuch as his epistemology, his view of the relation of the knower to the known, is grounded in a conception of the active human subject-as-knower. 'Man as the subject' constitutes for Marx both the 'point of departure' and the 'end result' of scientific enquiry.[13] Natural phenomena can be known by man only as they become objects of practical human interest. The scientist never confronts nature, *simpliciter*; he confronts a humanly transformed nature and, as he confronts himself, a reciprocally transformed human.

Marx's 'humanist' conception of nature is clearly at odds with Engels's 'naturalist' or 'positivist' view. If Marx subordinates nature to man, Engels subordinates man to nature. 'Nature' is for Engels what it could never be for Marx—a non-human realm of iron necessity to whose 'laws of motion' men are ultimately subject. Whereas Marx was interested in the study of nature in so far as it exemplified the historical operation and development of human powers and possibilities, Engels evinced an interest in human history only in so far as it provided a stage upon which natural processes unfolded and developed autonomously. Human history is for Engels— as for Aveling, Büchner, Kautsky, and other socialist Darwinists—a branch of natural history. Or, to put the contrast in Young–Hegelian terms: for Marx 'Man is always the subject' and nature the predicate;[14] for Engels and the socialist Darwinists, by contrast, nature is the active subject and man the predicate—the plaything or appendage of an autonomous nature.[15]

---

[12] Ibid. 372. On the purported connection between Vico and Marx, see Ch. 9 above.

[13] Marx, *Economic and Philosophic Manuscripts*, 136–7.   [14] Ibid. 145.

[15] Engels develops this naturalist or 'positivist' view in *Anti-Duhring* (1878) and the posthumously published *Dialectics of Nature* (1925). McLellan suggests that Engels's later positivist turn was prompted less by philosophical conviction than by considerations of political expediency: D. McLellan, *Engels* (London, 1977), 56–8.

10.4 MARX DISCOVERS DARWIN

Not surprisingly, perhaps, it was Engels who first recognized the supposed significance of Darwin's anti-teleological theory of natural selection for the 'scientific' understanding of human history. He had scarcely finished reading Darwin's *Origin of Species* in 1859 when he wrote to Marx: 'Darwin . . . is truly marvellous. Teleology, which has hitherto persisted, is now superseded. Never has such a magnificent attempt been made to discern historical development in nature.'[16]

Marx, then occupied with writing *Capital I*, had not yet read Darwin's *Origin*. But a year later, in 1860, he wrote to Engels: 'Although crudely developed in the English manner, this book contains the natural-historical basis [*die naturhistorische Grundlage*] of our outlook.'[17] A month later Marx wrote to Ferdinand Lassalle that Darwin's book, despite its 'crude English mode of development [*die grob englische Manier des Entwicklung*]', nevertheless 'deals the death-blow to teleology in the natural sciences'.[18] Darwin's having put an end to teleology in the natural sciences is, from Marx's radical-humanist perspective, entirely admirable, praiseworthy, and correct. Of course nature is without intrinsic design or purpose: that is man's prerogative. It is for this distinctly humanist reason that Marx praised Darwin's achievement of having finally banished the last vestiges of an immanent teleology in nature.

But Marx went further still. Two years later, in 1862, he tells Engels that he has just reread Darwin and now finds him 'amusing'. Darwin emerges, on Marx's rereading, as a nineteenth-century English bourgeois-turned-naturalist:

It is remarkable how Darwin recognizes among beasts and plants his English society with its division of labour, competition, opening up of new markets, inventions, and the Malthusian 'struggle for existence'. His [nature] is Hobbes's *bellum omnium contra omnes*, and one is reminded of Hegel's *Phenomenology*, where civil society is described as

---

[16] Engels to Marx, 12 Dec. 1859, *MEW* xxix. 524.
[17] Marx to Engels, 19 Dec. 1860, *MEW* xxx. 131.
[18] Marx to Lassalle, 16 Jan. 1861, in *MESC* 115; *MEW* xxx. 578.

a 'spiritual animal kingdom', while in Darwin the animal kingdom figures as civil society.[19]

Darwin is a 'crude English' theorist, not only because he reads into nature the categories of *laissez-faire* Manchesterism but because he underestimates the extent to which human purposes have been introduced and incorporated into supposedly 'natural' processes. The operations of 'nature' are nowadays no more 'natural' and autonomous than are the operations of the capitalist 'free market'. One need only think, for example, of the achievements of animal breeders and botanists in producing new breeds, strains, and hybrids—'mutations' that would not have occurred naturally and that have in their turn radically altered our social existence.[20] The opening chapter of his *Origin* notwithstanding,[21] Darwin fails to see that conscious human selection is, when weighed on the scales of human history, vastly more significant a factor in evolution than is natural selection through chance and accident. Because of human attempts to transform nature, 'natural history' is fast becoming 'human history'. Human purpose and *praxis* are replacing chance and accident as the motive force of evolution.

But if Marx thought Darwin amusing because he views nature in terms of civil society, he thought the socialist Darwinists contemptible because they view civil society in terms of nature. In 1868 Marx derided as 'shallow nonsense' Ludwig Büchner's early attempt (on the lecture circuit) to link Marx's theory with Darwin's.[22] (Marx's objections notwithstanding, Büchner's lectures were later expanded and published after Marx's death under the title *Darwinismus und Sozialismus*.) Two years later, Marx criticized Friedrich Albert Lange's *Die Arbeiterfrage*, which viewed the class struggle in 'Darwinian' terms as a 'struggle for life' and which added insult to injury by suggesting that this was also Marx's view.

[19] Marx to Engels, 18 June 1862, *MESC* 120; *MEW* xxx. 249.
[20] See e.g. Marx, *Capital I*, 632: 'An abstract law of population exists for plants and animals only, and only in so far as man has not interfered with them.'
[21] Charles Darwin, *The Origin of Species by Means of Natural Selection* (New York, 1958), ch. 1, 'Variation under Domestication', esp. 54–8.
[22] Marx to Kugelmann, 5 Dec. 1868, *MEW* xxxii. 579.

Marx's critique of Lange's book was, if anything, more vehement than his critique of Büchner's lectures:

Herr Lange has made a great discovery: the whole of history can be brought under a single all-encompassing law of nature. This natural law is the phrase (in this application Darwin's expression becomes a mere phrase) 'the struggle for life' . . . [But] instead of analysing the struggle for life as represented historically, in various definite forms of society, [Lange] merely translates every concrete struggle into the *phrase* 'struggle for life' . . . This is a very impressive method—for swaggering, sham-scientific, bombastic ignorance and intellectual laziness.[23]

For the socialist Darwinists Marx clearly reserved a special scorn.

But what of Marx's relation to Darwin and Darwinism? Of this much we may be certain: Marx clearly admired and agreed with Darwin's having finished off teleology in the natural sciences. Even so, he had at least two reasons for believing Darwin to be a 'crude English' theorist. First, Darwin takes nineteenth-century English market society as his implicit model. And, secondly, in emphasizing the role of chance and accident in natural selection, Darwin fails to appreciate the increasing importance of purposive human selection as the driving force in evolution. Darwin's theory of natural selection applies, at best, only to pre-human, pre-conscious natural history; it does not apply to the epoch of human history in which human beings consciously transform nature and thereby themselves. Darwin thus stands convicted on two counts, the first being that he is a provincial or 'crude English' theorist, the second that his theory is increasingly passé as humans come to make their own history by remaking nature.

This reading of Marx's relation to Darwin appears, however, to have a central flaw in the well-known and oft-cited fact that Marx wished to dedicate *Capital* to Charles

---

[23] Marx to Kugelmann, 27 June 1870, *MESC* 225; *MEW* xxxii. 685–6; cf. Marx's earlier, and equally caustic, estimates of Büchner and Lange (Marx to Engels, 14 Nov. 1868, *MEW* xxxii. 202–3). Lange's *Die Arbeiterfrage* (Duisburg, 1865) nevertheless continued to enjoy considerable popularity among German Socialists, going through six editions between 1865 and 1910. The sixth edition (Berlin, 1910) was edited and annotated by the SPD's historian and Marx's biographer, Franz Mehring.

Darwin.[24] How then explain—or explain away—this fact? Professor Avineri, having noted Marx's sceptical attitude to Darwin, can only surmise 'that Marx's intended dedication of *Das Kapital* to Darwin was evidently made tongue in cheek'.[25] Fortunately we need not accept Avineri's interesting but rather implausible explanation. For as we shall see, Marx never had any such intention.

10.5 THE MARX–DARWIN CORRESPONDENCE

As I noted earlier, the Marx–Darwin myth, as created and fostered by Engels and various socialist Darwinists, was made even more credible by the discovery of two letters written by Darwin, both apparently addressed to Marx. The first published disclosure of any correspondence between Marx and Darwin was made by Edward Aveling in 1897. According to Aveling, Marx had in June 1873 sent to Darwin a copy of the just-published second German edition of *Das Kapital* (the English translation by Aveling and Samuel Moore was not published until 1886, three years after Marx's death).[26] Disappointed by the English reading public's neglect of the first edition, Marx was determined to publicize the second edition by all possible means; accordingly, he sent inscribed copies of *Das Kapital* not only to Darwin but to his arch-foe Herbert Spencer.[27] The copy presented to Darwin bears this

[24] The episode is related unquestioningly by, *inter alia*, I. Berlin, *Karl Marx* (Oxford, 1963), 247–8; P. Gay, *The Dilemma of Democratic Socialism* (New York, 1952), 76; E. Lucas, 'Marx' und Engels' Auseinandersetzung mit Darwin', *International Review of Social History*, 9 (1964), 468–9; S. Avineri, 'From Hoax to Dogma—A Footnote on Marx and Darwin', *Encounter* (Mar. 1967), 30–2, at 30; B. Ollman, *Alienation* (Cambridge, 1971), 53; D. McLellan, *Karl Marx: His Life and Thought* (London, 1973), 424; V. Gerratana, 'Marx and Darwin', *New Left Review*, 82 (Nov.–Dec. 1973), 79; R. Colp, jun., 'The Contacts between Karl Marx and Charles Darwin', *JHI* 35 (1974), 329–38; J. Hoffman, *Marxism and the Theory of Praxis* (New York, 1974), 55–6; McMurtry, *Structure*, 163; J. Barzun, *Darwin, Marx, Wagner* (Chicago, 1981), 8; D. Boorstin, *The Discoverers* (New York, 1983), 619–20.

[25] Avineri, 'From Hoax to Dogma', 32.

[26] Aveling, 'Charles Darwin and Karl Marx', 243.

[27] See M. Rubel and M. Manale, *Marx without Myth* (Oxford, 1975), 291. Unfortunately Rubel and Manale do nothing to dispel the Marx–Darwin myth.

inscription: 'Mr. Charles Darwin / On the part of his sincere admirer / Karl Marx / London 16 June 1873'.[28]

Although usually prompt to acknowledge the gift of others' work, Darwin delayed his answer for nearly three months. In due course Marx received the following reply:

Oct. 1, 1873
Dear Sir
I thank you for the honour which you have done me by sending me your great work on Capital; & I heartily wish that I was more worthy to receive it, by understanding more of the deep & important subject of political Economy. Though our studies have been so different, I believe that we both Earnestly desire the extension of knowledge, & that this in the long run is sure to add to the happiness of Mankind.
I remain Dear Sir
              Yours faithfully
              Charles Darwin[29]

Although polite and non-committal in the extreme, Darwin's brief note was thought by Engels to be 'exceedingly charming' and by Aveling to be 'very beautiful'.[30] Even so, it hardly constituted—*pace* Engels and Aveling—an endorsement of Marx's science by a fellow scientist. Accustomed as he was to corresponding with zoologists, biologists, and paleontologists, Darwin was doubtless taken aback at receiving a

[28] H. E. Gruber, 'Marx and *Das Kapital*', *Isis*, 52 (1961), 582.

[29] First published in Aveling, 'Charles Darwin and Karl Marx', 243. The authenticity of Darwin's 1873 letter was challenged by L. S. Feuer ('Is the "Darwin-Marx Correspondence" Authentic?', *Annals of Science*, 32 (1975), 1–12). Feuer denounced the letter as a forgery—the product, he conjectured, of Aveling's ambition and an excessive enthusiasm for synthesizing Marxism and Darwinism. Among the slender shreds of evidence in favour of this conjecture Feuer cites the dastardly 'character of Aveling', whose misdeeds including forging his wife's handwriting. And—Feuer reasoned—if Aveling would stoop to forging Eleanor Marx–Aveling's handwriting, why not Darwin's? Aveling was without doubt a forger, and worse besides; but whatever his crimes, the forgery of Darwin's 1873 letter was not among them. For a convincing refutation, see R. Colp, jun., 'The Contacts of Charles Darwin with Edward Aveling and Karl Marx', *Annals of Science*, 33 (1976), 387–94. In the light of mounting evidence to the contrary, Feuer abandoned his forgery hypothesis. However, another of his conjectures—that Aveling, not Marx, was the intended recipient of Darwin's 1880 letter—has been brilliantly and independently confirmed (see n. 33 below).

[30] Engels to Eduard Bernstein, 3 May 1882, *MEW* 35, 315; Aveling, 'Charles Darwin and Karl Marx', 243.

weighty treatise on political economy. It was not mere polite-
ness or English understatement that led Darwin to 'wish I was
more worthy to receive [*Das Kapital*]'—a work foreign to him
not only in its subject-matter but in its language (he read
German only with great difficulty). 'Our studies', Darwin
rightly remarks, 'have been so different ... ' So different,
indeed, that Darwin, rather at a loss for words, finally resorts
to those platitudes of polite Victorian correspondence—'the
extension of knowledge' and 'the happiness of mankind'. His
duty duly discharged, Darwin relegated Marx's masterpiece to
a shelf in his library, where it remains to this day, most of its
pages still uncut.[31]

Marx's inscription of June 1873 and Darwin's acknowledgement of October 1873 were in fact the beginning and the end
of their correspondence. But what of the mysterious second
letter, in which Darwin supposedly declined Marx's offer to
dedicate *Capital* to him? Neither Aveling nor Engels makes
any mention of Marx's offer or Darwin's refusal. Not until
1931 did the editors of the Soviet journal *Pod Znamenem
Marxizma* ('Under the Banner of Marxism'), tell of Marx's
offer to dedicate the second volume of *Capital* to Darwin.
Although unable to locate Marx's letter, they produced from
the Marx–Engels *Nachlass* what they took to be Darwin's letter of refusal:

Oct. 13, 1880
Dear Sir
I am much obliged by your kind letter and the Enclosure—the publication in any form of your remarks on my writings really requires
no consent on my part, & it would be ridiculous in me to give consent to what requires none.—I shd. prefer the Part or Volume not be
dedicated to me (though I thank you for the intended honour) as it
implies to a certain extent my approval of the general publication,
about which I know nothing.—Moreover though I am a strong
advocate for free thought on all subjects, yet it appears to me
(whether rightly or wrongly) that direct arguments against christianity and theism produce hardly any effect on the public, & freedom of
thought is best promoted by the gradual illumination of men's
minds, which follow from the advance of science. It has, therefore,

[31] Only the first 105 pages of Darwin's copy (in his library at Down
House, Kent) were cut, presumably by Darwin himself.

been always my object to avoid writing on religion, & I have confined myself to science. I may, however, have been unduly biased by
the pain which it would give some members of my family, if I aided
in any way direct attacks on religion.—I am sorry to refuse you any
request, but I am old & have very little strength, & looking over
proofsheets (as I know by present experience) fatigues me much.—I
remain Dear Sir

Yours faithfully
Ch. Darwin[32]

This letter, which many scholars have considered to be
proof of Marx's intention to dedicate *Capital II* to Darwin, is
very curious indeed, and only deepens the mystery. In 1880
Marx was far from having completed *Capital II*; nor does that
work contain any 'direct arguments against christianity and
theism' or 'direct attacks on religion'. How then explain
Darwin's misapprehension? We now know—thanks to some
truly splendid detective work—that Darwin's letter was
addressed not to Marx but to Edward Aveling.[33] Moreover,
the 'Part or Volume' was not *Capital II* but Aveling's *The
Student's Darwin*—a work which did indeed contain 'direct
attacks on religion', Christianity in particular.[34] Darwin's letter of 13 October 1880 is in fact a reply to Aveling's letter of

[32] See Lucas, 'Marx' und Engels' Auseinandersetzung'; Colp, 'The
Contacts of Charles Darwin with Edward Aveling and Karl Marx'. A
Russian translation of Darwin's 1880 letter is included in *Pod Znamenem
Marxizma*, 1–2 (1931).

[33] See L. S. Feuer, 'The "Darwin–Marx Correspondence": A Correction
and Revision', *Annals of Science*, 33 (1976), 383–4; Feuer and P. T. Carroll,
'Further Evidence that Karl Marx was not the Recipient of Charles Darwin's
Letter dated 13 October 1880', ibid. 385–7; and particularly Colp, 'The
Contacts of Charles Darwin with Edward Aveling and Karl Marx'. See, fur-
ther, P. Thuillier, 'La Correspondence Darwin–Marx: Une rectification', *La
Recherche* (Apr. 1977), 394–5; and M. A. Fay, 'Did Marx Offer to Dedicate
Capital to Darwin? A Reassessment of the Evidence', *JHI* 39 (1978), 133–46.
Working independently of Feuer, Fay discovered the comedy of errors that
led to the mistaken identity of the recipient of Darwin's 1880 letter. See, fur-
ther, Fay, 'Marx and Darwin: A Literary Detective Story', *Monthly Review*
(Mar. 1980). For an accusation that some scholarly skulduggery was
involved in withholding recognition from Fay, see R. Colp jun., 'The Case of
the "Darwin–Marx" Letter, Lewis Feuer, and *Encounter*', *Monthly Review*
(Jan. 1981), 58–61.

[34] Aveling's *The Student's Darwin* (London, 1881) was issued as vol. 2 of
the International Library of Science and Freethought; see esp. 291–6.

12 October 1880, in which he requests permission to dedicate *The Student's Darwin* to Darwin.[35]

We can now conclude with some confidence that Marx never intended—'tongue in cheek' or otherwise—to dedicate *Capital II* to Darwin.[36] In the light of Marx's sceptical reconsideration of Darwin—and his hostile dismissal of the socialist Darwinists—this is hardly surprising.

10.6 PURPORTED POLITICAL IMPLICATIONS

More surprising, perhaps, have been the political reactions to this discovery. Scholars in China and the former Soviet Union have so far maintained a stony silence, refusing to discuss the matter or to revise the official accounts of the now-discredited Marx–Darwin connection. (Whether recent developments in the former Soviet Union will break the silence remains to be seen.) Their silence is, however, less surprising than the voluble reactions and retractions of one of the scholars whose labours contributed to this important find.

Lewis Feuer has recounted the story of the scholarly sleuthing that led to his independent co-discovery (with the late Margaret Fay) that Darwin's 1880 letter was addressed not to Marx but to Edward Aveling. Feuer expressed fears that this discovery might be put to nefarious political uses. 'Neo-Marxist circles', he hinted darkly, 'are now said to be trying to draw ideological comfort from the discovery that Marx never meant to dedicate a *Capital* volume to Darwin.' Theirs is, however, a curious kind of comfort: 'Somehow they think this confirms their rendition of Marx as an idealistic metaphysician, and not a materialist determinist.'[37]

One need not belong to a circle, 'Neo-Marxist' or otherwise, to take exception to Feuer's curious imputation, his inferences, and his use of evidence. In the first place he

---

[35] Fay ('Marx and Darwin') tells how Darwin's letter to Aveling found its way into the Marx–Engels *Nachlass*.

[36] Indeed, Marx expressed repeatedly his intention to dedicate the second and third volumes of *Capital* to his wife Jenny. See Engels, 'Vorwort', *Das Kapital II*, *MEW* xxiv. 26.

[37] L. S. Feuer, 'The Case of the Darwin–Marx Letter', *Encounter* (Oct. 1978), 76.

resurrects, and then relies upon, two rather shop-worn spectres. Marx, he suggests, had to be either 'an idealistic metaphysician' or 'a materialist determinist'. But surely, if 'Neo-Marxists' (by which Feuer apparently means 'Western', 'critical' and/or 'humanist' Marxists) derive comfort from anything, it is from the view—found, for example, in Alfred Schmidt's *Concept of Nature in Marx*—that Marx was neither an idealistic metaphysician nor a materialist determinist *simpliciter*. But Feuer was undeterred. Marx, he insists, was 'a materialist determinist', after all. In support of this claim he cites 'the fact that Marx, shortly after reading the *Origin of Species*, declared that Darwin's book provided him with 'a basis in natural science for the class struggle in history', and then stated plainly in his preface to *Das Kapital* in 1867 that his standpoint was one from which the evolution of society is 'viewed as a process of natural history'.[38] These passages, Feuer believes, suffice to show that Marx's conception of 'class struggle [is] founded on biological drives', and that such a view 'is about as far as one can get from a view of history that would regard its mainspring as man's quest to realize his essence, through an overcoming of whatever alienates him from himself'.[39] Feuer's evidence and his inference merit closer examination.

Feuer's first piece of evidence comes from a letter written by Marx to Lassalle early in 1861. 'Darwin's book', he told Lassalle, 'is very important and suits me as the natural-scientific basis of the class-struggle [*naturwissenschaftlische Unterlage des Klassenkampfes*]'.[40] What Marx means by this remark is not, *pace* Feuer, entirely clear. Considering that he immediately goes on to praise Darwin for having dealt 'the death-blow to "teleology" in the natural sciences', he might have meant only that his view of the class struggle resembled Darwin's view of the struggle for existence, in that both were anti-teleological. Far from showing that Marx was a 'materialist determinist', his (admittedly cryptic) remark suggests only that he shared Darwin's aversion to immanentist-teleological explanations. Feuer correctly notes that this letter was written

[38] L. S. Feuer, 'The Case of the Darwin–Marx Letter', *Encounter*, 76.
[39] Ibid. 78.
[40] Marx to Lassalle, 16 Jan. 1861, *MESC* 115; *MEW* xxx. 578.

shortly after Marx's first hasty reading of Darwin's *Origin*, but he fails to mention that Marx later formed a rather different opinion of its merits.

Feuer's second shred of evidence comes from Marx's Preface to the first edition of *Das Kapital*, written in 1867—five years after he had reread Darwin and found him 'amusing'. This piece of evidence is, accordingly, weightier than the first. His standpoint, Marx writes, is one from which 'the development of the economic social formation [*die Entwicklung der ökonomischen Gesellschaftsformation*] is viewed as a natural-historical process [*als einen naturgeschichtlichen prozess auffasst*]'.[41]

About Feuer's use of this remark two things may be said. First, his paraphrase and partial translation are not faithful to the original. Feuer says that Marx viewed 'the evolution of society' as 'a process of natural history'; but this is not what Marx says. He refers not to 'society', *simpliciter*, but specifically to 'the economic social formation' as having developed as 'a natural-historical process'. Secondly, Feuer omits to mention the relevant fact that Marx drew a distinction between 'natural history' and 'human history'. This is an unfortunate omission, inasmuch as Marx's remark is neither clear nor meaningful without a prior understanding of the significance of this distinction. When Marx says that he views 'the development of the economic social formation . . . as a natural-historical process', he means that economic changes have heretofore occurred without conscious human direction and control; in this respect they are (like) natural occurrences and belong, therefore, to 'natural history'. This, I take it, is what Marx had in mind when he told Engels that Darwin's *Origin* 'contains the natural-historical basis of our outlook'.[42] Darwin is remiss, however, in failing to provide a human-historical account of evolution in modern times. His theory of natural selection applies, at best, to pre-human 'natural' history; what is needed, Marx avers, is a theory of artificial, or human, selection applicable to 'human history'. Considered in this light, Darwin's theory is not mistaken; it is, rather, partial and incomplete. Precisely because natural history is fast

---

[41] Marx, *Capital I*, 10; *MEW* xxiii. 16.
[42] Marx to Engels, 19 Dec. 1860, *MEW* xxx. 131.

becoming human history, a Darwinian account of present and future developments will not suffice: that, after all, was why Marx objected so vehemently to socialist Darwinism, as espoused by Lange, Büchner, and others.

Feuer is therefore quite mistaken in viewing Marx as a socialist Darwinist whose conception of class struggle is 'founded on biological drives'. There is no good reason for supposing this to be Marx's view, and every reason for supposing that it is not. The final twist in Feuer's tale is, to say the least, ironic. Having made an important contribution to the de-mythifying of Marxism, Feuer went on to re-mythify it: 'the unknown German Social Democratic archivist who may have misclassified Darwin's letter [of 1880]' was, Feuer suggests, entirely justified in so doing. For, although Marx did not wish to dedicate *Capital* to Darwin, he might as well have, considering 'the well-established foundation of Marxism on Darwinian evolution'.[43] This, I have argued, is palpably untrue.

The Marx–Darwin connection can now be seen for what it is—a myth, pure but far from simple—and, one hopes, finally laid to rest. It has persisted for far too long and has in the interim done considerable harm. The myth has lent some semblance of credibility to the claim that Marx was himself a socialist Darwinist,[44] a crude biological reductionist,[45] and a 'positivist'.[46] No doubt Marx, who denied that he was even a Marxist, would reject all these labels; so too, I think, should we. If political theories—even supposedly scientific ones—are 'structures of intentions',[47] then we have long misunderstood the structure of Marxian theory because we have misunderstood Marx's intentions. Fortunately, with the Marx–Darwin myth out of the way, we can now read Marx's intentions

[43] Feuer, 'The Case', 78.
[44] See Büchner, *Darwinismus und Sozialismus*; Lange, *Die Arbeiterfrage*; Kautsky, *Ethik*; and the work of numerous modern commentators (see n. 24 above).
[45] Feuer, 'The Case', 78.
[46] S. Wolin (*Politics and Vision* (Boston, 1960), 358) speaks of Marx's 'acknowledged positivism', and A. Wellmer (*Critical Theory of Society* (New York, 1971), ch. 2) of his 'latent positivism'. For a critique, see Farr, 'Marx and Positivism'.
[47] See S. Wolin, 'Political Theory as a Vocation', *APSR* 63 (1969), 1078.

aright and begin anew the attempt to understand the structure of his theory.

10.7 CODA: REPLY TO A CRITIC

I am grateful to Mark Warren for criticizing my 'Marx and Darwin: A Reconsideration'.[48] Although ultimately unconvincing, the objections he raises are both interesting and important. Let me briefly reiterate and reply to these objections.

Warren first objects that I 'make Darwin the scapegoat for the various naturalistic fallacies smuggled into turn-of-the-century Marxism'.[49] This I do not do. These smugglings-in were due not to Darwin but, as I noted, to such self-styled socialist Darwinists as Lange, Büchner, and—not least—Engels. Warren's second and third objections are, respectively, that I 'misunderstand the nature of Darwin's unique contribution to evolutionary theories of history' and that I thereby 'miss the real and fruitful methodological connections between Marx and Darwin'.[50] The former objection rests, I think, upon a misunderstanding, the latter upon an as-yet unproven assertion.

Warren maintains that I have 'misunderstood the explanatory claims of Darwin's theory', in large part because I do not distinguish carefully between the *sources* of random variation across a population and the process whereby some of these are *selected* for success and others for failure. The sources of variation may, as Warren rightly notes, be multifarious, ranging from unconscious accident (e.g. genetic mutation) to conscious human design. But, whatever the *source* of variation, *success* is determined neither by chance nor design but by a process of natural selection. For nature—not human beings—selects those traits, features, characteristics, behaviours, etc. that are functional for (i.e. conducive to the adaptation and survival of) the species in question, and eliminates those that prove to be dysfunctional. (The pattern of Darwinian

---

[48] M. Warren, 'On Ball, "Marx and Darwin"', *Political Theory*, 9 (1981), 260–3.

[49] Ibid. 260.   [50] Ibid.

explanation is thus, broadly speaking, functionalist rather than teleological or purposive. More on this in a moment.) If I understand him aright, the nub of Warren's objection is this: although one may speak of artificial *variation*, it makes no sense to speak—as I do—of 'artificial *selection*' or, worse still, of 'selection through chance and accident'. Warren quite rightly chides me for the latter remark, which is inexcusably elliptical. I should have said instead that natural selection is sometimes made possible by chance and accident, thereby avoiding at least some of the ensuing confusion. Clearly while the *sources* of variation may be due to chance or accident, *selection* cannot be. Selection can, however, be either natural or artificial.

Interestingly, Darwin himself often spoke of 'artificial selection', and claimed to have modelled his theory of natural selection upon it.[51] In the late 1830s Darwin had numerous conversations with animal breeders, and avidly read and annotated pamphlets by Wilkinson and Sebright,[52] both of which contain the phrase 'artificial selection'. How then can selection, as distinguished from variation, be artificial? The following imaginary—but, I submit, none the less plausible— tale may provide an answer. Let us suppose that wild cows have smaller udders than domesticated cows. The explanation of the former is to be found (let us further suppose) in the fact that possessing large udders impedes a cow's ability to flee from predators; and so smaller udders, having greater survival value, are, over many generations, naturally selected for. Then along comes man, the domesticator of animals. He fences the cattle in and the predators out. What he values is not the cow's fleetness of foot but its ability to produce milk in ever-greater quantities. He therefore breeds cows for that purpose, and in succeeding generations more cows come in consequence to possess large udders. In the former case, small udders were naturally selected for; in the latter, larger udders were artificially selected. On this point Wilkinson and Sebright—and Darwin—are, so to speak, udderly clear and explicit. By artificially varying certain environmental conditions cattle-breeders can select out for replication traits or

---

[51] See Notebooks B and C in the Darwin Collection at the Cambridge University Library.

[52] See, respectively, offprints 62 and 63 in the Darwin Collection.

characteristics that they—and not Nature—deem necessary and/or desirable. It thus makes perfectly good sense to speak of purposive or artificial *selection*.

As for the 'real and fruitful methodological connections between Marx and Darwin', I must confess that I fail to find them. Certainly many Marxists—not the least among whom was Engels—claimed that such a connection did indeed exist. But what is the precise nature of this connection? For Engels, it was that Marx, like Darwin, had discovered certain 'laws' of development.[53] This claim is doubly doubtful, first because, as Popper suggests, Darwin's generalizations are not genuinely law-like;[54] and secondly because, as I tried to show, Marx was exceedingly sceptical if not scornful of the 'laws' formulated by (say) Malthus, and picked up not only by political economists and by natural scientists like Darwin but—worst of all—by such 'sham scientists' as Büchner and Lange.

Wherein then lies the 'real and fruitful methodological connection' of which Warren writes? It is to be found in the very similar 'pattern of explanation' which Warren claims to detect in the writings of Darwin and Marx. This pattern is broadly functionalist. On this view we 'explain' a phenomenon—whether natural or social—by showing what function it serves for the particular entity of which it is a part. The bird's hollow bones, the giraffe's long neck, and the scale of capitalist production are all explicable in terms of their respective functions. Economies of scale are like hollow bones and long necks, inasmuch as all enhance the efficiency, effectiveness, or profitability of the entity in question.

This 'functionalist' account of Marx's aims and achievements has been powerfully put by G. A. Cohen and persuasively challenged by Jon Elster. I have not the space to summarize Elster's critique of functionalist explanation generally,[55] and of Cohen's recasting of Marxian explanations in functionalist terms in particular.[56] Here it must suffice to say

[53] See Engels, 'Speech at Marx's Graveside', *MESW* 429.
[54] K. Popper, *Unended Quest* (London, 1976), 167–80. Cf. M. Scriven, 'Explanation and Prediction in Evolutionary Theory', *Science*, 130 (1959), 477–82.
[55] J. Elster, *Ulysses and the Sirens* (Cambridge, 1979), ch. 1.
[56] J. Elster, 'Cohen on Marx's Theory of History', *Political Studies*, 28 (1980), 121–8.

that both Cohen and Elster are right, or rather that each is half-right. Marx's methodology—his 'pattern of explanation'— is itself historically variable. Marx's distinction between 'natural' and 'human' history marks not merely a temporal but a methodological distinction. Explanations couched in terms of functions and natural selection may indeed be appropriate for the former but *not*, *pace* Cohen, for the latter. This was, after all, the basis of Marx's complaint that 'in Darwin progress is merely accidental' (or what Elster terms 'gradient climbing') and that *The Origin of Species* therefore yields little 'in connection with history and politics'.[57] The political actions and historical activities of fully conscious self-transforming human beings would be explained by reference to their aims, purposes, and intentions. (Note that I say 'by reference to' and not 'in terms of' the conscious intentions of purposive agents— because, of course, even in the era of 'human history', actions can misfire and produce unintended consequences. But the very identification of unintended consequences, as I have argued elsewhere,[58] requires reference to intentions.) Social changes and innovations will then be those 'artificially' selected for by rational-purposive beings. Marx's methodological point, I take it, is that different 'patterns of explanation' are appropriate to different historical epochs. The Darwinian pattern is appropriate to the era of pre-conscious 'natural history', but largely *passé* in the epoch of humanly created 'human history'.

Warren's claim that I 'dissolve the methodological connection' between Darwin and Marx, resting as it does upon an as-yet-unproven assertion—namely, that such a connection does indeed exist—simply assumes what he is obliged to prove. Although sceptical, I am prepared to agree with his parting remark that 'the methodological connection' between Darwin and Marx 'is interesting and deserves more serious attention'.[59] I hope that Professor Warren will one day give this supposed connection the attention it so clearly deserves. In any event, however, the point and purpose of my enquiry will not be affected by the outcome. My aim was simply to show that

[57] Marx to Engels, 7 Aug. 1866, *MEW* xxxi. 248.
[58] See my *Transforming Political Discourse* (Oxford, 1988), 8; and ch. 1.3 above, esp. 13–14.
[59] Warren, 'On Ball', 263.

Marx himself—quite unlike Engels and other latter-day Marxists—denied that there was a connection, methodological or otherwise, between his theory and Darwin's.

CONSTITUTIONAL INTERPRETATION: WHAT'S WRONG WITH 'ORIGINAL INTENT'?

There is a difference between the original meaning of the law and that applied in current legal practice. True, the jurist ... must have historical knowledge of the original meaning ... But he cannot let himself be tied by ... the intentions of those who first made the law. Rather, he has to take account of changed circumstances and hence define anew the normative function of the law. The legal historian, by contrast, is concerned only with the law's original meaning ...

Hans-Georg Gadamer

11.1 INTRODUCTION

The preceding chapters have, in one way or another, dealt with the interpretation of texts in political theory—or, more precisely, with problems that arise in attempting to understand puzzling aspects or features of those works. One interpretive strategy, that favoured by the 'new historians', requires the recovery of author's intention and the 'historical identity' of the text—the 'original intent', as it were, of the author and work in question. Such a strategy can work well, and sometimes brilliantly, for historians of political thought. But can it work as well for judges or jurists or indeed for ordinary citizens who wish to know the meaning of this or that constitutional doctrine or passage or phrase? I shall argue that the very strategy that can (depending of course on the problem being addressed) work so well for historians of political thought would be unworkable and well-nigh disastrous for jurists seeking to interpret the meaning of the US Constitution (and, by implication, other basic legal instruments). There are, I believe, good reasons for eschewing an 'originalist' strategy of legal interpretation. As I shall suggest, the hermeneutical tasks facing judges and jurists differ markedly and profoundly from those encountered by historians of political thought.

My aim in this chapter is accordingly to take another look at a current, or rather recurring, hermeneutical controversy. That controversy centres around a set of questions about what the Constitution 'means' and how it should be interpreted. Is the meaning of this particular (or perhaps indeed any) text extensionally equivalent to a (re)statement of its authors' beliefs and intentions? Or does the meaning of this (or any) text change over time and vary with the changing perspectives and interests of its interpreters? Various versions of the doctrine of 'originalism' answer the first question affirmatively and the second negatively. Critics of originalism tend to answer the first negatively and the second affirmatively.

Interesting as these questions (and answers) are to scholars, they are not, needless to say, purely academic. Such questions constitute what I have elsewhere called 'deadly hermeneutics'—deadly inasmuch as how they are answered has an important bearing upon people's lives and well-being.[1] I want here to take a critical second look at one way of addressing and answering these questions. That perspective—once called strict constructionism and, more recently, 'originalism' (or sometimes, in one particular version, 'original intent')—holds that the meaning of a text or utterance, generally speaking, is whatever its author initially intended (or could conceivably have intended) it to mean.[2] In the case of the Constitution, the task of the interpreter or 'interpretive community'—consisting not only of legal scholars, lawyers, judges, and Supreme Court Justices, but ultimately of ordinary citizens as well—is to discover what the Founders originally meant by this or that word, article, phrase, or passage.[3] Much has been

[1] See my 'Deadly Hermeneutics; or, *Sinn* and the Social Scientist', in Ball (ed.) *Idioms of Inquiry* (Albany, NY, 1987), 95–112.

[2] See S. Fish, *Is there a Text in This Class? The Authority of Interpretive Communities* (Cambridge, Mass., 1980), ch. 15.

[3] The US Constitution's interpretive community, Francis Lieber averred, includes not only the lawyers, judges, and courts but the entire citizenry. See

said in defence and in criticism of this doctrine.⁴ My aim here, however, is not to retread these well-travelled and by now deeply rutted roads but to suggest an alternate route to a familiar destination.

In making my way towards that destination I shall try to be critical of originalism without, however, trading in the caricatures that mar much of the decidedly polemical debate between the originalists and their critics. Judicial stereotypes, like racial or sexual ones, should be assiduously avoided. I know of no originalist, for example, who fits the stereotype of the flat-footed literalist whose principles would lead to the conclusion that the Air Force is unconstitutional because it— unlike the army, navy, and state militia—is not specifically mentioned or provided for in the Constitution. Nor am I aware of any non-originalist who holds that 'anything goes' and that judges can legitimately usurp the role of legislators by 'making' law on whim or as they see fit. Both are caricatures, and neither furthers the cause of criticism.

I propose to criticize originalism by advancing and defending two claims. The first, which I take to be straightforward and non-controversial, is that discovering an author's beliefs and intentions requires that one recover or reconstruct the

J. Farr, 'The Americanization of Hermeneutics: Francis Lieber's *Legal and Political Hermeneutics*', in G. Leyh (ed.), *Legal Hermeneutics* (Berkeley, Calif., 1992).

⁴ Strictly speaking, originalism is not a single doctrine but a fairly close-knit family of doctrines sharing a common assumption—namely, that judges and other interpreters must return to and regard as authoritative the original source, whether that source be construed as author, authorial intent, text, or, more broadly, the moral, historical, legal, and political context in which the author worked and/or the text was composed. I shall be dealing mainly with the 'original-intent' version of originalism. For a useful taxonomy of types of originalism, see P. Brest, 'The Misconceived Quest for Original Understanding', *Boston University Law Review*, 60 (1980), 204–38. In defence of originalism, see, *inter alia*, R. Bork, 'Neutral Principles and Some First Amendment Problems', *Indiana Law Journal*, 47 (1971), 1–35, and 'Tradition and Morality in Constitutional Law', in M. Cannon and D. O'Brien (eds.), *Views from the Bench* (New York, 1985); R. Berger, *Government by Judiciary* (Cambridge, Mass., 1977); H. Monaghan, 'Our Perfect Constitution', *New York University Law Review*, 56 (1981), 353–96. For criticisms, see, *inter alia*, R. Dworkin, *A Matter of Principle* (Cambridge, Mass., 1985), chs. 5–7; G. Leyh, 'Toward a Constitutional Hermeneutics', *AJPS* 32 (1988), 369–87; M. J. Perry, 'The Authority of Text, Tradition, and Reason: A Theory of Constitutional "Interpretation" ', *Southern California Law Review*, 58 (1985), 552–602, and *Morality, Politics, and Law* (New York, 1989).

language or idiom in which those beliefs and intentions were framed in the first place. Although fraught with difficulties, this task can be, and has been, performed by conceptual historians.[5] My second and more controversial claim is that there are compelling reasons why judges and Supreme Court justices—or ordinary citizens—are not now, and should not become, conceptual historians bent on reconstructing the world of words within which the Framers expressed their beliefs and framed their intentions.

My argument proceeds in the following way. I begin by sketching, very roughly and with the fewest possible strokes, a picture of the kind of un- or half-articulated beliefs that underlie and give point and meaning to human action and intention. This crude picture I then attempt to connect with current concerns about conceptual change and commensurability, in anthropology and elsewhere. These concerns, I argue, also have their counterpart in constitutional interpretation. The background beliefs and the discursive or linguistic conventions within which the Founders framed their intentions are in many respects remarkably different from our own. To recover and reinstate their intentions would perforce require that judges not only recover, but that they (and we) accept as valid and legitimate, the outdated or even discredited theoretical discourse of an earlier epoch. This, however, is a retrograde move that we cannot rationally make. Next, I suggest that, while one can of course sometimes discern the intentions of any particular individual Founder, one commits the 'single-author' fallacy if one attempts to impute a unique or univocal intention to the Founders as a group. Finally, I conclude by

---

[5] On the methods and justifications for constructing 'conceptual histories', see R. Koselleck, *Futures Past* (Cambridge, Mass., 1985). For the execution of particular conceptual histories, see O. Brunner, W. Conze, and R. Koselleck (eds.), *Geschichtliche Grundbegriffe* (Stuttgart, 1972–), 5 vols. to date; and R. Reichardt and E. Schmitt (eds.), *Handbuch politisch-sozialer Grundbegriffe in Frankreich, 1680–1820* (Munich, 1985–), 2 vols. to date. For more anglicized and Americanized versions of conceptual history, cf. A. Pagden (ed.), *The Languages of Political Theory in Early-Modern Europe* (Cambridge, 1987); T. Ball, J. Farr, and R. L. Hanson (eds.), *Political Innovation and Conceptual Change* (Cambridge, 1989); T. Ball and J. G. A. Pocock (eds.), *Conceptual Change and the Constitution* (Lawrence, Kan., 1988); and my *Transforming Political Discourse* (Oxford, 1988).

suggesting that the most persuasive critic of originalism is none other than the Father of the Constitution himself.

11.2 BACKGROUND BELIEFS AND THE PROBLEM OF COMMENSURABILITY

It might be best to begin by stating the obvious. Our intentions are necessarily framed against the backdrop afforded by our understanding of the world and how it works. This understanding not only includes beliefs about causal connections (if you wish to bring about Y, you must first do X, because X causes Y), but also certain assumptions about human nature —that is, about what kinds of creatures human beings are, what moves or motivates them, what ends they seek, and so on. These causal beliefs and these assumptions about human nature are in their turn part of a larger picture of the world and our place in it. As Isaiah Berlin observes:

Men's beliefs in the sphere of conduct are part of their conceptions of themselves and others as human beings; and this conception in its turn, whether conscious or not, is intrinsic to their picture of the world. This picture may be complete and coherent, or shadowy or confused, but almost always . . . it can be shown to be dominated by one or more models or paradigms: mechanistic, organic, aesthetic, logical, mystical, shaped by the strongest influence of the day—religious, scientific, metaphysical or artistic. This model or paradigm determines the content as well as the form of beliefs and behaviour.[6]

Correctly to characterize an agent's action—or an author's text—requires that one be able to identify the world-picture which informs the language within which his or her intentions are (or were) framed in the first place.[7] One must, in other words, see them as somehow fitting in with a whole network of background beliefs about the world and how it works.

[6] I. Berlin, *Concepts and Categories* (Harmondsworth, 1981), 154.
[7] See e.g. E. M. W. Tillyard, *The Elizabethan World Picture* (New York, 1944). The point applies not only to law and literature but to the natural sciences as well. See E. A. Burtt, *The Metaphysical Foundations of Modern Science* (New York, 1952); A. Koyré, *From the Closed World to the Infinite Universe* (Baltimore, 1957); and S. Toulmin, 'The Construal of Reality: Criticism in Modern and Postmodern Science', in W. J. T. Mitchell (ed.), *The Politics of Interpretation* (Chicago, 1983), 99–117.

Yet this often proves, in practice, to be extraordinarily difficult to do. Even in cases involving contemporaries with whom we presumably share a culture and a common language we are often at a loss to say what they are doing, much less why they act as they do. One need only think, for example, of the difficulties facing a secular observer who wishes to give an account of the actions and self-understandings of someone who has undergone a religious conversion. One can, of course, ask what this person is doing, or intends to do, and why. But one is unlikely to accept at face value any self-understanding in which even the most ordinary events are seen as evidence of divine providence.[8]

These difficulties are doubled when observer and subject share neither a culture nor a common language. In such circumstances the so-called commensurability problem becomes both obvious and acute.[9] The epistemological perils facing anthropologists are notorious, and the opportunities for mistranslation and other forms of cross-cultural mis-communication are legion.[10] How—to take merely one example among many —can one talk about self-interested behaviour in a culture or among a people whose language lacks the (modern Western) concept of 'economic man' or even of the individual self or 'person'? After all, as Clifford Geertz notes,

The Western conception of the person as a bounded, unique, more or less integrated motivational and cognitive universe, a dynamic center of awareness, emotion, judgment, and action organized into a distinctive whole and set contrastively both against other such wholes and against a social and natural background is, however incorrigible it may seem to us, a rather peculiar idea within the context of the world's cultures.[11]

The very terms that we take to be descriptive, or even constitutive, of who and what we are, or aspire to be, are not

---

[8] Cf. the amusing and instructive tale of the 'born-again' Christian outfielder, Pat Kelly, as told by Fish, *Is there a Text?*, 269–72.

[9] On various versions of the commensurability problem as it appears in the discourses of anthropology and other disciplines, see R. J. Bernstein, *Beyond Objectivism and Relativism* (Philadelphia, 1983), esp. pt. III.

[10] See e.g. C. Geertz, 'From the Native's Point of View', in P. Rabinow and W. M. Sullivan (eds.), *Interpretive Social Science* (Berkeley, Calif., 1979), ch. 6; and P. Winch, 'Understanding a Primitive Society', in B. R. Wilson (ed.), *Rationality* (Oxford, 1970).

[11] Geertz, 'From the Native's Point of View', 229.

always readily translatable into what we might call the moral languages of other cultures (nor theirs into ours). And even those terms for which translations are readily available—birth, death, marriage, friendship, worship, God, prayer, play, and many others—have very different meanings in different cultures.

Such problems of translation and interpretation—of grasping the meaning or point of alien practices and actions—arise most obviously and glaringly in anthropology and other disciplines that deal with other cultures and languages. But those problems are by no means unique to those disciplines. I want to suggest that the art of constitutional interpretation is fraught with dangers and difficulties at least as great, and possibly as intractable, as those facing any anthropologist.

Now this might seem absurd on its face. For we do, after all—so the argument might run—share with the Founders a continuous culture and a common language. We are able to recover and understand their intentions because they are, or were, framed in the very language that we still speak. It is of course true that we, like the Founders, are speakers of English. But it is no less true that this language has changed in several crucial respects. First, and most obviously, many of the 'same' words have quite different meanings for us than they did for the Founders. Garry Wills gives the following example:

'Your argument is obnoxious, but it will be liquidated once its specious character is discovered.' That sentence would not be considered friendly if spoken today. But its terms were not hostile in the eighteenth century. We need to translate: 'Your argument, though exposed to malice, will become clear when its attractive distinction is revealed.'

'Minor misunderstandings', Wills continues, 'can, cumulatively, become major if we forget the many small differences in usage between [the Founders'] time and our own.'[12]

Still, this problem, important as it is, is readily remediable with the aid of a good glossary or translation manual. But there is a second and perhaps more profound sense in which our language differs from the language in which the Founders

[12] G. Wills, *Explaining America* (New York, 1981), 280.

framed their intentions. What we call 'our language' (or theirs, for that matter) is not all of a piece. It is instead compounded out of those specialized sub-languages or idioms that we might for want of a better term call discourses.[13] Such discourses would today include, though by no means be restricted to, those that are conventionally classified as legal, literary, political, ethical, educational, scientific, economic, artistic, and athletic. Such sub-languages or discourses are not, of course, hermetically sealed, much less mutually exclusive. Each tends at times to transgress upon the other. (One need only think, for example, of the ways in which the discourse of sports is used today to describe and appraise political actions and practices.) Such transgressions are, indeed, one of the main sources of conceptual change and innovation.

The language of the Founders resembles ours in at least one respect: it was compounded out of a number of different discourses. But the important point to remember is that the discourses out of which it was compounded are in many respects quite different from those with which we are familiar. If we are to understand the meaning of their actions—in this case those linguistic actions or speech-acts that make up the arguments out of which and on the basis of which the Constitution was constituted—then we must know what their beliefs and intentions were. But these we cannot know without knowing something about the language in which those beliefs were expressed and intentions framed and made meaningful and intelligible in the first place. The conceptual and moral universe that the Founders inhabited is, of course, connected with—and is indeed partially constitutive of—the one that we now inhabit; but it does not coincide with our world at all possible points. To borrow a phrase from Gadamer, their historically specific 'prejudices' (or, if you prefer, prejudgements or standpoints: *Vorurteile*) are not wholly unrelated to ours, but neither are they entirely equivalent. Originalist claims to the contrary notwithstanding, the task of legal and constitutional interpretation is not to suspend or

---

[13] See J. G. A. Pocock, 'The Concept of a Language and the *métier d'historien*', in Pagden (ed.), *Languages of Political Theory*, ch. 1; J. B. White, 'Economics and Law: Two Cultures in Tension', *Tennessee Law Review*, 54 (1987), 161–202; and my *Transforming Political Discourse*, ch. 1.

forgo our own prejudices in favour of theirs, but to recognize, and if possible reconcile, our different understandings of how political society works and ought to be structured and governed.[14]

11.3 ORIGINALISM AND WILFUL IGNORANCE

The Founders subscribed to a particular view of politics and human nature. And this view in its turn provided the backdrop against which 'power' was conceived (and checked), 'liberty' understood (and promoted), and 'ambition' and 'faction' feared (and countered). It was within this theoretical horizon or discourse that they framed their intentions and couched their arguments in defence of the new design.

That much, at least, is part of a familiar story. But the story is incomplete without a more precise and detailed account of the connection between a particular kind of discourse and the intentions capable of being formulated within it. What was the Founders' discourse, and what intentions did it make possible and intelligible? Like many apparently simple questions, this one admits of no easy answer. Part of the difficulty is due to their having access to a number of discourses, not all of which were of a piece, much less mutually compatible. For the sake of simplicity I shall focus only upon two, the first being the political discourse of the republican tradition, the second the scientific discourse of 'faculty psychology'.

Historians have, of late, rediscovered the remains (or perhaps one should say the ruins) of an 'Atlantic republican tradition' that stretched from Aristotle and Polybius up through Machiavelli and Harrington to Montesquieu and the American Founding Fathers.[15] Very roughly, republicanism was the theory that viewed the *bios politikos*, the life of active citizenship, as the highest human calling and which, as a corollary, viewed the narrowly self-interested pursuit of private gain as an 'idiotic' (from the Greek *idion*) way of life unfit for free human

---

[14] See H.-G. Gadamer, *Truth and Method* (New York, 1984). Some of the legal and constitutional implications of Gadamer's hermeneutics are traced by Leyh, 'Toward a Constitutional Hermeneutics'.

[15] See J. G. A. Pocock, *The Machiavellian Moment* (Princeton, NJ, 1975).

beings. Not surprisingly, then, the concepts constitutive of the discourse of republicanism—'liberty', 'virtue', and 'corruption' among them—had different meanings for (say) Machiavelli or even for Montesquieu than they do for us. Thus 'liberty', for example, referred to the free citizen's ability and opportunity to take an active part in political affairs; 'virtue' to making full use of this liberty; and 'corruption' to the inability or unwillingness to use—and, if necessary, to take up arms to defend—one's liberty, choosing instead to pursue private gain and to lead a life of luxury and ease.[16] Thus the sort of privacy favoured in modern liberal societies was seen by republicans as a form of privation or loss of liberty.

The concepts of classical and Renaissance republicanism form scarcely any part of the discourse of such latter-day large-R Republicans as former President Ronald Reagan, of course; but neither are the rest of us on intimate terms with that tradition. We live, as Alasdair MacIntyre maintains, 'after virtue'; our ethics are not the ethics of virtue nor our politics the politics of *virtù*.[17] Confronted with an author or a text in which 'virtue' appears, we are likely to react much as Thomas Mann's Hans Castorp reacted to Settembrini's reliance on the discourse of 'virtue':

What a vocabulary! and he uses the word virtue just like that, without the slightest embarrassment. What do you make of that? I've never taken the word in my mouth as long as I've lived; in school, when the book said 'virtus,' we always just said 'valour' or something like that. It certainly gives me a queer feeling inside to hear him.[18]

This, indeed, is how modern readers might at first react to the proceedings of the Constitutional Convention and the various tracts and broadsides of the Ratification Debate. In the late 1780s 'Brutus' and 'Publius' and other latter-day mock Romans spoke of virtue, corruption, and liberty in ways that Machiavelli would have readily understood, but which we today can comprehend only with some difficulty, if at all. That this may be our loss, I do not deny; but what cannot be

---

[16] See my *Transforming Political Discourse*, ch. 3, esp. 48–54.
[17] A. MacIntyre, *After Virtue* (Notre Dame, Ind., 1981).
[18] T. Mann, *The Magic Mountain* (New York, 1966), 101.

denied, I think, is that this discourse has been largely lost to us, and is unlikely to be recovered, rehabilitated, and used once again as the common coin of communication. Yet it is upon our capacity to carry out just this sort of recovery and rehabilitation that originalism rests. That doctrine, as we shall see shortly, would require a Canute-like attempt to turn back the tide of conceptual change, and would doubtless meet with just about as much success.

The political and moral discourse of republicanism is not the only language lost to us; so too is at least one of the theoretical discourses employed by the Founders. Emphasizing 'the importance of the intellectual conventions of an age in defining an author's intentions', Daniel Walker Howe has recently reconstructed one of the discourses in which the Founders talked and thought about human nature. The authors of the Constitution and the *Federalist Papers*, Howe reminds us, had ready recourse to the concepts comprising 'faculty psychology'.[19] Faculty psychology holds that human beings are endowed with certain species-specific powers or 'faculties' which, taken together, constitute human nature. Human nature is therefore teleological, in that each faculty impels us towards certain sorts of ends. This teleological psychology comprises the theoretical model or background beliefs (or, in Berlin's sense, the paradigm) within which the Founders framed their intentions and argued their case.

To reread the Constitution, the records of the Constitutional Convention, and the *Federalist Papers* in the light cast by this recently recovered theoretical idiom is better to understand where the Founders stood and how they thought. But it is one thing to arrive at such historical understanding, and quite another to put it to present-day judicial use. To take the originalist position seriously enough to put it into (interpretive) practice would require that lawyers and judges accept that particular background theory as valid, or at any rate unproblematic, in arguing their cases and arriving at legal decisions. Were they to do so, however, they would be out of step with their contemporaries, including those whom we

[19] D. W. Howe, 'The Language of Faculty Psychology in *The Federalist Papers*', in Ball and Pocock (eds.), *Conceptual Change*, ch. 7.

nowadays call psychologists. No psychologist now subscribes to the tenets of faculty psychology, as though Freud (and even B. F. Skinner) had never lived or written a word. We can of course recognize and appreciate that the Founders found this particular theory persuasive. But human knowledge has grown; too much has transpired to allow us to accept this theory as authoritative, still less true. To the extent that the Founders framed their intentions in the idiom of this theory, we can recover those intentions, but we cannot return to them and make them our own. Anyone attempting to do so would be in a position analogous to a modern sailor who steers his ship by relying on old navigational charts and maps drawn in the belief that the earth was flat.

To understand what the Founders intended to convey or communicate requires that we recognize, as some say nowadays, 'where they're coming from'. It turns out that in the two aforementioned respects the Founders were coming from a place that no longer exists on modern maps of knowledge. To reconstruct earlier cartographic theories, and the maps drawn with their aid, is often illuminating; but we would not want to put those theories and maps to present-day navigational use. Yet that is precisely what originalists propose that we do, or at any rate aspire to do.

My contention is not that judges and the rest of us cannot adopt an originalist strategy; far from it. For certain purposes—to arrive at a better understanding of the Founders' historical context, for example—originalism functions as an admirable (if not readily attainable) regulative ideal. Nor am I claiming that judges can, or should, interpret the Constitution in any way they wish. No one, surely, wants judges to be able creatively to pull un- or extra-constitutional rabbits out of their own hats. My contention is, rather, that originalism in its several versions is defective, unwieldy, and probably unworkable as a guideline for arriving at judicial decisions. Originalism is not so much impossible in principle as it is misguided in its aims and unworkable in practice.[20] Since in our present political climate this is a contentious claim, I want to

---

[20] Although I take a somewhat dimmer view of originalism than does Perry (see n. 4 above), we agree that its defects are mainly practical.

restate and illustrate it by placing it in a more distant and, I hope, somewhat less contentious historical context.

11.4 A DISTANT MIRROR

The current call for a return to beliefs and intentions of the Founders is hardly novel. It is a call issued periodically by fundamentalists in different domains, whether literary, legal, religious, or otherwise. It appears at first glance to provide an attractively simple solution to an otherwise very complex problem: How do we moderns understand a text produced by predecessors who did not fully share our world, our language, our beliefs and presuppositions? Answer: we simply read the text as a statement of (actual or at any rate conceivable) authorial intent, which in turn fixes the meaning of the text then, now, and forever after. In fact, however, the purported answer turns out to be extraordinarily complicated, not only for the logical and conceptual reasons to which I have alluded already, but for several eminently practical reasons as well. The two turn out, moreover, to be quite closely connected.

We can look, by way of illustration, not at the Bible or the Constitution or the Qu'rān—texts around which passionate and protracted hermeneutical controversies continue to swirl—but at the distant mirror provided by the civil jurisprudence of late medieval and early modern Europe.[21] The story, in a nutshell, is this: Roman law, as codified by Justinian in the sixth century and subsequently glossed by Bolognese jurists in the twelfth, was synthesized in Accursius's Great Gloss of the mid-thirteenth century. The work of Accursius and other 'glossators' was necessary because, without their commentaries, clarifications, and cross-references, the text of the Justinian Code was well-nigh incomprehensible. Accordingly, Accursius's Gloss was widely regarded as enjoying equal authority with the Code. In the fourteenth century, the commentators who came to be known as Bartolists (after their most renowned representative, Bartolus of Saxoferrato)

[21] For a fuller version of the following, see D. Kelley, 'Civil Science in the Renaissance: The Problem of Interpretation', in Pagden (ed.), *Languages of Political Theory*, ch. 3.

devised cumbersome but workable techniques for interpreting and applying Roman law to the judicial problems being addressed in late-medieval European society. This they did not only by looking at the letter of the law, but by teasing out premises or principles believed to be latent in the law. Out of the archaic Code and accompanying Gloss they constructed a *ius commune*, a Common Law more attuned to the needs of their era.

By the fifteenth century, however, Renaissance grammarians challenged the Bartolists by claiming, with considerable justification, that newly refined philological techniques made it possible to rediscover and recover the original meaning of Roman law. Ancient texts could be restored to their original, and presumably authoritative, meaning. With the aid of this new broom, they claimed, much of the excess verbiage of 'interpretation' or 'commentary' could be swept away and the original meaning of the Roman law reinstated.

This seemed at first sight to be eminently sensible. But it was not long before the neo-Bartolists countered by pointing out that the original discourse of the Roman lawgivers, and the intentions it made possible, presupposed beliefs, legal contexts, and linguistic conventions remote and far removed from those of sixteenth-century Europe. To interpret the law in the light of an earlier lawgiver's 'original intent' would, therefore, mean removing the law from the contexts in which it did its unwieldy but invaluable work. Sundered from the language of the modern market-place and contemporary morality, the law would cease to be 'common', becoming not only more unwieldy and less workable, but largely unintelligible to those to whose conduct it was supposed to apply. The law would, in other words, cease to reflect the beliefs, inform the intentions, and regulate the actions and activities of those who were not legal scholars and specialists. The neo-Bartolists accordingly acknowledged that, while the historical reconstruction or recovery of original meaning or initial intent had its place in judicial reasoning, jurists ought not to attempt the impossible feat of recovering the past in order to return to it.

There is in this sixteenth-century case, I think, a lesson to be learnt by late-twentieth-century Americans—and a warning for those willing, ready, and even eager to eschew an intervening history of interpretation and commentary and return directly to the original intent of the Founders. The lesson is not that such a return is impossible either in principle or in practice. Far from it: modern conceptual historians, like Renaissance grammarians, can and regularly do restore the world of words within which intentions were initially framed, whether by law-givers in Rome or in Philadelphia. Theirs is, to be sure, an exceedingly difficult task; but it can be, has been, and is still being, performed—and sometimes at a very high level.[22] The difficulty that needs to be recognized and addressed by both proponents and critics of originalism is of a rather different sort. Even supposing that one can arrive at some approxima-tion of the Founders' intent or original meaning, what weight, if any, is it to be given? And this becomes especially important in the light of the fact that the recovery of the Founders' beliefs and intentions requires that one not only understand but presumably *accept as authoritative* the discourse(s) in which their intentions were framed in the first place. Of course conceptual historians have no difficulty in 'accepting' such the-oretical idioms; theirs is acceptance 'for the sake of argument' (and for the sake of historical understanding: they wish, that is, to restore the contexts which render intelligible the beliefs, intentions, arguments, and actions of agents long dead). The arguments in which they engage are, however, largely—and non-pejoratively—academic.

The judge or Supreme Court Justice, by contrast, is faced with a very different—and distinctly non-academic—task. His or her task is not to recover and restore the idioms and inten-tions of lawgivers long dead, but to render decisions that apply to law-benders and law-breakers now living—and to do so, moreover, in terms that are more or less intelligible to those whose conduct is being judged. Of course this is, and remains, a regulative ideal to which reality all too rarely cor-responds. No one could fail to recognize that there are excep-tions, breakdowns, and failures aplenty: many a criminal goes to prison with only the vaguest understanding of the letter of the law under which he has been charged, tried, and sen-tenced. The larger point, however, is that the criminal's con-

---

[22] See n. 5 above.

temporaries should be able to understand the law, even if the criminal does not. It is in the final analysis a question of criminal intent, not original intent, and of the intelligibility of the law to those whose conduct and/or conscience is being appealed to. An originalist jurisprudence is blind and deaf to considerations of either sort. And that, I submit, is only one of its flaws.

11.5 THE SINGLE-AUTHOR FALLACY

Another of the flaws afflicting originalism is to be found in its treatment, not of texts in general, but of the Constitution in particular. Originalists who look to the intent of the Framers propose to treat the Constitution as if it were the product of a single author. But in fact it is possible to give only the most minimal and abstract characterization of the (shared) intention(s) of the Founders. They intended the Constitution to be the binding legal basis of a system of government in which each branch would balance and check the others and in which there was a division of powers between the federal government and the several states. Beyond that, agreement ends and intentions differ. As the record of the Constitutional Convention clearly shows, the articles, sections, clauses, sentences, and even single words that comprise this text were originally the result of oft-times contentious and even quarrelsome collaboration, and an almost endless series of compromises among its many authors.[23] And, if the diaries, memoirs, and correspondence of individual Founders are any indication, few were fully satisfied with the final result.[24]

To attempt to treat the Constitution as one would a text by a single author is to commit the single-author fallacy—that is,

---

[23] Cf. M. Farrand (ed.), *The Records of the Federal Convention of 1787*, 4 vols. (New Haven, Conn., 1966); and P. B. Kurland and R. Lerner (eds.), *The Founders' Constitution*, 5 vols. (Chicago, 1987).

[24] Though not alone among the Founders, Hamilton came to believe the Constitution a failure. 'Perhaps no man in the United States', he wrote in 1802, 'has sacrificed or done more for the present Constitution than myself; and contrary to all my anticipations of its fate . . . I am still laboring to prop the frail and worthless fabric' (quoted in J. C. Miller, *Alexander Hamilton* (New York, 1959), 543).

the fallacy of simply assuming, without argument or evidence, that all the authors of a collectively drafted document agreed on all particulars and shared identical intentions. To see just what relevance this has for contemporary constitutional interpretation, particularly from the standpoint of 'original intent', I want to examine a case that, for a time, captured considerable interest in the United States.

The case I wish to examine—*Perpich* et al. v. *Department of Defense*—involves a gubernatorial challenge to the constitutionality of Section 522 of the Defense Authorization Act for Fiscal Year 1987.[25] Section 522, otherwise known as the Montgomery Amendment, severely restricts the grounds upon which state governors may withhold consent to permit their National Guard units from participating in training missions outside the United States. The Montgomery Amendment was added when several state governors balked at the Pentagon's decision, late in 1986, to expand its practice of sending National Guard units to Central America on expeditions rather euphemistically described as 'training' missions (they were, in fact, attempts by the Reagan Administration to intimidate the Sandinista Government which then ruled Nicaragua). Led by Governor Perpich of Minnesota, the governors filed suit in Federal District Court. The gist of the plaintiffs' suit was that the Montgomery Amendment violates the Militia Clause (Article I, Section 8) of the Constitution, which reserves to the states the right to oversee the training of their respective militia. On 6 December 1988 the 8th US Circuit Court of Appeals found for the plaintiffs, citing in its decision 'the intent of the Founders' in drafting the Militia Clause.

Among the many ironies in this case was that the Reagan Administration—which, in the persons of Attorney-General Edwin Meese III, Solicitor-General Charles Fried, and at least one unsuccessful nominee for the Supreme Court (Judge Robert Bork) had been a staunch advocate of the 'original-intent' variant of originalism—had the tables turned on it. The Court of Appeals' decision was couched precisely in terms of the intentions of the Founders. It turns out that a judicial strategy of original intent, far from being the consis-

25 Cf. 10 United States Codes 672 (f), Sect. 522.

tently conservative blade that Judge Bork and Attorney-General Meese expected it to be, can cut in quite unexpected directions. When the Reagan Administration appealed to the Supreme Court, the Court overturned the Appeals Court decision.[26] And since this may yet prove to be a landmark case, its historical origins are perhaps worth reviewing here.

Coming as it did in the Bicentennial year of 1987, the governors' lawsuit was well timed. For it reopened one of the questions that were so heatedly debated in Philadelphia during the hot summer months of 1787. That question was, who is to control each individual state's 'militia'—the federal government or the states themselves?[27]

On the one side were the champions of a strong central government, including Alexander Hamilton, who favoured nationalizing the state militias by putting them under the control of the central government. They feared that an irregular state militia might take up arms against neighbouring states and even against the federal government itself.[28] Their fears were not without foundation. The memory of Shays's Rebellion in western Massachusetts (1786–7) was still fresh in their minds. And their worst fears would be realized some seventy-four years later when the southern states seceded from the Union and turned their respective militias against the federal government. On the other side, however, were those who wanted the states to retain exclusive control over their own militia. They feared that an all-powerful central government would ride roughshod over the rights reserved to the states, using federally controlled state militias to stifle dissent.

As so often happened during the Constitutional Convention, neither side carried the day entirely and a compromise was eventually devised. The results of that compromise can still be seen in Article I, Section 8, which empowers the Congress to 'raise and support armies' and to 'provide and maintain a navy', both of which are to be under the exclusive jurisdiction of the federal government. As for the several state

[26] Decision and eighty-one-page opinion in US Court of Appeals, for the Eighth Circuit, No. 87–5345 (6 Dec. 1988).
[27] See Farrand (ed.), *Records*, ii. 129–37, 158–9, 323, 352–3, 380–3, 570, 595; Kurland and Lerner (eds.), *Founders' Constitution*, i. 173–211.
[28] See n. 25 above; and Hamilton, *Federalist 29*.

militias, the new Constitution gave Congress the power 'to provide for calling forth the militia to execute the laws of the union, suppress insurrections, and repel invasions'.

This still did not satisfy sceptical decentralizers, who insisted that the extent of congressional control over the state militia be spelt out more fully and more precisely. And so, in the succeeding paragraph of Section I, Article 8, we see the further fruits of that heated debate. It begins by specifying that the Congress is 'To provide for organizing, arming, and disciplining the militia, and for governing such parts of them as may be employed in the service of the United States', and concludes by 'reserving to the states respectively, the appointment of the officers, and the authority of training the militia according to the discipline prescribed by congress'. In short, the centralizers who favoured full federal control of the militia succeeded in giving the Congress some measure of control over the state militia. And the states-rights-minded decentralizers succeeded in limiting the extent of congressional control. Each side got the proverbial half-loaf.

The governors' lawsuit claimed—and the Court of Appeals subsequently agreed—that the Montgomery Amendment reneges on the crucial compromise of 1787 by giving an additional and arguably unconstitutional slice to the federal government. Article I, Section 8, specifies that 'the authority of training the militia' is to be left to the individual states, provided that this training accords with congressional guidelines regarding the appropriate regimen or 'discipline'. Citing 'the intent of the Founders', the Appeals Court agreed with Governor Perpich's claim that the Montgomery Amendment goes well beyond this. By forbidding states to withdraw their militias from foreign countries without declaring an official state emergency, that amendment is inconsistent with the original intent of the Founders.

And yet one could argue, I think, that the Appeals Court decision did not go as far as it might have done, had it considered the language in which the Founders framed their (several) intentions and their final (univocal) compromise. A close reading of Article I, Section 8, scarcely suggests that the Congress can deploy state militias outside American borders for any purposes whatsoever, whether they be engaged in actual combat or in training exercises. After all, 'the laws of the union' do not apply outside US borders; an 'insurrection', in the eighteenth-century parlance of the Founders, was a domestic, not a foreign, uprising; and an 'invasion' can by definition be 'repelled' only after an invader has already crossed a country's borders. All this suggests that the original intent of the Founders—or, at any rate, the result of their compromise—is that state militias are only to be deployed *domestically*, that is, intra-nationally, not internationally. If so, not only the Montgomery Amendment but the Governor's lawsuit and the Court of Appeals' decision are alike in resting upon a constitutionally false premiss.

More than that, the Appeals Court decision commits the single-author fallacy. For while the Appeals Court judges were surely right in their recovery and reconstruction of the intentions of some Founders, they did not succeed in recovering and respecting the intentions of Hamilton and others who wished to place the several state militia under federal control. But of course to raise questions about the particular intentions of individual Founders is perforce to undermine the entire thrust—and (dare I say it?) the intent—of the original-intent variant of originalism.

11.6 MADISON'S CRITIQUE OF ORIGINALISM

If the foregoing arguments against originalism should prove to be less than completely convincing, let me turn, finally, to that last refuge of scoundrels and scholars, the Argument from Authority. My authority is none other than the Father of the Constitution himself, James Madison. I choose Madison simply because he, in his role as Founder, is one of those to whose beliefs and intentions originalists are duty-bound to look for advice and guidance. Ironically, however, Madison sides with those who hold that the reader or interpreter must have some say in determining what a text 'means'. At the very least, originalism runs into real problems when an author intends that his words should not be interpreted originalistically. Indeed, to put the point in a slightly more sophisticated (though admittedly anachronistic) way, we might say that

Madison, not unlike modern 'reader-response' or 'reception' theorists, holds that texts are by their very nature essentially incomplete: even though a particular text has an author(s) it nevertheless needs a reader(s) or interpreter(s) to round it out and give it its full meaning.[29] It is, I submit, something like this position to which Madison himself subscribed, and for reasons that might best be termed conceptual or linguistic.

In *Federalist 37* Madison remarks that 'All new laws, though penned with the greatest technical skill, and passed on the fullest and more mature deliberation'—as the document drafted in Philadelphia surely was—'are considered as more or less obscure and equivocal, until their meaning be liquidated [i.e. clarified] and ascertained by a series of particular discussions and adjudications'.[30] Madison then goes on to enumerate three reasons for subscribing to this reception-theory account of constitutional meaning. The first has to do with 'the obscurity arising from [the] objects' of constitutional deliberation. The more complex the object, the greater the possibility of mistake or misunderstanding. The second has to do with 'the imperfection of the human faculties'. The powers of human reason and understanding are by nature imperfect, occasionally defective, and invariably limited, and must therefore be checked or compensated for. Important as they are, however, these two reasons for a 'reception-theory' approach get short shrift in comparison to the third.

Madison's third and weightiest reason has to do with the nature of language itself: 'the medium through which the conceptions of men are conveyed to each other', he complains, 'adds a fresh embarrassment. The use of words is to express ideas. Perspicuity therefore requires not only that the ideas should be distinctly formed, but that they should be expressed by words distinctly and exclusively appropriated to them. But', he adds,

no language is so copious as to supply words and phrases for every complex idea, or so correct as not to include many equivocally

---

[29] For different variants of reception theory, see Fish, *Is there a Text?*; S. R. Suleiman and I. Crosman (eds.), *The Reader in the Text* (Princeton, NJ, 1980); H. R. Jauss, *Toward an Aesthetic of Reception* (Minneapolis, 1982); and, more generally, R. C. Holub, *Reception Theory* (London, 1984).

[30] This and all following quotations come from Madison, *Federalist 37*.

denoting different ideas. Hence, it must happen, that however accurately objects may be discriminated in themselves, and however accurately the discrimination may be considered, the definition of them may be rendered inaccurate by the inaccuracy of the terms in which it is delivered. And this unavoidable inaccuracy must be greater or less, accordingly to the complexity and novelty of the objects defined. When the Almighty himself condescends to address mankind in their own language, his meaning, luminous as it must be, is rendered dim and doubtful by the cloudy medium through which it is communicated.[31]

Thus Madison maintains that the medium through which human beings communicate is not contingently but necessarily a 'cloudy' one. Perfect clarity is not only impossible for human beings using human language; it would be impossible even for God, were He to deign to talk to us in any human tongue.

Now if God cannot make His meaning perfectly clear, it follows that even the most god-like human legislator cannot frame and communicate his intentions with perfect precision and clarity. Not only can he not do it, says Madison, he cannot even *hope* to do it, given the nature of human language itself. The opacity of language is not, Madison insists, a failure or shortcoming of any particular language; it is, rather, an ineliminable feature of all language and hence, by implication, of all authors and speakers and therefore of all utterances and texts.

Madison's reflections on language and meaning are, I believe, fatally damaging to the doctrine of originalism. For that doctrine assumes that language is (or is at any rate capable of being) a transparent medium in which meanings and intentions can be framed and communicated in an absolutely unambiguous way. But this, according to Madison, is impossible. Language is not, and can never be, a wholly transparent medium. Thus the doctrine of original intent rests upon what Madison might have termed the Fallacy of Perfect Clarity.

Originalist doctrine also depends upon another doubtful assumption, the one that Nietzsche called the Dogma of Immaculate Perception and that I call the Dogma of

---

[31] Here Madison evidently follows Locke, *Essay Concerning Human Understanding*, bk. III, chs. 9, 10.

Immaculate Reception. That dogma holds that a reader or listener or interpreter is, or can (or should) be, an empty vessel—a veritable *tabula rasa* on which a speaker, author, or text imprints its message. But human communication, as Madison certainly acknowledged, is a two-way street. It involves not only speakers and authors but also listeners and readers. The speaker or author is not simply the active agent and the listener or reader an inactive patient or passive receptacle. Both are and must be participants in any act of communication. As Madison puts it, the meaning of even the most carefully drafted law will be 'more or less obscure and equivocal, until [its] meaning be liquidated and ascertained by a series of particular discussions and adjudications'. And these discussions and adjudications can, and arguably must, begin in and be mediated through the theoretical, moral, legal, political, and/or scientific discourse of our day, and not simply that of the Founders alone. So it would appear that Madison foresaw —and arguably attempted to forestall, or failing that, to add his own voice to—the debate over originalism.

11.7 CONCLUSION

The thrust of the foregoing account, if correct, is that the doctrine—or perhaps one should say the dogma—of originalism is specious in the eighteenth-century sense of that term— that is, flashily attractive. Its obvious attractions aside, that doctrine, I have argued, is specious in the twentieth-century sense of being erroneous, false, or misleading. As a strategy of legal or constitutional interpretation, 'original intent' is, in fact, afflicted with a number of heretofore unnoticed difficulties. But, if past experience is any guide, it is unlikely that this doctrine will be dislodged by argument, much less dropped altogether, at least as long as it satisfies some influential faction's political agenda and rhetorical requirements. And that, arguably, is what accounts for originalism's continuing appeal among jurists. The attractions of originalism among historians of political thought, I have argued, is a rather different—and decidedly less weighty—matter.

12

THE MYTH OF ADAM AND AMERICAN IDENTITY

> It is notorious that American culture is haunted by
> myths, many of which arise out of the attempt to escape
> history and then regenerate it.
>
> J. G. A. Pocock

12.1 INTRODUCTION

Contrary to a modern conceit, the 'politics of identity'—to use
a still-fashionable phrase—is not a new variety of politics but
is almost as old as politics itself. The ancient Greeks distinguished themselves from foreigners or 'barbarians' (so called
because their languages sounded to Greek ears like nonsensi-
cal yammering: 'bar bar bar'). In Athens, women and slaves
and metics (resident aliens) lacked the requisite identity—that
of free male native-born Athenian—to be citizens. (Distinguished as he was, Aristotle, as a metic, could not partici-
pate in the affairs of the *polis* whose praises he sang.) The
politics of identity (or 'identity–difference') is now, and always
has been, about inclusion and exclusion, about belonging and
being cast out or aside.[1]

Or, to put the point in the terms of the contemporary 'com-
munitarian-liberal' debate, the politics of identity is about
defining and claiming membership in a community of one or
another sort. All communities are 'imagined communities' in
that they are maintained and legitimated by their members'
shared self-images, images that shape and make possible their
interpretations of who they are and where and to whom they
belong.[2] These, more than any articulate theory or doctrine,

[1] W. E. Connolly, *Identity/Difference* (Ithaca, NY, 1991).
[2] B. Anderson, *Imagined Communities* (London, 1991).

determine the shape and mark the boundaries of a community, giving its members a sense of belonging and of shared identity. Humans are self-interpreting animals whose sense of self and identity depend in important ways on the communities to which they belong and with which they identify.[3]

In late-eighteenth- and early nineteenth-century America there developed a new way of identifying oneself and interpreting one's relation to one's community. Americans claimed to belong to a nation composed not only of individuals but of individualists—or 'rugged individualists', in Herbert Hoover's later phrase. America was said to be not only a new nation but a new type of nation, and Americans a new type of people. America was, in short, a new kind of community—a non-communitarian community, as it were, populated by a new kind of individual.

'What, then, is the American, this new man?', asked Crevecœur towards the end of the eighteenth century.[4] It is a question asked many times since, and in any number of idioms and accents. But it is at bottom a question, or rather a series of questions, about individual and collective identity: Who am I? Where do I come from? Who are my people and what is my relationship with them? How am I related and what do I owe to those who are, and are not, my people? These questions have been posed, if not answered to everyone's satisfaction, by almost every American writer one cares to name. White or black, red or yellow, man or woman, many have tried their hand at solving the riddle of American identity. No one can claim that the riddle has been solved or doubt that this terrain is anything but hotly contested.

My aim here is to look at one way of framing these questions about American identity, as a way of shedding some light on the (im)possibility of reimagining a different kind of national community. I want to examine the claim that there is, or once was, a native American mythology—a myth already presupposed in Crevecœur's question. The American,

---

[3] C. Taylor, 'The Liberal–Communitarian Debate', in N. Rosenblum (ed.), *Liberalism and the Moral Life* (Cambridge, Mass., 1989); Taylor, *Multiculturalism and 'The Politics of Recognition'* (Princeton, NJ, 1992).

[4] Hector St John de Crevecœur, *Letters from an American Farmer* (1782; New York, 1963), 63.

according to this myth, is a 'new (kind of) man', the likes of whom has not been seen before, except perhaps in the biblical account of Creation. The 'American Adam' is innocent and uncorrupted, as was Adam before the Fall, living without Eve (and therefore free from sin and temptation) in the Eden of the New World.[5] This is an early and recurring expression of the Americans' self-identification as innocents, bereft of ideology and imperial ambition, of American 'uniqueness', and the other markers by which Americans would come to define themselves to each other and to the rest of the world. And, arguably, this self-definition and sense of identity persists even today.

Anyone who wishes to make, much less sustain, such a claim must, of course, recognize that America is today largely, though by no means exclusively, a secular, modern, and presumably post-mythic culture. Most Americans, when asked who they are and how they see themselves, are not likely to answer—very readily anyway—in mythic, much less 'Adamic' terms. I want nevertheless to suggest that this myth, or something like it, supplies the scaffolding or framework within which otherwise puzzling odds and ends come together and make a certain kind of sense. If this myth be present, and as pervasive as I believe it to be, then we must begin by asking just where this cultural equivalent of the Loch Ness Monster is to be found in a modern (or perhaps postmodern) and presumably post-mythic culture.

The creators and practitioners of the genre now known as 'American studies' long ago taught us to look to literature and other forms of popular culture for the traces and themes of a native American mythology. And, as R. W. B. Lewis, Leo Marx, and Henry Nash Smith have shown, such themes and traces abound in highbrow and lowbrow literature, in nineteenth-century dime novels and modern detective stories, in Hollywood movies and Madison Avenue ads.[6] But in its search for an American mythology this interpretive genre encounters a singular difficulty. One of the characteristics of a genuine mythology—as distinguished from the ersatz

---

[5] R. W. B. Lewis, *The American Adam* (Chicago, 1955).
[6] Ibid.; L. Marx, *The Machine in the Garden* (New York, 1964); H. N. Smith, *Virgin Land* (Cambridge, Mass., 1950).

contrivances that are quite consciously created for political purposes or literary effect—is its pervasiveness in all a society's thought-forms, whether literary and artistic or philosophical and scientific.[7] Moreover, a genuine myth, as Marcel Detienne maintains, is a mode of thought that does not know its name and is unaware of its status as myth.[8]

It is the unselfconscious quality of myths and those who hold them, says Sheldon Wolin, that shows modern or postmodern 'myths' to be nothing of the kind. The postmodern era is characterized by the proliferation of ersatz myths—in movies, literature, art, advertising, and other forms of popular culture—and the absence of any genuine ones. And among postmodern societies, America has gone farther than most. What in postmodern America passes for mythic themes

are more in the nature of post-mythic strategies than direct expressions of myth. They are evocations of the archaic in the midst of a modernizing society which, by its own self-understanding, is committed to the systematic extirpation of mythical thought. They are myth-making self-conscious of itself, aware that it is engaged in a premeditated act of fabrication. There is, consequently, an irreducible element of alienation that accompanies contemporary mythologizing.[9]

My aim here is to agree with one part of Wolin's diagnosis and to disagree with another. While it is certainly true that art, literature, movies (e.g. *Star Wars*), and other modern media are wont to employ post-mythic strategies and even to concoct ersatz myths, it is less certain that genuinely mythical themes are altogether absent from other aspects of contemporary American culture. I want to suggest that several surviving features of an American mythology are to be found in some rather unlikely and heretofore unsuspected places. In the domains of academic analytical philosophy, in futurology, and in certain postmodernist political visions we can, I believe, find quite unselfconscious expressions and articulations of mythic themes. Since so sweeping a claim cannot be substanti-

[7] See e.g. M. Eliade, *Myths, Rites, Symbols* (New York, 1976), i. 2–7.

[8] M. Detienne, 'Rethinking Mythology', in M. Izard and P. Smith (eds.), *Between Belief and Transgression* (Chicago, 1982), 43–5.

[9] S. Wolin, 'Postmodern Politics and the Absence of Myth', *Social Research*, 52 (1985), 217.

ated here, I shall confine myself to three recent works in these genres. The texts I have chosen to examine might at first sight appear to be rather unpromising candidates—John Rawls's *A Theory of Justice*, Gerard O'Neill's *The High Frontier*, and Richard Rorty's *Contingency, Irony, and Solidarity*. The first is by a distinguished American philosopher, the second by an eminent physicist and futurologist, and the third by a prominent postmodern thinker. Despite their very different subject-matters, all are alike in drawing upon, and being more fully intelligible in the light of, the same native myth, the myth of Adam in the Edenic garden of a new world.

My plan is to begin by briefly saying what I mean by myth generally, and by a native American mythology in particular. I shall then take a fresh look at several foundational features of Rawls's theory of justice, claiming that much of its intelligibility, and even perhaps its persuasiveness, derives from several mythic features implicit in the imagery of his argument. I then go on to examine O'Neill's proposals for the colonizing of space. His highly technical vision of the American future is, I believe, fraught with mythic presuppositions and Adamic imagery. So too, I contend, is Richard Rorty's vision of a postmodern culture consisting of the self-creating contingency-embracing individuals whom he calls 'strong poets'. Finally, I shall conclude by connecting the pervasiveness of the Adamic myth to some of the difficulties encountered in contemporary debates among political theorists about 'identity' and 'community'.

12.2 THE MYTH OF ADAM

'A myth', says Mark Schorer in his luminous study of Blake, 'is a large, controlling image that gives philosophical meaning to the facts of ordinary life; that is, has organizing value for experience.' Myths, in other words, 'are the instruments by which we continually struggle to make our experience intelligible to ourselves . . . Without such images, experience is chaotic, fragmentary, and merely phenomenal.' Not even the most rational thinker among us is immune to the appeals of myth, thus understood. 'Rational belief', Schorer continues, is secondary. We habitually tend to overlook the fact that as human beings we are rational creatures not first of all but last of all, and that civilization emerged only yesterday from a primitive past that is at least relatively timeless. Belief organizes experience not because it is rational but because all belief depends on a controlling imagery, and rational belief is the formalization of that imagery.[10]

I shall suggest, a little later on, that two paradigms of rational belief—analytical philosophy, and science turned into technology and applied to particular problems—can to some extent be understood as formalizations and articulations of mythic themes and images. And much the same can be said of the 'postmodern' mode of thinking that is critical of both.

However illuminating and suggestive, Schorer's characterization of myth is deficient in one important respect. It is simply not true that 'experience' and our 'interpretation' of it are two separable things. On the contrary, as modern postpositivist philosophers of science and hermeneutically minded literary critics remind us, experience without interpretation is impossible; indeed, it is not experience at all. All experience—artistic, literary, moral, religious, scientific, political, or otherwise—is (in Gadamer's phrase) 'always already' interpreted or 'preinterpreted'; even the barest, most unvarnished scientific observation, for example, is 'theory-laden'.[11] Far from being two separable things, experience and interpretation constitute a single indivisible whole. Thus, for example, devout Christians do not have experiences upon which they subsequently superimpose a 'Christian' interpretation or structure of meaning; rather, they have Christian experiences.[12] Nor, for that matter, do scientists make observations upon which they then place a 'scientific' interpretation; rather, they make scientific observations.[13] Much the same is true of the activity

---

[10] M. Schorer, *William Blake: The Politics of Vision* (New York, 1959), 25–6.

[11] Cf. N. R. Hanson, *Patterns of Discovery* (Cambridge, 1958); H. I. Brown, *Perception, Theory and Commitment* (Chicago, 1979), chs. 6, 7. See also S. Fish, *Is there a Text in This Class? The Authority of Interpretive Communities* (Cambridge, Mass., 1980).

[12] See Fish, *Is there a Text?*, 269–72.

[13] S. Toulmin, 'The Construal of Reality: Criticism in Modern and Postmodern Science', *Critical Inquiry*, 9 (1982), 93–111.

of political, literary, artistic, and social-scientific interpretation.[14]

For our present purposes, the most important difference between a philosophical or scientific theory and a myth is that the former tends to be more self-conscious and tentatively held than the latter. A theory can accordingly be more readily criticized than a myth, if only because the latter often supplies the symbolic frame of reference in terms of which the former assumes a socially shared meaning (so, at any rate, I shall suggest in connection with Rawls's theory of justice). We may say of theories what Leslie Stephen said of doctrines: 'The doctrines which men ostensibly hold do not become operative upon their conduct until they have generated an imaginative symbolism.'[15] To disinter such symbolic frames and to trace them to their source is somewhat akin to what Foucault called 'archeology' and later, and in a somewhat different (and decidedly Nietzschian) version, 'genealogy'.[16] This, indeed, is just the sort of enquiry in which students of American culture have long been engaged.

In attempting to discover and to sketch the 'outlines of a native American mythology', R. W. B. Lewis's *The American Adam* (1955) proved to be one of a select band of books that have decisively influenced the course of American literary criticism and, more generally, the methodology of American studies. Lewis did for high-brow literature what Henry Nash Smith (in *Virgin Land*) had earlier done for popular pulp literature and political oratory, and what Leo Marx (in *The Machine in the Garden*) was later to do for the anomalies afflicting both: namely, to disinter and examine the half-submerged ideals and imagery in terms of which Americans tended to think of themselves as a people possessing a distinctive national character and culture.

That ideal and its constitutive imagery can be roughly recounted in this way. America was—and, at its best, still is—a pastoral nation, a veritable Eden in the New World. The

---

[14] H.-G. Gadamer, *Truth and Method* (New York, 1984), 431–47.
[15] Quoted in Schorer, *William Blake*, 25.
[16] M. Foucault, *The Archaeology of Knowledge* (New York, 1976), pt. IV; 'Nietzsche, Genealogy, History', in *Language, Counter-Memory, Practice* (Ithaca, NY, 1977), 139–64.

scene of perpetual rebirth and rejuvenation, this pastoral paradise is permanently without a past. The American, the 'new
man' of whom Crevecœur wrote, can be compared to Adam
before the Fall. The American Adam thus represented

a radically new personality, the hero of a new adventure: an individual emancipated from history, happily bereft of ancestry, untouched
and undefiled by the usual inheritances of family and race; an individual standing alone, self-reliant and self-propelling, ready to confront whatever awaited him with the aid of his own unique and
inherent resources.[17]

Clint Eastwood and the Marlboro Man (and his Camel-
smoking counterpart) are merely the latter-day Hollywood
and Madison Avenue versions of a venerable myth, the myth
of the American Adam.

Although the imagery is biblical, the context of its invoca-
tion is identifiably and distinctly American. The Americans
were the first people to make a 'case against the past'. What
Lewis's lawyerly turn of phrase obscures is that the case was
not a well-constructed and articulated argument but, myth
that it was, an interlacing structure of sentiment, symbol, and
feeling. The Adamic myth's most memorable expressions are,
arguably, literary (as when, in Cooper's narrative, Natty
Bumppo, reversing the direction of time itself, traverses the
distance from old age to ageless youth). But its most self-
conscious and articulate expressions are, *pace* Lewis, political.
Here Paine is perhaps a more representative spokesman than
Jefferson.[18]

Besides being a pamphleteer and propagandist, Thomas
Paine was among the earliest and most adept articulators of
the Adamic myth and its political implications. 'The case and
circumstances of America', wrote Paine, 'present themselves as
in the beginning of a world.' America is 'the only spot . . .
where the principles of universal reformation could begin'. To
make such a beginning Americans must think and act as if
they were the first people ever to think. This stricture he duly
applies to himself. In thinking and writing about politics, he

[17] Lewis, *American Adam*; cf. C. L. Sanford, *The Quest for Paradise*
(Urbana, Ill., 1961).
[18] *Pace* Lewis, *American Adam*, 15–19.

assures us, 'I followed exactly what my heart dictated. I neither read books, nor studied other people's opinions. I thought for myself.'[19] As Adam turns philosopher, new truths emerge as in the clear light of morning. Heretofore hidden from view, the eternally valid principles of justice are at last accessible to the pastless, present-minded American. Finally freed from 'the errors of tradition', Americans can see that 'The wrong which began a thousand years ago is as much a wrong as if it began to-day.' And, he adds, 'the right which originates today, is as much a right as if it had the sanction of a thousand years. Time with respect to principles is an eternal NOW.'[20] Once emancipated from the prejudices of the past, we will finally be free to consult and to be guided by Reason alone: 'The present age will hereafter merit to be called the Age of Reason, and the present generation will appear to the future as the Adam of a new world.'[21]

Whether we turn to Paine or to Jefferson, to Crevecœur or Cooper—or even to Adam's nemeses Melville and Hawthorne—we are struck by the omnipresence of Adam in the Garden of the New World. To students of American cultural history this is, of course, a familiar story. Less familiar, perhaps, is the tale concerning the continued presence of Adam in some unsuspected places, including modern American analytical philosophy.

12.3 RAWLS IN EDEN

Published in 1971 to a chorus of critical praise, John Rawls's *A Theory of Justice* continues even now to excite scholarly controversy. Despite the defects duly noted by its critics,[22] *A Theory of Justice* is a monumental work, and all the more remarkable because it was written in an age in which 'normative' or 'prescriptive' political philosophy was presumed to be

[19] T. Paine, *The Rights of Man* (Garden City, NY, 1973), 455.
[20] Quoted in M. Drukman, *Community and Purpose in America* (New York, 1971), 62.
[21] Paine, *Rights of Man*, 505.
[22] See N. Daniels (ed.), *Reading Rawls* (New York, 1975); B. Barry, *The Liberal Theory of Justice* (Oxford, 1973); and R. P. Wolff, *Understanding Rawls* (Princeton, NJ, 1977).

dead and buried. If nothing else, Rawls has proved that the genre is still vital and very much alive. Without wishing to detract from Rawls's achievement, I should like to enquire into the sources of his theory's appeal, at least some of which seems to lie less in its theoretical argumentation than in its imagery and symbolism. And its very imagery, it seems to me, is inescapably mythic, drawing less upon its ostensible philosophic forerunners than upon the symbolic resources of a native American mythology.

Rawls, rightly enough in some sense, sees himself as the inheritor of the social-contract tradition. Like Hobbes, Locke, and Rousseau, he begins with his own version of a pre-civil state of nature, which he calls 'the original position'. This *Gedanken*-experiment he quite clearly regards as a moral and methodological fiction meant to make a point about objectivity and impartiality.[23] More originally still—and utterly unlike any of his philosophical predecessors—Rawls imagines that people placed in the original position suffer from a kind of metaethical amnesia. Once situated behind an imaginary 'veil of ignorance', they do not know who they are or where they have come from, or to what race, sex, or generation they belong, what their talents and/or handicaps are, and so on. Thus deprived of all contingent and particular features of their personalities, social status, and situation, such disinterested hypothetical choosers are therefore presumably equipped to arrive at, and to articulate, general and impartial principles of justice.[24] The first, and primary, principle is that extending equal liberty to all individuals takes precedence over other values, including human happiness. The second stipulates that inequalities are justifiable only in so far as they work to everyone's advantage and are attached to offices or positions open to all.[25] The two principles of justice at which Rawls's ideal choosers arrive are of less interest here than is the situation and circumstance under which he has them make their imaginary choice. In the technical terms favoured by modern mathematically minded game theorists, the situation in which Rawls places his hypothetical choosers is an N-person, non-zero-sum co-operative bargaining game in which players make

[23] J. Rawls, *A Theory of Justice* (Cambridge, Mass., 1971), ch. 3.
[24] Ibid. 136–50.   [25] Ibid. 60.

choices on the basis of incomplete information about their respective positions. The logical and mathematical properties of this game-theorist's fantasy interest me less than its mythic possibilities.

The conventional interpretation of Rawls's theory is, so to speak, Eurocentric. Rawls's rational choosers are presumed to be ideal Rousseauian citizens solicitous only of the General Will, or Kantian moral agents, making ethical choices not from any particularistic 'phenomenal' perspective but from the wholly disinterested 'noumenal' vantage-point of the perfectly rational person. There is much to recommend this way of reading Rawls. It is the perspective adopted by almost all of his defenders and critics.[26] Indeed, it is the position adopted by Rawls himself.[27] I want to suggest that there exists a second, more distinctive—and more identifiably 'American'— perspective from which Rawls's theory of justice may be read and understood.

Like Paine's Adamic American, Rawls's hypothetical choosers are placed 'as in the beginning of a world'. Unencumbered by the past, by tradition, or by the memory of previous practices, they alone are able to articulate, for the first time, truly universal principles of justice. Having been tainted by tradition, particularity, and partiality (sexual, racial, class, generational, or otherwise), earlier principles and theories of justice were clearly deficient. These old theories and principles can now be criticized, discredited, and set aside. Situated behind the veil of ignorance, Rawls's rational choosers choose not for themselves alone but for all of mankind and for all time.[28] Like Paine, Rawls thinks that principles of justice discovered by disinterested Reason are eternally valid:

This standpoint . . . enables us to be impartial, even between persons who are not contemporaries but who belong to many generations. Thus to see our place in society from the perspective of this position is to see it *sub specie aeternitatis*: it is to regard the human situation not only from all social but also from all temporal points of view.[29]

---

[26] See e.g. Wolff, *Understanding Rawls*, pt. III.
[27] Rawls, *A Theory of Justice*, sects. 3, 40.   [28] Ibid. 137, 289–93.
[29] Ibid. 587. Rawls subsequently eschewed such universalist claims: see his *Political Liberalism* (Cambridge, Mass., 1993).

Or, as Paine put it, 'Time with respect to principles is an eternal NOW.'[30] A well-honed historical sensibility, derived from diligent study of the past, is therefore philosophically irrelevant. History, as Henry Ford said, is bunk.

Stripped of a past and of all particularity, Rawls's hypothetical choosers are, in effect, amnesiacal orphans. They are orphans, indeed, in much the same sense that Billy Budd is. Melville's adamic anti-hero was also without a past, uncertain of his parentage (though distinctly European and quite possibly aristocratic), and—as his very name suggests—perpetually alive with the Spring-like possibility of rebirth and renewal. But Billy Budd suffered from a singular defect—a stammer which soon proved to be a fatal flaw. His failure to communicate in the clinch—when confronted with the absolute evil represented by the 'serpentine' Claggart—leads to his literal death and symbolic crucifixion.[31]

A far cry from Rawls's theory of justice, surely; but not so far as one might think. Both are, after all, concerned with justice and injustice. And it is a grievous and malign act of injustice that renders Billy Budd mute. Moreover, Billy Budd's inability to communicate, just when it is most important that he do so, shares several features of the imaginary situation in which Rawls places his ideally rational choosers. For, being ignorant of their particular circumstances, they are incapable of communicating anything about them. Thus they too are mute about their individual interests and idiosyncracies. Billy Budd and Rawls's rational choosers are solitary figures, unable (because of ignorance, isolation, or impediment of speech) to communicate to others anything about their respective circumstances or situation. The upshot, unsurprisingly, is that the solitary individual is in all cases thrown back upon his own resources. Unable to rely upon others, each relies solely upon himself.

Several 'communitarian' critics have suggested that Rawls's theory of justice is deficient inasmuch as it is predicated upon a peculiarly narrow and unsatisfactory conception of human selfhood and moral agency. This, says Michael Sandel, is the

[30] Quoted in Drukman, *Community*, 62.
[31] H. Melville, *Billy Budd*, in *Four Short Novels* (New York, 1959), esp. 207–8, 246.

vision of a solitary 'unencumbered self'.[32] Unencumbered by enduring connections to other similar selves, and even to its own past, this paragon of Emersonian self-reliance is, so to speak, at home in the homeless condition that Rawls calls the original position. Indeed, according to Rawls, it is only in this position that valid principles of justice can be chosen. Only individuals unencumbered by the past, by history, by memory or tradition are capable of rationally and disinterestedly choosing such principles. Sandel suggests, quite rightly I believe, that the theory is flawed because no rationally or humanly satisfactory self can ever be wholly unencumbered in the way that Rawls's hypothetical choosers are assumed to be. But, having disagreed with Rawls's argument and his conclusions, Sandel goes on to trace his vision of moral agency, autonomy, and self-sufficiency to the same philosophical parentage that Rawls claims. Liberalism in general, and Kant in particular, Sandel says, are the culprits. It is this Kantian conception of selfhood and moral agency that we now need to transcend.[33]

Perhaps. But is it not equally plausible to suggest that Rawls's theory of justice has even deeper roots in a quite unselfconsciously held native American mythology, the myth of Adam, and that whatever appeal it possesses might owe as much to Paine or Emerson as to Kant? And, if so, does it not then follow that extricating ourselves from its confines is likely to be an even more difficult and onerous task, raising as it does questions about our very identity—about who we are as a people, where we have come from, and what we can hope to achieve and to be?

I shall conclude by answering these questions in the affirmative. But first I want to turn to a second, and seemingly very different, author and text.

---

[32] M. J. Sandel, 'The Procedural Republic and the Unencumbered Self', *Political Theory*, 12 (1984), 81–96; *Liberalism and the Limits of Justice* (Cambridge, 1982). Cf. J. H. Schaar, *Legitimacy in the Modern State* (New Brunswick, NJ, 1981), ch. 7.

[33] Sandel, *Liberalism*, 175–83.

12.4 O'NEILL IN SPACE

The breaking-out of narrowing confines has long been a hallmark of the Adamic myth. Crevecœur's farmer, Cooper's Natty Bumppo, and Twain's Huck Finn are all alike in taking their leave, heading for the frontier or the territories, leaving their pasts behind, and seeking their freedom and their fortunes in the open space of the West. The actual physical frontier having been closed, according to Frederick Jackson Turner's reckoning, before the end of the last century, Americans had no new places to go, no new space to conquer. Only when they ran out of space, said Hegel earlier in that same century, would the Americans then confront their past and become a people with a genuinely historical consciousness.[34] As Richard Hofstadter observed:

Time is the basic dimension of history, but the basic dimension of the American imagination is space. . . . What Americans have lacked in a sense of time they have tried to make up by an enlarged sense of space. Their thoughts tend not to run backward into an antiquity they do not know but rather outward into a larger geographical theater of action, the theater not of the past but of the future. . . . For Americans, uprooted from many soils and stemming from many ancestries and thrust into the open natural environment of the new continent, the very possibility of freedom quickly became associated with the presence of empty space, and also with the freedom to move, to get away from the physical proximity of others, to escape from society itself into the innocence of nature.[35]

This ahistorical and 'spatial' sensibility is a fundamental feature of the American Adam. He is, as Lewis reminds us, a hero not in time but in space.[36] His twofold freedom—freedom from the past, and the freedom to move in and through space—is deeply ingrained, as only myths can be, in our national consciousness (and perhaps even more deeply etched in our shared subconscious). The first of these freedoms is

[34] G. W. F. Hegel, *Lectures on The Philosophy of History* (New York, 1956), 85–6. Cf. G. A. Kelley, 'Hegel's America', *Philosophy and Public Affairs*, I (1972), 3–36.
[35] R. Hofstadter, *The Progressive Historians* (New York, 1969), 5–6.
[36] Lewis, *American Adam*, ch. 5.

exemplified in the situation in which Rawls places his ideally rational choosers. The second, I want to suggest, is to be found in Gerard O'Neill's vision of the American future.

O'Neill is no armchair visionary. A distinguished physicist, O'Neill left his post at Princeton to head his own Geostar Corporation and has for some time served as a consultant for the National Aeronautics and Space Administration (NASA). He claims not to write science fiction, a genre in which he professes not to be greatly interested; nor does he wish to spin out utopian schemes. He insists that his proposals for 'space habitats' require no suspension of credulity or any leap of literary imagination. All are predicated upon presently existing scientific and technological capabilities.[37] It is now technically possible for human beings to create, to live and work within, and to travel between, space habitats. With a wealth of technical detail, O'Neill describes the construction of such 'space colonies'. Large, slowly rotating stations in space, several miles in diameter and constructed of lunar material, could house hundreds, even thousands, of people. Fascinating though they are, the technical details do not concern me here. I am more interested in O'Neill's vision and, so it seems to me, its essentially mythical imagery and rationale.

In effect, the whole mythic message of O'Neill's *The High Frontier* is that Turner and Hegel were mistaken. The geographic and physical frontier of the American West may well be closed forever. But for Americans the *idea* of the frontier is not, and never will be, dead or *passé*. And this is not an idea that exists exclusively in the historical past—an abomination for Adam—but in a present perpetually alive with possibilities for self-assertion and exploration. The 'high frontier' of outer space is in its very nature infinitely open, presenting an unlimited horizon of limitless possibility, of renewal, regeneration, and rebirth. Americans need never confront the closure and finitude of the 'steady state' society and an economy of scarcity.[38] That being the case, they are forever able to strike

[37] G. K. O'Neill, *The High Frontier* (New York, 1978), 116. See also the lavishly illustrated volume by T. A. Heppenheimer, *Colonies in Space* (New York, 1978).

[38] Ibid., ch. 2. The idea that small is *not* beautiful and that the 'steady state' economy is abhorrent recurs throughout O'Neill's work. See e.g. his *2081* (New York, 1981). O'Neill's ethic of economic growth mirrors one of

out, in Huck Finn fashion, for the territories, thereby thumbing their noses at Aunt Sally—and Hegel—and anyone else who wants to 'sivilize' us by restricting our freedom.

One is understandably tempted to think that colonies in outer space would be the very antithesis of the agrarian ideal. The pastoral paradise that was Eden before the Fall—and America afterwards—could scarcely be imagined to exist in an environment so utterly 'unnatural' and so dependent for its existence upon technology and engineering expertise. After all, the machine in the garden, as Leo Marx reminds us, was seen as an anomaly in the Eden of the New World.[39] True enough. But O'Neill's extraterrestrial Eden turns Marx upon his head (if I may be forgiven for saying what an earlier Marx once said about Hegel). In effect—and apparently quite unconsciously—O'Neill gives us The Garden in the Machine. The controlled climate, seasons, sunlight, and water supply make the space station an ideal environment for farming.[40] Crops can be grown year-round. There are no pests or insects to destroy the crops. But there are birds to charm the space colonists with their songs, and beautiful butterflies for the birds to eat. Better still, 'there need not be mosquitoes—or cockroaches, or rats'. Nor need there be pollution, poverty, or unemployment.[41]

In an imaginary 'letter from space', a newly emigrated colonist describes the New World to a friend still living on earth: 'It's a comfortable life here. Fresh vegetables and fruit are in season all the time . . . We grow avocados and papayas in our own garden, and never need to use insecticide sprays. Of course we like being able to get a suntan without ever being bitten by a mosquito.'[42] In a later editorial aside, O'Neill adds: 'how delightful would be a summertime world of forests without mosquitoes!' Space colonists 'can take along the useful bees while leaving behind wasps and hornets'.[43] There are, moreover, no volcanic eruptions, floods, earthquakes, hurricanes, typhoons, or tornadoes.[44] Made even better than the original by Yankee ingenuity, this is an Eden without wasps.

the distinguishing features of the American national character: see D. M. Potter, *People of Plenty* (Chicago, 1954), pt. II.

[39] Marx, *Machine*, 4.   [40] O'Neill, *High Frontier*, 51, 71–8, 118–20.
[41] Ibid. 221.   [42] Ibid. 9.   [43] Ibid. 49.   [44] Ibid. 112.

Even as pains and dangers are minimized, pleasures are maximized. Clothing could be light, or perhaps discarded altogether. And in this Edenic habitat human existence could be eroticized as never before. 'Can one imagine a better location for a honeymoon hotel', O'Neill asks, 'than the zero-gravity region of a space community?'[45] Evidently not, for he later returns to the topic. In another letter from space, a mother writes—rather more rapturously than most mothers, one suspects—to her daughter back on earth:

[Your father and I went] to the Floating Island Hotel for our weekend. Most of the hotel, like the lobby and restaurants—and the showers—are at one-tenth gravity, but those bedrooms! My dear, it's just indescribable. Of course, you could watch TV or listen to music if you want, but really, as Dad says, those rooms are designed for just one thing. I can't imagine you [and your husband] not getting along well together, but if you ever have a problem . . . bring him up here for a second honeymoon! You may never want to go back. Now that we've found out what it's like, I can tell you it's going to be a lot harder for us to leave![46]

Little wonder, then, that this couple confide in another letter that they are 'more likely to move farther out [into space] than to go back [to earth]'.[47]

Life in this demi-paradise is made possible by an escape from a darkening Old World—not Europe this time, but the planet earth itself—and an earth-bound state of mind that O'Neill describes as 'planetary chauvinism' and 'the planetary hang-up'.[48] Over-populated, its atmosphere poisoned, its air and water polluted, its inhabitants perpetually warring over increasingly scarce resources, the planet earth is, at the end of the twentieth century, a place unfit for human habitation, still less for adventure and exploration. Nothing is left save to escape from an earthbound past into an idyllic future in the endless vastness of space.[49]

As Lewis describes it, 'the American myth saw life and history as just beginning. It described the world as starting up again under fresh initiative, in a divinely granted second

---

[45] Ibid. 97.   [46] Ibid. 214–15.   [47] Ibid. 10.   [48] Ibid. 35, 50.
[49] Ibid. 234. For a powerful but unintended antidote to O'Neill's ersatz Eden in space, see H. Arendt, 'The Conquest of Space and the Stature of Man', *Between Past and Future* (New York, 1969), 265–80.

chance for the human race, after the first chance had been so disastrously fumbled in the darkening Old World.'[50] No longer Europe, but the entire planet earth, must now be abandoned. The Adams of the twenty-first century abandon their planetary past and light out for the timeless territory of space, there to tend their celestial Garden. Only in space, O'Neill maintains, can mankind attain immortality. While we remain on the earth, he warns, we are an endangered species, vulnerable to slow poisoning or to sudden nuclear annihilation. Once dispersed through the galaxy, however, the human species will become unkillable.[51] Space promises to conquer time and mortality itself. It is the medium of perpetual rebirth and regeneration. O'Neill's is a vision at once hopeful and bleakly pessimistic—and, if I am right, deeply and genuinely mythic in its imagery and its appeal.

12.5 RORTY IN BLOOM

My third and final illustration of the claim that the Adamic myth is to be found today in unlikely places is Richard Rorty's *Contingency, Irony,* and *Solidarity.* The following précis does scant justice to a book that is at once ingenious and (intentionally?) irritating, and replete with brilliant rereadings of familiar texts. I have, I hope, given Rorty his due in another place.[52] Here I want to redescribe Rorty's project, and in a way that he might find uncongenial and unrepresentative of his intentions. But, as a postmodern thinker who holds that readers may read and interpret texts without regard to authorial intention, he can have no grounds for complaint or objection.

Rorty describes himself as a 'postmodern bourgeois liberal'. He is 'postmodern' in that he holds that 'modernity' generally—and 'the Enlightenment project' of emancipating men and women through reasoned criticism and the rational reform of social and political institutions in particular—has failed, leaving us in what Jean-François Lyotard calls 'the

[50] Lewis, *The American Adam,* 5.   [51] O'Neill, *2081.*
[52] R. Rorty, *Contingency, Irony, and Solidarity* (Cambridge, 1989). See my review-essay, *History of the Human Sciences,* 3 (1990), 101–4.

postmodern condition'.[53] This condition is characterized by a thoroughgoing scepticism as regards claims to truth or even to the validity of arguments advanced in support of such claims. Rorty is 'bourgeois' in the sense that he accepts without dissent the institutions of the society in which he lives, i.e. a capitalist or free-market or (in Marx's term) 'bourgeois' society. And, not least, Rorty is 'liberal' in that he sees society (or at any rate this society) as populated by self-interested individuals who aspire towards autonomy even as they eschew cruelty towards other similarly situated selves. Whether one can be all three at once and without contradiction—a possibility raised by Rorty's critics[54]—does not concern me here. I am interested, instead, in the 'Adamic' assumptions and implications of Rorty's picture of a postmodern American society.

His is indeed a 'picture' rather than a theory or a sustained and systematic argument. A distinguished 'analytical' philosopher turned postmodern renegade, Rorty now eschews the very idea of reasoned argument and analysis. He favours instead the essentially rhetorical and aesthetic strategy of redescribing the familiar world in new, unfamiliar, and more 'attractive' ways, so as to persuade people, not by argument—as a philosopher might do—but by painting a new and attractive picture of a possible world.[55] It is worth noting, as students of myth remind us, that this non- or anti-argumentative mode of presentation and persuasion is a key feature of mythic thinking.[56] So we might without undue distortion read Rorty as a postmodern myth-maker and his vision of a liberal society as an attractive postmodernist myth.

Following Rorty's own method, I propose not to advance an argument, but to paint a picture. I want, that is, to redescribe his project in an alternative vocabulary and imagery —the idiom and the image of the American Adam. I shall suggest that Rorty is a thoroughly 'American' thinker in that his idiom and imagery are identifiably Adamic. This is not, of

[53] Cf. J.-F. Lyotard, *The Postmodern Condition* (Minneapolis, 1986).

[54] See the symposium on Rorty's *Contingency* in *History of the Human Sciences* (n. 52 above).

[55] Rorty, *Contingency*, 9.

[56] On the non-discursive or 'pictoral' character of myth, see nn. 7, 8, 10 above.

course, how Rorty describes his project and his stance as a 'postmodern bourgeois liberal'. Both come out of his encounters with thinkers who are, in the dismissive multicultural phrase, dead white European males.[57] He makes repeated reference and expresses debts to Derrida, Foucault, Nietzsche, Nabokov, Orwell, and Oakeshott. And if Rorty owes anything to any American thinker, it is—by his own oft-stated admission—to Dewey and, in a different way, to Harold Bloom.

Rorty borrows Bloom's notion of the 'strong poet'—the arch-individualist who creates but is not created, who wills into existence the world in which he (yes, he is identifiably male) lives alone and unencumbered. The strong poet is, in Bloom's and Rorty's description, driven by 'the anxiety of influence', the fear that his thoughts and language might be borrowed or derivative, that he might be beholden or indebted to anyone, ancestor or contemporary, for anything. Capable even of 'giving birth to [him]self', the strong poet is the unencumbered self *par excellence*.[58] 'In my view', Rorty writes, 'an ideally liberal polity would be one whose culture hero is Bloom's "strong poet" . . .'[59]

Now many things might be said about Bloom's and Rorty's vision of the strong poet driven by the anxiety of influence. One might say, with Wendell Berry, that Bloom's is 'an adolescent critical theory'.[60] Or one might simply note that the vision is unoriginal and old hat, at least in America. (Paine, for one, articulated the anxiety of influence in terms only slightly different from, and hardly less adamant than, Bloom's.) Oddly, Bloom seems not at all anxious about (or even aware of) having been influenced by at least one earlier European thinker—namely, Nietzsche. His (and Rorty's) idea of the 'strong poet' is almost palpably Nietzschian, and

---

[57] It strikes me as curious that many critics of the 'canon' of works by 'dead white European males' are at the same time apt to be extravagant admirers of Nietzsche, Heidegger, Lacan, Foucault, de Man, and Derrida (the last of whom, though not yet dead, is certainly white, European, male, and mortal).

[58] H. Bloom, *The Anxiety of Influence* (New York, 1973). On 'giving birth to himself', see Bloom, *Agon* (New York, 1982), 43–4. Rorty, *Contingency*, 29.

[59] Ibid. 53.

[60] W. Berry, *What Are People For?* (San Francisco, 1991), 165.

arguably another (and nicer) name for Nietzsche's *Über-mensch.*

Ostensibly European sources aside, I want to suggest that the image of the strong poet driven by the anxiety of influence has an even older, and more distinctly American, ancestry. In America the anxiety that one might be beholden to or influenced by an ancestor or predecessor is hardly a new notion. Bloom's (and Rorty's) anxiety of influence can be found in the Adamic aspirations and boasts of Paine, Crevecœur, and Emerson. Paine wished to think thoughts and speaks words that no one had ever thought or spoken before. So did Crevecœur's new man. And so too did Emerson, who imagined a self-creating individual without ancestors, free of the dead weight of the past, and unencumbered even by the burden of friendship.

If Bloom gives us (as Berry says) an adolescent theory of criticism, Rorty gives us an adolescent theory of politics. Rorty's vision of a society whose culture hero is the unencumbered postmodern bourgeois-liberal strong poet animated by anxiety about being beholden or answerable to others is not only an adolescent vision—it is nothing less than our Adamic myth, our picture of ourselves in relation to others, past, present, and future. It is a profoundly anti-communitarian vision with a long history and deep cultural roots. Until and unless we recognize this, the communitarian critique of liberal individualism will deal only in surfaces and appearances.

12.6 IDENTITY AND COMMUNITY

I began by suggesting that a genuine mythology is apt to appear not only in the art and literature of a culture but in virtually all of the thought-forms through which its aspirations, hopes, and fears are conceived and communicated. It may well be true that our national literature, as Lewis lamented more than thirty years ago, has lost much of its mythic richness, resonance, and vigour. But this does not mean that American culture has been denuded of all mythic traces and themes. It may mean merely that these have to be searched for elsewhere. Perhaps, then, Weber and Wolin are mistaken in suggesting that science and technology, and the increasing rationalization of everyday existence, necessarily entails the thoroughgoing 'disenchantment' (*Entzauberung*) of the social world. Far from being wholly abandoned or out-grown or somehow transcended, myths may instead be trans-ferred from traditional symbolic spheres—religion, art, and literature, for example—to newer, non-traditional spheres such as science, analytical philosophy, and postmodern criticism. Such, at any rate, appears to have been the fate of the myth of Adam in America.

But Adam's fate need not be ours. We need not accept or acquiesce in the thoughtways of our peers or predecessors. If they have shown nothing else, communitarian critics of liberal individualism have at least called attention to the faults and flaws of Adamic individualism—of the ideal of an 'unencum-bered self' shorn of all connection with others—and to the need to critically reconsider, and perchance replace, this flawed ideal of individual (and, by implication, collective) con-duct.[61] We Americans have, like Huck Finn, too often tried to escape to the territory to the west—a frontier more of myth and mind than of matter—in order to evade responsibility and avoid growing up. As Wendell Berry observes, 'Huckleberry Finn fails in failing to imagine a responsible, adult community life.' And this, he adds, is not the failure, in fiction, of a par-ticular author or his character, but 'of our life, so far, as a society'.[62]

We appear to be left in a modern, or perhaps a postmod-ern, version of limbo. On the one hand are those who, know-ingly or not, celebrate our Adamic condition as disconnected individuals, without memory, bereft of history and ancestors, autonomous and self-creating Adams or strong poets. On the other hand, however, are those who see 'us' as having no national or collective identity, Adamic or otherwise. Each of us must base his or her identity on a particular facet or fea-ture which we share with some and which, no less impor-tantly, distinguishes or divides us from others. According to

---

[61] See Sandel, *Liberalism*; A. MacIntyre, *After Virtue* (Notre Dame, Ind., 1981); R. N. Bellah *et al.*, *Habits of the Heart* (Berkeley, Calif., 1985); Taylor, 'Liberal–Communitarian Debate'.

[62] Berry, *What Are People For?*, 77.

the adherents and champions of 'identity politics', one must act not as a citizen or an American *per se*, but as one who is female or male, gay or straight, black or Indian or hispanic (etc.). This view of identity would appear, at first sight, to be the antithesis of Adam: one's history and identity, far from being forgotten, are as indelible as a tattoo; one cannot escape from one's group past, which is ever-present. One's community, and the identity one adopts and on which one acts, are inherited conditions: one is born a woman, or black, or gay; and, just as one had no choice in who, or what, one was born, one is not wholly free to choose (much less invent) one's personal or political identity. Against the Adamic vision of the unencumbered self, identity politics presents an alternative vision of the eminently encumbered self, a socially situated self bearing the burdens of one's group's past as a badge of identity.

In one sense, then, the current concern with 'identity' represents the apotheosis of the Adamic myth. Does the emphasis on identity then supply a corrective to the excessive individualism of that venerable myth? I want to conclude by suggesting that it does not. The current preoccupation with identity merely grasps the other horn of a continuing national dilemma.

The champions of Adamic individualism and the proponents of identity–difference are agreed on one crucial point: both eschew citizenship and, with it, 'community' in any broader and more inclusive sense. Each is alike in grasping one horn of a persistent American dilemma. On the one side are those who wish to belong to a community of one—an unencumbered sovereign self or a 'majority of one', in Thoreau's phrase.[63] On the other are those who wish to belong to a small and select community based on gender, or race, or sexual preference. But—and this is the important point—both are alike in denying the possibility of communality, of shared sympathy (and antipathy), of common joys and sorrows. Each is, in de Tocqueville's sense, shut up in the solitude of their own heart, individual, or group.[64] But neither

---

[63] H. D. Thoreau, 'Civil Disobedience', *Selected Writings* (New York, 1952), 19.
[64] De Tocqueville, *Democracy in America*, II. ii, ch. 2.

heart is, so to speak, a civic heart. From a political point of view such an identity is partial, partisan, and even, one might say, prejudiced. Such prejudice, properly understood, need not be a bad thing. After all, our prejudices, as Gadamer reminds us, provide a place to begin or to stand, not to stay.

The problem with contemporary 'identity politics' is that, while it supplies some with a place to stand initially, it provides no one a place to stay. Its ersatz rootedness ratifies our rootlessness and celebrates our partialities. The politics of identity offers, as it were, a homeless shelter rather than a home. And this is because identity politics, like Adamic individualism, offers no sustainable civic vision, no wider view of political possibilities for the community of which we might yet be full members and citizens.

SELECT BIBLIOGRAPHY

ARENDT, H., *The Human Condition* (Chicago, 1958).
—— *Between Past and Future: Eight Exercises in Political Thought* (New York, 1968).
ASHCRAFT, R., *Revolutionary Politics and Locke's 'Two Treatises of Government'* (Princeton, NJ, 1986).
AVELING, E., 'Charles Darwin and Karl Marx: A Comparison', *New Century Review* (Mar.–Apr. 1897), 232–43.
AVINERI, S., 'From Hoax to Dogma—A Footnote on Marx and Darwin', *Encounter* (Mar. 1967), 30–2.
BAIN, A., *James Mill: A Biography* (London, 1882).
BALL, T. (ed.), *Idioms of Inquiry: Critique and Renewal in Political Science* (Albany, NY, 1987).
—— *Transforming Political Discourse* (Oxford, 1988).
—— and Farr, J. (eds.), *After Marx* (Cambridge, 1984).
—— and Pocock, J. G. A. (eds.), *Conceptual Change and the Constitution* (Lawrence, Kan., 1988).
—— Farr, J. and Hanson, R. L. (eds.), *Political Innovation and Conceptual Change* (Cambridge, 1989).
BARKER, E., *Essays on Government* (Oxford, 1951).
BARRY, B., 'The Strange Death of Political Theory', *Government and Opposition*, 15 (1980), 276–88.
BAUMGOLD, D., 'Political Commentary on the History of Political Theory', *APSR* 75 (1981), 928–40.
BELLAH, R. N., MADSEN, R., SULLIVAN, W. M., SWIDLER, A., and TIPTON, S. M., *Habits of the Heart* (Berkeley, Calif., 1985).
BENTHAM, J., *Works*, ed. J. Bowring, 11 vols. (Edinburgh, 1838–43).
—— *Collected Works*, ed. J. H. Burns, J. R. Dinwiddy, and F. Rosen (London, 1968–).
BERLIN, I., *Vico and Herder* (New York, 1976).
—— *Against the Current* (London, 1979).
—— *Concepts and Categories* (Harmondsworth, 1981).
BERRY, W., *Home Economics: Fourteen Essays* (San Francisco, 1987).
—— *What Are People For?* (San Francisco, 1991).
BLUHM, W. T., *Theories of the Political System* (Englewood Cliffs, NJ, 1965).
BORALEVI, L. C., *Bentham and the Oppressed* (Berlin, 1984).
BÜCHNER, F. C. C. L., *Darwinismus und Sozialismus* (Leipzig, 1894).
COBBAN, A., *Rousseau and the Modern State* (London, 1964).

COCHRANE, C. N. *Thucydides and the Science of History* (London, 1929).

COLLINGWOOD, R. G., *Autobiography* (Oxford, 1939).

—— *The Idea of History* (Oxford, 1946).

COLLINI, S., Winch, D., and Burrow, J. *That Noble Science of Politics* (Cambridge, 1983).

COLP, R., jun., 'The Contacts of Charles Darwin with Edward Aveling and Karl Marx', *Annals of Science*, 33 (1976), 387–94.

COMTE, A., *System of Positive Polity* (1854; trans. R. Congreve, London, 1877).

—— *A General View of Positivism* (1857; trans. J. H. Bridges, New York, 1957).

CONDREN, C., *The Status and Appraisal of Classic Texts* (Princeton, NJ, 1985).

CONNOLLY, W. E., *Political Theory and Modernity* (Oxford, 1988).

—— *Identity/Difference* (Ithaca, NY, 1991).

CRANSTON, M., and Peters, R. S. (eds.), *Hobbes and Rousseau* (Garden City, NY, 1972).

CRANSTON, M., *The Noble Savage: Jean-Jacques Rousseau* (London, 1991).

CRIMMINS, J. E., *Secular Utilitarianism* (Oxford, 1990).

CROCKER, L. G., *Rousseau's Social Contract* (Cleveland, 1968).

DAGGER, R., 'Metropolis, Memory and Citizenship', *AJPS* 25 (1981), 715–37.

—— 'Understanding the General Will', *WPQ* 34 (1981), 359–71.

DARWIN, C., *The Origin of Species by Means of Natural Selection* (1859; New York, 1958).

DERATHÉ, R., 'La Religion civile selon Rousseau', *ASJJR* 25 (1962), 161–80.

DIETZ, M. G., 'Trapping the Prince: Machiavelli and the Politics of Deception', *APSR* 80 (1986), 777–99.

DRUKMAN, M., *Community and Purpose in America* (New York, 1971).

DUNN, J., 'The Identity of the History of Ideas', *Philosophy*, 43 (1968), 85–116.

—— *The Political Thought of John Locke* (Cambridge, 1969).

ELSTER, J., *Ulysses and the Sirens* (Cambridge, 1979).

—— 'Cohen on Marx's Theory of History', *Political Studies*, 28 (1980), 121–8.

Études sur le Contrat social (Paris, 1964).

EUBEN, J. P., 'Political Science and Political Silence', in P. Green and S. Levinson (eds.), *Power and Community: Dissenting Essays in Political Science* (New York, 1970), 3–58.

FARR, J. 'Marx and Positivism', in T. Ball and J. Farr (eds.), *After Marx* (Cambridge, 1984), 217–34.

—— 'The Americanization of Hermeneutics: Francis Lieber's *Legal and Political Hermeneutics*', in G. Leyh (ed.), *Legal Hermeneutics* (Berkeley, Calif., 1992), 83–102.

—— DRYZEK, J. S., and LEONARD, S. T. (eds.), *Political Science in History: Research Programs and Political Traditions* (Cambridge, 1995).

FARRAND, M. (ed.), *The Records of the Federal Convention of 1787*, 4 vols. (New Haven, Conn., 1966).

FAY, M. A., 'Did Marx Offer to Dedicate *Capital* to Darwin?', *JHI* 39 (1978), 133–46.

—— 'Marx and Darwin: A Literary Detective Story', *Monthly Review* 31 (Mar. 1980) 40–57.

FEUER, L. S., 'Is the "Darwin–Marx Correspondence" Authentic?', *Annals of Science*, 32 (1975), 1–12.

—— 'The "Darwin–Marx Correspondence": A Correction and Revision', *Annals of Science*, 33 (1976), 383–4.

FISH, S., *Is there a Text in this Class? The Authority of Interpretive Communities* (Cambridge, Mass., 1980).

FOUCAULT, M., *Discipline and Punish* (New York, 1977).

—— *Language, Counter-Memory, Practice* (Ithaca, NY, 1977).

—— *Power/Knowledge* (New York, 1980).

GADAMER, H.-G., *Truth and Method* (New York, 1984).

GEERTZ, C., 'From the Native's Point of View', in P. Rabinow and N. M. Sullivan (eds.), *Interpretive Social Science* (Berkeley, Calif.), ch. 6.

GILBERT, F., 'The Humanist Concept of the Prince and the Prince of Machiavelli', *Journal of Modern History*, 11 (1939), 449–83.

GOLDSMITH, M. M., *Hobbes's Science of Politics* (New York, 1966).

GUNNELL, J. G., *Between Philosophy and Politics: The Alienation of Political Theory* (Amherst, Mass., 1986).

HABERMAS, J., *Theory and Practice* (Boston, 1973).

HADARI, S. A., ' "Persuader sans convaincre" ', *WPQ* 39 (1986), 504–19.

HADDOCK, B. A., 'Vico on Political Wisdom', *European Studies Review*, 8 (1978).

HALÉVY, E., *The Growth of Philosophic Radicalism* (London, 1929).

HAMILTON, A., Madison, J., and Jay, J., *The Federalist Papers* (New York, 1982).

HOBBES, T., *English Works*, ed. W. Molesworth, 11 vols. (London, 1839).

—— *Latin Works*, ed. W. Molesworth (London, 1839).

HOBBES, T., *Leviathan*, ed. C. B. Macpherson (Harmondworth, 1968).

HOROWITZ, A., *Rousseau, Nature, and History* (Toronto, 1987).

HUGHES, H. S., *Consciousness and Society*, rev. edn. (New York, 1977).

KAUTSKY, K., *Ethik und Materialistische Geschichtsauffassung* (1906; 2nd edn. Berlin and Stuttgart, 1922).

KELLY, C., 'To Persuade without Convincing: The Language of Rousseau's Legislator', *AJPS* 31 (1987), 321–35.

KUHN, T. S., *The Structure of Scientific Revolutions* (Chicago, 1963; rev. edn., 1974).

KURLAND, P. B., and LERNER, R. (eds.), *The Founders' Constitution*, 5 vols. (Chicago, 1987).

LANGE, F. A., *Die Arbeiterfrage* (Duisburg, 1865).

LASLETT, P. (ed.), *Philosophy, Politics and Society*, 1st ser. (Oxford, 1956).

—— and Runciman, W. G. (eds.), *Philosophy, Politics and Society*, 2nd ser. (Oxford, 1964).

—— Runciman, W. G., and Skinner, Q. (eds.), *Philosophy, Politics, and Society*, 4th ser. (Oxford, 1972).

LEIGH, R. A., 'Liberté et autorité dans le *Contrat social*', in *Jean-Jacques Rousseau et son œuvre* (Paris, 1964).

LESLIE, M., 'In Defence of Anachronism', *Political Studies*, 18 (1970), 433–47.

LEWIS, R. W. B., *The American Adam* (Chicago, 1955).

LEYH, G., 'Toward a Constitutional Hermeneutics', *AJPS* 32 (1988), 369–87.

—— (ed.), *Legal Hermeneutics* (Berkeley, Calif., 1992).

LICHTHEIM, G., *From Marx to Hegel* (New York, 1971).

LOBKOWICZ, N., 'On the History of Theory and Praxis', in T. Ball (ed.), *Political Theory and Praxis* (Minneapolis, 1977), 13–27.

MACHIAVELLI, N., *The Prince and the Discourses* (New York, 1950).

MACINTYRE, A., *A Short History of Ethics* (New York, 1966).

—— *After Virtue* (Notre Dame, Ind., 1981).

—— 'The Indispensability of Political Theory', in D. Miller and L. Siedentop (eds.), *The Nature of Political Theory* (Oxford, 1983).

MACK, M. P., *Jeremy Bentham* (London, 1962).

MACPHERSON, C. B., *The Political Theory of Possessive Individualism* (Oxford, 1962).

MCMANNERS, J., *The Social Contract and Rousseau's Revolt against Society* (Leicester, 1968).

MCLELLAN, D., *Karl Marx: His Life and Thought* (London, 1973).

MCMURTRY, J., *The Structure of Marx's World-View* (Princeton, NJ, 1978).

MARX, K., *The Economic and Philosophic Manuscripts of 1844* (New York, 1964).

—— *Capital I* (New York, 1967).

—— *Critique of Hegel's 'Philosophy of Right'* (Cambridge, 1970).

—— and F. Engels, *The German Ideology* (New York, 1963).

—— —— *Selected Works* (New York, 1969).

—— —— *Werke*, 39 vols. (Berlin, 1968–).

MARX, L., *The Machine in the Garden* (New York, 1964).

MASTERS, R. D., *The Political Philosophy of Rousseau* (Princeton, NJ, 1968).

MATTINGLY, G., 'Machiavelli's Prince: Political Science or Political Satire?', *American Scholar*, 27 (1957–8), 482–91.

MILL, James, *History of British India* (London, 1818; 3rd edn., 1826).

—— 'The Church, and its Reform', *London Review*, 1 (1835), 257–95.

—— *Fragment on Mackintosh* (1835; 2nd edn. London, 1870).

—— 'Schools for All', in W. H. Burston (ed.), *James Mill on Education* (Cambridge, 1969), 120–93.

—— *Analysis of the Phenomena of the Human Mind*, 2nd edn. (London, 1878).

—— *Political Writings*, ed. T. Ball (Cambridge, 1992).

MILL, John Stuart, *Autobiography*, ed. J. Stillinger (Oxford, 1971).

—— *The Early Draft of John Stuart Mill's Autobiography*, ed. J. Stillinger (Urbana, Ill., 1961).

—— *Auguste Comte and Positivism* (1865; Ann Arbor, Mich., 1961).

—— *The Subjection of Women* (London, 1869).

—— *Collected Works*, ed. J. M. Robson *et al.* 29 vols. (Toronto, 1963– 89).

MILLER, D., 'The Resurgence of Political Theory', *Political Studies*, 38 (1990), 421–37.

MILLER, J., *Rousseau: Dreamer of Democracy* (New Haven, Conn., 1984).

—— *Democracy is in the Streets* (New York, 1987).

—— *The Passion of Michel Foucault* (New York, 1993).

MITCHELL, W. J. T. (ed.), *The Politics of Interpretation* (Chicago, 1983).

NIETZSCHE, F., *The Genealogy of Morals* (Garden City, NY, 1956).

NOONE, J. B., *Rousseau's Social Contract* (Athens, Ga., 1980).

OKIN, S. M., *Women in Western Political Thought* (Princeton, NJ, 1979).

O'NEILL, G. K., *The High Frontier* (New York, 1978).

—— *2081: A Hopeful View of the Human Future* (London, 1981).

PACKE, M. St J., *Life of John Stuart Mill* (London, 1954).

PAGDEN, A. (ed.), *The Languages of Political Theory in Early-Modern Europe* (Cambridge, 1987).

PAINE, T., *The Rights of Man* (Garden City, NY, 1973).

PATEMAN, C., *The Sexual Contract* (Stanford, Calif., 1988).

PERRY, M. J., *Morality, Politics, and Law* (New York, 1989).

PETERS, R. S., *Hobbes* (Harmondsworth, 1967).

PITKIN, H. F., *Fortune is a Woman: Gender and Politics in the Thought of Niccolò Machiavelli* (Berkeley, Calif., 1984).

PLAMENATZ, J., 'The Uses of Political Theory', *Political Studies*, 8 (1960), 37–47.

—— 'In Seach of Machiavellian *virtù*', in A. Parel (ed.), *The Political Calculus* (Toronto, 1972), 157–78.

POCOCK, J. G. A., 'The History of Political Thought: A Methodological Enquiry', in P. Laslett and W. G. Runciman, (eds.), *Philosophy, Politics, and Society*, 2nd ser. (Oxford, 1964), 183–202.

—— *The Machiavellian Moment* (Princeton, NJ, 1975).

PRICE, R., 'The Senses of *virtù* in Machiavelli', *European Studies Review*, 3 (1973), 315–45.

RAWLS, J., *A Theory of Justice* (Cambridge, Mass., 1971).

REES, J. C., *John Stuart Mill's 'On Liberty'* (Oxford, 1985).

RICARDO, D., *Works and Correspondence*, ed. P. Sraffa, 11 vols. (Cambridge, 1962).

RORTY, R., *Contingency, Irony, and Solidarity* (Cambridge, 1989).

—— J. B. Schneewind, and Q. Skinner (eds.), *Philosophy in History* (Cambridge, 1984).

ROUSSEAU, J.-J., *Political Writings of Jean-Jacques Rousseau*, ed. C. E. Vaughan (Cambridge, 1915).

—— *Œuvres complètes* (Paris, 1959–).

RYAN, A., *Property and Political Theory* (Oxford, 1984).

SANDEL, M. J., *Liberalism and the Limits of Justice* (Cambridge, 1982).

—— 'The Procedural Republic and the Unencumbered Self', *Political Theory*, 12 (1984), 81–96.

SCHMIDT, A., *The Concept of Nature in Marx* (London, 1971).

SCHORER, M., *William Blake: The Politics of Vision* (New York, 1959).

SEMPLE, J., 'Foucault and Bentham: A Defence of Panopticism', *Utilitas*, 4 (1992), 105–20.

—— *Bentham's Prison* (Oxford, 1993).

SHAPIRO, I., 'Realism in the Study of the History of Ideas', *HPT* 3 (1982), 535–78.

SIMON, W. M., *European Positivism in the Nineteenth Century* (Ithaca, NY, 1963).

Skinner, Q., 'The Ideological Context of Hobbes's Political Thought', *Historical Journal*, 9 (1966), 286–317.
—— 'Meaning and Understanding in the History of Political Thought', *History and Theory*, 8 (1969), 3–53.
—— *Foundations of Modern Political Thought* (Cambridge, 1978).
—— *Machiavelli* (Oxford, 1981).
—— 'Some Problems in the Analysis of Political Thought and Action', in J. Tully (ed.), *Meaning and Context: Quentin Skinner and his Critics* (Princeton, NJ, 1988), 97–118.
—— 'The State', in T. Ball, N. Farr, and R. L. Hanson (eds.), *Political Innovation and Conceptual Change* (Cambridge, 1989), ch. 5.
SMITH, A., *Wealth of Nations* (Oxford, 1979).
SMITH, B. J., *Politics and Remembrance* (Princeton, NJ, 1985).
SMITH, H. N., *Virgin Land* (Cambridge, Mass., 1950).
SOREL, G., 'Étude sur Vico', *Devenir social*, 2 (Oct.–Dec. 1896), 787–817, 906–41, 1013–46.
STAROBINSKI, J., *Jean-Jacques Rousseau, la transparence et l'obstacle* (Paris, 1957).
TAGLIACOZZO, G. (ed.), *Vico: Past and Present* (Atlantic Highlands, NJ, 1981).
—— (ed.), *Vico and Marx: Affinities and Contrasts* (Atlantic Highlands, NJ, 1983).
—— and WHITE, H. V. (eds.), *Giambattista Vico: An International Symposium* (Baltimore, 1969).
TALMON, J. L., *Origins of Totalitarian Democracy* (New York, 1952).
TAYLOR, C., 'The Liberal–Communitarian Debate', in N. Rosenblum (ed.), *Liberalism and the Moral Life* (Cambridge, Mass., 1989).
—— *Multiculturalism and 'The Politics of Recognition'* (Princeton, NJ, 1992).
THOMAS, P., 'Marx and Science', *Political Studies*, 24 (Mar. 1976), 1–23.
THOMAS, W., 'James Mill's Politics: The Essay on Government and the Movement for Reform', *Historical Journal*, 12 (1969), 249–84.
—— 'John Stuart Mill and the Uses of Autobiography', *History*, 56 (1971), 341–59.
—— *The Philosophical Radicals: Nine Studies in Theory and Practice, 1817–1841* (Oxford, 1979).
THOMPSON, W., *Appeal of One Half the Human Race* (London, 1825).
THUCYDIDES, *History of the Peloponnesian War*, trans. R. Crawley (New York, 1951).
TULLY, J., *A Discourse on Property* (Cambridge, 1980).
—— (ed.), *Meaning and Context: Quentin Skinner and his Critics* (Princeton, NJ, 1988).

TULLY, J., *An Approach to Political Philosophy: Locke in Contexts* (Cambridge, 1993).

VICO, G., *The New Science* (1744; Ithaca, NY, 1984).

VIROLI, M., *Jean-Jacques Rousseau and the 'well-ordered society'* (Cambridge, 1988).

WARREN, M., 'On Ball, "Marx and Darwin"', *Political Theory*, 9 (1981), 260–3.

WATKINS, J. W. N., *Hobbes's System of Ideas* (London, 1965).

WENZ, P. S., *Environmental Justice* (Albany, NY, 1988).

WHITE, J. B., *When Words Lose their Meaning* (Chicago, 1984).

WHITFIELD, J. H., *Machiavelli* (Oxford, 1947).

WILLIFORD, M., 'Bentham on the Rights of Women', *JHI* 36 (1975), 167–76.

WOLFF, R. P., *Understanding Rawls* (Princeton, NJ, 1977).

WOLIN, S., *Politics and Vision* (Boston, 1960).

—— 'Political Theory as a Vocation', *APSR* 63 (1969), 1062–83.

—— 'Postmodern Politics and the Absence of Myth', *Social Research*, 52 (1985) 217–39.

WOLTMANN, L., *Die Darwinsche Theorie und der Sozialismus: Ein Beitrag zur Naturgeschichte der Menschlichen Gesellschaft* (Dusseldorf, 1899).

INDEX

DATE DUE